Praise for Robert G. Kaiser's

Act of Congress

"A crackling page-turner. . . [Kaiser] delivers a clear under-standing of the issues as well as the exhausting, exhilarating and often appalling political process. His extensive original reporting and deep research lend both richness and authority to the lively text."   —*The Plain Dealer*

"One of the best books on the [legislative] process in a long time."   —*Bloomberg*

"Certain to become a classic, this rich and beautifully crafted book tells the story of a rare moment of congressional suc-cess. Who would have thought such a thing possible?"
        —Lawrence Lessig, professor at Harvard Law School

"The great value of Robert G. Kaiser's *Act of Congress* is its refusal to accept the Washington cliché that the Dodd-Frank legislation represents a moment when Congress worked the way it is supposed to."   —*The New York Review of Books*

"Riveting. . . . Kaiser offers an insightful primer on how laws are made, from conception to passage, as well as the char-acters and culture of the U.S. Congress, observed from an astonishing perspective most citizens never see."   —*Booklist*

"Congress is the most powerful, and least well-understood, branch of the American government. Luckily, Robert Kaiser is here to explain it to us. Required reading for anyone who is affected by Washington, which is, as Kaiser demonstrates in this book, all of us."
—Ezra Klein, columnist, *The Washington Post*

"A tour de force, an unparalleled account of the difficulty of legislating in an intensely polarized political era. Robert Kaiser brings decades of experience to the task, deftly showing how lawmakers balanced policy goals and political risk to build bicameral majorities for landmark Wall Street reform."
—Sarah Binder, professor of political science at George Washington University

"Intricate [and] incisive. . . . [Kaiser] finds the drama in arcane parliamentary procedure and paints extraordinary fly-on-the-wall scenes of legislative sausage making. . . . His absorbing true-life political saga exposes the good, the bad, and the ugly in Congress."   —*Publishers Weekly*

"*Act of Congress* is easily the best book on Congress I have read in decades. It is a stupendous achievement—richly informative, a pleasure to read, wise in its assessments of why Dodd-Frank was able to succeed and how this case is more exception than rule in these difficult governing times. . . . A classic."
—Thomas E. Mann, Senior Fellow, Governance Studies, The Brookings Institution

"*Act of Congress* is the first book to describe in detail what it takes to legislate in the 'new' Congress. Robert Kaiser was present at the creation of the Dodd-Frank Act. His reputation as a straight-shooting reporter earned him open access to the staffs of Congressman Barney Frank and Senator Chris Dodd, and extensive interviews with the key players in both parties. The result is an enlightening, sobering tour de force. Any teacher who hasn't read this book should have his syllabus examined." —Samuel L. Popkin, author of *The Candidate*

"Robert Kaiser's *Act of Congress* is a great read. He makes a complex issue and an arcane process understandable and interesting. Readers get a real sense for the interplay of politics and policy and of personality and structure that goes into passing major legislation. Not just for Congress junkies, Kaiser's book is a fascinating 'How Done It.'"   —Barbara Sinclair, professor emerita of American politics at UCLA

"Bob Kaiser has written a captivating and insightful account of the Dodd-Frank reform of financial services regulation. He convincingly explains both the successes of key actors and why, in the current Congress, such successes are increasingly rare."   —Congressman David E. Price

"Richly detailed. . . . Remember that old saw about making sausages and making laws—that you don't want to know too much about either one? Kaiser disproves it with this lucid . . . book."   —*Kirkus Reviews*

"This book is essential reading for students of Congress and national policy making, for everyone interested in the policy response to the Great Recession, and for citizens who care about the dysfunction of American national government."   —Steven S. Smith, professor of political science at Washington University

"Robert Kaiser's triumph is to make this complex subject an intimately human tale. Thanks to reporting and insight, the story of Dodd-Frank is revealed not simply as a collision of public and private interests on Wall Street, but as a kind of case study in the anthropology of modern Washington. A great story by a journalist singularly well-equipped to tell it."   —John Harris, editor in chief of *Politico*

"The most detailed, fascinating and sophisticated case study of congressional law making to appear in years. . . . It's a great read." —Dr. Gary C. Jacobson, professor of political science at the University of California, San Diego

Robert G. Kaiser

Act *of* Congress

Robert G. Kaiser has been on the staff of *The Washington Post* since 1963. He has reported on the House and Senate; was a correspondent in Saigon and Moscow; served as national editor and managing editor; and is currently associate editor and senior correspondent. He has also written for *Esquire, Foreign Affairs*, and *The New York Review of Books*. His books include *Russia: The People and the Power*; *So Damn Much Money*; and, with Leonard Downie Jr., *The News About the News*. He has received an Overseas Press Club award, a National Press Club award, and was a Pulitzer Prize finalist. He has also been a commentator on NPR's *All Things Considered*. He lives in Washington, D.C.

Act *of* Congress

Act of Congress

HOW AMERICA'S ESSENTIAL INSTITUTION WORKS,
AND HOW IT DOESN'T

Robert G. Kaiser

VINTAGE BOOKS
A DIVISION OF RANDOM HOUSE LLC
NEW YORK

FIRST VINTAGE BOOKS EDITION, JANUARY 2014

Copyright © 2013 by Robert G. Kaiser

All rights reserved. Published in the United States by Vintage Books,
a division of Random House LLC, New York, and in Canada by Random
House of Canada Limited, Toronto, Penguin Random House Companies.
Originally published in hardcover in the United States by Alfred A. Knopf,
a division of Random House LLC, New York, in 2013.

Vintage and colophon are registered trademarks of Random House LLC.

The Library of Congress has cataloged the Knopf edition as follows:
Kaiser, Robert G.
Act of Congress : how America's essential institution works,
and how it doesn't / Robert G. Kaiser.
p. cm.
Includes bibliographical references and index.
1. United States. Congress.
2. United States. Dodd-Frank Wall Street Reform
and Consumer Protection Act.
3. Financial services industry—Law and legislation—United States.
4. Global Financial Crisis, 2008–2009. I. Title.
HG181.K35 2013
346.73'082—dc23
2012038245

Vintage Trade Paperback ISBN: 978-0-307-74451-7
eBook ISBN: 978-0-307-96218-8

Author photograph © Lucian Perkins
Book design by Maggie Hinders

www.vintagebooks.com

Printed in the United States of America
10 9 8 7 6 5 4 3 2

This book is for

Hannah Jopling

Contents

Preface

Work on this book began in early December 2008 with an appointment in the cavernous office of Congressman Barney Frank of Massachusetts—Room 2252 of the Rayburn House Office Building on Independence Avenue in Washington, D.C., my hometown. I have an unlikely connection to the Rayburn Building, one that came to mind that day, my first visit in several years. In the summer of 1960, just before I started college, I had a construction job helping to lay the Rayburn Building's elaborate foundations.

Just a year later, after my freshman year, I was a delegate to the National Student Congress in Madison, Wisconsin. One of the most formidable student politicians I met there was a Harvard delegate who talked too fast in a thick, New Yorkish accent, who had mastered *Robert's Rules of Order*, who seemed to know everything about any topic that came up, and who loved to make wisecracks. That was Barney Frank of Bayonne, New Jersey, then twenty-one years old.

I was just eighteen, but I already knew I wanted to be a reporter. I had spent the previous semester working on my college newspaper, where I discovered that this was the life for me. Frank wanted to somehow participate in politics and public life. We both got what we hoped for, and over the years our paths crossed from time to time. We maintained friendly relations.

A few weeks before I visited him in Rayburn 2252, Frank and I had spoken on the phone about the Great Crash that had just shaken the foundations of the global economic system. As chairman of the House Financial Services Committee, Frank was more than a casual observer.

"Your next book should be about this stuff," he had said on the phone. He knew that I had recently finished a book on lobbying and money in Washington, but he didn't realize how timely his suggestion was. At that moment I was eagerly looking for a new project, and this phone call got me thinking.

I did not want to write a book about the Great Crash, an event centered on Wall Street in New York, beyond the world I know best. My subject is Washington and the politicians who inhabit it. That phone call led to the thought that with cooperation from Frank and other members, I might be able to write an interesting book based on Congress's response to this catastrophe. I had long thought Congress was America's least understood important institution. I had been trying to figure it out for four decades. Maybe I could finally get to the bottom of its mysteries.

When I saw Frank in his office, I proposed that I become the historian of the congressional response to the Great Crash, specifically of the effort I knew Frank and his Senate counterpart, Christopher Dodd of Connecticut, were planning—a new rulebook for American high finance. I'd heard Frank speak of "a new New Deal," a reference to the legislation enacted in Franklin D. Roosevelt's first term that helped save American capitalism in the Great Depression. Frank's ambitions sounded big, even historic. And a new president shared this goal, so it might actually be achieved. Would Frank talk to me as this story unfolded? Would he allow his staff to tell me what was going on backstage? My ambition, I said, would be to use the story of what he and Dodd did as a kind of case study that would explain the modern Congress.

Frank agreed. More important, he asked nothing in return—no assurances, no right to read drafts of what I would write or to approve the way I used the material he provided. The idea that a reporter he knew would record his effort to make some history evidently appealed to him.

Next I needed to convince Dodd that he should help too. I had first met Dodd in the late 1970s, when he was a popular junior congressman from Connecticut. At the time I was *The Washington Post*'s reporter in the Senate, so did not have a lot to do with the House. I got to know

Dodd better in the early 1980s, when he became an active critic of the Ronald Reagan administration's Central American policy. We were just a year apart in age, and had both grown up in the Washington area in the 1950s, when his father was a congressman and senator.

Dodd had given me a revealing interview for my book on lobbying. I realized then that he was an astute student of the Senate. I hoped he would see the merit of helping with this project. I confess it also occurred to me that he might feel a little competitive about Barney Frank, as House and Senate committee chairmen with overlapping jurisdiction tend to do, and would want to make sure that his side of the story was well covered in this book.

We first discussed all this in his "hideaway" in the Capitol, Room S-236. The room was part of the original Capitol building, built between 1796 and 1800. Room S-236 was a fine space about thirty feet by twenty feet with a high ceiling and a large window that looked west across the Mall toward the Washington Monument and Lincoln Memorial. There were several dozen hideaways in the Capitol for senior senators (and none for members of the House); this was one of the finest, as befit a committee chairman with twenty-eight years of service in the Senate.

Dodd, in his own words, was "a believer in symbols." On this occasion he was eager to explain the oil portraits on his walls. "This is Samuel Morse," inventor of the telegraph. In 1844, Morse sent one of the earliest telegraph messages from this very room to a convention in Baltimore, about thirty-five miles away. "That is the original senator from Connecticut, Roger Sherman, the only one of the founders who signed the Articles of Confederation, the Declaration of Independence, the Constitution, and the Bill of Rights. And that one is Oliver Ellsworth," coauthor of the Connecticut compromise at the Constitutional Convention that created the Senate as an upper house of the legislative branch. Dodd obviously loved this history, and loved the fact that he was a part of it.

He too agreed to be interviewed periodically, and to share information about his maneuverings as the story unfolded. Dodd was somewhat more circumspect than Frank; he wanted to be able to approve quotations attributed to him from our interviews. I agreed, hoping this would prove to be an insignificant condition. It did. Dodd never tried to withhold or alter a quotation that I wanted to use in this book.

Both men also did something that proved critical to my research: They told their staffs that they could cooperate with me. In the modern Congress, staff members tend to disappear from public view. Many talk to reporters, but usually anonymously, and nearly always with a purpose: to advance the political interests of their bosses. Dodd and Frank gave me an unusual kind of access to the staffs of the Senate Banking and House Financial Services committees, which vastly improved my ability to understand the legislative saga recounted here.

So I would have the chance to follow an important piece of legislation from first conception to final passage through both houses of Congress—if Dodd and Frank could fulfill their shared ambition to pass a regulatory reform bill. I hoped that this story would illuminate the culture of Congress, an institution that can appear mighty strange from afar, but ought not seem foreign.

That was a lesson I had learned over nearly half a century of exposure to the House and Senate. The Congress of the United States is a typically American institution. Its charter, the U.S. Constitution, is an inspirational document that persistently summons to service what Abraham Lincoln called "the better angels of our nature." But—also typically—what the Constitution describes and what humankind creates are often just rough approximations of one another. From its inception in 1789, Congress has been razzed and ridiculed by skeptical citizens who, in a typically American way, expect the worst from their elected officials, and get it just often enough to confirm their prejudices. Will Rogers, the early-twentieth-century humorist, made a pretty good living ridiculing Congress with quips: "This country has come to feel the same when Congress is in session as when the baby gets hold of a hammer," for example.

Also typically, though the founders expected that Congress would become the principal engine of American democracy and the venue for working out the country's most difficult problems, they provided few tools to assure this outcome. Instead they hoped and expected that intelligent citizens would pay attention to Congress, run for Congress, and take Congress seriously. Many of the founders themselves decided to participate in the House and Senate, suggesting that they anticipated similar interest on the part of future generations of the nation's best and brightest.

But, typically, those high-minded thoughts clashed with the cruder realities of a republic whose governmental institutions could make some men rich and others poor, could favor one section over another, could reward and punish for reasons that were decidedly not high-minded. Exchanges of favors and petty corruption became congressional reflexes, as did the flight from responsibility in the face of large national problems. In the modern age the task that requires the most time and energy for a typical member of Congress is raising money to run for reelection. Legislative statesmen and -women are few. Occasionally a career in Congress has appealed to the best and brightest citizens, but in our time that has not been common. We may get a representative Congress, but we don't get a distinguished one.

By the early twenty-first century, Americans had lost touch with the institution in which the founders had invested such hope. In surveys of civic knowledge, both the population at large and America's students regularly embarrass themselves with their ignorance about their Congress. A *Newsweek* poll in 2011 found that less than 40 percent of Americans knew the term of office of a U.S. senator (six years). When the same question was posed to Arizona high school students, just 15 percent knew the right answer. How Congress does its many jobs remains a mystery to most Americans. This of course doesn't mean Americans can't judge the House and Senate. Voters hold overwhelmingly negative views of their Congress; its approval ratings in public opinion polls have been dreadful year after year.

Yet Congress has always attracted enthusiasts, people intrigued by the congressional circus and the individuals who perform in it. I am one of them. I grew up in a Washington household consumed by politics (my father was a government official of modest importance), and learned the basics at an early age. In my first job in journalism I was a copyboy for the Associated Press in the Press Gallery of the House of Representatives. That was in 1962, when I was an eighteen-year-old college student. Whenever I could sneak away from the Press Gallery at noon, I'd exploit my press credential to go down to the speaker's office on the second floor of the Capitol for his almost daily press conference. The speaker was John W. McCormack, an Irish pol from Boston with a serious dandruff problem. McCormack favored dark, pin-striped suits that highlighted the dandruff. His noon press conference began with a ceremonial brushing away of the flakes by William "Fishbait" Miller of Pascagoula, Mississippi, a then famous congressional character who had the title of doorkeeper of the House of Representatives. When Miller had finished the cleanup, McCormack would answer reporters' questions, usually about pending House business, with a Boston accent thick enough to slice. The room was full of tobacco smoke, much of it from McCormack's cigar. I found the spectacle irresistible.

A year later I went to work for *The Washington Post* and was further exposed to Congress, one of the *Post*'s most important subjects. In 1967 *Esquire* magazine asked me to write a profile of one of the most powerful members of Congress at the time, Wilbur Mills of Kensett, Arkansas. Seven years later Mills became notorious for a drunken escapade with a stripper named Fanne Foxe, a passenger in the congressman's car when it was stopped near the Lincoln Memorial by a park policeman. Ms. Foxe tried to flee by splashing through the reflecting pool in front of the memorial. She and Mills were arrested. Mills eventually admitted he was an alcoholic, a frailty I had missed.

The Mills I knew was the self-contained and self-controlled chairman of the most powerful committee in the House, Ways and Means, which is responsible for everything related to the raising of government revenue—taxes, and much else besides. When I trailed him around the Capitol, everyone he met greeted him as "Mister Chairman." At home in Kensett and Searcy, Arkansas, he was the fortunate son, a hero in his own time. He enjoyed strolling down Wilbur D. Mills Avenue in Kensett, a one- and two-story town fifty-five miles northeast of Little Rock. Mills was small and mousy, which was deceptive, because he was so smart. He graduated second in his class from Hendrix College in Conway, Arkansas, then made the leap to Harvard Law School. He knew the tax code better than any other member of Congress. And he had big political ambitions, which led him in 1972 to run for president.

It was a quickly forgotten candidacy with one enduring consequence. As a way to position himself as a friend of the elderly on the eve of his presidential campaign, Mills sponsored a change in the law providing for an annual cost-of-living adjustment in Social Security benefits. Benefits have kept up with inflation ever since, preventing millions of senior citizens from falling into poverty in their retirement years.

Chairmen of House committees can wield considerable power.

In 1977 I became the *Post*'s Senate correspondent, a job that gave me a wonderful education. My most memorable experience was a trip to

Louisiana in 1979 with Senator Russell B. Long, the son of Huey ("The Kingfish") Long, one of the most gifted American politicians of the New Deal era. Huey Long was a faker and demagogue but also a talented exploiter of the populist sentiments provoked by the Great Depression. He was a genuine radical who served as governor of Louisiana and then as a senator for three years, until he was assassinated by a relative of a political opponent in 1935. Russell was seventeen at the time.

When we traveled together in July 1979, Russell Long was chairman of the Senate Finance Committee, the Senate's equivalent of Ways and Means. He was famous for his brainpower and his aphorisms. One of the best was his definition of tax reform: "Don't tax you, don't tax me, tax that fellow behind the tree!" I had covered Long extensively, but never had the chance to talk to him at length until that trip. We spent several days together—Long and I and Henry Heltz, a retired Louisana policeman who drove the senator around the state in a white Mercury sedan.

The high point of our travels was a visit to the town of Tioga in the center of the state. Tioga is home to the summer encampment of the United Pentecostal Church. Thousands of the faithful gather every summer in a giant tabernacle, the size of two football fields, tucked among groves of towering pines. They worship, sing, pray, often speaking in tongues, and listen to the exhortations of many preachers. The worshippers seemed intent on spiritual redemption, but Long's interest was political. These people vote as a bloc, he told me, and vote the way their leaders tell them to.

Soon after we had joined the throng, the Reverend T. F. Tenney, the church's leader, announced that "the featured ones here tonight are Jesus Christ and then Russell Long." Murmurs of approval followed.

Now it was Long's turn to speak from the pulpit: "Many of you knew my father. I've tried to follow along in his tradition. But I regret to say there's been a lot of mistakes made in Washington. . . . Some of those decisions of that Supreme Court have been very misguided decisions. It leads me to wonder whether those justices start their sessions the way we do in the United States Senate—with a prayer." Now the murmurs became loud amens, punctuated with applause. "I want to make a little contribution," Long continued, "so there won't be any doubt how I feel about the matter—the fine job you're doing here. It may not be much, but it's the largest contribution I've made at any one time."

He handed a check to the bespectacled, round-cheeked Reverend

Tenney, who was obviously delighted. He held it up to the crowd. "I have a check here signed by Russell B. Long on the American Bank in Baton Rouge for $5,000," he announced. The tabernacle filled with high-pitched groans of appreciation. "Praise the Lord!" Reverend Tenney said. Then, after a theatrical pause, he turned to Long and asked, "When are you running again?" Reverend Tenney led the crowd in laughter at his own joke. But it wasn't a joke. Long would be on the ballot a year later. The last time he'd visited the tabernacle had been six years earlier, a year before his previous campaign, in 1974. These Pentecostalists were his faithful supporters. He visited them as just another pandering politician.

And yet Russell Long was a serious legislator. He was notorious for the favors he did for the oil and gas industries, both important to the Louisiana economy, but he was also the author and principal defender of the Earned Income Tax Credit, one of the government's least appreciated and most important programs to help the working poor, supported by both parties. Thanks to Long, low-income workers in the United States don't pay any income tax, and can receive money back from the Treasury through this tax credit—today about $6,000 a year for a family with three children. Benefits from the program add up to tens of billions a year. Huey Long would have approved.

It was easy to poke fun at Russell Long, and at Wilbur Mills; easy too to be cynical about their motives and behavior. But they taught a more complicated lesson: The same politician can combine admirable qualities with dreadful ones, can demonstrate both pathetic human frailty and a keen interest in helping ordinary people, sometimes courageously, in the course of a career, or even the course of a week on Capitol Hill.

Congress is more than its colorful characters, who in fact have always represented a small minority of the membership. Congress is a system and a culture. It is a wonderful laboratory in which to pursue one of the reporter's favorite questions: How does it work?

I realized this during the biggest story I covered during my years assigned to the Senate—the ratification of the Panama Canal treaties. Now largely forgotten, for a few years in the 1970s there was no bigger political issue in America than the Panama Canal. The two treaties, negotiated over six months in 1977, would slowly relinquish American control of the canal, built by the United States in the early twentieth century, to Panama, while committing Panama to remain neutral forever and guarantee access to the canal to ships of all nations.

The treaties provoked sharp controversy. Conservative Republicans saw giving up the canal as a sign of American weakness. Senator Jesse Helms of North Carolina and Ronald Reagan, who first ran for president in 1976, were leaders of a popular movement to hold on to the canal, a symbol of Yankee imperialism throughout Latin America, but to those conservatives a proud American accomplishment and asset. Proponents of the treaties argued that they were a proper acknowledgment that the United States had no right to claim Panamanian territory—which we had done, in effect, by ruling the Panama Canal Zone unilaterally for seventy-five years. Returning the canal to Panama would help our diplomacy in Latin America, treaty supporters said, and put the United States on the right side of history.

Ratifying treaties, the founders decided long ago, requires two-thirds approval in the Senate—sixty-seven votes. The first head counts taken by Senate leaders early in 1978 showed at least thirty strong no votes, and perhaps more. The outcome would be close.

The Senate debate on the treaties dragged on for two months. Many members behaved like buffoons—no surprise, but startling to see at close range in such an important debate. But some also showed signs of nobility. The best, I thought, was Senator Howard Baker of Tennessee, the Republican leader, who led a deeply divided Republican caucus. At least two dozen of the thirty-eight Senate Republicans were die-hard opponents of ratification. Baker had presidential ambitions for 1980 and knew conservatives viewed him warily, but nevertheless decided to support the treaties, provided they were modified slightly. This, Baker told me privately, was the right thing to do, though he knew it could cost him dearly in the political arena. In fact it probably ended his career.

Sixty-eight senators—one more than needed—voted to ratify each of the two treaties. Just enough members of both parties were afraid to take responsibility for sabotaging a treaty that President Jimmy Carter and his senior diplomats said was of vital importance to the United States in its Latin American backyard. Courage—particularly Baker's courage—was a necessary ingredient, but fear probably influenced more votes.

These stories and others like them had fed my fascination with the Congress, and taught me that on Capitol Hill reality was elusive. I hoped that this time, with the unusual access I had been granted, I might finally get inside the legislative process and explain the reality—explain how the modern Congress works. I spent two years reporting this story, and conducted hundreds of interviews. Besides Dodd and Frank, a dozen key members of both houses, from both parties, agreed to talk with me repeatedly while the legislation was pending.

Ultimately, Dodd and Frank were able to construct and pass one of the most ambitious pieces of legislation that Congress has enacted in many years, a bill now named for both of them—"Dodd-Frank." But its final contents were uncertain for months, and important matters were resolved only in the wee hours of June 25, 2010, by the senators and House members who took part in the special conference committee empowered to reconcile differences between the similar bills passed earlier by House and Senate. Many years of experience had not prepared me for the intricacy, the improvisations, the difficulty, or the drama involved in passing this big bill.

Dodd-Frank is full of imperfections—"no bill is ever perfect," as Senator Dodd put it. Its principal authors revealed their own imperfections as they steered their versions of regulatory reform toward final passage. Their huge "piece of legislation," as new laws are called on Capitol Hill, will have unintended consequences—every big bill does. The effects of many of its provisions won't be known until regulatory agencies write and apply "rules" under which they will enforce the law. Those rules will be challenged in court and altered in practice. Eventually Dodd-Frank will be amended by additional legislation. Only the next big financial crisis will fully test the new law, if it remains in effect when that crisis arrives. In Washington, nothing is forever, no argument is ever finally resolved.

This book is about the process that produced the bill. My hope is that these pages will explain the essence of a vitally important American institution.

Key Participants

SPENCER BACHUS, Republican of Alabama, the senior or "ranking" Republican on the House Financial Services Committee, 2009–11.

MICHAEL BARR, assistant secretary of the treasury for financial institutions.

MELISSA BEAN, Democrat of Illinois, active member of the House Financial Services Committee and of the New Democrat Coalition of centrist Democrats.

MICHAEL BERESIK, Democratic staff member of the House Financial Services Committee.

MARIA CANTWELL, Democratic senator from Washington state.

JULIE CHON, Democratic staff member of the Senate Banking Committee who made herself an expert on derivatives.

WILLIAM LACY CLAY JR., Democratic member of the House of Representatives from Missouri, whose father held the same seat in Congress.

RODGIN COHEN, chairman of the New York law firm of Sullivan & Cromwell, one of the country's leading banking lawyers and a Democrat.

BOB CORKER, Republican member of the Senate Banking Committee from Tennessee.

CHRIS DODD, Democratic senator from Connecticut and chairman of the Senate Banking Committee, 2007–11.

ANTHONY DOWD, former investment banker who served as an informal aide to Paul Volcker during negotiations with Congress on financial regulatory reform.

WILLIAM D. DUHNKE III, minority (Republican) staff director of the Senate Banking Committee.

DIANA FARRELL, deputy director of the National Economic Council in the White House and one of the authors of the Obama administration's regulatory reform proposals.

CAMDEN FINE, president of the Independent Community Bankers of America.

BARNEY FRANK, Democratic congressman from Massachusetts and chairman of the House Financial Services Committee.

AMY FRIEND, chief counsel, Senate Banking Committee.

COURTNEY GEDULDIG, aide to Senator Bob Corker, Republican of Tennessee, specializing in Banking Committee issues.

TIMOTHY GEITHNER, secretary of the treasury.

GARY GENSLER, chairman of the Commodity Futures Trading Commission, one of the two principal regulators (with the Securities and Exchange Commission) of the exotic financial instruments called derivatives.

ANDREW GREEN, aide to Senator Jeff Merkley, Democrat of Oregon, who worked on regulatory reform issues.

JUDD GREGG, Republican senator from New Hampshire, who joined the Banking Committee in September 2009.

JEB HENSARLING, congressman from Texas, a leader of conservative Republicans on the House Financial Services Committee.

ROBERT HOLIFIELD, staff director of the Senate Agriculture Committee, appointed to that job by Blanche Lincoln, Democrat of Arkansas, when she became the committee's chairman in September 2009.

STENY HOYER, Democratic congressman from Maryland and majority leader of the House of Representatives.

PAUL KANJORSKI, Democratic congressman from Pennsylvania, the second-ranking Democrat (after Barney Frank) on the House Financial Services Committee.

LARRY LAVENDER, minority (Republican) staff director of the House Financial Services Committee and old friend of its ranking Republican member, Spencer Bachus.

CARL LEVIN, Democratic senator from Michigan, chairman of the Permanent Investigations Subcommittee of the Senate Committee on Homeland Security and Governmental Affairs.

BLANCHE LINCOLN, Democratic senator from Arkansas and, after September 2009, chairman of the Senate Agriculture Committee.

FRANK LUNTZ, Republican pollster and political strategist, author of "The Language of Financial Reform," a pamphlet offering guidance to Republican members of Congress on how to effectively oppose financial regulatory reform.

SHAWN MAHER, Chris Dodd's former staff director (2007–9) of the Senate Banking Committee, who became deputy director of President Obama's office of legislative affairs in 2009.

PATRICK McCARTY, staff aide working for Senator Blanche Lincoln and Robert Holifield on the Senate Agriculture Committee.

Mɪтсн McConnell, senator from Kentucky, Republican leader of the Senate.

Jeff Merkley, the junior senator from Oregon and a new Democratic member of the Senate Banking Committee.

Andrew Miller, staff aide to the Democratic majority on the House Financial Services Committee.

Jonathan Miller (no relation to Andrew Miller), staff aide to the Senate Banking Committee and Dodd's advisor on consumer issues.

Mark F. Oesterle, minority (Republican) counsel to the Senate Banking Committee, Senator Richard Shelby's expert on regulatory reform.

Nancy Pelosi, congresswoman from California and speaker of the house (2007–11).

Ed Perlmutter, Democratic congressman from Colorado, active member of the House Financial Services Committee.

Jack Reed, Democratic senator from Rhode Island, senior member of the Senate Banking Committee.

Harry Reid, Democratic senator from Nevada, majority leader of the Senate.

Jeanne Roslanowick, staff director of the House Financial Services Committee, Barney Frank's most influential aide.

Jim Segel, special counsel to Barney Frank who handled political matters including cultivating the Democratic members of the Financial Services Committee.

Richard Shelby, Republican senator from Alabama, the senior or "ranking" Republican on the Senate Banking Committee.

Ed Silverman, an old friend and former aide of Senator Dodd's, who became staff director of the Senate Banking Committee in May 2009.

David Smith, chief economist, House Financial Services Committee. With Jeanne Roslanowick and Jim Segel, one of Barney Frank's most influential aides.

Kara Stein, staff aide to Senator Jack Reed of Rhode Island, who worked with him on derivatives.

Nathan Steinwald, staff aide to Democratic senator Mark Warner of Virginia on Banking Committee issues.

Lawranne Stewart, counsel to the House Financial Services Committee and an important expert on Jeanne Roslanowick's team.

Paul Volcker, former chairman of the Federal Reserve Board (1978–84), and proponent of new regulations to limit banks' investments of their own capital. The Obama administration embraced this idea and called it the "Volcker rule."

ELIZABETH WARREN, law professor at Harvard who first proposed creation of a new government agency to protect consumers of financial products.

MARK WARNER, Democratic senator from Virginia and member of the Senate Banking Committee.

MAXINE WATERS, Democratic congresswoman from California, senior member of the Black Caucus and of the House Financial Services Committee.

MEL WATT, Democratic congressman from North Carolina, member of the House Financial Services Committee, and one of Barney Frank's favorite colleagues.

NEAL WOLIN, deputy secretary of the treasury.

EDWARD YINGLING, president of the American Bankers Association, who actively lobbied Congress against the consumer protection agency.

MARK ZANDI, independent economist and author of a book on the financial crisis admired by Republicans and Democrats. Zandi's testimony in Congress was often influential.

Principal Organizations and Institutions

COMMODITY FUTURES TRADING COMMISSION (CFTC). Established by Congress in 1974, the CFTC is an independent federal agency whose purpose is to assure an open and honest market in the financial products variously known as swaps, futures, and derivatives. In 1998, with the support of the Clinton administration, Congress barred the CFTC from making any new regulations of the booming market in "over-the-counter derivatives," often exotic swaps that became extremely popular with the mathematical wizards of Wall Street. The Dodd-Frank Act formally regulated this market and gave substantial new powers to the CFTC.

CONSUMER FINANCIAL PROTECTION BUREAU (CFPB). The new consumer protection agency established by the Dodd-Frank bill, with powers to regulate most American financial firms offering services and products to the public. The CFPB is an independent agency under the Federal Reserve Board, though the Fed cannot interfere with its operations.

FEDERAL DEPOSIT INSURANCE CORPORATION (FDIC). The agency established by the Glass-Steagall Act of 1933 that insures the deposits in virtually every bank in the United States. The FDIC is a principal regulator of smaller banks that are not federally chartered, and of state-chartered savings banks. When a bank fails, the FDIC is responsible for winding up its affairs and protecting the money of its depositors.

FEDERAL RESERVE BOARD (THE FED). The Federal Reserve is the central bank of the United States, whose primary responsibilities are to set interest rates, preserve the value of the dollar, stabilize prices, maximize employment, and regulate the nation's largest financial institutions. It is an independent agency run by a Board of Governors whose seven members are appointed by the president to fourteen-year terms. Its chairman—Ben Bernanke in the period covered by this book—is one of the most powerful figures in Washington.

HOUSE AND SENATE OFFICES OF THE LEGISLATIVE COUNSEL. Both houses of Congress maintain large staffs of lawyers and legislative experts whose job is to turn members' policy ideas into clear, concise, and legally effective legislative language. Both are nonpartisan offices that will draft a bill for any member or committee. House and Senate "Leg Counsel" (pronounced "ledge counsel") are among the most important and least publicized or understood institutions in Washington. Without their expertise, the House and Senate would be unable to function as legislative bodies.

HOUSE COMMITTEE ON AGRICULTURE. One of the twenty standing committees of the House. All legislation affecting American agriculture must originate in this committee. It has jurisdiction over the Department of Agriculture and the Commodity Futures Trading Commission, which means it provides oversight of those agencies often by holding hearings on their activities.

HOUSE COMMITTEE ON FINANCIAL SERVICES. Another of the standing committees of the House, known until 2001 as the Banking Committee. In the period covered by this book Barney Frank of Massachusetts was its chairman. The committee's jurisdiction includes the federal laws and regulations governing the financial industry, housing, international economic organizations, bank and financial regulators, the Treasury Department, and the Federal Reserve.

HOUSE COMMITTEE ON RULES. The Rules Committee manages the flow of legislation to the floor of the House as an agent of the leadership of the party that controls the House of Representatives. In the modern era the membership has consisted of nine members of the majority party, and four members of the minority. The committee decides what bills will be voted on, what amendments will be considered, and how much time will be allocated to debate amendments and the underlying legislation.

HOUSE OF REPRESENTATIVES. The larger of the two branches of Congress, with 435 members, allocated to the states by population. The seven states with the smallest populations each have just one member of the House; California, the biggest state, has fifty-three House seats. Members of the House serve two-year terms. Under Article I of the Constitution, the House and Senate have equal legislative powers. For a legislative proposal to become law, it must be approved by both bodies, and then signed by the president.

NATIONAL ECONOMIC COUNCIL. A White House agency, created by Bill Clinton in 1993, intended to raise the profile of economic policy issues inside the executive branch. The council develops policy ideas for the president and tries to coordinate executive branch activities that affect the national economy. In the period covered by this book, the NEC was chaired by Lawrence Summers, the former treasury secretary and president of Harvard University.

OFFICE OF THE COMPTROLLER OF THE CURRENCY (OCC). Oldest and biggest of the bank regulators, OCC was established by Congress in 1863. It regulates all nationally chartered banks and savings banks. It is run by the comptroller, who is appointed by the president and confirmed by the Senate to a five-year term. OCC is an independent unit within the Treasury Department.

OFFICE OF THRIFT SUPERVISION (OTS). A regulatory agency set up in 1989 to supervise the nation's federally and state-chartered savings banks, usually known as savings and loans or thrifts. OTS was established in reaction to the savings and loan scandals of the 1980s, but over time it developed a reputation as a lax regulator. Important institutions that it regulated collapsed in the Great Crash, and it lost all support in Congress. The Dodd-Frank bill abolished it, giving its responsibilities for regulating savings banks to the FDIC, OCC, and the Federal Reserve.

SECURITIES AND EXCHANGE COMMISSION (SEC). The SEC is the principal government regulator of stock markets. Established in 1934 as part of the New Deal, the SEC regulates stock offerings and stockbrokers, and sets rules for the buying and selling of shares. The Dodd-Frank bill gave the SEC (with the CFTC) new regulatory authority in the derivatives markets.

SENATE COMMITTEE ON AGRICULTURE. The Senate's version of the Agriculture Committee, with the same responsibilities as the House Committee. Senator Blanche Lincoln of Arkansas became the Agriculture Committee's chairman in September 2009.

SENATE COMMITTEE ON BANKING, HOUSING AND URBAN AFFAIRS. The Senate counterpart of the House Financial Services Committee, which has essentially the same jurisdiction, and was primarily responsible for drafting financial regulatory reform legislation. Chris Dodd of Connecticut was chairman of Banking in the period covered in this book.

SENATE OF THE UNITED STATES. The Senate consists of one hundred members, two from each of the fifty states. The founding fathers created it to assuage the concerns of smaller states, particularly southern states, assuring them they would have a loud voice in the affairs of the new nation. Senators serve six-year terms; one-third of Senate seats are contested in elections every two years. The Senate has the same legislative powers as the House, plus several powers reserved for it in the Constitution, including the confirmation of judges and executive branch appointees, and the ratification of international treaties.

TREASURY DEPARTMENT. The executive branch department responsible for managing the finances of the United States government, including collecting taxes, selling government bonds and notes, producing and managing coins and currency, paying the government's salaries and bills, and supervising and regulating national banks. The secretary of the treasury is the president's senior advisor on all these matters and economic policy generally. Treasury and the National Economic Council shared responsibility for financial regulatory reform issues in the first Obama administration.

Act *of* Congress

CHAPTER ONE

"I Could Hear Everyone Gulp"

Thursday, September 18, 2008, was a fine late-summer day in Washington—blue skies, temperatures in the seventies. But the politicians on Capitol Hill were in no mood to notice the weather. They were thoroughly distracted by chaos in the financial markets brought on by a series of seismic events: the nationalization of the government-supported agencies that provided most of the financing for home mortgages, Fannie Mae and Freddie Mac; then the sudden death of one enormous Wall Street institution, Lehman Brothers; and a unprecedented government bailout of another, the American International Group (AIG), a huge insurance company that traded financial products too. The stock market was suffering convulsions. The Dow Jones Industrials fell 504 points on Monday the 15th, the day Lehman Brothers went broke, then jumped 142 points on Tuesday, when the Federal Reserve Board, the American central bank, saved AIG, then dropped another 449 points on Wednesday, when several huge financial institutions were teetering.

The United States Congress is normally immune to emotional reactions. It is a ponderous institution, usually cautious and always reactive. But some events break through the protective layers of ceremony and custom that typically insulate the House and Senate from high emotion. One such event was unfolding in those September days.

"This is what a Category 4 financial crisis looks like," members of

Congress and other Washingtonians read on the front page of their morning newspaper that Thursday. Steven Pearlstein, *The Washington Post*'s economics columnist, captured the sinking feeling that gripped the nation's capital: "Giant blue-chip financial institutions swept away in a matter of days. Banks refusing to lend to other banks. . . . Daily swings of three, four, five hundred points in the Dow Jones industrial average. What we are witnessing may be the greatest destruction of financial wealth that the world has ever seen—paper losses measured in the trillions of dollars. . . . Finance is still a confidence game, and once the confidence goes, there's no telling when the selling will stop."

Open-ended bad news, a national and global disaster bound to get still worse—this was a formula for unbridled fear among members of the House and Senate. They all knew that they would be blamed for whatever had gone wrong whenever angry voters got a chance to register their reactions. The politicians always got blamed—this was an article of their professional faith. Fear of being blamed might be the single most potent motivator in the House and Senate. When Congress actually does something dramatic or unexpected, fear is often the best explanation.

This financial crisis had undermined congressional confidence. In normal situations members and especially senior leaders exude a sense of being on top of events, in control. This is an act, and often misleading, but rarely exposed. During this week in September, the actors stumbled. Congress was visibly on the defensive. Its pretentious facade crumbled. On the 16th, when leaders of the House and Senate met with Hank Paulson, the secretary of the treasury, and Ben Bernanke, chairman of the Fed, the fear was palpable.

That meeting was scheduled as Paulson and Bernanke were finalizing the plan for the Fed to put $85 billion into AIG, transforming the gigantic firm into a ward of the state. Paulson realized they needed to give key members of both houses advance warning for what was about to happen. For decades, administrations of both parties had realized that Congress usually did not want to do much, but it always wanted to be consulted.

Paulson had arranged for such a consultation with Harry Reid, the Democratic senator from Nevada who was the majority leader. They would meet at 6:30 p.m. in the conference room of the Senate Rules Committee in the Capitol. The majority leader invited key senators and congressmen, including the chairmen of the two committees that had jurisdiction over the Fed, Senator Chris Dodd of Connecticut and Representative Barney Frank of Massachusetts. There were only a few chairs in the room, so all stood.

When Paulson and Bernanke explained what was going to happen, the room was hushed. "There was an almost surreal quality to the meeting," Paulson later recounted. "The stunned lawmakers looked at us as if not quite believing what they were hearing."

Frank and Dodd both marveled that the Fed had the legal authority to simply make $85 billion available to AIG without anyone else's approval; theoretically these two men were responsible for overseeing the Fed. That evening they discovered that the central bank had powers they never knew existed. At the end of the meeting Senator Reid was blunt: "I want to be absolutely clear that Congress has not given you formal approval to take action. This is your responsibility and your decision." That was the true voice of Congress, covering its own flanks before all else.

Now, on the 18th, Speaker Nancy Pelosi had gathered the leaders of her Democratic majority in her grand office on the second floor of the Capitol. On this day the stock market had perked up, apparently encouraged by rumors that the administration was planning some new initiative to help banks cope with their suddenly rotten housing assets. We need to get Hank Paulson up here to talk with us, Pelosi told her inner circle. "I'll call him and set up a meeting for tomorrow." After this meeting broke up, she put in a call to the treasury secretary. She wanted to be consulted.

For Paulson, a large, energetic man of high intellect, rich Wall Street experience, and no detectable political talent, this was another in a long string of very bad days. At nine that morning the vice chairman of Morgan Stanley had called to warn that his investment bank was teetering. The world's banks refused to lend money to one another—credit markets were truly frozen. Disaster loomed. Paulson spent the next several hours exploring alternative responses to the crisis with Treasury colleagues. He spoke to President George W. Bush on the phone and arranged a meeting with him for that afternoon to discuss what to do. In a conference call with Bernanke and other Fed officials, everyone agreed that they would have to make a formal request to Congress to appropriate hundreds of billions of dollars to save the financial system.

No member of Congress was invited to join these conversations.

This was typical of modern practice in a crisis: The executive would formulate a response, then bring it to Capitol Hill for approval. In this case, Paulson and Bernanke both realized how hard it would be to get Congress to put up so much money to bail out banks.

Paulson was walking from the Treasury to the White House next door when he took Pelosi's call on his cell phone. She asked that he and Bernanke come up to Capitol Hill the next morning to brief the Democratic leadership.

"Madame Speaker," Pelosi recalled Paulson replying, "it cannot wait until tomorrow morning. We have to come today." Paulson explained "just how bad things were" and said he would be asking Congress for emergency powers. "We need legislation passed quickly. We need to send a strong signal to the market now."

Paulson asked Pelosi to assemble a bipartisan group of senior members from both House and Senate to hear from him and Bernanke. Soon after this call ended, Bernanke and Paulson sat down in the Oval Office to explain the grim facts to President Bush: The administration would have to ask for an emergency appropriation of half a trillion dollars to save the financial system and prevent another Great Depression. The dazed president approved this plan.

Pelosi conveyed Paulson's impatient message to her colleagues. They were taken aback. Paulson wanted an urgent meeting with House and Senate leaders, but waited for Pelosi to call him before saying so? "He hadn't called us!" recalled Steny Hoyer, the number two Democrat in the House of Representatives. Pelosi told Hoyer the meeting was set for 7 p.m. Her staff invited the relevant members; Pelosi herself called Harry Reid, who invited the key senators.

Thanks to a sense of grandeur that animated the many creators of the Capitol of the United States, members of the House of Representatives and the Senate work in extraordinary physical spaces. Some are ridiculously ornate, some feel like transplanted Greek temples, some are quite beautiful. All convey a sense of importance—the sort of rooms that history is made in. Members often volunteer the thought that the Capitol's splendor influences the attitudes of those who work in it.

Speaker Pelosi's conference room on the second floor of what is called the Capitol's west central front was a good example. It measures about fifteen feet by forty under vaulted ceilings decorated with classical designs and scenes from antiquity that look Roman. Ornate gilded moldings separate the ceiling from the walls that Pelosi's decorator had painted in a soothing coffee-with-cream tone. A beige carpet with a repeating diamond motif covered the marble floor. The room was dominated by a handsome mahogany table at least twenty-five feet long, big enough to accommodate twenty-two armchairs. Another thirty of the same chairs lined the walls—seats for staff when large meetings were convened. Above the table a giant crystal chandelier hung from the vaulted ceiling. Three windows looked west over the magnificent Mall; the view included the Washington Monument and Lincoln Memorial in the distance. There was just one piece of art on the walls, an oil portrait of Abraham Lincoln as a young Illinois congressman, painted early last century—another reminder of the history made in this building.

The meeting in the conference room on this evening was unusual in many ways, but it provided a clear view of the congressional leadership reacting spontaneously to unexpected bad news. Pelosi took her usual seat in the middle of the long table, with her back to the windows. Harry Reid sat on her right. The table was decorated with three bouquets of fresh flowers and two bowls of nuts and chocolates—Ghirardelli chocolates from Pelosi's hometown, San Francisco. The guests sat facing Pelosi and Reid: Bernanke, Paulson, several of his aides, and Chris Cox, a former Republican congressman from California who was the hapless chairman of the Securities and Exchange Commission, theoretically the regulator of many of the financial institutions now dead, dying, or endangered.

The others present were the two Republican leaders, Senator Mitch McConnell of Kentucky and Representative John Boehner of Ohio, who sat on Pelosi's left; Dodd and Frank and the senior Republican members of their committees, Senator Richard Shelby of Alabama and Representative Spencer Bachus, also of Alabama; and other members of the leadership of both houses: Democratic senators Dick Durbin of Illinois, Chuck Schumer of New York, and Patty Murray of Washington; Republican representative Roy Blunt of Missouri; and Democratic representatives Rahm Emanuel of Illinois and James Clyburn of South Carolina. Pelosi had ordered that only a handful of staff be allowed into the room, and six or eight were present.

Of this group, only half a dozen had a reasonably good understanding of the financial markets: Dodd and Frank, Shelby and Bachus,

Schumer—an ardent supporter of his constituents—and Emanuel, a former investment banker. As Paulson had discovered in his two years in Washington, the gulf that divided Capitol Hill from Wall Street was wide and deep. Too many members of Congress neither understood finance, nor wanted to learn about it. A prominent Republican in the House had confided to Paulson that "one third of our guys are real knuckle-draggers"—cavemen, primitives. After two years on the job, Paulson knew this to be true.

Pelosi quickly turned the meeting over to Paulson, who anticipated a hostile reception when he asked members of Congress to approve hundreds of billions for the banks. They already suspected he was just trying to bail out his old friends on Wall Street, he had told Bernanke at the White House that afternoon, after their meeting with Bush. "They'll kill me up there [on Capitol Hill]. I'll be hung out to dry."

Bernanke, an economics professor at Princeton before becoming a Federal Reserve Board governor in 2002, volunteered to speak first to exploit his considerable credibility. He had no Wall Street experience; he was an academic, an egghead, whose specialty was the Great Depression. He had the sort of rigorous, specialized expertise that can intimidate members of the House and Senate.

Paulson understood the mission. His chief of staff, Jim Wilkinson, a veteran of the Bush White House staff, had laid it out for him as he left the Treasury for Capitol Hill: "This is only going to work if you scare the shit out of them." Paulson knew that Bernanke could do this best. So when Pelosi turned her meeting over to Paulson, he reported briefly on their session with President Bush that afternoon and on the president's decision to propose new legislation, then asked Bernanke to describe the state of the financial system.

Bernanke handled himself like a professor leading a seminar, but a seminar with an unusual subject: the possible end of the world as we know it. He assumed no prior knowledge on the part of his class. He explained: They were facing a grave financial crisis. There had been a loss of confidence, and the markets were not working. There was a credit freeze. The commercial paper markets had ceased to operate. The stock market had dropped by more than a thousand points. The efforts he and Paulson had made to restore normalcy had proven inadequate, so they were now asking Congress to support an unprecedented appropriation of hundreds of billions of dollars to shore up the banks and head off total collapse. Bernanke said that he had been studying the Great Depression for his entire adult life. "If we don't act in a very huge way, you can expect another Great Depression, and this is going to be worse," he said sternly. "It is a matter of days before there is a meltdown in the global financial system." And he warned, "Our tools are not sufficient" to deal with this crisis.

"This is a save-your-country moment," said Cox of the SEC, implying that hundreds of billions of dollars was a tolerable expense under such extreme circumstances. It's time to come together and act, Cox said. He knew his former colleagues, knew that wrapping the cause in the flag could help.

Senator Reid noted that the stock market was up sharply that day, suggesting that maybe they didn't have to be so afraid. Bernanke dismissed this news—the market was up based on rumors that this meeting was going to take place, and that new government action would follow. If the expected actions didn't materialize, Bernanke said, the market would plummet.

"I kind of scared them," Bernanke said later. "I kind of scared myself."

When Bernanke had finished his brief, terrifying lecture, Paulson spoke. In all his years at Goldman Sachs (thirty-two of them until he became treasury secretary in 2006), "I've never seen anything like this," Paulson said. They were living through a once-in-a-century event. To salvage the situation, "we have to buy residential and commercial mortgages and mortgage-backed securities [from the banks that held them]. We need hundreds of billions of dollars to start off." Congress, Paulson said, had to pass legislation at once—the next week—to allow Treasury to begin buying these toxic assets. Without action they faced a financial calamity. The country could collapse.

In the words of Senator Dodd, there was "an eerie, jaw-dropping silence in the room." No one present had ever lived through a comparable moment. Now the usual, jaunty cockiness of these men and women evaporated. "I could hear everyone gulp," said Senator Schumer. "People who talk for a living somehow couldn't think of anything to say," Dodd marveled.

Bernanke made another point based on his academic research: There are no examples in history of a meltdown in the financial system that was not accompanied by a depression in the rest of the economy. Main Street is tied to Wall Street. That is why the Congress needed to act quickly, he said—if it didn't act, a depression-type situation would result. Congress should pass a simple piece of legislation authorizing these purchases, Paulson said. He urged again that this be done quickly, without the issue becoming politicized.

"I chuckled when I heard that," said Jaime Lizarraga, a Pelosi aide who was in the room, and who knew from experience how politicized the House of Representatives had become. Partisan warfare had dominated Congress since the 1980s.

Members asked technical questions, many stemming from the fact that they didn't really understand what Paulson was proposing. The members knew they had a responsibility to push Paulson for explanations, but they weren't always certain what to ask. How would the toxic assets be valued? Boehner wanted to know. We would pay more than their apparent current value, Paulson said, hoping they would become more valuable over time. Who would manage this process? Frank asked. Either the Treasury or a new entity to be created for the purpose, Paulson said. Wouldn't the announcement of this plan reassure markets and help restore some confidence? Dodd asked. Yes, said Paulson, an announcement of the plan should have "a salutary effect."

Senator Shelby was worried about the cost. Could it be as much as $500 billion? Yes, Bernanke answered, it could be that much. The program should be "big enough to make a difference," Paulson added, but said he didn't want to put a number on it now. Shelby, sitting next to his friend and colleague Dodd, who then chaired the Banking Committee they had served on together for years, whispered into Dodd's ear: "Chris, they should have listened to you, they should have listened to you!" Dodd had been holding hearings on the frailties of the housing market for two years without persuading the administration or Bernanke that a breakdown was at least possible and perhaps likely.

Congressman Frank, who by reputation possessed the quickest mind in the House of Representatives, began to think ahead. They could do this, he said, but conditions had to be set. There had to be guidelines for the compensation received by executives of the firms that would be helped. Warrants were needed to protect taxpayers' interests—securities issued by the bailed-out firms that would allow the government to buy their shares at a fixed price, in hopes that over time such warrants would become valuable, and help repay the government. Practical ways had to be found to help more people avoid foreclosure, Frank insisted.

The idea of a government role in setting bankers' compensation alarmed Paulson. If you insist on that, he said, the auctions could fail, because some banks and financial institutions might refuse to take part in a program that threatened to limit their executives' pay. "If you put in a compensation requirement," Paulson said, "I cannot say it [his auction scheme for purchasing toxic assets] will work."

"If there are no compensation requirements," Frank snapped back, "I cannot say it will pass" the House of Representatives.

And if a bill isn't passed? someone asked. "Heaven help us all," replied Paulson, a practicing Christian Scientist. At this point, said one of the staff in the room, "the meeting was starting to get tense."

Spencer Bachus and his senior aide, Larry Lavender, a former Alabama businessman with a glorious white handlebar mustache, had another idea. Instead of the complicated plan for auctioning off toxic assets, why not just inject capital directly into the troubled banks by buying their shares? This had been done successfully in similar situations—in Sweden, for example, in a banking crisis there in 1992. Ultimately Swedish taxpayers lost almost nothing because they owned a piece of their banks, which eventually returned to profitability. Bachus and Lavender had been discussing the possibility for months as they watched the American crisis unfold, and Bachus asked about it now.

Paulson shot it down dismissively. Simply buying shares would not have the positive impact on the banks that was needed. "If you want something that will work," he said, "this [his plan] is it."

We need to leave this room saying that we're going to write a bill, Pelosi said, but her Senate counterpart, Harry Reid, was nervous about the timing: "If you think we can pass a bill next week to give you $500 billion, you don't understand the Senate. . . . It takes me two weeks to pass a bill to flush a toilet around here."

Mitch McConnell, the Republican leader in the Senate, demurred: "If what is at stake is saving the country, we can do this in record time."

Schumer, the New York Democrat, said the administration had to offer something significant on foreclosures. Inevitably the Paulson plan would be seen as a bailout for the banks. Little people had to be seen to benefit as well as the big bankers. "We have to have a fore-closure mitigation effort in order to pass this" in the Senate. "If we don't help homeowners," Schumer added, "we will be damned."

Shelby of Alabama, a former Democrat who converted to the GOP in 1995, agreed that "doing something for distressed homeowners" ought to be part of the package. But he also expressed reluctance to support Paulson's request, the only member at the table to do so.

The tension was subsiding. Apart from Shelby, a clear consensus was taking hold. Cox's admonition seemed apt; it did feel like a "save-your-country moment."

Reid again expressed concern about Paulson's timetable. Pelosi reminded Reid that his Republican counterpart, McConnell, had just said the Senate could move with record speed on a matter of such importance, and McConnell nodded in agreement. We have to work together on the bill, Paulson said, and Congress (scheduled to begin a recess the next day) has to stay in session until it's done. Reid then suggested that he and Pelosi formally designate Dodd and Frank, chairmen of the most relevant committees, to work with Treasury on language for a bill. Frank insisted that the first step be a draft from Treasury laying out what the administration wanted.

The final, surprising sign of a consensus came from John Boehner of Ohio, the House Republican leader, a man whose many conservative colleagues reflexively opposed government interventions in the market. His conservatives kept Boehner on a short leash. "This is a national crisis," Boehner said. Congress, he noted, had low approval ratings (in public opinion polls—he was right about that!). "We need to rise above politics and show the American people we can work together." This was about saving the economy, preserving people's savings, Boehner continued, and they had to work in a bipartisan way. "I will be here as long as it takes. Let's lock arms and get it done." McConnell said it was important that they all talk that way when they left the room.

After an hour and a half the meeting broke up. Participants walked into the corridor to confront the battalion of television cameras waiting for them. There seemed to be a shared urge to brag about how united they were. Pelosi spoke first: "We just had what I believe was a very productive meeting where we heard from the Administration and from the chairman of the Fed, an initiative to help resolve the financial crisis in our country."

Senator Reid said Congress was "ready to react to any administration plan. We need to hear from them. Next week should be very, very interesting."

Said Paulson, "I think we saw the best of the United States of

America in the Speaker's office tonight. This country is able to come together and do things quickly when it needs to be done for the good of the American people. . . . We're coming together to work on an expeditious solution which is aimed right at the heart of this problem which is illiquid assets on financial institution balance sheets."

Bernanke said, "I thank the congressional leadership for a very, very positive meeting. We look forward to working closely with Congress to resolve this financial crisis and get our economy moving again."

Boehner said he believed a package could be approved by Congress "within a matter of days."

What had happened in that room over ninety stomach-churning minutes was so rare as to be unique in the experience of everyone sitting around Pelosi's conference table. None of them had ever had to confront such an event—the economic equivalent of 9/11, Dodd called it.

The meeting was unique in another respect—the grim warnings Bernanke and Paulson delivered were a surprise. Unlike normal interactions between the executive branch and Congress, "nobody had a heads-up, no ground work had been done," in the words of David Smith, chief economist to the House Financial Services Committee and one of the few staff allowed in the room. If anyone at the table doubted Bernanke's unexpected conclusion that a second Great Depression could be imminent, he or she didn't say so that night. Who were they to question these two experts, who seemed so scared themselves? In such a situation, it is instinctive for members of Congress to defer to the executive's authority.

Members of Congress in the modern era are used to having homework done for them by staff. They rely on facts, figures, and arguments prepared by others. Announcing one's position on a controversial matter without knowing what your party leaders or colleagues are thinking is also rare, and risky too, as John Boehner soon discovered. His statesmanlike commitment to "rise above politics and show the American people we can work together" disappeared after a week under pressure from the Republican Study Committee, the most conservative and largest element of his membership, which decided it wanted no part of Paulson's "bailout."

Over the next fifteen days Congress took the financial world on a terrifying joyride. Paulson submitted a ridiculously incomplete three-page bill to Congress that would have given him a blank check to spend $700 billion, the amount finally agreed upon inside the Bush administration. Dodd and Frank went to work in their committees and converted that document into a 450-page bill full of limitations and conditions that Paulson and his successors would have to respect. This was a classic act of legislative improvisation, a reminder of the many ways legislating is like performing jazz. Dodd and Frank were the bandleaders, their colleagues on the Senate and House committees, the sidemen. The players inspired and accommodated one another, and produced a bill that was intended to create something akin to harmony—the Troubled Asset Relief Program, or TARP.

But harmony was elusive. The House of Representatives voted against the bill on September 29, 228–205. Democrats supported the bill 140–95, but House Republicans opposed it decisively, 133–65, despite the Republican administration's pleas for support. The world's stock markets responded cataclysmically. The Dow Jones Industrials fell 777 points, the biggest point drop ever recorded. Paper losses for that day alone totaled $1.2 trillion.

There followed forty-eight hours of hectic activity in the Senate, whose version of the bill was "sweetened" with benefits for a few special interests favored by some House Republicans. The collapse on Wall Street after the first vote and the fears expressed to members by bankers and businessmen at home who suddenly discovered that no one could lend or borrow also had an impact. Two days after the House voted the bill down, the Senate passed its version 74–25, and two days after that, the House voted on the Senate's revised bill. This time it passed, 263–171, because thirty-two Democrats and twenty-six Republicans who originally voted no reversed course and supported the bill.

The tumultuous events that filled the fifteen days after that meeting in Speaker Pelosi's conference room brought out the worst in the United States Congress. Many members could never grasp what was happening in the financial markets, and pandered shamelessly to scared constituents whose understanding of the crisis was even weaker. Representative Brad Sherman, a liberal Democrat from California, was one of the panderers: "We're told not to worry because this $700 billion is not going to cost anything," Sherman said after voting against the plan. "Wall Street gets its money now, and we get it back never."* "Undermining the basic principles of Americans and pushing hundreds of billions of dollars on the backs of hard-working taxpayers is absolutely wrong and irresponsible," said Representative Tom Price, a leading conservative from Georgia. "It is also not the American way." Many of the conservative Republicans in the House simply refused to entertain any plan for government action to stabilize the markets. In the book he wrote later, Paulson recorded this comment from one of them: "I've been talking about deregulation and free markets my whole life. You're asking me to change my view, and there is no way I can do that." This was an example of the powerful tug of ideology that colors so much of the work of the modern Congress.

The fifty-eight vote switchers in the House looked particularly feckless. For many of them, the courage of their no-vote convictions lasted only hours—just until they saw the sky falling as a result of the first House vote against the bill. Liaquat Ahamed, Pulitzer Prize–winning author and financial expert, noted eight months later that the financial markets actually survived the bankruptcy of Lehman Brothers, often cited as the event that pushed global markets over the edge. Ahamed noted that the Dow Jones Industrial Average—one of the basic measurements of the stock market—fell only 279 points, or 2.5 percent, in the two weeks that followed Lehman's bankruptcy. But the same index fell nearly 2,700 points in the two weeks following the no vote in the House—a decline of nearly 25 percent. Subsequent reversal of the House vote did not restore confidence, Ahamed wrote. "The specter had been raised that America's dysfunctional political system might paralyze the country in dealing with the worst banking crisis since the Great Depression." Congressional fecklessness had consequences.

Hours after the second House vote on October 3, President Bush put his signature to the bill, and Paulson had the money he needed to bail out the banks. Almost immediately, he had to change course. As the global financial system teetered, Paulson's cocky certainty that auctions of toxic assets were the answer evaporated. Auctions proved much too complicated to execute quickly, and speed was suddenly critical. On the very afternoon that Bush signed the bill into law, Paulson asked his staff to figure out how to do just what Spencer Bachus had

---

* Thirty months later, in the spring of 2011, all the bailout money advanced to banks had been repaid.

suggested on September 18—use government money to invest directly in troubled banks. Luckily, the TARP legislation allowed him to do so, in part because Pelosi and her staff had insisted on it. They weren't experts, but they could have good instincts.

"In my time in Washington," Paulson wrote after he had returned to the private sector, "I learned that, unfortunately, it takes a crisis to get difficult and important things done." This is an old lesson, relearned by newcomers to the nation's capital on a regular basis. A genuine crisis increases the political risks of inaction to the point where they appear greater than the risk of doing something that proves imperfect. In this episode, efforts by Bernanke, Paulson, and their associates to scare members of Congress reflected their appreciation of this old rule. A really scared member can support policy changes that ordinarily would be unthinkable. In a crisis, voters expect action.

In the end fear triumphed. The final, negotiated version of the bill provided $700 billion—more than the annual defense budget, including the wars in Afghanistan and Iraq—to rescue the very financial institutions that helped push the world into this catastrophe.

The fecklessness and fear that proved so important in this episode were symptoms of the most fundamental reality of the United States Congress: It is an utterly human institution. Institutions aren't feckless or fearful, people are. On occasion people can also be serious, courageous, and creative. How Congress behaves is a function of human choices, not institutional imperatives. Human frailties produced the Great Crash of 2008, leaving it to human resourcefulness to try to repair the damage and reduce the chances of a recurrence of such destructive behavior.

At the beginning of 2009, the interested parties—bankers, lobbyists, members of Congress and their staffs—all seemed to understand that a big legislative event was in the offing. The crash and its aftermath had put financial reform on the agenda. Disaster called for action of some kind. The outgoing Republican administration, its incoming Democratic successor, and the Democratic Congress agreed about that. Congress would act.

CHAPTER TWO
———

The Man Who Wasn't Gray

Barney Frank was nervously excited about the prospect of legislating new regulations for the American financial industry. As chairman of the House Committee on Financial Services, once known as the Banking Committee, he would be the single most important player in the House of Representatives on these issues. He had been a big player throughout the fall, exposing his political neck to help Paulson get the authority he wanted to bail out troubled banks. That had been painful, but now Frank saw a chance to make some history. The opportunity to rewrite the rulebook would create the biggest moment of his long career, and he knew it. He had been preparing for it for nearly half a century.

In the House of Representatives, the standard-issue member is the human equivalent of gray. This is obvious in the cloakrooms just off the House floor at the southern end of the Capitol, where the men and women whose gold-colored lapel pins announce their status as members mill about and schmooze with one another. It is obvious during business hours in any House committee hearing room, or on the floor when legislation is being debated. These are earnest citizens whose bland faces could easily disappear in any crowd of prosperous Americans. Most of them are instinctually polite, good-natured, and careful. Few if any suffer from a deprivation of ego, but their vanity is generally held in check. They may want to be loved, admired, and—most of all—reelected every two years, but most of them have no interest in standing out from the crowd. Like student body presidents everywhere, they have succeeded in life by not offending.

Barney Frank is one of the rare exceptions. From the time he was a student politician at Harvard in the late 1950s, Frank was delighted to be special and often eager to be rude. ("I would rather be rude than bored," he liked to say.) His singularity began with his physical appearance, which was never conventional. Keeping his shirts tucked in was a constant struggle, one he often lost. His shoes were famously so scuffed that the shiny black surface (always black, easier that way) disappeared. His weight went up and down erratically, but he was never slim. His black hair resisted his sporadic efforts to arrange it atop his head. His face was distinctive too, built around a plump nose, chipmunk cheeks, and a small mouth formed by slim lips above a prominent chin, with a hint of a second one below. He wore thick eyeglasses. He always talked faster than anyone around him—so fast, and with such a thick Bayonne accent, that some had trouble understanding his words. Articulation was the victim of speed. His friends thought the main reason he talked so fast was to keep up with his brain. Often, what he was saying was original, and hilarious. He loved the art of the quip.

Frank was an unlikely Harvard fixture—a Jew who grew up just across the Hudson River from New York, whose father ran a truck stop much frequented by the criminal element, in a world of northern New Jersey dominated by corrupt politics and the mob. When Frank was six his father, Sam, spent a year in prison for refusing to testify in a grand jury investigation of his older brother, Harry Frank, whose auto dealership had a cozy relationship with the Jersey City Democratic machine. The family truck stop weathered this storm and young Barney completed a relatively normal childhood with a distinguished academic record. His older sister, Ann, had broken all family precedent by winning admission to Radcliffe College at Harvard; Barney followed her to Cambridge. Neither of their parents had gone to college, and no one from their world had been to Harvard.

As an undergraduate and later a graduate student and junior member of the Harvard faculty, Frank became a famous campus character, widely admired and enjoyed. He staked out a distinctive political position as a fervid but practical liberal who consistently rejected the radicalism of the early 1960s propagated by Students for a Democratic Society (SDS) and anti–Vietnam War activists. When *The Harvard Crimson*, the student-run newspaper, praised SDS members for participating directly in electoral politics, working for candidates in the 1962 election instead of just marching in protest, Frank wrote a critical letter to the editor: "Long before peace marchers discovered the inefficacy of effervescence there were many students who realized that their political ideals could best be effected within the political process." He was referring to himself. Later Frank regularly debated SDS leaders in public, often ridiculing their radical pose.

Frank was on a path to a Ph.D. in government from Harvard when his career was transformed by an invitation to work for the 1967 Boston mayoral campaign of Kevin White, an appealing, upper-class Irish politician. When White won, he asked Frank to work in his office. At first Frank refused—he had to write a dissertation to complete his Ph.D., and under the rules of the Harvard government department he had to finish it within two years. White then successfully lobbied the chairman of the department, a friend and neighbor, to waive that rule so Frank could work for him as his chief aide.

This was Frank's first experience in government and he loved it. He quickly established a reputation as the hardest-working member of a reform administration full of hard workers. He became White's right-hand man on both politics and policy and soon knew everyone who mattered in Boston.

After three years with White, Frank was invited to Washington to work as administrative assistant—chief aide and office manager—for Michael J. Harrington, a newly elected antiwar Democratic congressman from Massachusetts who was just four years older than Frank. Frank loved being on Capitol Hill, but stayed for only a year, because an opportunity arose in Boston that he decided he had to seize. The state representative from Boston's Ward 5 had decided to retire, and Frank saw a chance to run for office in his own right. The unfinished Ph.D. and the Barney Frank who was pursuing it were both now artifacts of history. At the age of thirty-two, he had found his true calling.

Ward 5 had historically elected moderate Republicans to the state House of Representatives, the lower house of the state legislature, but registered Republicans constituted less than 20 percent of the electorate, and Frank thought he could win the seat. He first had to win a Democratic primary, and did so easily, organizing a spirited campaign manned by scores of volunteers, including many of his former students. In the general election he faced a serious Republican with roots in the district, but in Boston, 1972 was a Democratic year. Massachusetts was the only state George McGovern carried against Richard

Nixon. McGovern did especially well in Ward 5. For years afterward, Frank joked that he was one of the very few politicians in America who could attribute electoral victory to George McGovern's coattails. Frank easily won the seat.

The Massachusetts House turned Frank into a legislator. He loved the action, loved the variety of issues and arguments. He realized that this was a job that played both to his intellectual strengths and to his personal weaknesses. "My short attention span, jumping around, some of my weaknesses in other contexts became advantages as a legislator," he later observed. "I am much better at doing a lot of things quickly than doing a couple of things over a long period of time. When you are dealing with seven or eight issues a day at the State House, that becomes an advantage."

"Even as a freshman, he was eight lengths ahead of everybody else," according to Jim Segel, a former Harvard student of Frank's who was also elected to the Massachusetts House in 1972. "He just has this natural ability. He sees the essence of things. He sees what's important. He can strategize and see paths better than most. He also combines a big talent for operating inside with communications skills that make him effective outside, an unusual combination."

While serving in the legislature, Frank decided he ought to get a law degree. He persuaded Harvard Law School to admit him despite its rule that a student could not hold a regular job while studying law. He did so well that he was invited to join the Law Review with the best students at the end of his first year; he declined the honor to concentrate on politics. He served four terms in the legislature and became perhaps the most famous state legislator in America, a favorite with both the Boston media and national political reporters. Frank understood that reporters were suckers for a clever quip.

In his fourth term Frank's enthusiasm for the statehouse began to wane. His fortieth birthday in 1980 put him into a funk. "He was depressed," Segel recalled. Segel knew one reason why. Shortly before that birthday, Frank had invited him to breakfast at the Ritz-Carlton in Boston to confide that he was gay, and wanted to come out of the closet. This news was not a surprise, Segel said years later. But it did surprise him that Frank wanted to make a public affirmation of his sexual orientation. Segel, by then a close friend and confidant, told Frank he shouldn't come out "if he wanted a political future." Frank protested: "Everybody thinks I'm gay anyway." No, replied Segel, most people didn't think about his sexual orientation. Some thought he was asexual. "No one is asexual," Frank replied. He was worn out by hiding his orientation, and by denying himself a personal life.

Later in 1980 another unexpected resignation, this one involuntary, ended Frank's agonizing and opened a new door to his ambition. Father Robert Drinan, a Jesuit priest and liberal Democratic member of the U.S. House from Massachusetts's 4th District, had to resign when Pope John Paul II ordered that no priest serve in an elected political office. Drinan's resignation came just three days before the filing deadline for a place on the ballot. Frank urgently needed to collect at least two thousand signatures from voters in a district where he didn't live. He got six thousand. Nearly a dozen Democrats joined the race, but Frank prevailed.

Running a successful campaign brought out the worst in Frank. He never liked campaigning, and was no good at being nice to people he didn't care about. He hated being criticized. He drove his staff to distraction. In the general election campaign he ran against a conservative dentist and former member of the John Birch Society who had no political experience. Many politicians and political reporters in Massachusetts assumed that Frank would coast to victory in the heavily Democratic district, but Frank understood that as a Jewish outsider in a largely Catholic constituency, in a year when Republicans, led by Ronald Reagan, were going to do well even in Massachusetts, victory was far from guaranteed. The possibility that he might lose really upset him. "I was worried," he admitted later.

"Part of our job," said Jim Segel, who was the campaign manager for his old friend, "was to keep Barney away from people. He was alienating everyone he came in contact with. . . . If he wasn't such a good friend, I would have walked out. You have to love Barney Frank to like him." Years later, Segel said, "I'm not sure his staff voted for him. He was an impossible candidate!" Frank never conquered this dark side; it has tripped him up periodically throughout his career.

But he did conquer the Birch Society dentist, Richard Jones. Reagan carried the 4th District and the commonwealth of Massachusetts, but Frank won—by just eight thousand votes. Swimming against a powerful national tide, he had become a member of the House of Representatives.

In the House Frank followed the same path to prominence that had worked for him in the Massachusetts legislature. First he mastered the rules of procedure. Then he cultivated his reputation as an insightful quipster whom reporters could count on for apt and colorful quotations. He did his homework on issues that interested him. Finally he established himself as a serious player who couldn't be pushed around or marginalized. It was a bravura performance for a new member, and it was noticed. When polled by news organizations, Frank's colleagues chose him as the most promising freshman member; in 1981 there were seventy-one others to choose from.

His position was nonetheless insecure. After the 1980 census, Massachusetts had to give up one of its twelve House seats. The state's redistricting commission, controlled by conservative Democrats whom Frank had alienated in the legislature, decided in December 1981 to give up Frank's seat and force him into the district of Margaret Heckler, a popular eight-term member who was a Massachusetts-style moderate Republican. Heckler routinely won more than 60 percent of the vote, and Frank was initially convinced he couldn't beat her in a new district composed primarily of her old constituents. He told family members that he was going to retire after a single term rather than face the pain of losing to Heckler. He moaned to staff and friends about the unfairness of it all, a pose that struck many of them as self-pity. It was surely evidence of his distaste for selling himself to voters in a campaign. "Anyone who tells you he likes campaigning," Frank has said, "is either a liar or a sociopath."

Frank's closest allies and friends refused to let him off the hook. Segel warned him that supporters would be furious if he ducked a contest with Heckler. "People busted their ass to help you get that seat. Now it's tough and you're walking away. That's what they're going to think."

After weeks of agonizing, Frank agreed to make the run. The first poll conducted for his campaign brought discouraging news: Heckler led 52–34 in the reconfigured district. But the political terrain of 1982 proved favorable for Frank. There was a recession and Reagan's popularity had waned. Frank waged the best campaign of his career, raising $1.5 million to do so—a huge sum for a House race at the time, and $500,000 more than Heckler. His television commercials were brilliant. The best featured an unidentified white-haired woman speaking into the camera about Social Security: "All this talk about cutting social security is really making me nervous. That's why I'm glad Barney Frank is in Congress. Barney helped stop the Republicans from cutting cost-of-living and Medicare benefits, and he'll keep fighting to protect our social security. How can I be so sure Barney will do the right thing by us older people? Because," said Elsie Frank, "he's my son."

Heckler came off badly in a series of joint appearances and debates—she wasn't ready for the likes of Frank—and in November he thumped her by sixty thousand votes, enhancing his status in the state and nationally. Now, Frank confided to friends at the time, he felt he had a job that he loved and could keep for the rest of his working life. His assessment was correct—over the next twenty-eight years, through fourteen more reelection campaigns, he never faced a really serious challenge at the polls.

He did, however, find numerous other challenges, including harrowing ones involving his private life. In 1987 he decided to announce his sexual orientation to the world, making him the first member of Congress to voluntarily acknowledge his homosexuality. He did this with considerable trepidation in May 1987 in an interview with *The Boston Globe*, and was surprised how well the news was received in his district, and in Washington. For years afterward he chastised himself for taking so long to come out. The decision to do so had allowed him, at age forty-seven, finally to lead the life of a gay man without fear of being exposed.

Unfortunately for Frank, it came too late to head off the worst scandal of his career. In his years in the closet, Frank sometimes turned to male prostitutes for sex. One was Steven Gobie, whom Frank had found through a classified ad. Frank and Gobie went from a paid sexual relationship to an odd friendship that Frank later compared to a mentoring relationship. Gobie, a manipulative con man, took advantage of Frank by using his Capitol Hill basement apartment (famous among his friends as an ill-kempt, unappealing habitation) to run a prostitution business that offered both male and female companionship. Frank paid Gobie as a personal aide, and paid for his lawyer and psychiatrist. Frank ended the relationship and kicked Gobie out of his apartment in August 1987, three months after his interview with the *Globe*.

Two years later, hoping to exploit his relationship with Frank by turning it into a book or movie, Gobie revealed that he'd run a prostitution service out of Frank's apartment. Frank acknowledged their relationship but said he ended it as soon as he learned about the prostitution service. He asked the House Ethics Committee to investigate. The committee concluded, eleven months later, that he should be reprimanded, a mild punishment.

Some Republicans tried to stiffen the penalty to "censure," or even to expel Frank from Congress, but their proposals lost badly on the House floor. During the floor debate a chastened Frank enumerated his many errors of judgment, saying, "Those mistakes were mine." He also offered an explanation: "There was in my life a central element of dishonesty," Frank said. "Three years ago I decided concealment wouldn't work—I wish I had decided that long ago." The House voted for the reprimand 408–18.

Again Frank's colleagues were supportive, and his constituents went on reelecting him by large majorities. But this episode left a scar; Frank would never escape its taint. At best, it was a reminder of his unusualness—of the fact that Barney Frank was indeed a singular fellow, and never gray.

In the House, the best way to achieve real power is to keep getting reelected every two years, and then to be lucky. So it was with Frank. One key bit of luck came in 2002, when John LaFalce of Buffalo, New York, decided to retire from the House—the third time a retirement gave Frank's career a boost. LaFalce was the senior Democrat on the Financial Services Committee, and Frank was next in seniority, so he became the "ranking minority member," or Democratic leader of Financial Services.

Frank's next bit of luck came from George W. Bush, whose unsuccessful policies at home and abroad helped Democrats regain control of the House in November 2006. For the first time since 1995, the chairmen of the House committees—powerful potentates who generally enjoy a great deal of discretionary authority from both senior party leaders and other members—would be Democrats. One of them was Frank.

By the time he got power, he had one of the best reputations on Capitol Hill. Just two months before the 2006 election, *Washingtonian* magazine asked congressional aides to rank members in various categories. They chose Frank as the brainiest, the funniest, and the most eloquent member of the House. Frank's colleagues in both parties routinely referred to him as the smartest member. Not all of them appreciated his stinging partisanship, imperious manners, or obvious satisfaction with his own capabilities, but Frank enjoyed the respect of his fellows.

As a serious student of numerous issues including housing, military spending, civil rights law, and banking, Frank was one of the rare policy experts in the House. Over the nearly three decades that he had served in Congress the legislative branch had changed profoundly. By 2009 the number of members who cared about and understood complex issues of national policy had shrunk dramatically.

One wise observer of this transformation was Lee Hamilton of Indiana, a Democrat who was first elected to the House in 1964 and stayed until he retired in 1999. Initially, Hamilton said years later, he was one of many members who really cared about policy, and were happy to work on complicated, substantive matters. But from about 1980 onward, politics began to eclipse policy as most members' primary concern. By the mid-1990s, both parties battled every two years for control of the House, waging ever more expensive campaigns based increasingly on expensive television advertising. Fundraising became a primary concern for every member who ever worried about reelection. Policy lost its primacy. "Politics became more important," Hamilton said, and the House changed. He was not sad to leave when he did.

Frank understood his special status. It was obvious in September and October 2008, during the darkest days of the financial crisis, when Democratic colleagues flocked to him for explanations of what was happening that they could use at home during their reelection campaigns. Most House Democrats (172 out of 235 who voted) had supported TARP, the bailout bill, and all knew that their vote would be unpopular at home. Frank tried to help them explain, first to themselves and then to their constituents, that passing TARP was extremely unpleasant but also necessary to prevent an economic catastrophe. He promised to help pass subsequent legislation to help homeowners threatened with foreclosure and to limit the compensation of bankers who got bailed out. In early December 2008, weeks after the election that produced a much bigger Democratic majority in the House, Frank noted proudly that not one Democrat had lost his or her seat because of voting for TARP. The policy expert could be good at politics too.

CHAPTER THREE

What Is to Be Done?

The TARP legislation that bailed out the nation's banks caused political turmoil, but it actually represented a cautious, conservative approach to a radical problem. Both Hank Paulson and the Democrats who controlled Congress in 2008 had decided in the heat of the crisis that their goal should be to hold the old system together and prevent a catastrophe. No serious effort was made either to call to account the profligate institutions and individuals who contributed to the crash, or to meaningfully alter the financial landscape—by forcing the biggest institutions to break up into smaller pieces, for example. Confronted by disaster and panic, the relevant officials in the executive branch and in Congress seemed to share the same instinct: Keep the old ship afloat.

As he began to contemplate how to change the rules, Barney Frank was not inclined to alter that conservative approach. He thought of himself as a proud liberal, a direct descendant of John F. Kennedy and Lyndon B. Johnson, a believer in the power of government to improve the lives of ordinary Americans. He also took pride in being a realist who declined to tilt at windmills. He said, repeatedly and unabashedly, that he believed in the market, and in capitalism. But he felt strongly that to be efficient, stable, and fair, a capitalist economy needed good rules. His vision of regulatory reform was a set of new, improved rules to govern essentially the same universe of financial firms and banks that already existed.

He had no desire to take control of the issue himself. In a conversation three days before Christmas 2008, Frank said it would not be his job to invent a new New Deal. He would leave that, at least initially, to the incoming administration of Barack Obama. "Our visions generally coincide," he said. "I'll count on them to fill in a lot of the blanks."

This was consistent with the well-established balance of power between the executive and legislative branches. That balance was evident in the emergency response to the Great Crash. As we have seen, the first proposals for action did not come from the institution that the founding fathers expected would make most national policy, the Congress. In Article I, Section 8 of the Constitution the founders enumerated congressional powers that dwarf those reserved for the president, described in Article II. Only Congress can coin money, raise and spend government revenue, ratify treaties, declare war, regulate foreign trade and interstate commerce, and "provide for . . . the general welfare." The founders did give the president the power to disapprove (veto) acts of Congress, but then gave Congress authority to overrule (by a two-thirds vote) any presidential disapproval.

The founders lived in simpler times, and did not foresee the enormous growth of the government, nor the increasing complexity of American life as the country grew into a continental powerhouse. By the twentieth century, a succession of strong presidents established the ascendancy of executive power. The fact that the presidential administration is responsible for day-to-day management of a huge government has made it the dominant force. Congress retained its ultimate powers—the executive could spend no money not appropriated by vote of Congress, nor impose any form of regulation or control not authorized in explicit legislation approved by House and Senate—but in the modern era it initiated new laws or policies less and less often. Typically, the modern Congress responds to proposals from the executive.

Frank had begun the legislative process that would produce regulatory reform nearly six months earlier, two months before the bankruptcy of Lehman Brothers signaled a disaster. He did so by summoning witnesses from the executive branch. On July 20, 2008, he held a hearing on "Systemic Risk and the Financial Markets," taking testimony from Paulson, Bernanke, Cox of the Securities and Exchange Commission, and Timothy Geithner, then the boyish president of the Federal Reserve Bank of New York.

An effective committee chairman uses hearings to lay an intellectual and political foundation for legislation. They give members and staff a chance to think through the issue at hand. They provide a way to exploit the expertise of outsiders—government officials, academics, practitioners. Hearings provide a forum for testing legislative ideas against reality, giving the interests or individuals affected by proposed legislation a chance to explain how they think it might affect the real world.

Frank began the process, but not alone. No chairman ever organizes a hearing, proposes a new bill, writes it, or wins its passage by himself. In the modern Congress most chairmen don't even originate the idea for such a hearing, though Frank was, sometimes, an exception to that rule. Hearings, like virtually everything else of substance that occurs in Congress, are organized and often orchestrated, even scripted, by staff.

Edward M. Kennedy slipped an important truth into the memoir he wrote just before he died: "Ninety-five percent of the nitty-gritty work of drafting [bills] and negotiating [their final form] is now done by staff. That . . . marks an enormous shift of responsibility over the past forty or fifty years." Could Kennedy really mean that staff took care of nearly all the important work? Yes, he could mean just that.

Perhaps the definitive demonstration of staff influence on hearings was provided by a fellow named Harley Dirks, the senior clerk in the 1970s of a subcommittee of the Senate Appropriations Committee. Dirks was known for scripting hearings so carefully that he knew in advance exactly how they would proceed. He demonstrated this talent in 1976 when half a dozen of his hearings were canceled to accommodate a tight legislative schedule. Nevertheless, the Government Printing Office produced thousands of pages of "transcripts" of those hearings that read as if the meetings had actually taken place. Dirks had embellished his scripts, which were based on statements provided by government agencies and senators' offices, to create this false impression, even including purported off-the-cuff remarks by senators and witnesses. When his maneuver was exposed in the press, Dirks had to resign.

Frank had a talented staff. Unconventionally, he did not hire his own staff director for the Financial Services Committee, but retained the woman that his predecessor as the senior committee Democrat had picked in 2001. She was Jeanne Roslanowick, eight years Frank's junior, a graduate of the Catholic schools of Erie, Pennsylvania, Marquette University in Milwaukee, the University of Massachusetts (a master's in public affairs), and Yale Law School. From an early age she had unusual ambitions for a woman of her generation. "I can remember crying in my room when JFK was assassinated, and saying someday I want to go to Washington and do something important," she recalled.

After several frustrating years practicing law in a Washington firm, she applied for and got the post of counsel to one of the House Banking Committee's subcommittees. For the next three decades Roslanowick worked for the committee. Once such careers were commonplace; numerous long-serving aides provided institutional memory, continuity, and expertise. Those who rose to senior positions enjoyed considerable status on Capitol Hill and in Washington. But in the 1980s the lobbying industry began to boom, and smart firms in this expanding marketplace began offering big salaries to senior staff on Capitol Hill who knew the legislative process, had personal relationships with members and their aides, and could help clients try to influence congressional decisions. Some like Roslanowick rebuffed offers to double, triple, or even quadruple their congressional salaries to come "downtown" as lobbyists, but a great many succumbed. A revolving door began to spin that eventually swept nearly four hundred defeated or retired members of the House and Senate and more than five thousand staff members downtown. By the time Roslanowick became the staff director under the newly minted Chairman Frank in January 2007, long-serving senior staff were rare in the House, and many of her former colleagues were eager to lobby their newly influential old friend Jeanne on behalf of the special interests they represented.

Roslanowick, a handsome, wide-beamed woman with straight brown hair and a ready grin, was a pro's pro. She was widely recognized as one of the best staff directors in Congress, a woman who knew her subject matter, hired excellent people, and knew how to manage her chairman and other members—a critical talent. Frank thought she gave him "an extraordinary combination of substance and ability, and she is complementary to me, in the sense that she's good at dealing with people." Frank knew his own weaknesses.

He let Roslanowick choose nearly all the staff, interviewing her choices, usually for just a few minutes before they were formally hired. "To write good laws," she once observed, "you've got to have really good staff—people who understand how members think, and really know the substance." She had a big staff of nearly sixty, thanks in part to Frank's good relations with Nancy Pelosi, the Democratic leader in the House, who had allowed him to increase the committee budget and staff.

On substantive matters, Roslanowick had one peer on the committee staff, David Smith, its chief economist. Frank personally hired Smith in 2007. The two had known each other since 1972, when Frank worked for Mayor White and Smith was a professor at the University of Massachusetts's Boston campus. His was a classic liberal biography. A native New Englander, his only advanced degree was a master's in education from Harvard, but he spent many years working on community development projects in Boston with like-minded liberal activists. At one point Smith moved his family into Roxbury, a black neighborhood where he was working at the time. In 1981 Smith began a decade-long stint on Senator Kennedy's Washington staff, dealing with economic issues. In 1990 he moved to New York to work for David Dinkins, the newly elected mayor, first as commissioner of business development, then as a senior budget officer. In 1995 the president of the AFL-CIO invited him to create a public policy staff for the labor organization, and Smith became a spokesman for labor's causes in Washington. Frank asked him to join the Financial Services Committee staff when he became chairman at the beginning of 2007. "I needed someone around who was my age and knew how to talk to me," Frank explained. In fact, Smith was five years younger than his boss, but still over sixty. "Forgetting that these [congressional staff] jobs were for kids," he explained later, "I said yes."

Unlike most chairmen—and most members too—Frank almost never read a prepared statement or question at a hearing. So when he opened that hearing in July 2008 he spoke extemporaneously. Keeping in mind that this was two months before the collapse of Fannie Mae, Freddie Mac, and Lehman Brothers, Frank's comments reveal his state of mind long before his committee actively took up the issue of writing a new financial rulebook: "When I was about to become chairman of this committee, in [late] 2006, I was told by a wide range of people that our agenda should be that of further deregulating [financial markets]. I was told that the excess regulation . . . was putting American investment companies and financial institutions at a competitive disadvantage. . . . [But] things have changed. . . . I believe the evidence is now clear that we are in one of the most serious economic troubles that we have seen recently, in part because of an inadequacy of regulation. . . .

I believe there is a consensus now among people in the Administration, among many of us in Congress, and among people in the financial industry, that an increase in regulation is required."

That consensus had existed for months. In the small universe of people who worried about such things, it was fashionable even before the crisis struck to discuss the topic of reforming the rules for banks, investment banks, hedge funds, and other players in our vast financial casino. The experts realized that the financial sector had become both much bigger and much more complicated since the 1980s, and many considered the existing rules inadequate. The end of the housing bubble and the unexpected collapse of Bear Stearns—the first big Wall Street institution to fail—solidified the consensus. There was striking evidence of this at the end of March 2008, just a fortnight after Bear Stearns died. Two speeches, from men who represented the executive branch or wanted to, made the point.

The first speech was delivered at Cooper Union in New York on March 28 by Senator Barack Obama, then one of the two leading candidates for the Democratic presidential nomination. In an address on economic policy, Obama included a section on financial reform. "It is time for the federal government to revamp the regulatory framework dealing with our financial markets," he said. "We need to create a 21st-century regulatory framework" to account for the many ways the financial system had changed. He outlined the "core principles for reform that I intend to pursue as president."

Just three days later, Treasury Secretary Paulson introduced a "blueprint for regulatory reform" with words similar to Obama's: "Our current regulatory structure was not built to address the modern financial system," Paulson said, enumerating the many new complexities that were beyond the reach of a system that was "developed after the Great Depression." He and his colleagues had been working on this blueprint for a year.

The utter inadequacy of the regulatory arrangements both men proposed to change hadn't yet been demonstrated—that would happen dramatically six months later, in September, when the big crash came. But there was already plenty of evidence of their shortcomings, which was why Obama and Paulson could enunciate principles for reform that sounded remarkably similar.

Both proposed creating a new regulator of "systemic risk," meaning threats to financial stability. This would be a new kind of super-regulator with authority over all sorts of financial institutions, not just banks whose deposits are insured by the government. Both men proposed changes to the mortgage industry that had contributed so much to the turmoil in the markets. Both referred to the need to better regulate how much money financial institutions keep on hand to meet unexpected demands on their resources—capital and liquidity requirements. Both recommended rationalizing the crazy quilt of government agencies that shared the job of regulating financial markets, including the merger of some existing federal agencies. Both mentioned the need to do something about the private ratings agencies that had been caught out in the housing bust because they had given Triple A ratings—the best possible—to bonds based on dubious home mortgages. Obama did not mention new consumer protections in his speech—though he later embraced the idea of a consumer financial protection agency—but Paulson did. He recommended creation of a new "business conduct regulator with the responsibility to vigorously protect consumers and investors." Obama spoke of the need to crack down on stock traders who try to manipulate the markets, one example of bad business conduct.

Obama the candidate was outlining a plank in his campaign platform. Paulson, the senior government official, more cautiously described the ideas in his blueprint as a basis for discussion and debate. He explicitly ruled out trying to adopt reforms while the markets remained in turmoil: "Once we are through this period of market stress, we need to begin the serious work of modernizing and reforming the [regulatory] structure, which will require a great deal of discussion and many years to complete." When he said that, Paulson was still playing by the old rules. Until the Great Crash, the typical model for congressional action on financial reforms involved many years of ponderous deliberation. The old rules suddenly expired in September, when the crash came. Paulson helped rip them up. By enacting the bailout legislation, Congress announced its recognition that the world had changed.

The impulse to act after the crash was encouraged by an embarrassing realization: For about thirty years, both Congress and the executive branch had been kidding themselves and the country about regulation of the financial sector. Both Democrats and Republicans had embraced a philosophy of deregulation, broadly agreeing on a great unraveling of the regulatory regime that the government imposed in the 1930s to try to prevent a recurrence of the 1929 stock market crash and the Great Depression that followed. Congress was complicit in the crash of 2008 in ways no member stood up to announce, but a great many understood.

The individual most closely associated with this sweeping deregulation was Alan Greenspan, chairman of the Federal Reserve Board from 1987 to 2006, the longest-serving chairman in Fed history. A smallish man of gentle demeanor and scratchy voice, Greenspan managed to create a charismatic public persona from raw material that might remind you of the class nerd who got only As and spent Saturday nights playing chess. As his long tenure at the Fed continued, his reputation as "the maestro" who could keep the American economy humming was burnished to the point of gleaming. Congress loved him. By the time George W. Bush had nominated him for a fifth term in June 2004, the Senate confirmed him by acclamation.

The maestro played the Congress like the clarinet he had mastered as a young man, and the Congress never challenged him. In 1994 Congress gave Greenspan's Fed the power to regulate the subprime mortgages that ultimately proved so poisonous, but Greenspan refused to exercise the power.

Greenspan's enthusiasm for deregulation was a product of his personal ideology as well as his economic analysis. As a young man he was a follower and friend of Ayn Rand, the libertarian author of *The Fountainhead* and *Atlas Shrugged*, whose philosophy combined a fervid opposition to government interference in economic matters with a rigorous defense of "rational egoism," or self-interest. Given his unabashed enthusiasm for deregulation over many years, Greenspan may be the best available witness to explain what went wrong in 2007–8.

In late October 2008, about six weeks after the crash, he testified before the House Committee on Oversight and Government Reform. Its chairman at the time was Henry Waxman, a California Democrat. At the hearing Greenspan did something rare in Washington and even rarer on Capitol Hill: He admitted making a big mistake.

His basic error, Greenspan testified, was to believe that "the self-interests of lending institutions" could be relied on to protect the solvency of banks and other lenders—that self-interest would make bankers sufficiently cautious that they would avoid mortal risks and protect their shareholders. "Those of us" who believed this, he said, "myself especially, are in a state of shocked disbelief" after witnessing the collapse of Bear Stearns, Lehman Brothers, Wachovia, Countrywide Savings & Loan, Washington Mutual, and the others whose imprudent behavior destroyed them. He explained, using the esoteric language he always favored, that these firms had relied on "a vast risk management and pricing system [that combined] the best insights of mathematicians and finance experts supported by major advances in computer and communications technology. . . . This modern risk management paradigm held sway for decades. The whole intellectual edifice, however, collapsed in the summer of last year [2007, when the housing bubble burst]." Greenspan said he had discovered "a flaw in the model that I perceived is the critical functioning structure that defines how the world works, so to speak."

Waxman interrupted him: "In other words, you found that your view of the world, your ideology, was not right, it was not working."

"Absolutely, precisely," Greenspan replied. "You know, that's precisely the reason I was shocked, because I have been going for 40 years or more with very considerable evidence that it was working exceptionally well." Yes, that paradigm had indeed worked well—until it didn't. The years of its success had lulled not only Greenspan, but the overwhelming majority in Congress that eagerly followed his every cue. When the paradigm failed, lives were shattered, retirement nest eggs disappeared, millions lost their jobs and their homes.

As the new Congress convened in January 2009, Frank and his staff remained in a waiting mode. When the new administration was ready to present its ideas, the Financial Services Committee would consider them, improve on them if it could, and enact reforms. In Frank's view this decision did not suggest diminished ambition on his part, just a recognition of the obvious realities. The administration would "do most of the drafting" of the reform legislation, Frank explained, because "we don't have the staff to do that."

He fully intended to put his mark on what he saw as the third great "regulatory wave" to save capitalism from its own worst excesses. The first, he thought, came early in the twentieth century, when Theodore Roosevelt (president from 1901 to 1907) and Woodrow Wilson (1913–21) busted the giant trusts that formed in the late 1800s and imposed some basic rules on American corporations that regulated child labor, hours, working conditions, and workers' rights.

The second was Franklin Roosevelt's New Deal, which created regulatory structures for the banking and securities industries that had survived for eight decades. Bank examinations by federal regulators, insurance on bank deposits, and the Securities and Exchange Commission to police stock markets, the three fundamental reforms of the New Deal, gave investors and consumers confidence in the system, creating an orderly environment for American business and finance that allowed them to prosper, Frank thought.

Now the third wave could address a new problem made obvious by the crash of 2008, the need for more effective regulation of financial risk. Frank agreed with Greenspan—the crash proved that market pressures alone could not protect the system from dangerous risk taking by high-flying financiers. He saw the need for a new systemic risk regulator, a government body empowered to limit or ban risky behavior by major players in the now enormous financial sector.

As Frank thought about it, the risk regulator's principal concern would be "leverage," Wall Street's word for borrowed money. New rules were needed, especially to "control everything that involves leverage." Giving government officials the power to prevent private firms from taking excessive risks was, Frank understood, a substantial departure from past practice. He thought it was overdue.

A bank is leveraged when its liabilities are greater than its equity—that is, when the money it could owe to others exceeds its own tangible assets, its real money. Leverage is part of banking, a critical source of bank profits. But in the run-up to the Great Crash of 2008, America's biggest financial institutions were leveraged to their gills. The big Wall Street firms had leverage ratios ranging from 25:1 (Goldman Sachs) to 32:1 (Morgan Stanley and Bear Stearns). That meant that for every dollar Morgan Stanley had on hand in invested capital and past profits, it had potential liabilities of $32. Leverage was wonderful when the value of a bank's assets kept rising, as they did during the housing bubble that lasted into 2007.

Someone who owned a $100,000 house whose value rose to $200,000 had a $100,000 gain. But someone who borrowed an amount thirty-two times his own capital to buy thirty-two such houses would have had a gain of $3.2 million, less the interest he paid to borrow that money. That lucky investor profited hugely from the risk he had taken, at least on paper. The heavily leveraged banks enjoyed just such a happy position—until the bubble burst and values measured on paper disappeared.

Frank's first formal contacts with the new administration to discuss financial regulatory reform came on February 2, 2009. The chairman met separately with the new treasury secretary, Timothy Geithner, and the former treasury secretary and new director of President Obama's National Economic Council, Lawrence Summers. He also met that day with Ben Bernanke of the Fed. "I'm going to start coordinating with them what we do about reforms," Frank said that day, before he met those men.

Those meetings illustrated the committee chairman's power, or at least his stature. They occurred in Frank's big office on the second floor of the Rayburn House Office Building, the newest and biggest of the three marble monsters that provide office space and hearing rooms for all 435 members of the House. Frank's suite, 2252, included an office that measured twenty-five by forty feet, under a ceiling twenty feet high. The large windows behind the chairman's desk were always covered with blue velvet curtains; daylight never penetrated. Frank rarely left his lair for any meeting—he hated wasting time in taxicabs traveling downtown, and he expected government officials to come to him. (Despite his power, a committee chairman is not provided with a car and driver; senior officials of the executive branch are.)

Not only did those important men come to see Frank on his own turf, but he met with them as a thoroughly independent actor. No other member of the Financial Services Committee and no one from the House leadership was present. Only Roslanowick and Smith joined Frank for meetings of this kind. Ultimately, Frank's colleagues on the Financial Services Committee, all seventy of them, would have a chance to debate and vote on proposed new regulations, but in this critical first stage when reforms were first being conceived, Frank and his staff were on their own.

He agreed that day with both Summers and Geithner that a new systemic risk regulator should be their first priority. At this early moment in the new administration there were dreams of quick action in Congress. Rahm Emanuel, President Obama's new chief of staff who had just relinquished his seat in the House to take that job, had already pressed Frank to act quickly. Emanuel hoped something could be enacted, by the House or by Frank's committee, before Obama met the leaders and finance ministers of the richest countries—the Group of 20—in early April.

New administrations often dream of winning speedy action from Congress on their priorities, but this almost never happens. "Congress" and "speedy action" are words that seldom appear together; Congress's default speed is "slow." Quick congressional action on TARP in the fall of 2008 was an important exception, but that was a rare occurrence, the result of urgent fear that did not exist in the case of regulatory reform. Saving the economy was easier to understand than writing new rules for the financial industry.

"We have a conceptual agreement" on the need for a new kind of systemic risk regulation, Frank said a few days after those February 2 meetings. The agreement was that the Federal Reserve Board's regulatory authority should be expanded so it could monitor risk taking by big financial institutions and insist on changes in their behavior, if that was warranted. "We will now be awaiting their sending us some paper that will explain what we're doing," Frank said.

Frank's position as the would-be recipient, and not the initiator or author, of a plan for regulatory reform was formalized on February 25 at a White House meeting with Obama. Lesser officials came to him, but for a meeting with the president, Frank traveled to the White House. Even speakers and majority leaders did that.

On this occasion, as Frank described the meeting, "the president did gently but clearly make the point that he did not want us drafting this bill because it was after all pretty complicated stuff and he hoped that the drafting could be done in the executive branch. I told him I was not only willing for that to happen but eager." This was consistent with past practice. Most of the New Deal legislation was written by the Roosevelt administration eighty years earlier. Ever since, the executive branch has regularly initiated important new laws.

In that same meeting, by Frank's account, he also reasserted his ultimate authority. "If there is this view on Rahm [Emanuel]'s part that we would simply rubber-stamp it"—the proposal the administration would draft—"that's clearly a nonstarter," he remembered telling the president.

Frank's principal interest was the politics of reform, not the technical details. In early 2009 he spoke repeatedly about "the greatest breach between elite and public opinion that I have ever seen" as a consequence of the financial crisis. In Frank's view this wasn't surprising. Saving the system required bailing out banks, but bankers were among the most unpopular people in the society. The millions of dollars bankers paid themselves were unimaginable to the average American household earning about $50,000 a year. The "elite"—educated people who understood how grave the crisis was, and how important it was to prop up the only institutions that could provide credit, the lifeblood of capitalism—might accept the need for bank bailouts, might even favor them, but Frank did not expect most people to be supportive.

"People think we are only helping the banks," he said in early March. There had to be concrete evidence that regular folks were being helped too. At a news conference on March 5 he presented an agenda he hoped would provide political cover. First, the House would again pass a bill banning most subprime mortgages, the loans to marginal customers that had done so much damage when the housing bubble burst. It had passed one in 2007, but the Senate let it die. Then he proposed to enact, again for the second time, a bill on credit cards that would limit card issuers' ability to jack up interest rates and fees. Finally he promised to press the Justice Department to aggressively pursue those who contributed to the Great Crash: "We want to know what proposals there are to recover funds from people who caused this loss of taxpayer dollars and investor dollars . . . and we want to know whether or not there are going to be criminal prosecutions." Hearings would be held, he promised.

Frank hoped that these measures plus a new program announced by the Treasury Department to try to head off some foreclosures on home mortgages would help create "the political space" the new Obama administration would need to persevere with the bailouts and stabilize the economy. As the Ides of March approached, he was cautiously hopeful that he was succeeding. Then, on March 15, the country learned that AIG, which had received a federal bailout of more than $170 billion, was about to pay employees of the division that had nearly bankrupted the company $165 million in bonuses. Frank's optimism suddenly disappeared.

CHAPTER FOUR

An Orgy of Outrage

Nothing animates Congress like a sudden scandal, particularly a scandal that voters might decide to blame on members of the House and Senate. So the sudden scandal over bonuses at AIG that erupted on the weekend of March 14–15, 2009, created a hurricane of frenzied activity on Capitol Hill.

The congressional version of frenzied activity usually consists of rhetorical excess—typically, a combination of indignant posturing and aggressive blame avoidance. So it was in this instance, a classic example of a contemporary political firestorm. The storm had no substantive content, but it blew Barney Frank off course, altering the context in which financial regulatory legislation would be written in the House. And it revealed traits of the modern Congress that affect any serious legislative undertaking.

AIG—The American International Group, Inc.—received the biggest bailout of the financial crisis. Hours after the bankruptcy of Lehman Brothers, Paulson and Bernanke realized that AIG would also collapse unless the government stepped in, and they were afraid to let it sink. Eventually the Federal Reserve and Treasury made available $182.3 billion to stabilize the company.* The Federal Reserve pro-

---

* The two government agencies took shares in AIG in return for the bailout money. The last of those were sold to the public in December 2012. Altogether, Treasury and the Fed made $22.7 billion in *profits* from the bailout.

vided the first rescue—a loan of $85 billion of its own money, made available to the company under a provision of the Federal Reserve Act that members of Congress had never understood. This was the action that had stunned Senator Dodd and Congressman Frank the previous September. The government provided its final increment of support for AIG in March 2009, on the same day AIG reported a loss of $100 billion for 2008, the largest annual loss ever recorded by an American corporation.

AIG's principal business was insurance, and the insurance companies it owned were all in good shape. But the company also included a division called AIG Financial Products that behaved like a hedge fund, the Wall Street term for a speculative investment fund. AIGFP engaged in much riskier behavior than selling life or casualty insurance. Its primary business was "derivatives," the exotic financial instruments that played a big role in the Great Crash, and would come to bedevil members of the House and Senate. Derivatives trading was not regulated by the federal government, so the operations of AIGFP, as it was known, were mostly hidden from public view. During the housing bubble, AIG offered "credit default swaps," a type of derivative that amounted to insurance on the securities that Wall Street created from subprime mortgages. For a fee, AIGFP would guarantee to cover losses on those securities incurred by the banks, hedge funds, and others who bought them.

For years this business was hugely profitable, but when the housing market crumbled and those mortgage-based securities went bad, AIG's corporate leaders discovered the huge risks that AIGFP had assumed. Because of the company's internal financial arrangements, the ensuing losses threatened to bring down the entire AIG empire, with potentially profound consequences. For example, AIG's insurance companies held the money for and guaranteed the pensions of 30 million Americans. Government officials at Treasury and the Fed were persuaded that numerous other financial institutions at home and abroad could have collapsed if AIG went under. AIGFP had outstanding derivatives deals with more than two thousand counterparties around the world. Its failure, Bernanke concluded, "would be disastrous."

Every bailout in the fall of 2008 was unpopular in the country and in Congress, none more so than AIG's. For the government officials sponsoring the bailouts—first the Bush administration and Bernanke, and then the new Obama administration—it was never easy to explain the need to provide billions to gigantic financial institutions. The economy was crumbling into a deep recession, millions saw their 401(k)s and nest eggs shrink almost overnight, and the fat cats of Wall Street were being taken care of. Where was the justice in that? Both citizens and members of the House and Senate gagged on this arrangement.

The challenge for bailout proponents began with the basic theory that persuaded Paulson and Bernanke to act in the fall of 2008—that the world economy really was on the verge of a collapse that could have been worse than the Great Depression of the 1930s. Both men, and a great many serious economists, were quite certain of this, but neither citizens nor congressmen could see or feel the danger. As Frank liked to say, "You can't prove a counterfactual." In other words, politicians can't sell—and often can't understand—a proposal that something both expensive and politically unappealing has to be done to head off a disaster that isn't yet evident.

Paulson and Bernanke—and the world's bankers—all understood that the credit markets, providers of the capital that is the lifeblood of capitalism, were seizing up in mid-September, but citizens still got cash from their ATMs and paid their bills with checks the banks honored. Bernanke and Paulson did convince the group of leaders that met in Pelosi's conference room on September 18, but many other members, and countless voters, resisted their apocalyptic message. Wrapping one's mind around the complexities of the global financial system was hard. Damning the fat cats and bemoaning a system that seemed rigged to their benefit was much easier.

AIG was hardly a household name; most members and most citizens knew nothing about it. What they learned upset them. The news media reported that days after receiving its bailout, some of the company's top insurance salesmen enjoyed a $440,000 retreat to a posh California resort, a reward for good work. Then came disclosures that many of the billions the Federal Reserve and Treasury had provided to AIG had been used to pay in full its obligations to the biggest investment and commercial banks, including many foreign ones. Detested or not, AIG was now effectively a state-owned enterprise; in return for the bailouts, the government eventually held about 90 percent of its stock.

Then on that March weekend came news reports that AIG was pay-

ing $165 million in "retention bonuses" to employees of AIG Finan-
cial Products. The Treasury Department had actually leaked the story
with its own spin, providing reporters with accounts of the efforts
made by Secretary Geithner to avoid paying the bonuses, or to force
AIG to restructure them. But the company's lawyers said there was no
legal alternative to paying, and the government's lawyers decided they
were right.

Paying looked like rewarding the people of AIGFP for almost
destroying AIG and maybe even the world economy. No amount of
Treasury spin could alter that fact. The story was front-page news in
The Washington Post and *The New York Times* on Sunday, echoed on
the Sunday television talk shows. Suddenly, Washington had a new
scandal.

That AIG was paying these bonuses wasn't literally news. The company had disclosed its bonus arrangements in filings with the Securities and Exchange Commission a year earlier. In late January, the
Bloomberg news service had reported the same story. After his staff
read the Bloomberg account, Congressman Paul Kanjorski, a Pennsylvania Democrat who chaired the Financial Services subcommittee
on capital markets, issued a press release expressing "outrage" that
AIG was going to pay bonuses to employees of "the very business unit
that . . . caused the company to lose billions of dollars and seek a federal bailout."

But the news media ignored Kanjorski's press release, as they had
ignored the company's SEC filings earlier. News coverage often drives
congressional behavior, but the news media are fickle. It is difficult to
know when they will seize on a particular story. This one only came
to life in Washington after that Sunday, when the two most important
newspapers and the talk shows gave it high visibility—high enough for
members of Congress to notice.

On Monday, members of the House and Senate flooded the air-
waves with horrified denunciations of the bonuses. Perhaps most
colorfully, Senator Charles Grassley, an Iowa Republican, proposed
that executives of AIG "follow the Japanese model . . . resign, or go
commit suicide." (An aide to Grassley said later that the senator didn't
really want anyone to kill himself.) Republicans in the House introduced legislation demanding that the Obama administration simply take the bonuses back—how, or on what legal authority, was not
explained. Grassley cosponsored a bill that would authorize taxation

of the bonuses at a 70 percent rate. Dozens more vented their anger that day. So did President Obama, who expressed his own "outrage" at a White House event and urged AIG employees to voluntarily return the bonuses.

Nancy Pelosi was proud of her ability to anticipate political trouble, and this smelled like big trouble. Her staff immediately began pressing Frank's staff to do something to distance House Democrats from these bonuses. Pelosi's concern was public relations, not substantive policy. Her priority was to protect the new Democratic members elected in 2006 and 2008, who created the Democratic majority that made her speaker. So Pelosi asked if the House could pass a tax that would largely confiscate these bonuses. Or could they pass a "sense of Congress" resolution that pressed AIG's bonus-receiving employees to repay the bonus money to the government voluntarily? She and her colleagues in the Democratic leadership decided to pursue both options.

Six weeks earlier, in his role as a subcommittee chairman, Congressman Kanjorski had summoned the president of AIG, Edward Liddy, for a private tongue-lashing based on the Bloomberg story on the bonuses. Kanjorski also scheduled a hearing for March 18 to examine the bailout of AIG and its impact. The hearing was on the schedule long before the scandal erupted that weekend.

Kanjorski's initiative reflected a tension between him and Frank and their staffs that periodically colored the work of the Financial Services Committee. It was the sort of difficult relationship that can affect proceedings in Congress in ways that members almost never discuss and outsiders can rarely see.

Kanjorski, three years older than Frank, was elected to the House in 1984 by the voters of Pennsylvania's 11th Congressional District, a swath of central Pennsylvania that includes Scranton and Wilkes-Barre. In 2009 Kanjorski ranked second among the Democrats on Financial Services. He resented Frank's prominence, his glib intelligence, and his chairmanship.

Kanjorski was an odd duck, a tall, balding, angular man with a booming bass voice who marched to his own eccentric drummer. He knew more about financial issues than most members, but his senior colleagues considered him unpredictable and unreliable. Steny Hoyer of Maryland, the Democratic House majority leader, teased Frank about his health when he became chairman in 2007. "You better take good care of yourself, Barney," he cautioned; if anything happened to Frank, who had a quintuple heart bypass operation in 1999, the leadership would face a grim predicament: Kanjorski would be next in line to serve as chairman, a prospect that also worried younger Democrats on the committee.

For Frank, managing Kanjorski was part of the challenge of being chairman. Just two weeks before the March 18 hearing, the two had sparred at a private meeting of the Democratic members of Financial Services. Kanjorski "totally surprised me by essentially saying that he was going to be in charge" of drafting financial regulatory reform legislation, and that he was going to do this "in a totally bipartisan way, working with the most conservative Republicans," Frank recounted. "I had to disagree with him and say . . . that I had no confidence that he would achieve anything working with the most right-wing Republicans, and that in fact we could not leave out the [Obama] administration. His response was to make a silly statement that he didn't come here to simply do what the administration told him to do and if that was the case, he would just go off and sulk—those weren't his exact words, but they were the meaning." More to the point, "I had told him that I wanted to deal with the [regulatory] restructuring at the committee level"—it was too important to be handled by a subcommittee. Of course, it was also Frank's chance to make history.

Frank was trying hard to be an evenhanded chairman. He wanted to mimic Lyndon Johnson, who was the most successful Senate majority leader of modern times, perhaps of any time, long before he became president. Frank loved the third volume of Robert Caro's monumental biography of LBJ, *Master of the Senate*, and particularly its chapter on Johnson's first two years as Democratic leader, 1953–54, when Republicans were in the majority and Johnson was minority leader. Johnson's objective, Frank explained, was to persuade Democratic senators that it was in their political interest to be loyal to him. Frank hoped for a similar standing with his Democratic colleagues on Financial Services.

There were forty-one of them, and twenty-nine Republicans. Frank had tried to persuade Pelosi to shrink the unwieldy Financial Services Committee at the beginning of 2009. At first she agreed, but then decided she couldn't. She wanted to put more members of the classes of '06 and '08 on Financial Services, known as "a money committee," from which it was easier to raise campaign contributions. (The financial interests that cared most about its work had a lot of money to donate.) So for political reasons, the committee did not shrink, but grew. More than 15 percent of the House of Representatives were members of Frank's committee.

He wanted his Democratic members to feel they were important, so when he felt he could, Frank supported Kanjorski's initiatives. On that March 18 this meant stepping aside to let Kanjorski chair the AIG hearing he had organized. By the time it convened a few minutes after ten on the morning of March 18, about a third of the members of the full committee were in their big, leather-covered, swiveling chairs, sitting in four rows shaped like crescents across the east side of the vast room, under a thirty-foot ceiling. This was actually quite high attendance; most hearings in the committee's hearing room on the first floor of the Rayburn Building attracted just a handful of members.

This one drew not only two dozen members of Financial Services, but also a large contingent of reporters and photographers, and fifty television cameras in the hearing room and the hall outside. Their presence colored the event. Cameras, especially cameras belonging to the television networks, can turn congressional hearings into a kind of preening contest. In the heat of the AIG bonus flap, many wanted to preen.

The hearing convened on the third day of the firestorm, which had alarmed Liddy and other AIG executives. Paulson had recruited Liddy to run the company after the government became its de facto owner. He was the retired president of Allstate Insurance Company, and agreed to try to salvage AIG for a salary of $1 a year.

The job had proven difficult. Perhaps the trickiest element was unwinding the deals made by AIGFP that still threatened the company's survival. These were complicated derivatives contracts used by the banks and financial firms that were AIG's counterparties to hedge against unforeseen developments—interest rate changes, commodity price fluctuations, or a decline in American housing values, among countless others. Some were simple and straightforward—AIG would pay, for example, if a particular mortgage-based security lost its value. Some were extremely complex, and customized for an individual client. AIGFP built up a huge portfolio of fifty thousand derivative contracts with a "notional value" of $2.7 trillion. This meant that AIGFP had accepted theoretical or "notional" commitments to counterparties that would have required putting up $2.7 trillion if every single deal totally collapsed. Only nuclear war might have created that much havoc, but the $2.7 trillion number did convey a sense of the enormity of this business. Liddy's goal was to do whatever was necessary to end those contracts, which often meant negotiating with the counterparty to find a way to terminate whatever commitment AIGFP had made to it originally. This could involve settlements for large amounts of money, and it could require considerable expertise. The people who best understood many of the customized derivatives were the people who devised them.

This was the origin of the retention bonuses that caused this furor. The pre-crash management of AIG had negotiated the bonus arrangements early in 2008, when AIG began absorbing bruising losses on its mortgage-backed derivatives. Company executives feared the flight of their knowledgeable employees at AIGFP just when their expertise was most needed to minimize the losses. That's why they negotiated a package of $400 million in retention bonuses in early 2008 that would be paid to key people, part of it a year later, a larger part two years later. This was bait intended to lure the key people into staying.

After the bailout of AIG in September 2008, the Federal Reserve Bank of New York became the company's overseer, with a veto over its important decisions. Fed officials and the outside lawyers they retained focused on these bonuses, hoping to find a way to limit or eliminate them. This was the first time that lawyers working for the government concluded that the contracts were legally binding, and that trying to evade them could leave management vulnerable to punitive damages in court. Potentially more serious, as Liddy would try to explain to members of the Financial Services Committee that day, if bonuses were limited or denied, the firm could lose the very people it needed most. Liddy and his Fed overseers knew AIG was still in danger, and that the billions invested in it by Treasury and the Fed remained at risk. They also noted that the really guilty parties, the men whose decisions created the disaster at AIGFP, were long gone and would receive no bonuses.

Seventy-three employees of AIGFP received bonuses, most between $1 million and $6.4 million, on Friday, March 14, so by the time the storm of protest erupted, the money was paid.

The bonuses provoked an angry public reaction. AIG hired guards to protect the Greenwich, Connecticut, office building that housed AIGFP. According to *The Washington Post*, "death threats and angry letters flooded e-mail inboxes. Irate callers lit up the phone lines.

Senior managers submitted their resignations. Some employees didn't show up at all."

The politicians wanted revenge, but exacting it could have put taxpayers at still greater risk, and also appeared to be illegal. This was a classic congressional confrontation between the high emotion of the moment and the real-world complexity of the situation. As usual, complexity got short shrift.

The hearing began with the obligatory round of self-important "opening statements," a congressional custom that seems to have been invented to aggravate everyone subjected to it. Most citizens are spared the bloviation typical of opening statements because they are only rarely picked up by the news media. But aficionados of C-SPAN, the cable network that broadcasts many congressional hearings, have had to sit through long hours of this warm-up rhetoric that can delay the questioning of witnesses.

Frank at least had imposed rules of brevity on opening statements in the Financial Services Committee—one minute each. That wasn't difficult to observe on this occasion, because most who spoke only wanted to join the chorus of outrage, which could be done quickly. For example, Gary Ackerman, a Democrat from Long Island: "There's a tidal wave of rage throughout America right now, and it's building up, and it's expressing itself at this latest outrage which is really just the tip of the iceberg. And that rage is because the taxpayer knows that they are the ultimate sucker on the list of who pays for all of the greed that has been going on in the marketplace for years and years."

Randy Neugebauer, a Texas Republican, said, "I'm going to go ahead and say that I'm outraged as well, but what I would like to be is enlightened. What we really need to know is what the plan is. . . . So I hope we'll . . . get a little bit less enraged and more engaged in getting our money back for the American taxpayers."

Chairman Frank offered a practical suggestion: "We're the effective owners of this company. What we ought to be doing is exercising our rights as the owners to bring lawsuits to say, 'These people performed so badly, the magnitude of the losses was so great, that we are justified in rescinding the bonuses.' "

And then he said something startling—something that alarmed his own staff: "We will be asking Mr. Liddy to give us the names of the [bonus] recipients. . . . We will be asking for the names. If Mr. Liddy declines to give us the names, then I will convene the committee to vote a subpoena for the names." There was no mistaking Frank's threat—he wanted to humiliate and intimidate the individuals receiving bonuses.

This was "an appalling mistake," in the view of Dave Smith, Frank's senior aide. "This was a big deal that was unnecessary and inappropriate. It served no public policy purpose." He and Roslanowick both made clear their displeasure with this threat to Frank, who "was defensive about it," in Smith's words. The men and women who worked for Frank held him in a high regard, so took it badly when he disappointed them, as he did on this occasion. They thought he had succumbed to the political frenzy, and had joined in scapegoating the wrong people, unsympathetic as they were.

Finally it came Liddy's turn to testify. He had prepared with care. Appearing before a hostile congressional committee is tricky; expensive Washington lawyers train people like Liddy how to do it, and help them prepare their remarks. Liddy handled himself well. He tried to combine explanation with contrition, and he sprung a surprise peace offering designed to mollify the members.

"Make no mistake, had I been CEO at the time, I would never have approved the retention contracts that were put in place over a year ago. It was distasteful to have to make these payments, but we concluded that the risks to the company, and, therefore, the financial system and the economy, were unacceptably high." He meant the risks of not paying the bonuses to the people of AIGFP.

"Why pay these people anything at all? Here's why: I'm trying desperately to prevent an uncontrolled collapse of that business. This is the only way to improve AIG's ability to pay taxpayers back quickly and completely, and the only way to avoid a systemic shock to the economy that the U.S. government's help was meant to relieve."

Then the surprise: "This morning I've asked the employees of AIG Financial Products . . . who received retention payments in excess of $100,000 or more to return at least half of those payments. Some have already stepped forward and offered to give up 100 percent of their payment. . . . We will work to ensure the highest level of employee participation in this effort in the days ahead."*

It was a nice try, but members had come to make a scene, to demon-

---

* Ultimately, bonus recipients returned $45 million of the $168 million paid out in bonuses in March 2009.

strate their indignation without, in most cases, any concern for facts or nuances, and a scene they would make. This was of course perfectly understandable. Liddy was defending paying millions to financial wizards who personified the villains of the Great Crash, the Wall Streeters who seemed to evade any accountability for their contributions to a grievous economic disaster. On this day members were determined to give Liddy a thrashing, no matter what he said.

"Lynch mobs are never attractive, and they aren't improved when composed of good guys," Dave Smith observed, flattering the members with that description. During that long afternoon, the committee did seem to take on the characteristics of such a mob.

California Democrat Brad Sherman declared AIG guilty of "criminal wrongdoing."

Stephen Lynch of Massachusetts, also a Democrat, accused Liddy of "outrageous . . . unbelievable . . . arrogant" behavior that was "probably illegal" to boot—his comments all based on a misreading of the bonus plan at AIG. When he finished his peroration, Lynch asked Liddy, "Do you have anything to say for yourself?"

Liddy tried to explain that no bonuses were paid under the provisions Lynch had attacked, and noted that although Lynch said repeatedly that "you" had done things he disapproved of, in fact "these contracts were all put together before I was at AIG. . . . So I take offense sir at the use of—"

Lynch cut him off: "Well, offense was intended, so you take it rightfully."

Alan Grayson of Florida played the role of prosecutor. He wanted Liddy to provide the names of the individuals in AIGFP who had been responsible for the credit default swaps that proved so toxic. Liddy had said earlier there were twenty or twenty-five of them.

Grayson: "I want to know who they are. Names, please."

Liddy: "I don't know them."

Grayson: "Well, how can you propose to solve the problems of the company that you're now running if you don't know the names of the people who caused that problem?"

Frank too returned to the issue of naming names—in his case, of the bonus recipients. The death threats to AIG employees had given him pause, and he had agreed to write to the FBI and the Connecticut state police to ask their assessment of the danger to individuals if their names were publicized. But he continued to growl.

"Many of us get these kinds of threats. Clearly those threats are despicable . . . and I would say to my colleagues, the rhetoric can get overheated so we ought to be very careful . . . but this is an important public subject. And my guess is that there are probably threats aimed without too much specificity about people who work there. . . . I ask you to submit the names of the people who've received the bonuses, noting that they've paid them back or not. . . . If you feel unable to do that, then I will ask this committee to subpoena them."

The overheated rhetoric continued for nearly four hours. Some members did at least acknowledge Liddy's dollar-a-year contribution but that did little to lighten the atmosphere of inquisition.

The very next day, March 19, Pelosi brought to the floor of the House her ideas for how to make political hay from the ongoing orgy of outrage. She proposed a bill imposing a surtax at a rate of 90 percent on the families of all employees of bailed-out firms receiving cash bonuses, provided their reported annual income exceeded $250,000. In other words, this was a bill to confiscate most of the bonuses paid to AIG employees—but also people who worked for any of the Wall Street institutions that received substantial federal assistance during the financial crisis. Wall Street bonuses have long been a basic part of remuneration packages, so such a tax could alter the lives of a lot of people.

Under normal procedures, the Ways and Means Committee is first to consider a tax bill. It holds hearings, "marks up" the legislation—agrees on final provisions and wording—and reports the bill to the Rules Committee, which then decides the way the full House will consider it, and how much time will be reserved for amendments and debate. In this instance, Pelosi pushed the hastily drafted bill onto the floor without any hearings or markup, a most unusual procedure.

Her second offering was a sense of Congress resolution complimenting President Obama for his handling of the bonus flap and urging recipients of the AIG bonuses to give them back. This one was pure window dressing, containing no practical consequences whatsoever.

The tax bill was called up for consideration by Charles Rangel, then the chairman of the Ways and Means Committee, responsible for all tax bills. A week earlier Rangel said it would be wrong to use the tax code to "punish" bonus recipients, but now he supported the 90 percent tax with gusto. "Most all Americans believe that a bonus is something that is paid as a reward for a job well done," Rangel began. But the bonus recipients at AIG, he suggested, were guilty of "threatening the community in which we live, and indeed our country and the financial structure of the world" with their speculative behavior. "The whole idea that they should be rewarded with millions of dollars is repugnant to everything that decent people believe in."

The debate on the bill provided yet another opportunity for members to put their AIG outrage vividly on the record. One after another, the denunciations rang out. This debate hit the high watermark of congressional anger over the bonuses at AIG. Nearly every Democrat and half the Republicans voted for the confiscatory tax, which passed 328–93.

After that the debate on Pelosi's sense of Congress resolution was perfunctory. The vote on it followed party lines, and it was approved 255–160, never to be heard of again.

And then, quite suddenly, the hurricane subsided. "It was like a tempest—[it] whirled through here, we went crazy, and then the air went out of the balloon with a whoosh," was the way Jeanne Roslanowick remembered it. "Rage having been appropriately expressed, without consequence, we moved on."

This is one of the odd features of the modern Congress, and it can be baffling. The civics book presumption might be that strong expressions of congressional anger signify meaningful intentions to do something substantive, to legislate some change in the situation that provoked the anger. But in fact the anger is usually not a means to an end, but an end in itself. Members who advertise their anger often decide that doing so is enough, especially in cases when they are trying to align themselves with a popular cause.

Blame avoidance is not just a slogan; on Capitol Hill it has become a way of life. Members fear negative television commercials in their next campaign, and look for ways to deny their opponents the fodder for such commercials. A classic 1986 article by political scientist R. Kent Weaver, "The Politics of Blame Avoidance," argued convincingly that "politicians are motivated primarily by the desire to avoid blame for unpopular actions rather than by seeking to claim credit for popular ones." Weaver concluded that much of the responsibility for this behavior lies with the voters, whose "negativity bias" makes it more useful to politicians to be against what they see the voters are against than to try to divine and pursue more positive objectives. More voters usually agree on what's bad than on what might be desirable.

The House passed its tax-the-bonuses bill on Thursday, March 19. As takes place nearly every Thursday, members of the House and Senate left Washington to spend the weekend at home. Over that weekend, the mood began to change. On Sunday evening, speaking on *60 Minutes*, President Obama expressed concern about congressional efforts to tax away the AIG bonuses and questioned the constitutionality of passing laws to punish specific people. On Monday, Harry Reid said he would put off consideration of any bonus-related legislation for a month or more.

The next day, March 24, Frank convened another hearing of the Financial Services Committee, this time to hear testimony from Secretary Geithner and Chairman Bernanke. The news media were expecting, or hoping for, more of the fireworks of the previous week; more than two dozen cameramen and women were waiting for the witnesses when they arrived. Most members of the committee were in their chairs. But from the beginning, this was a calm, even benign event, with no hint of the fire and brimstone of the first hearing on AIG bonuses six days earlier.

Frank was eager to change the subject. He was personally embarrassed by the vote to tax away the bonuses, and admitted later that he'd had "serious reservations about our tax approach. If I thought it was going to become law, I would have had to bite the bullet and vote against it." He sought to establish a new tone with his opening remarks, in which he ignored the bonus issue and tried to bring his colleagues' attention back to the much bigger matter on their agenda: regulatory reform. For Frank, giving regulators the power to "resolve" failing financial firms—to force them out of business in a controlled process akin to the way the Federal Deposit Insurance Corporation can force failing banks to close, usually by merging them with healthier institutions—was, after risk regulation, the most important goal for regulatory reform. AIG exemplified the need for such a power.

Geithner and Bernanke gave testimony that echoed Frank. (The staffs of all three had consulted in advance.) They spoke repeatedly of the need for a new way to wind down companies in the financial sector that weren't federally chartered banks. "Resolution authority," the term of art for the power to close down a failing firm and settle its outstanding debts and commitments, became a theme of that hearing. Both Bernanke and Geithner gave detailed explanations for the decision to bail out AIG, emphasizing the chaos and fear that had seized the financial markets the previous September. They explained their anxiety about what could have happened if AIG went down. They both expressed personal anger over the bonuses AIG had paid, but also presented their view that they were helpless to prevent the contractually provided payments.

Both men made a strong impression on their audience. Geithner had stumbled out of the gate as the new treasury secretary, barely escaping a flap over his personal income taxes during his Senate confirmation hearings. In his first appearances on the Hill he had looked hesitant and weak—for the political sharks in Congress, the equivalent of blood in the water. Some of Washington's talking heads began to speculate that he would be forced out of office. This hearing marked a turning point. Any fair-minded person watching would have been struck by the contrast between the members who wanted to criticize these witnesses and Bernanke and Geithner, who were thoughtful, articulate, and persuasive. The members, often reading questions prepared for them by staff, repeatedly advertised their own misunderstanding of the basic facts. Some used the terminology of high finance incorrectly.

One such was Carolyn Maloney of New York City, the third-ranking Democrat on the committee. Though married to an investment banker and the representative of thousands of employees of the financial industry, Maloney could appear uncomfortable discussing complicated financial issues. She preferred blacks and whites to grays. In this hearing she implied that bailing out AIG had not really been necessary, suggesting that the Fed had taken AIG's word for it that a bailout was required. Then she criticized the government for failing to impose any controls on the firm's compensation practices. "AIG came back several times for more money," she observed, "and at each point, we could have put restrictions on executive compensation or management or a number of ways [*sic*]."

Bernanke said the Fed bailed out AIG because of an impending catastrophe, not because of a request from the company. He pointed out, accurately, that "we did impose considerable restrictions on executive compensation and the process for setting it," a fact Maloney seemed not to know. She then changed the subject to the contracts AIG had signed promising to pay the controversial bonuses.

"A contract can be changed," she declared, not explaining how it could have been done unilaterally in this case, and then she changed the subject again. Expressing skepticism about the assertion that

AIG's failure would pose a "systemic risk," she asked about AIG's counterparties, the entities it had made deals with. Some, she noted, were municipal governments, and asked Bernanke: "Do you consider municipal—municipalities systemic risk?"

Bernanke diplomatically interpreted the question as meaning, Could the failure of a municipal government pose a systemic risk? "As I discussed in some detail in my [prepared] testimony," Bernanke replied, the biggest risk was "the loss of confidence in the system as a whole and the likelihood that we would have seen a run on banks."

Maloney wasn't interested in that point. AIG, she went on, "had counterparties that were a number of foreign banks. Do you consider bailing out foreign banks a systemic risk to the American economy?"

Again Bernanke gave Maloney the benefit of a logical interpretation of her question. Yes, he replied, it was "essential" that AIG meet its obligations. There was no way legally to refuse to make the payments AIG owed and hope to preserve the confidence that makes the financial system work.

Maloney didn't argue, but shifted her ground yet again. "Basically, could this systemic risk have been contained at a much lower cost, Mr. Bernanke? Obviously—"

But she could never explain what she thought was obvious, because her five minutes of questioning—Frank's allotment to each member—had expired. Frank cut her off with a whack of his gavel.

Maloney was one of half a dozen members who tried to poke holes in Geithner's and Bernanke's testimony; none succeeded. The three-hour hearing was a reminder of how little real expertise there was on the Financial Services Committee. (Those who were experts—fewer than ten of the seventy-one committee members—mostly chose not to participate in the hearing, or asked questions about financial regulatory reform, not AIG bonuses.) Bernanke and Geithner deflected every criticism, largely with facts. No member directly challenged their facts. Geithner and Bernanke offered a coherent, consistent argument. No member offered a different argument, or directly challenged theirs. They were the pros; the skeptical members challenging them, from both parties, looked like amateurs.

On March 25, eleven days after the firestorm erupted, when the Financial Services Committee met again, the change in mood was striking. This meeting was called to consider another bill written to assuage the public anger, this one banning "unreasonable or excessive bonuses" by financial firms that received bailouts from the government. This was called the "Grayson-Himes" bill, named for two of the freshmen Pelosi was eager to protect, Alan Grayson of Florida and Jim Himes of Connecticut. The bill was unenforceably vague but sounded good.

The ranking Republican, Spencer Bachus of Alabama, engaged in a little truth telling. The spectacle in recent days of members "covering themselves" with expressions of bonus outrage "really got out of control," Bachus said. It was a "disservice to the country" to rush to legislate without proper hearings or reflection. "I have grandchildren now, and sometimes they just have to take time out." Bachus suggested that Congress take a time-out of a month before doing anything further on bonuses.

One of Frank's key allies on the committee was Congressman Mel Watt of North Carolina, an African American lawyer from Charlotte first elected to the House in 1992. Watt was calm, smart, and thoughtful—a Phi Beta Kappa graduate of the University of North Carolina and an editor of Law Review at Yale Law School. On this occasion he too engaged in unusual truth telling.

"I was part of the mob last week [at the hearing on AIG bonuses]," he said. "I do however want to express some growing trepidation. . . . It does appear we are changing the rules in the middle of the process." If a bill like Grayson-Himes were to be enacted, Watt said, it could drive people working for the firms that received TARP aid to quit their jobs and go to work for competitors whose pay policies would not be affected by congressional action. This could weaken the companies that have to repay the TARP money they received. He would vote for the bill anyway, because his angry constituents expected him to, but he wasn't enthusiastic.

This sort of congressional candor was rarely heard in the open. Watt knew this bill was going nowhere—the Senate would not take it up. He knew it was a symbolic response to the tempest that had already subsided. Watt was talking indirectly about a dilemma faced often by smart members of Congress who understand that their constituents will not, and probably cannot, see some issues the way they see them—as really complicated.

The ferocity of public anger over the AIG bonuses scared Frank, and forced him to reconsider his approach to one of the two key elements of regulatory reform. In a conversation on March 13, the day before the uproar began, he talked about the inevitability of making the Federal Reserve Board the new strategic risk regulator. Yes, not everyone liked this idea, the Fed did not have a big fan club, "but what's the alternative?" No other institution had the expertise and authority this role would require, or the standing to tell a big financial company that its behavior was too risky and had to change.

This was "the Henny Youngman principle," Frank explained, referring to the stand-up comedian's famous line when he was asked, "How's your wife?"

"Compared to what?" Youngman replied.

If you don't want the Fed to be the new risk regulator, said Frank, "I ask you, compared to what? Who do you like instead?"

Just a week later he had changed his mind. The Fed's reputation had been badly damaged by the revelation that it had known about but could not prevent payment of the AIG bonuses. Congress would never reward it now with vastly increased powers.

"I think we have to start from scratch," Frank said. "There's going to have to be some committee" of regulators that serves as the new risk regulator. This troubled him, because it was messy. How could a committee regulate? What staff would actually do the work? "Where they borrow their people from, I don't know." This change of heart was permanent. Frank never again tried to revive the idea of using the Fed alone as the risk regulator.

But he thought the consequences of the AIG firestorm went further. "Now our capacity to govern is at risk," he said. He had hoped that the Democratic sweeps of 2006 and 2008 meant "government is back." The combination of a smart Democratic president (though Obama wasn't Frank's first choice; he had been a Hillary Clinton supporter) and Democratic majorities in Congress should launch a period of creative government that could begin to undo the damage he felt had been caused over many years, since Ronald Reagan won the White House in 1980.

But the crash punctured a broadly based sense of prosperity that the housing bubble had created, caused a deep recession that baffled many ordinary citizens, and led to bailouts that seemed to benefit only the principal malefactors. The public was furious. It was "the bitterest possible pill" to realize that "paradoxically, the deregulators (the conservative Republicans) are temporarily benefiting from the disaster they caused. . . . Because [voters think] the whole government stinks, everything the government does is terrible. The Republicans get a temporary advantage." It made no difference that the AIG bailout occurred when George W. Bush was president and Republican appointees were making all the decisions. "Whoever is in power at the time" bears the brunt of a popular backlash. "We have to do things [to respond]," said Frank. "A lot of us had qualms about that tax bill that we passed yesterday [to expropriate the AIG bonuses]," one of those "things." But that vote was easy for Frank to rationalize. He was trying to calm the public anger before it blew Congress off a rational course of action toward sensible reforms. "I really think that our ability to govern—and I don't mean we the Democrats, I mean our ability as a country to govern ourselves—is at risk," he said, repeating himself.

The new Congress and the new Obama administration had been in office barely two months. No serious legislative work had yet been done on financial regulatory reform. For weeks Frank had been frustrated by the obvious fact that "last year wouldn't end," as he put it: The events of 2008 still dominated the political landscape. They frustrated Frank's plan to turn the page and begin afresh by writing those new rules.

The sorry spectacle produced in the House of Representatives by the furor over AIG's bonuses brought out some of the worst features of that institution: blame avoidance, ignorance, emotionalism, an urge to posture and pander. To fulfill his ambitions for regulatory reform, Frank and his staff would have to find ways to overcome them.

CHAPTER FIVE

A Politician for Life

Chris Dodd had to wait an unusually long time to become chairman of an important Senate committee. He arrived in Washington at age thirty in 1974, a member of the new class of House members called "Watergate babies" who won seats in the Democratic landslide of 1974, three months after Richard Nixon resigned the presidency. Six years later, in 1980, Dodd won his Senate seat. Then he waited twenty-seven years to become chairman of the Banking Committee.

This was a lesson in the ways of the Senate. Seniority was all-important, but only relative seniority could make a chairman. By the time Democrats won control of the Senate in the 2006 elections, Dodd was more senior than all but eight of his Democratic colleagues. But on all three of his principal committees—Banking, Foreign Relations, and Health, Education, Labor and Pensions (HELP)—one colleague "outranked" him. "This is not a meritocracy here, you have to wait your turn," Dodd explained. "You have to check the heartbeat and pulse and everything" of your colleagues. The senior Democrat on Banking had been Paul Sarbanes of Maryland, a reticent gentleman "whose heart beat once an hour," in Dodd's words. On Foreign Relations it was Joe Biden of Delaware, the same age as Dodd and full of life. And the chairman of HELP was Dodd's close pal and mentor, Ted Kennedy, twelve years Dodd's senior but still vigorous.

Then Sarbanes decided not to seek a sixth term in 2006. When the 110th Congress convened in January 2007, Dodd became the new chairman of the Committee on Banking, Housing and Urban Affairs. Its broad jurisdiction included responsibility for banking, insurance, financial markets, housing, urban development and mass transit, international trade and finance, and economic policy.

Politics had dominated Chris Dodd's world since childhood. His father was Thomas J. Dodd of Norwich, Connecticut, who graduated from Yale Law School in the depths of the Great Depression. The elder Dodd worked as an FBI agent, then as a federal prosecutor. In 1946 he joined the American prosecution team at the Nuremberg trials of Nazi war criminals. When he returned to Connecticut, Dodd began practicing law and dreaming of a political career. His big Irish American family—six children, Chris the fifth—was a political asset. In 1952 he won election to the House of Representatives.

Chris, born in 1944, was just eight years old when his dad first went to Washington. Tom Dodd was ambitious, and ran for the Senate just four years later. He lost by 12 percentage points to the Republican senator Prescott Bush, father of George H. W. Bush. Two years later Dodd tried again and easily won Connecticut's second Senate seat against a long-forgotten Republican incumbent.

As a teenager Chris lived with his parents in Washington. He attended Georgetown Prep, a Catholic school in the Maryland suburbs. Politicians and their wives from both parties regularly showed up at the Dodds' house in Georgetown for cocktails and dinner parties—a common form of socializing in a long-ago Washington quite unlike the modern version. In those days most Senate couples maintained a principal residence in Washington; today few do.

Chris Dodd enrolled in Providence College, the Dominican school in Rhode Island that was his father's alma mater. The younger Dodd majored in English literature.

In Chris's senior year, Tom Dodd became the target of Washington's most famous muckraking journalists, Drew Pearson and Jack Anderson, who wrote a daily column that appeared in *The Washington Post* and hundreds of other papers. Pearson was vain and could be ruthless; facts mattered less to him than exposing and damaging those he disagreed with or found unworthy. His younger sidekick, Anderson, had developed a relationship with one of Tom Dodd's key aides who had turned against his boss after concluding that he was corrupt. Dodd fired this aide and three others. They then broke into the senator's office, stole embarrassing documents from the files, and fed them to Anderson and Pearson, who launched a crusade.

In column after column, they accused Dodd of helping people who had contributed to his campaigns or gave him gifts and converting campaign contributions to his personal use. The drumbeat of accusations prodded the Senate to undertake a formal investigation in 1966. At that time the Senate had no code of ethics, no requirements that senators disclose their sources of income, and no rule forbidding the use of campaign contributions for personal expenses. All these would come later. But in 1964 the Senate had created a new Select Committee on Standards and Conduct, which began an investigation of whether Dodd's behavior discredited the Senate.

While this investigation continued, Chris Dodd graduated from Providence and joined the Peace Corps. He was working in the small rural town of Monción in the Dominican Republic when he read in a local newspaper that the Senate had censured his father. This was, he said years later, devastating news for which he was ill-prepared. "There was nobody to talk to" in Monción, and he knew few details of the case his father's colleagues had brought against him. He didn't come home from the Dominican Republic until the following year.

The evidence against Tom Dodd was overwhelming. The vote to censure him was 92–5. The resolution of censure said his conduct was "contrary to accepted morals, derogates from the public trust expected of a Senator, and tends to bring the Senate into dishonor and disrepute." He was only the seventh senator in American history to be censured.

After the Peace Corps, Chris Dodd volunteered for the U.S. Army Reserve, serving four months on active duty, then entered law school at the University of Louisville, which had a program that led to a degree in two years instead of the usual three. Senator John Sherman Cooper of Kentucky, a moderate Republican and pal of Tom Dodd's, had recommended the program to Chris.

After Tom Dodd's censure by the Senate, the Connecticut Democratic Party refused to endorse him for reelection and chose another candidate. Dodd forced a primary against the man chosen by his party and lost. He ran for reelection anyway as an Independent. His devoted son Chris, who never publicly accepted the idea that his father had done something seriously wrong, worked on his campaign that summer before starting law school in September. The Republican Lowell Weicker won the three-way election, completing Tom Dodd's humiliation.

Six months later, Chris Dodd recalled years afterward, he called his father to report his election to Law Review. "Having not always lived up to his standards of excellence, I was finally giving him some good news," Dodd remembered. "So he was rather excited, and he was bellowing around the house for my mother to get on the phone." But he couldn't find her and asked his son to call back later. That night Tom Dodd suffered a fatal heart attack. He was just sixty-four.

Chris Dodd finished law school in 1972 and joined a firm in New London, not far from his father's birthplace in Norwich. Years later Dodd remembered liking the fact that the firm discouraged its lawyers from running for public office—a rule that would insulate him from any temptation to follow his father's path, he remembered thinking.

Morgan McGinley, then a reporter covering politics for *The Day* in New London, has a different memory. At the predominantly Republican firm that Dodd joined, McGinley said, "they kidded him that he didn't know a lot of law, but he sure could bring in business." Everybody understood, McGinley said, that Dodd had come to eastern Connecticut to run for Congress.

McGinley's memory seems the more accurate one. Dodd took the first possible opportunity to run for Congress, declaring his candidacy for a House seat in May 1974, after his older brother, Thomas Dodd Jr., a college professor, decided not to run. The speech he gave to announce his candidacy included this revealing passage: "Lest there be any question in anybody's mind as to whether or not I am running on my name, let me tell you what I have said time and again—I am my father's son, but I am not my father, and I don't believe anyone should or will be chosen as a candidate for this office because of his or her name. Don't misunderstand me, no one could be prouder of my father and his record than I am, but I haven't asked nor will I ask you or anyone else to support me because my name is Dodd."

He didn't have to. There was "great loyalty" to Tom Dodd, said McGinley, "especially among blue-collar voters." And Chris Dodd could connect with constituents at least as well as his father did. "Chris Dodd is just a likable person," as McGinley put it, and as others would put it for the next four decades. He was friendly, open, and easy to talk to.

That spring and summer of 1974 was probably the most challenging period in Chris Dodd's political career. He faced two serious rivals for the nomination who also had familiar last names and ties to the district. One was Douglas Bennet, a Harvard Ph.D. in history and former aide to several senators in Washington whose father had run for the same seat years earlier. The other was John M. Bailey Jr., son of the longtime Democratic state chairman. They "debated sixty times" before the Democratic town committees in nearly every community in the sprawling second district, Dodd recalled years later. "Sometimes the three of us outnumbered the audience by two. It was a wonderful experience." It culminated on July 22, 1974 (Dodd remembered the date nearly forty years later), in a memorable one-day district convention in Thompsonville. The event was held in a Knights of Columbus hall without air-conditioning on a hot day. "It was really an old cattle barn," Dodd remembered. "It was 120 degrees!" He recalled home-made signs and an enthusiastic crowd, which voted overwhelmingly for Dodd.

Winning that nomination was the last big political challenge Dodd faced for three decades. He combined a gift for politics with remarkable good luck. The luck began barely two weeks after that cow barn convention, when Nixon resigned to avoid being removed from office, setting up one of the great Democratic landslides in history in November 1974. Dodd won his race with 56 percent of the vote.

So "at the ripe old age of thirty I was sitting in the halls of Congress," Dodd said. "It was a little overwhelming. . . . I look back at it now and it's somewhat frightening what we didn't know." His life experience beyond his education consisted of two years in the Dominican Republic mastering Spanish and trying to help poor peasants, and barely a year of law practice in New London. But the young Dodd was well served by his natural political skills. At the end of his first term, he found himself involved in a leadership fight among House Democrats, serving as one of three coordinators of a reformer's campaign for the job of House majority leader. The reformer, Richard Bolling of Missouri, narrowly lost, but was so impressed with young Dodd that he asked Speaker Thomas P. (Tip) O'Neill to make him a member of the Rules Committee that Bolling chaired.

Dodd joined that influential committee, which determined what bills reached the floor for votes, and under what circumstances, at the beginning of his second term, then an unusual honor for a junior congressman. As a member of Rules blessed by the leadership, Dodd was an instant insider. But he didn't like it. Joining Rules meant "you put yourself in a cocoon. All you could say was no. Just saying no to people was not what I wanted to do in public life." He wanted to pass bills and change the world.

Dodd's original campaign manager was a man named Al Goodin, who had worked for Tom Dodd and shared Chris's desire to restore the Dodd name in Connecticut. "He never had more than an eighth grade education," Dodd said, "but he had this wonderful gift for sizing people up." Goodin helped Dodd build a local political organization that served him well for years, first by persuading a Norwich jeweler, Stanley Israelite, to run Dodd's home office. Israelite spent three decades as Dodd's main man in Connecticut.

Reelection was never difficult. Dodd cruised to victory in 1976 and again in 1978. "I might have stayed in the House" for many years, Dodd said, "had I not been sentenced to Rules." When Abraham Ribicoff, a three-term senator, announced his intention to retire—"it was May 3, 1979," Dodd recalled more than thirty years later—"at that point this was not a hard choice. I was six years in the House [it was actually four years and four months]. I was not going to sit there for the next twenty years waiting to climb up to be chairman of the Rules Committee at age eighty."

It was not a hard choice, but also not one he would announce publicly for nineteen months. Another Democratic congressman was interested in the Senate race, and Dodd wanted to line up as much support as he could quietly, before making any announcement. By the time he was ready his potential rival had abandoned the idea of running. After that, "the nomination was basically mine for the asking," Dodd said. In January 1980, he formally declared his candidacy.

The political terrain of 1980 proved tricky. Though Democrats outnumbered Republicans in Connecticut, Jimmy Carter was an unpopular president there. Ted Kennedy defeated Carter in the state's Democratic primary, and Ronald Reagan, the Republican candidate, appealed to many swing voters in the state. In early October, Dodd recalled, "the bottom fell out of the Carter campaign in Connecticut"—Dodd's own polls showed Reagan pulling into a clear lead. "I honestly thought the day before that election that if Carter lost Connecticut by 100,000 votes, then I couldn't possibly win."

Dodd was too pessimistic. His Republican opponent proved to be an asset. That was James Buckley, the brother of the conservative celebrity William F. Buckley, who had already served one term in the Senate—from New York. Though he had long been a part-time Connecticut resident, this history didn't help Buckley. Nor did his stiff patrician manner. And Dodd's charms had clearly won over a great many Connecticut voters. On election day, Reagan defeated Carter in the state by 150,000 votes, but Dodd beat Buckley by a similar margin. "It took my breath away," he said.

That was the last exciting election Dodd faced. In 1986, 1992, 1998, and 2004, winning reelection proved about as difficult as eating breakfast. In those contests he won 65, 59, 65, and 66 percent of the votes. "For decades he was the state's most appealing politician," said *The Day*'s Morgan McGinley.

Dodd's approach to the job of senator was atypical. From the beginning of his career he looked for ways to make things happen. For sixteen of his thirty years in the Senate, Republicans were in the majority, but this did not deter Dodd. It did, however, shape his approach to legislating. He was a proudly liberal Democrat who constantly cultivated Republican partners to push the legislation he cared most about. "You shop around for people of like mind who are willing to work on something, and they can become part of it," he explained shortly after leaving the Senate in 2011. That meant sometimes compromising to win the collaboration of others. Dodd believed in compromise, a fundamental ingredient of the legislative process since the earliest Congresses. "Why are you in the Senate? What's the point?" To make things happen—that was always his answer.

He liked to list the Republican "partners" with whom he'd worked on various legislative endeavors: Arlen Specter of Pennsylvania, with whom Dodd created a "children's caucus" in the early 1980s that recruited like-minded colleagues from both parties to try to pass laws to help kids and their parents; Orrin Hatch of Utah, with whom he coauthored one of his early big bills providing federal aid for child care for working mothers; Dan Coats of Indiana and Kit Bond of Missouri, who helped with the law Dodd considered his single biggest accomplishment, the Family and Medical Leave Act, requiring employers to provide up to twelve weeks of unpaid leave to allow employees to care for ill family members or newborn children; Mitch McConnell of Kentucky, cosponsor with Dodd of a bill to provide federal aid to states to modernize voting technologies after the troubled 2000 presidential election; Rick Santorum of Pennsylvania, who worked with Dodd to enact a bill providing federal funds for the study of autism. This was a partial list.

In modern Washington legislative patience is uncommon, but Dodd always had it. He worked for eight years to pass the Family and Medical Leave Act. The business community fought the bill ferociously, but Dodd prevailed. President George H. W. Bush vetoed the bill twice, but Dodd and his allies persisted. Bill Clinton embraced the act in his 1992 presidential campaign, then signed it into law in February 1993. It has changed the lives of millions of Americans.

Curiously, his capacity for patient persistence coexisted with a flamboyant personal life as a bachelor who liked women. (As a law student Dodd was married to Susan Mooney, a former speechwriter for his father; they were divorced, without children, in 1982.) Dodd was seen with Bianca Jagger and Carrie Fisher on his arm. He and Ted Kennedy famously caroused together around Washington in the 1980s, often in the company of young women. After meeting Jackie Clegg, a Mormon from Utah, on a ski trip in 1988, Dodd finally began to settle down—though they weren't married until June 1999, when he was fifty-six. They have two daughters, born in 2001 and 2005. Dodd entered the state of fatherhood at an age when most men are becoming grandfathers.

Dodd never lacked for ambition. When the job of Democratic leader came open in 1994, he ran and lost by a single vote to Tom Daschle of South Dakota. The next year he accepted President Bill Clinton's offer to become general chairman of the Democratic National Committee and held the job for two years, acting as a spokesman for the party. When Daschle lost his Senate seat in 2004, Dodd was again a candidate for Democratic leader, but withdrew before a vote was held when he realized that Harry Reid of Nevada was his colleagues' clear choice. In 2007, when Dodd was sixty-two, he decided to take a shot at the presidency; he understood that this was his last chance at the big prize that so many members of the Senate allow themselves to dream of.

In politics, Dodd once explained, dreaming of the presidency was "a siren call" to which too many succumbed. "You get elected to the city council someplace," and that's enough to prompt "some people" to say, "'You know, someday I could be president of the United States!'" He was talking about himself, though he actually skipped the city council and started in Congress.

Dodd had announced his candidacy in early January, entering what would be a crowded field. Even his oldest supporters were dubious—in polls, Dodd was never favored for the presidential nomination by more than one percent of Democrats. But reaching for that brass ring proved irresistible.

The world was not waiting for a President Dodd. Though liked and respected by many Democrats, he never emerged from a crowded field that included Hillary Clinton, John Edwards, and Barack Obama. By October he decided to make his biggest play in Iowa, whose caucuses began the primary season and offered a long shot opportunity to surprise the field. Dodd moved his family to a small house in Des Moines. He enrolled his oldest daughter in a Des Moines kindergarten. They spent most of November and December campaigning around the state. Dodd opened thirteen offices across Iowa and spent most of his remaining money on the effort.

The prolonged absence of the chairman of the Banking Committee did not play well in Washington. *The Washington Post* published a story in November noting that Barney Frank's House Committee on Financial Services held eighty-two hearings and passed dozens of bills in the first ten months of 2007 in a flurry of activity related to worsening conditions in the housing market (which led to the Great Crash ten months later). Dodd's Banking Committee, by contrast, had held thirty-two hearings but passed no legislation related to the housing crisis, nor acted on several dozen bills already passed by the full House and forwarded to the Senate for consideration. One of those House bills would have virtually banned the subprime home mortgages that turned out to be an important cause of the Great Crash. Dodd's committee never took up the House bill, so it died. Frank was frustrated that Dodd's presidential ambitions had derailed his efforts, preventing them both from fully exploiting the chairmanships they had waited years to achieve.

Despite discouraging polls in Iowa, Dodd soldiered on. He was all smiles and optimism in his public appearances. His good nature didn't help. When the caucuses met on January 3, 2008, he won less than .01 percent of the votes cast, finishing dead last. The next day he announced he was abandoning his candidacy.

This outcome was humiliating, but it was worse than that. Voters in Connecticut were upset with their senior senator for the first time in his career. Many expressed displeasure with the Dodd family's move to Iowa, halfway across the country. As the leading paper in Connecticut, *The Hartford Courant,* put it later, "Things were turning sour in Connecticut, and the folks wanted him back home."

In early January the Dodds reoccupied their homes in Washington and East Haddam, Connecticut. The chairman of the Banking Committee finally began to focus on the job he already held.

CHAPTER SIX

Back in the Game

Chris Dodd returned to Washington at the beginning of 2008 determined to assert his authority as chairman of the Banking Committee. Like all of his colleagues, Dodd was sensitive to criticism in the press. He wanted to respond to complaints that his presidential campaign had hobbled the Banking Committee during 2007. And he was on the defensive in Connecticut, where polls showed a disquieting absence of enthusiasm for his reelection in 2010. He scheduled a news conference in the Senate Press Gallery on January 23, 2008, to talk about his agenda for the new year.

In Iowa Dodd hadn't had much luck attracting attention from the news media, so he must have been heartened when several dozen reporters and seven television cameras crowded into the Press Gallery that morning. But he undermined his cause by reading a 2,700-word statement praising the accomplishments of his Banking Committee during the year he was largely absent. This took twenty-one minutes, and exhausted the attention span of many of the reporters.

In the previous twelve months, Dodd said, "the committee has passed seventeen pieces of legislation—all with strong bipartisan support—and held thirty-five hearings." He enumerated a mind-numbing list of bills that the committee had produced, from reforming the National Flood Insurance Program to stiffening the penalties for companies that "do business with terrorists." Many had never been enacted by the Senate, the House, or both. Few of Dodd's remarks were reported or broadcast. Like so many "news" conferences in Washington, this one was a bust.

Something truly important that would help Dodd fulfill his ambition to make a mark as chairman happened that same month, but got almost no public attention: the hiring of a lawyer named Amy Friend to be chief counsel of the Banking Committee. She was hired without being interviewed by Dodd, who barely knew her at the time. In the months to come she would became his most important collaborator, almost his alter ego. She would have more influence on the process of writing the new rules for American finance than most senators—probably more than all senators other than Dodd. Her hiring was reported by just one Washington publication, a daily trade paper called *American Banker.*

Friend was forty-nine years old when she joined the committee. Her generation was one of the first to fully exploit the new opportunities available to females in the 1970s and 1980s. Like many women her age, Friend recalled, she did not think of herself as a feminist or a standard-bearer for other women. From the time she was a child, she just assumed she could do whatever she wanted to do; gender was irrelevant. Her parents, both educators, agreed. They raised her in the suburbs of New York, then of Philadelphia. She had to switch schools at the age of fifteen, from a big central high school in Emerson, New Jersey, "that emphasized sports" to Lower Merion High outside Philadelphia, one of the country's best academic public high schools (and also Kobe Bryant's alma mater). Friend remembered the switch as traumatic, "but I coped," and then thrived. The experience convinced her she could handle difficult challenges.

She hoped (with many Lower Merion classmates) to enroll at the University of Pennsylvania, an Ivy League school, but she failed to win admission. She spent one unhappy year at Penn State, reapplied to Penn, and was accepted as a transfer student. She quickly found her intellectual footing. In 1980 she graduated magna cum laude with a Phi Beta Kappa key. Her major was psychology.

In her senior year, Friend attended a campus rally for Edward M. Kennedy, who was challenging the sitting Democratic president, Jimmy Carter. After the rally she volunteered to work for Kennedy, and was soon the campus coordinator for his campaign. "It was the Kennedy magic" that lured her, she said. She had a vivid childhood memory of the days after John Kennedy was assassinated, when her parents watched television all weekend. "I had never seen them so serious, so somber." At age twenty-two, still a college senior, she ran in the Pennsylvania Democratic primary for a seat as a Kennedy delegate to the 1980 Democratic National Convention, and won—a life-changing experience that lured her to Washington. After graduating from Penn, she worked for a year as a paralegal in a Washington law firm, then applied to Georgetown Law School. While a student there she worked part-time on the staff of the Senate Judiciary Committee, which Kennedy chaired. Upon completing law school she spent three years at Washington law firms. This period was most memorable for the husband it produced—another lawyer she met at her first law firm. In 1987 she got a chance to work for Chuck Schumer, then a congressman from New York City, and jumped to Capitol Hill. Friend spent the subsequent twenty-three years in public service, where she felt she belonged.

She worked in the House for eleven years, the last six of them in staff positions on the House Committee on Financial Services. For Friend, one of the best aspects of the job was the opportunity it offered to build networks of people with similar interests. She made two friends during those years who would prove important to her role with Dodd in 2008–10—both good examples of the way those networks created on the Hill can have enduring importance for their members.

One was Shawn Maher, a bright, intense New Yorker who worked for Representative Joseph P. Kennedy II, Robert Kennedy's son, then a congressman from Massachusetts. Maher figured out that the svelte, attractive Friend was smart, competent, and efficient. Another was Jeanne Roslanowick. She was already an important figure on the committee staff in the early 1990s. She was also a feminist who liked helping other women's careers. Roslanowick also took a shine to Friend, ten years her junior.

Maher brought Friend to the Senate Banking Committee in 2008. After years on Dodd's personal staff, Maher had become staff director of the committee when Dodd became chairman in 2007. He had stayed in touch with Friend after she left the Hill in 1998 to become assistant chief counsel of the Office of the Comptroller of the Currency, a division of the Treasury Department that regulated the country's national banks. Friend liked working at OCC. The regular hours of a federal agency helped her cope with a full home life populated by that husband, a daughter, and a son. Professionally it gave her a whole new set of contacts in the banking industry, among lobbyists, and in the Federal Reserve and other regulatory agencies.

When Maher first approached Friend about coming to work at Senate Banking in early 2007, she resisted, fearing the impact of such a job on her domestic tranquillity. Maher persisted. He offered to enhance her title to "chief counsel," symbolically significant in title-conscious Washington. Roslanowick, with whom Friend consulted throughout this process, had urged her to insist on the elevated title.

Maher offered her the opportunity to talk to Dodd before accepting the job if she thought it necessary. Friend had met Dodd years earlier and knew him to be affable and a good boss with a serious sense of purpose. Members who are dumb, lazy, or imperious are soon identified within the tribe of Capitol Hill aides, as are the good ones who can be fun to work for. Dodd was one of the latter. That was enough for Friend. She took the job without talking to Dodd.

In January she moved into a cubicle in the crowded suite of offices occupied by the Banking Committee staff on the fifth floor of the Dirksen Senate Office Building. As cubicles go it was a nice one, with a big window looking north at Washington's magnificent Union Station. Friend's workspace was small but adequate. She could overhear her neighbors' phone calls, and they hers. Her salary was $153,500 a year, more than three times the national median family income, but a fourth or less the earnings of a successful Washington lobbyist or law partner, which Friend could easily have been.

At that news conference on January 23, Dodd promised an "aggressive" legislative program to confront the steadily worsening housing crisis, but at the time neither he, nor Maher, nor Friend had an inkling of how serious that crisis would become. In March they got the first clear warning: Bear Stearns, one of the largest New York investment banks and a big player in the market for securities based on subprime mortgages, disappeared—merged by the Federal Reserve Bank of New York into JPMorgan Chase to prevent its collapse. The Fed extended $30 billion to JPMorgan to consummate the deal, the first big bailout of the year.

The Banking Committee held a hearing on the failure of Bear Stearns, but concentrated its legislative energies on an ambitious housing bill. Barney Frank had already steered similar legislation through the House. Dodd pursued what was the normal procedure in the Banking Committee by looking for bipartisan support for the legislation. By late May he had a deal with Richard Shelby of Alabama, the ranking Republican on Banking, who had himself been the committee chairman in the previous Congress, from 2005 until the Democrats took over in early 2007. The Banking Committee "reported" (approved) its housing bill on May 20 by the lopsided vote of 19–2.

By traditional standards it was a big and important bill. It provided billions of dollars to try to help stabilize the housing market, prevent foreclosures, encourage construction of affordable housing, and create a new, independent regulator for Fannie Mae and Freddie Mac, the two government-sponsored enterprises (GSEs) that owned or insured more than $5 trillion in home mortgages. Their full names were the Federal National Mortgage Association and the Federal Home Loan Mortgage Corporation.

As the bill neared final passage in July 2008, the financial markets showed signs of extreme anxiety about the health of Fannie and Freddie. The Bush administration asked that Congress add provisions allowing the government to guarantee their debts and even to seize control of them if the crisis got out of hand. Hank Paulson hoped the debt guarantee plus the "bazooka" (Paulson's term) he was authorized to use to nationalize the two firms in an emergency would reassure the markets. He said he doubted the bazooka would be needed.

The housing bill occupied Dodd, Maher, and Friend for months. President Bush signed it into law toward the end of July, and then it was August in an election year. Congress dispersed. The Democratic National Convention convened in Denver in the last week of August; the Republicans met in Minneapolis the first week of September.

And then on September 6, barely six weeks after Congress had given him the authority to do so, Paulson fired the bazooka. The government abruptly put Fannie and Freddie "into receivership"—it took them over, wiping out their shareholders (though preserving the investments of their bondholders, of whom the biggest was China). "I had not known the extent of the companies' problems," Paulson explained later. That was the beginning of the Great Crash. Chris Dodd and his staff found themselves on the front lines in the worst economic crisis in eight decades.

After the stomach-churning meeting in Pelosi's office on September 18, Dodd got deeply involved in the legislative response. His usual Republican partner, Shelby, decided he wanted no part in the TARP legislation, so Dodd looked for other Republican collaborators, and found them in Judd Gregg of New Hampshire and Bob Corker of Tennessee, who helped him manage the bailout legislation through the Senate.

In October, Maher, Friend, and several colleagues turned to the obvious question raised by the Crash: How should Congress respond? They and Dodd produced a statement that he read on the Senate floor on November 6, two days after the election that gave Barack Obama the presidency and the Democrats increased majorities in both House and Senate. Dodd announced that he would be staying at the Banking Committee. Senator Joe Biden's election as vice president meant Dodd could have claimed the chairmanship of Foreign Relations, Biden's previous job. Dodd loved Foreign Relations, but as a candidate for reelection in two years, he knew that Banking was more useful politically. "There is no more important way right now that I can serve the people of Connecticut and our country than as Banking Committee Chairman," he said. He intended to write legislation "to modernize our nation's framework of financial regulation."

Dodd offered his first thoughts on what that might entail. Regulators would have to become "strong cops on the beat," not enablers of risky behavior. The regulatory system should be reorganized so that regulated institutions could not "shop" for the easiest overseer, as they had in the past. The system needed to better regulate the risks that financial institutions were taking, which required more information about their behavior, and greater transparency, so outsiders and investors could see what they were up to. "Last but certainly not least," Dodd said, "we need to accept the fundamental premise that consumer protection and economic growth are not in conflict. On the contrary, they are inextricably linked. If we learn nothing else from this crisis, it is that the failure to protect consumers can wreak havoc on the financial system." Dodd promised stronger regulations on mortgage lending and credit cards. "Consumer protection should be on an equal footing with supervision that ensures the safety and soundness of our financial system."

Dodd's outline was consistent with the past statements of the president-elect, with the recommendations of the outgoing secretary of the treasury, Paulson, and with the early thinking of Barney Frank and his staff in the House. Neither Obama nor Frank had put the same emphasis on consumer protection, but Paulson had, and the idea was gaining currency when Dodd spoke.

Soon after the new Congress convened in early January, Dodd invited the Democratic members of his committee to dinner in a private room of Charlie Palmer Steak, a sleek emporium of red meat located on the ground floor of an office building at the foot of Capitol Hill. Dodd's Press Gallery news conference was Washington theater, but this dinner, attended only by senators and a few Dodd aides, was Washington reality. The news media knew nothing about it.

There were eleven Democrats besides Dodd on the Banking Committee, and seven of them came to dinner. The Great Crash was fresh in the minds of all present. Its full impact was still unfolding. The principal topic at the dinner table, according to the notes of one of the diners, was what Dodd was calling "regulatory modernization."

Dodd conveyed a message that he had received from the president-elect's transition team—as Rahm Emanuel had told Barney Frank, Obama "wanted a product by early April," when he was scheduled to meet with the G-20. Dodd understood, as Obama would soon, that this was an "unrealistic" deadline for writing legislation that would inevitably be complicated and controversial. But he suggested that they should all be grateful for the opportunity now before them. "For whatever reason, we're here at this moment—it's historic," Dodd said. "We have a chance to make a difference. This is our moment."

Everyone present explicitly or tacitly agreed that they should produce "something with real teeth, not just a rap on the knuckles," in the words of Robert Menendez of New Jersey. Dodd's enthusiasm for the enterprise was clear. He said he wanted "street-smart" advice: "I want to listen to people who will tell us the down-and-dirty of how this should work." He wanted finally to pass new regulations for the credit card industry, to make it harder for card issuers to exact large fees from their customers. He wanted to ban subprime mortgages—home loans to people who did not qualify for them under traditional standards.

There were shades of differing opinion. Schumer of New York expressed concern about new regulations that could put New York at a competitive disadvantage to London and other global financial centers. Schumer had so faithfully represented New York's financial interests for years that he was known as "the senator from Wall Street"— a role he quickly abandoned, at least outwardly, after the crash. At this dinner he urged that international collaboration on new bank regulations be encouraged. Menendez noted that if confidence were not restored in American financial institutions, their competitive position could not be improved.

Tim Johnson of South Dakota, who spoke with difficulty because of an unusual brain aneurysm he had suffered in 2006, gently asserted his special status as the best Democratic friend of the big banks on the Banking Committee. Was it really necessary, he asked Dodd, to write ambitious new rules for financial firms, since the Fed had finally issued regulations that would largely eliminate subprime mortgages, the biggest cause of the crash? Dodd said he thought it was necessary.

Johnson's concern for the big banks was a classic example of the way special interests can dominate the decision making of members of Congress. South Dakota, curiously, had become a hub of banking activity—an only-in-America story.

After the Supreme Court ruled in 1978 that banks issuing credit cards could charge their customers the highest interest rate allowed in the state where the bank was chartered, South Dakota passed a law allowing banks to charge any interest rate they liked. Citibank, then losing money on its credit card business because it was regulated in New York state, whose strict usury limit set maximum credit card interest at 12–18 percent per year on unpaid balances, saw an opportunity. Walter Wriston, the famous CEO of Citi at the time, flew to South Dakota to talk to the governor about bringing Citi's credit card operations to the state. South Dakota's politicians demonstrated their enthusiasm by passing a law allowing Citi to take over a South Dakota bank. Citi did so and made the South Dakota bank the proprietor of its national credit card business. Under that Supreme Court decision, there would be no legal limit on the interest rates of Citi's credit cards.

Other banks with credit card businesses followed Citi's lead. Thousands of new jobs came to South Dakota. In the 1980s, Sioux Falls, the state's biggest city, grew faster than any other city in the upper Midwest. In gratitude, South Dakota's two senators and lone House member became loyal foot soldiers for the banking industry and Citi in particular. They were also the recipients of hundreds of thousands of dollars of campaign contributions from banks and bankers. Consumers around the country did not do so well; some credit card interest rates soared above 20 percent.

That night at Charlie Palmer Steak, Dodd said he wanted to follow Banking Committee tradition and produce a bipartisan bill on regulatory modernization. No Democrat demurred. He reported that the new White House team had invited him and Barney Frank to meet with Obama and his key aides to talk about regulatory reforms. And he warned them that the crisis wasn't over yet—"the danger of falling off a cliff is still real."

The meeting with Obama took place on February 25. Dodd asked the White House to invite Shelby, whose cooperation Dodd considered critical if regulatory modernization were to succeed in the Senate. So Shelby and the ranking Republican on the House Committee, Spencer Bachus, another Alabamian, joined Dodd and Frank in the Oval Office. Geithner, Lawrence Summers, and Rahm Emanuel were also present.

Dodd urged that consumer protection be a central element of regulatory reform. "The basis of this bill ought to be restoring consumer confidence and consumer protection, because it was basically what happened to individual home buyers that was the source of all that eventually unfolded," he recalled saying. Friend, who sat in an anteroom waiting for the meeting to end, remembered Dodd's report afterward: "They looked at me like I was crazy" when he said that. But consumer protection soon became an important part of the new administration's proposed legislation.

(Friend also remembered how President Obama had come out of the Oval Office to meet the staff waiting in the anteroom, saying he wanted to shake hands with "the ones who are going to do the work." Obama asked the White House photographer to take pictures of him with his arms around Friend and several colleagues. "I remember thinking how amazing that was, that the president actually was acknowledging the staff.")

This was the meeting at which Obama said he hoped the House and Senate committees would allow the administration to draft the regulatory reform legislation. Frank, as we know, liked this suggestion. Dodd and his staff understood that the administration would offer draft legislation, but from the beginning they expected the Senate to produce its own version that might be quite different from either the administration's proposals or a House version produced by Frank.

If Dodd was indeed going to draft a bill with Republican support, this seemed inevitable. No one expected Senate Republicans to support legislation written in the liberal House or by a new Democratic administration. As the process of writing new rules began, the small tribe of intensely interested parties—bankers and their Washington representatives, lobbyists, lawyers who specialized in banking regulation, academic experts—generally expected the new administration and Barney Frank's House committee to agree on tough new regulations that a bipartisan group of senators would tone down and moderate. Edward L. Yingling, president of the American Bankers Association, the banking industry's principal Washington lobbyist, was a typical member of this tribe. Beginning early in 2009, Yingling consistently predicted a tough bill from the House and "something better from the Senate," meaning something easier for the banks to swallow. He hoped and expected that the Senate would ultimately dominate the legislative process, as it often did.

Shelby's performance in the Oval Office that day reinforced the view that he could prove to be a useful partner. "It was an excellent conversation," Frank noted the day after the meeting. "One of the hopeful things was Dick Shelby saying that he plans to be very supportive of this and he and Dodd appear to be ready to work together." Frank was impressed by the different attitudes adopted by Shelby and Bachus, who was much more cautious.

When Obama asked those present to share their opinions, Bachus "had no substantive thing to say, but talked about the need not to get too public with all this," Frank recalled. "While I didn't say so, it's clear to me that he has this problem with his caucus, which is so right-wing-dominated, and he wasn't able to say much because he's not clear if anything he says will be sustained." Frank could not resist giving Bachus a rhetorical jab: "I said that there were four caucuses present—two House and two Senate, obviously—and that three of the four of us could probably work together, but that in fairness to Spencer, it was very unclear that he could deliver his own caucus." This was the sort of remark that infuriated Bachus, a bright but inarticulate man who felt Frank did not take him seriously.

But Frank's analysis appeared accurate. Bachus was indeed nervous about his standing with the leadership of the Republican caucus, which viewed him suspiciously, and Shelby did seem ready to work out a bipartisan bill. That day at the White House he agreed that the first items of business should be the creation of a new systemic risk regulator to curb reckless behavior by financial institutions, and a new mechanism to resolve those that fail—ease them out of business.

A fortnight after that Oval Office meeting Shelby put his thoughts on the record in an interview. He confirmed that he, Dodd, and Frank saw many of the issues in similar terms. The existing regulators "failed us" by allowing the Great Crash to happen. "I believe that we have to have a new regulatory regime for our financial system. . . . I think we're going to have to have a powerful regulatory body that approves or disapproves new [financial] products, that will put the old system in play.

"A lot of people say, 'Let the market work.' You can't let the market work where the market is manipulated to such an extent that it would bring down our economy and half the world. I think that's what we're looking at. This would be, in my view, sweeping legislation. We've got to do it right. We cannot afford to let interest groups, whoever they are, subordinate the interest of the nation to their particular whim or needs, which they've always done."

This was not an analysis you would have heard from the big financial institutions or their sympathizers. It was the voice of one of the most interesting characters in the Senate. "Even some of my Republican friends say I have a populist, progressive streak," Shelby said in another interview. "I am not a doctrinaire, anti-government person."

Shelby spent his first twenty-five years in elected office as a Democrat—a progressive Democrat by Alabama's standards, because he avoided the racist posturing typical of many whites in that state's politics. Born in 1934, Shelby grew up with six sisters in a working-class family. His father, Ozie Houston Shelby, was a draftsman for U.S. Steel. These origins mattered. "He's from across the tracks, so to speak. That gives you a different view," in the words of Mike House, an Alabamian who has known Shelby for years.

Six feet four with a broad, handsome face, Shelby got to the University of Alabama on his talent as a defensive end. A knee injury ended his football career prematurely, but he thrived as a student of political science and won a place in the University of Alabama School of Law. Classmates there report that he cultivated the manner of a courtly southern gentleman even in his twenties. As a law student he fell for an undergraduate named Annette Nevin, a bright, pretty, and independent daughter of educators. She accepted Shelby's Delta Chi fraternity pin just three weeks after they met, and married him soon after her graduation. "I liked his energy level, his wit, his presence," she said years later. She became a formidable political asset.

Shelby began his professional career as a small-town plaintiff's lawyer, and discovered he had a talent for it. Juries liked him. Annette also wanted a career, and she pursued it in an unusual way. When their firstborn son was two years old, she moved herself and Richard Jr. to Baton Rouge, Louisiana, to pursue a Ph.D. in communications at Louisiana State University. Shelby continued his law practice in Tuscaloosa. Every weekend he drove 350 miles to Baton Rouge to see his wife and son. When Annette got her degree, she began her academic career as a professor at the University of Alabama.

As a young man Shelby led a purposeful life, accumulating friends, influence, and money. In 1970 he launched the political career he'd long been plotting by running for the Alabama state Senate. He won easily, and the leadership of the state Senate quickly embraced him. He was chosen for a seat on the most powerful committee in Montgomery, the Senate Rules Committee, which managed the flow of legislation. Shelby has always felt comfortable in a legislative body.

In 1978, the U.S. congressman representing Tuscaloosa and its environs unexpectedly announced his retirement. Shelby and his wife had been preparing for such a possibility; they had built the Tuscaloosa Title Co. into a strong real estate business that assured their financial security. Shelby jumped into the House race and won the seat. In Washington he made friends easily and pursued his own education, particularly on international issues. He joined the Boll Weevils, a caucus of conservative House Democrats, mostly southerners. When Ronald Reagan came to town in 1981, Shelby often voted for his legislative proposals.

In 1986, after four terms in the House, and against the advice of many friends and supporters, Shelby decided to challenge Admiral Jeremiah Denton, a former prisoner of war in North Vietnam whom Alabamans sent to Washington as a Republican senator in 1980. "I was going up or out," Shelby explained years later. Denton wasn't much of a senator, but he was a war hero. Running against him was the first (and, as it turned out, last) serious political risk Shelby ever took. Annette went on leave from her professorship at the business school of Georgetown University in Washington to help run the campaign.

Shelby had more charm than Denton, and more friends in Alabama. Speaking grandly in a mellifluous baritone from his high altitude, Shelby also looked and sounded a lot more like a senator than the admiral did. Senator Denton had rarely been seen at home, a fact eagerly exploited by the Shelby campaign, particularly in a withering television commercial that Shelby's political consultant, Carter Eskew, remembered gleefully: "We had footage of Denton having a meltdown at a press conference where he said, 'I don't have time to come back home and pat babies' butts and [still] get things done in Washington.' It caught his essence, his condescension to the voters of Alabama." The spot appeared scores of times on Alabama television stations. Shelby squeaked into the Senate, winning by just 6,233 votes.

Shelby took two important lessons from this experience. The first reflected the trouble he'd had raising money to challenge Denton and pay for those commercials: Never stop raising campaign money. He became famous for his aggressive fundraising, and for the size of his campaign bank account. By the time he and Dodd began working on financial regulatory issues—two years before Shelby's next campaign—he had more than $15 million in the bank. The second lesson was elementary: Make regular appearances in Alabama. Senator Shelby pledged to hold a public town meeting in each of Alabama's sixty-seven counties at least once a year, a pledge he kept for the next quarter century.

When he first ran for the state Senate in 1970, Republicans were still a rare breed in Alabama. Over the next two decades Richard Nixon's Southern Strategy bore its historic fruit, assisted by Democrats' embrace of the civil rights revolution and the changing demographics of the American Sunbelt. The old Confederacy, once a Democratic stronghold, became Republican territory. By 1994, when Republicans won control of Congress for the first time since the early 1950s, Republican senators from the southern states outnumbered Democrats twelve to ten. Then in January 1995, Shelby made that thirteen to nine; he became a Republican.

The switch was a little awkward. Shelby had said repeatedly that he had no plans to change parties, once describing himself as "a lifelong Democrat—I was born one." But when Democrats lost control of the Senate, he had a new incentive to convert. The Republicans promised to recognize his seniority (eight years in the Senate already) and offered to preserve his chairmanship of an appropriations subcommittee if he came across the aisle. He would have lost it to a Republican had he not switched parties. Appropriating federal dollars was Shelby's favorite activity—especially when he could direct them to Alabama.

A traveler visiting the university campuses of Alabama would encounter the Senator Richard C. and Dr. Annette N. Shelby Center for Engineering Technology at Auburn University; Shelby Hall, the largest science building at the University of Alabama in Tuscaloosa; the Richard C. and Annette N. Shelby Interdisciplinary Biomedical Research Building at the University of Alabama, Birmingham; the Shelby Center for Science and Technology at the University of Alabama, Huntsville; and the Shelby Hall for Engineering and Computing Sciences at the University of South Alabama in Mobile. Each of these was funded with an "earmark," a special appropriation of millions of federal dollars ushered through Congress by Senator Shelby. He had no prouder accomplishments than these memorials.

The Shelbys were an unconventional Republican couple in today's Senate. Their principal residence was in Washington's patrician Georgetown neighborhood, where they lived in a relatively modest brick house worth more than $1 million. They had a fancy big house in Tuscaloosa too, but weren't there often. Shelby lacked the political anxiety that drove so many of his colleagues to leave their families at home and commute every weekend back to their constituents. He never had a serious opponent after beating Jeremiah Denton. The Shelbys read books at home in the evening. They went out to dinner with certain colleagues—with the Dodds repeatedly during 2008 and 2009. They traveled the world, and especially liked Paris; in 2008–9, the Shelbys found reasons to make three trips to Paris, all connected to official business, so taxpayers paid for them all.

"At home he still plays that good ol' country boy—'I'm just Richard'—but he's not," said an old friend from Alabama who has known Shelby for decades. "He loves New York, he loves Paris, he loves to travel—he likes all those things, but he downplays it when he's at home. He has the ability to live in both worlds."

Shelby was more conservative than most Democrats, but also instinctively more moderate than most of the younger Republican firebrands who dominated the Senate Republican caucus. Though popular with many of his Republican colleagues, Shelby was also the object of some suspicion because of his Democratic past. He understood this, and the understanding reinforced his natural predilection for caution. Shelby did not take political risks.

Chris Dodd believed in the Senate of the United States. Many liberal Democrats of his political stripe complained bitterly about the Senate's inefficiencies, particularly the cloture rule that allowed forty-one senators to block action on any piece of legislation by threatening a filibuster, or endless debate. They complained about the ease with which individual members could tie up the entire body with parliamentary maneuvers that were often just expressions of personal pique. To Dodd these were annoyances, sometimes exasperating, but to dwell on them was fruitless, and in his view foolish. The Senate could act when it had to—as it had in the fall of 2008, when the economy teetered on the edge of collapse, and the Senate speedily approved unpopular bailouts that saved the day. The House had proven unable to act on that occasion, at least initially, and made the crisis worse. But Dodd's beloved Senate came through. "Whoever thought this place could act . . . in a limited amount of time to produce the right result for the country in the face of overwhelming public negative reaction? A great moment in the Senate," he said afterward. The key to success was compromise.

Most candidates for the modern Senate, Dodd noted, promise that "if they get elected they'll be their own person, that they'll be independent," but that is the antithesis of what makes an effective senator. The key talent is the ability to compromise, to work things out with people of different persuasions. No candidate for the Senate promises to be a great compromiser, Dodd once observed, "and yet that's exactly what you need to be able to do" to serve your constituents and "make the institution work."

The point of being a senator was "to get something done," one of Dodd's favorite phrases. In the course of three decades in the Senate, he had gotten a great deal done. Now, in the aftermath of the Great Crash, he saw an opportunity to accomplish a lot more.

In February 2009, Dodd surprised his staff by suggesting that the time was ripe to enact credit card legislation of the kind he had discussed at that dinner in January at Charlie Palmer Steak. "We were all scrambling to formulate the financial reform bill," Amy Friend recalled, "and he said, 'I want to move credit cards.' And we just looked at him and said, 'Why? Why now? We're not ready.' " Friend feared that introducing credit card legislation then would deflect attention from the more pressing job of writing the big regulatory reform bill.

Credit cards had been on Dodd's agenda for years. He introduced his first bill to reform credit card practices in 1987, which would have required card issuers to disclose interest rates and all fees in every credit card application or solicitation. He tried several times to limit the banks' ability to raise fees and interest rates, particularly on delinquent cardholders. Every time the banking lobby, traditionally one of Washington's most effective, called in its chits with other senators and blocked Dodd's efforts.

In early 2009, Friend recalled, Dodd understood that because of the crash and subsequent bailouts, the big banks were suddenly among America's least popular institutions. He wanted to exploit their momentary weakness to finally pass a credit card bill to ban the industry's most unpopular practices, including retroactive rate increases and rate increases based on a cardholder's failure to pay any bill on time—not just the credit card bill.

Dodd was far from alone in sensing that the time was right for credit card legislation. In January a Credit Cardholders' Bill of Rights was reintroduced in the House, which had passed the bill in September 2008. This was one of several responses to the economic crisis that came out of Frank's committee, won House approval, and died in the Senate. Frank told his staff in February that he wanted the credit card bill to move quickly through the House (which it did). Dodd wanted to go down the same path. But his preferred method, as always, was to travel that path with a Republican partner, ideally Shelby. Initially Shelby was cool to the idea of a credit card bill, but Dodd persisted. At the end of March, staff for both men spent a long weekend trying to negotiate a deal, but failed. On the last day of the month, Dodd's bill was "reported out" by the Banking Committee by the closest possible vote, 13–12. Every Republican voted no; so did Senator Tim Johnson of South Dakota.

This was widely seen as a rebuff to Dodd and a sign that the Senate was unlikely to pass credit card legislation. Banking lobbyists were delighted. But Dodd promised to soldier on. "This is going to be difficult. I knew that," he told reporters after the vote. "Unless you bring it up and push it, you never get people to sit down [to negotiate]."

In fact, staff negotiations had already made substantial progress. Shelby and Bob Corker of Tennessee both said publicly that there should be a way to achieve a bipartisan consensus. Privately, Shelby told Dodd, "Don't make me vote against this." On the day of the committee action, Shelby signaled his willingness to deal by enumerating the elements of Dodd's proposal that he could accept, including banning gimmicks that card issuers used to raise interest rates and limiting the marketing of cards to young people. The argument he used against the bill—that it might restrict access to credit at a time when the economy could ill-afford to discourage consumers from buying things—seemed rather esoteric when contrasted with the obvious popularity of knocking the credit card issuers down a peg.

The banks could never find a way to generate public sympathy for their position. Their influence in Congress was greatest when they could make their case quietly, out of public view. In this case, they couldn't hide from the obvious public hostility.

Right after the committee vote, Amy Friend realized that the tenor of the negotiations had changed. Shelby's two key aides, William D. Duhnke III and Mark F. Oesterle, "quite literally came knocking on our door" and announced that they were ready to work out a compromise. "It became obvious that Shelby had ordered them to make a deal," she recalled.

Dodd and his aides decided that the Republicans had realized they could not afford to be defenders of the unpopular credit card policies of the banks. The White House encouraged this conclusion by making credit card reform a highly visible issue during April. President Obama summoned the executives of the largest card-issuing institutions for a lecture about the need to give card users some breaks. The president spoke out repeatedly on the need for credit card reform.

On May 11, Dodd and Shelby announced agreement on a revised bill. It was not significantly different from the one Republicans earlier voted against; on some issues it was actually somewhat tougher on the card issuers. *American Banker* reported the view of many following the legislation that reforms had become "politically unstoppable." A week later the full Senate approved the Dodd-Shelby bill 90–5. Both South Dakota senators voted no.

The House quickly embraced the Senate version, which was also tougher than the one the House had passed earlier, and President Obama signed the bill into law. For the first time since the Great Crash, the government had taken action that punished some of the biggest banks. The new rules would cost them hundreds of millions in lost fees and interest charges that would no longer be legal.

For Chris Dodd and his staff, the credit card bill confirmed that collaboration with Shelby was the best way to enact significant legislation. "Shelby and I have a very good relationship," Dodd said after the credit card bill was passed. He observed that when they cooperated, results followed; when they didn't, success was much less likely. Dodd intended to follow this model again as the Banking Committee began the much larger job of writing the regulatory reform legislation.

CHAPTER SEVEN

"Downtown" Takes the Lead

Barney Frank, as we have seen, expected the Obama administration to do "most of the drafting" of the financial regulatory reform legislation, and Chris Dodd expected his Banking Committee to rewrite it significantly. Inside the new administration, a small group of intense officials working on the regulatory issues had a different idea: They would produce the bill, and the president would persuade both House and Senate to enact it.

That idea had come from the president. In the early days of Obama's administration, when he met for the first time with this group to discuss regulatory reform, the president told them, "This is a bill I want the administration to write," one participant recalled. Obama said the subject matter was complicated and highly technical. A new regulatory regime had to be coherent and consistent. Individual members of Congress, Obama accurately observed, have a way of caring a lot about the piece of a bill that they care about, but don't worry about how that bit connects with any other piece. In this case, when the goal was to both modernize and reregulate the huge financial sector, it was essential that all the pieces work together. One set of like-minded authors who could write the entire package would produce the best result, Obama said. He wanted his team to figure out what ought to be in the new rulebook.

Diana Farrell was an important member of this group. Born in 1965, she had worked on regulatory reform issues on the Obama transition team under Summers, who now ran Obama's National Economic Council, where Farrell was his principal deputy. Farrell had the reputation of being unusually smart and creative. She had worked for years for McKinsey & Co., the giant consulting firm, most recently running the company's own think tank. She had spent years in McKinsey's financial institutions group, consulting with big international banks and learning about global capital markets. She felt lucky to have had so much relevant experience when she was tapped to work on regulatory reform.

Farrell was exhilarated by the "intense, blank-sheet-of-paper sessions" with her new colleagues in which they brainstormed the challenge of writing new rules. "We had really intellectual debates involving smart people," she said. The key players included Cass Sunstein, a Harvard law professor and prolific author of books and articles; Michael Barr, a University of Michigan law professor, former Rhodes Scholar, and expert on financial institutions; Patrick Parkinson, one of the best economists on the staff of the Federal Reserve Board and an expert on financial markets whom the Fed had lent to the new administration to help with regulatory reform; and Neal Wolin, a summa cum laude graduate of Yale who also had a master's degree from Oxford and a Yale law degree. Wolin served as general counsel of the Treasury Department under Bill Clinton, then worked as a senior executive of the Hartford Group, an insurance and financial services company. In the new administration Wolin was deputy secretary of the treasury; Barr was assistant secretary for financial institutions; and Sunstein was administrator of the White House Office of Information and Regulatory Affairs, responsible for overseeing all federal regulations.

The brainstorming continued from January through March. Often this group met day after day after day. "We had a lot of meetings where, all night long, everybody was hashing it out on the intellectual level," Farrell remembered. They began with fundamentals: "What's the philosophy of what we want to do? What went wrong [and caused the Great Crash]? What . . . should the future of the system be like?" Farrell loved the opportunity to ask such basic questions: "I don't think people get that luxury very often."

The first objective was to produce a white paper, outlining the administration's plan for reforms, which would guide the drafting of actual legislation. As these intense intellectuals talked and argued, they found that most of what they thought should be done had already been suggested by the academics and other experts who had been studying financial regulation for years. They reaffirmed, in effect, the consensus that had produced those speeches from Paulson and Obama in March 2008, six months before the crash, that outlined similar components of needed reform. The difference, Farrell noted, was that until the crash in the fall of 2008, "modernizing the system and doing things that people [experts] knew had to happen" was politically impossible. The crisis made them possible.

During the boom years that preceded the crash, Barr observed, "there was simply no room for challenges to the belief that the market was perfection incarnate, the last word. Now there's room to question perfection of the market." That meant room for a new role for government and regulation, the subject that most animated this group.

Every week or two the brainstormers met with Summers and Secretary Geithner to report on their progress, and to seek guidance. Obama sometimes joined the discussions. As this process continued, the administration officials directly involved met repeatedly with staff of the House and Senate committees, consulted by telephone, and met occasionally with Dodd and Frank.

By the second half of April, Jeanne Roslanowick, Frank's chief aide, thought the administration was making good progress. "They are farther along than we had hoped," she said a few days after meeting with the team writing the white paper. "Conceptually we are largely in the same place. We agree about the essential elements of reform."

Who would play the role of systemic risk regulator remained a matter of disagreement. The administration team had not been affected by the AIG bonus flap the way Frank and Roslanowick had, and still hoped to make the Federal Reserve the risk regulator, Roslanowick reported. But she and Frank both believed that was politically impossible. The Fed would have to share this role with others. "There's going to need to be some give-and-take." Overall, she liked the administration team: "You see people in the room who are on top of all the issues, who know what they're doing, who are working collaboratively."

The officials drafting the white paper spent literally hundreds of hours consulting with Roslanowick and her colleagues, Amy Friend and other key staff on the Senate committee, outside experts, market participants, and government regulators. Members of Congress, revealingly, were rarely consulted personally.

Frank was an important exception. Rahm Emanuel, now in the White House but a longtime friend and admirer of Frank's since they served together in the House from 2003 through 2008, made it clear early in the process that the White House would give great weight to his judgment on the politics of regulatory reform. "Rahm and I have a very good relationship," Frank explained. "Rahm has a lot of confidence in my judgment about the House." In one meeting with Geithner and Summers, Frank said, Emanuel told them that when Frank said something had to be done to help him get a bill through the House, "we've got to accommodate Barney." For Frank, Emanuel's blessing was "very helpful." As we have seen, Frank met quite regularly with Geithner and Summers.

One contentious issue that Frank knew was politically dicey was whether or not to merge the two agencies that would enforce any new regulations of derivatives, the financial instruments that made it possible to hedge against price fluctuations of commodities, interest rates, and exchange rates, and to bet on future movements of stock and bond markets. The most basic of these were futures contracts, derivatives that allowed commodity users and traders to hedge against price changes in markets they depended on. For example, wheat farmers bought futures contracts promising to deliver wheat at a specific price to protect the value of their crops; airlines bought futures contracts for aviation fuel to protect against sudden changes in the market price; international corporations bought futures contracts for foreign currencies important to their businesses, to hedge against sudden changes in those currencies' values. Those older forms of derivatives had been joined in recent years by more exotic derivatives, most notably credit default swaps, a kind of insurance that dealers traded to try to guarantee the value of bonds. AIG's collapse was caused by reckless trading of credit default swaps, which played an important part in the Great Crash.

For nearly thirty years during which the market for derivatives grew exponentially, they remained unregulated. Congress finally addressed the issue in 2000, passing the Commodity Futures Modernization Act of 2000, but it rejected meaningful regulation, instead assuring participants in the derivatives markets that they would remain unregulated. The only regulation would be in the form of general "safety and soundness" supervision of the entities dealing in derivatives by their traditional regulators, the Securities and Exchange Commission

(SEC), a New Deal agency created in 1934 to regulate securities dealers, and the Commodity Futures Trading Commission (CFTC), created by Congress in 1974, to ensure safe and reliable futures markets.

This law divided responsibility for the firms handling derivatives
contracts between the SEC and CFTC, based on the underlying securities or indices. It was not a neat division. The SEC generally regulated those that were based on the stocks of individual companies and
small baskets of stocks, and exchange-traded foreign currency options.
The CFTC was responsible for futures contracts based on commodities prices, but also futures based on stock prices and many other stock
indices such as the Dow Jones Industrials average.

This division made no logical sense, but logic had little to do with
it. This was part of a classic clash of congressional jurisdictions. The
SEC was under the "jurisdiction" of the Senate Banking Committee
and the House Financial Services Committee, which provided "oversight" of the agency, authorized its budgets, and controlled legislation
relevant to it. The Senate committee considered nominees for members of the SEC, whose appointments had to be confirmed by the full
Senate. The CFTC, however, was from its inception under the jurisdiction of the House and Senate Agriculture committees.

Over time, two factors made this division significant. One was the
stunning growth of derivatives trading into a business that was measured in trillions of dollars. The second was the dramatic increase in
the cost of congressional election campaigns, beginning in the late
1970s. This was one of the most consequential changes in American
political history. Once it became accepted political wisdom that candidates for the House and Senate needed pollsters, direct mail firms,
and television commercials to win election and reelection, they had
to raise vast amounts of money. In 1950 senators could get elected
by spending $100,000 on their campaigns; by 1980 that number was
typically several million dollars; by 2010 many Senate candidates spent
$20–$30 million to win or retain their seats. Multimillion-dollar races
became common in the House as well.

So members became hungry for money. Those who belonged to
the House and Senate Agriculture committees discovered that they
could raise millions of dollars from people interested not only in
subsidies for wheat farmers, sugar quotas, and the like—the obvious and usual business of the committees—but also, and in larger
numbers, from interests who cared about CFTC regulations and
policies, which could affect their derivatives business. This was the

financial sector, which by the twenty-first century was the most profitable piece of the American economy. In the two years leading up to the elections of 2008 (when those participating in these events had last faced the voters), financial interests contributed $8.7 million to members of the House Agriculture Committee, compared to the $7 million donated by agribusiness interests. For the Senate committee the numbers were even more striking: $29.3 million given to members of both parties by financial interests, versus $10.8 million given by agribusiness.

When this relationship was pointed out to Chairman Frank, he acted surprised. "Interesting," he said. Frank is one of many members who raise money from the interests potentially affected by the decisions they make who insist that the money given to them has no effect on their votes. Proving the contrary, of course, is usually difficult—motivation is an elusive factor in all human behavior, including politics. About 45 percent of the $2.2 million that Frank raised for his 2008 election (he ran against a virtual unknown who posed no real threat) came from the financial, insurance, and real estate industries.

Frank did, however, understand that challenging the jurisdiction of the Agriculture Committee would start a fight he could not win by himself. He considered jurisdictional fights between committees counterproductive and annoying. If the Obama administration decided it wanted to merge the CFTC into the SEC—a reform favored by dispassionate experts for many years as an obvious way to simplify the regulatory structure, assure consistent regulation, and save the money spent on overlapping responsibilities—it would have to propose and sell the idea itself, he said. He understood the logic of a merger, but he also appreciated the potential political cost of picking a fight. He preferred a less contentious solution: Give both agencies identical laws and rules to enforce. "It is theoretically possible to have the exact same rules in each entity, so that all you're getting is duplication," as Frank put it in early April. A little duplication of effort didn't bother Frank, especially if it bought political peace between him and Collin Peterson, the Minnesota congressman who chaired the House Agriculture Committee.

At a meeting in February with Speaker Pelosi and two outside experts she had invited to discuss regulatory reform, Peterson made a clumsy move to claim jurisdiction over all derivatives trading. He argued that credit default swaps and other types of derivatives were ultimately traded as futures, and his committee was "in charge of futures," Frank recounted soon after the meeting. Peterson's ploy flopped. "I was pleased to see that he got very little sympathy" from members of the House Democratic leadership at the meeting, Frank continued. "His solution, which seemed to me somewhat simplistic, was rejected by Nancy's experts.* I made the point that this was a matter that cut across jurisdictions," so responsibility should be shared between Agriculture and Financial Services. Pelosi agreed.

The Obama administration officials writing the white paper ultimately decided that merging the CFTC into the SEC could cost more politically than it would be worth. The white paper, entitled "A New Foundation: Rebuilding Financial Supervision and Regulation," was released on June 17. Instead of suggesting that the SEC absorb the CFTC, it proposed "to harmonize the statutory and regulatory regimes" administered by both agencies to eliminate "gaps and inconsistencies"—Frank's idea.

This was typical of the decisions conveyed in the white paper, which were generally cautious. In a memorandum for its clients analyzing the document, the Wall Street law firm of Davis Polk & Wardwell described the document as "far less revolutionary than some either feared or hoped for and reflects an 'art of the possible' approach to regulatory reform by the Obama Administration." Davis Polk noted the decision to avoid "the most difficult . . . turf battles," specifically mentioning that "it does not propose a CFTC-SEC merger" or seek a sweeping reorganization of the alphabet soup of agencies providing financial regulation. The only agency the administration proposed to abolish was one that had lost all support in Congress: the Office of Thrift Supervision, a regulator created in 1989 in the wake of a huge savings and loan debacle in the 1980s that cost the government nearly $125 billion to cover all the losses. OTS had proven ineffectual in the years before the Great Crash, and no prominent politician defended it. The white paper proposed merging OTS into the major regulator of federally chartered banks, the Office of the Comptroller of the Currency, a division of Treasury.

The administration had indeed chosen a pragmatic path to reform. Its authors concluded that the best reforms would create incentives to

---

* Vincent Mai, a New York investor and contributor to liberal causes, and Professor David Moss of the Harvard Business School.

encourage good behavior and discourage malfeasance in the financial sector. The white paper did not propose breaking up the big banks or restoring the enforced separation of retail banking from investment banking contained in the Glass-Steagall Act of 1933 and repealed in 1999. There was little political support for those moves, a fact that exasperated some liberal commentators and economists. Neither Frank nor Dodd had any appetite for trying to transform the financial sector, which had grown into a huge part of the American economy. Like the two chairmen, the Obama administration's white paper came down on the side of better, more intrusive regulation rather than punitive new limits on the size of financial institutions.

But the white paper did propose profound changes in the relationship between the government and the financial sector. *The Wall Street Journal*'s headline on its main news story the next day made the point: "Historic Overhaul of Finance Rules." It was more important than most reports issued by the White House.

The administration's outline of reforms became the template eventually followed by both the House and Senate in the legislative process that produced Dodd-Frank. The topics covered in the white paper were the topics covered in the final version of the new law, and many of Dodd-Frank's provisions followed the white paper's recommendations. It demonstrated the influence of the executive branch in shaping legislation of this scope and significance.

These were the principal proposals in the white paper that would become the substance of the congressional debate in the months ahead:

- Create a new systemic risk regulator to identify risky behavior by large financial firms of all kinds, not just the federally insured banks that were the traditional focus of government regulators. AIG was the definitive example of a huge financial firm that could pose an enormous systemic risk, but under existing rules was not subject to meaningful federal regulation. The white paper proposed giving this authority to the Federal Reserve Board, despite Frank's warnings that Congress would not support "rewarding" the only agency that had the authority to head off the Great Crash by regulating subprime mortgages, but chose not to do so—the same agency supervising AIG when the decision was made to pay those bonuses.

    One of the most striking powers of the systemic risk regulator, barely mentioned in the white paper, was the ability to regulate the activities of large financial firms, and to acquire information from them about their activities, and refer behavior considered too risky to the regulator responsible for overseeing that firm. In effect, there would be no privacy for big financial firms, no hiding activities from scrutiny by regulators. Authors of the white paper hoped the use of this power would enable regulators to limit or terminate risky behavior by financial institutions before it posed a risk to the system. This was a radical idea, new in the history of American capitalism. It survived the legislative process, and became part of Dodd-Frank, without ever being debated or much discussed in the House or Senate.

The white paper also proposed requiring big financial institutions to hold more capital, in effect insisting that they have a bigger cushion of cash to help them survive future crises.

The white paper proposed creating a new category of the biggest financial firms that would receive the closest scrutiny from regulators and face the strictest regulations. First the House Financial Services Committee and later Senate Banking rejected this idea because both decided it implied that the biggest firms would be seen as "too big to fail," and could count on government support in future crises. Politics, specifically the strong reaction against any more "bailouts," soon killed this idea.

- Establish a new way to put failing financial firms out of business— a resolution regime in the jargon of regulatory reform. This had been one of Paulson's and Bernanke's priorities, and the Obama administration embraced it, as did Frank. The idea was to give regulators the powers they would need, for example, when next confronted with a failing firm like Lehman Brothers, to close down the company in an orderly way, without setting off the kind of chain reaction that Lehman's sudden collapse initiated. When regulators "resolved" such a firm, they could enforce decisions about which creditors got paid, how much they got paid, and so on.

- Create a powerful new Consumer Financial Protection Agency to regulate consumer credit, from credit cards to home mortgages and other kinds of loans. This idea alarmed banks, and pleased liberals. It grew from the realization that mortgage brokers, particularly, had induced or duped millions of families to take out mortgages they could not afford, without regard for their ability to repay what they borrowed. This became the single most controversial element of regulatory reform, though experts did not consider it one of the most important.

- Regulate—many for the first time—the markets on which derivatives of all kinds were traded, from futures contracts on the price of wheat to instruments that allowed investors to gamble on future moves in interest rates or currency values. As we have seen, derivatives based on home mortgages played a big role in the Great Crash, costing those who held them losses of hundreds of billions of dollars.

- Require firms that turn home mortgages and other forms of debt such as auto loans and credit card debt into securities—bonds—to put some "skin in the game." This somewhat esoteric idea grew directly from the excesses in the mortgage market that contributed so much to the crash. Since 1970, the government has permitted "securitization" of mortgages. This means pooling together a batch of home loans and selling the pool to investors. The original lender can, through securitization, realize most of the value of, say, a thirty-year mortgage months after it is issued. The lender can use that money to issue new mortgages, then securitize them and keep the process going. Once the new bond was sold, the originator of the mortgages no longer had any financial interest in them. This proved to be an effective way to direct trillions of dollars into the housing market. Securitization became a principal business of Fannie Mae and Freddie Mac, the two government-supported entities that collapsed and were taken over by the government in September 2008.

  Mortgage lenders, particularly unregulated brokers working independently from regulated banks, used securitization to blow air (money, actually) into the vast housing bubble that burst in the financial crisis. This was made easy by the privately owned rating agencies, particularly Moody's, Standard & Poor's, and Fitch, which decided that the mortgage-based bonds were totally safe—Triple A rated, the same as United States Treasury bonds.

The high ratings created ever more demand for the securities, further inflating the bubble.

The white paper proposed that securitizers be required to retain a 5 percent interest in whatever bonds they created, to give them an incentive to pay attention to the quality of the underlying loans. This too was an idea already championed by Frank.

- Empower regulators to require financial firms to adopt compensation policies for their executives that would discourage them from taking risks that "threaten the[ir] safety and soundness." Executive pay should reward decisions that create "long-term shareholder value" rather than short-term results that can turn to dust in a crisis—as happened in 2008. The white paper also supported requiring companies to offer shareholders the chance to express their opinion on executive compensation packages. This was a hot topic, hotter after the AIG bonus flap, and another departure from traditional practices. Regulators had never questioned compensation packages.

- Require hedge funds to register with the SEC. This modest reform would finally bring pools of capital totaling more than a trillion dollars into the universe of regulated financial firms. Hedge funds—aggressively managed funds usually consisting of the capital of wealthy individuals and the assets of pension funds and endowments of private institutions—held more than $1 trillion in assets on the eve of the Great Crash. They were not significant contributors to the market turmoil of 2008–9, but many of them lost a lot of money.

President Obama introduced the white paper at a White House event on June 17. He gave a speech on the need to use government to stabilize the financial system and control the excesses of the free market. The speech reflected the view of the white paper's authors that it would be best for the House and Senate to embrace their plan, not mess with it. "I look forward to working with leaders in Congress," Obama said, "to see these proposals put to work so that we can overcome this crisis and build a lasting foundation for prosperity."

But it was not going to be so simple. This was made clear the next day when Geithner testified on the white paper before the Senate Banking Committee. Geithner handled himself adroitly and was generally well received, but not one senator embraced the administration's plan as outlined in the white paper without some qualification. Dodd set the tone with an opening statement that described the writing of new rules as "the most important thing this committee will have done in the last 60 or 70 years or the most important thing any one of us are going to do as a member of this committee for years to come." Obviously, he wasn't thinking about simply ratifying the White House's proposals.

Dodd and nearly every other member who spoke expressed skepticism about giving the Fed more authority as systemic risk regulator. Dodd quoted a professor he'd talked to as saying, "giving the Fed more responsibility at this point is like a parent giving his son a bigger, faster car right after he crashed the family station wagon." Senator Shelby said the Fed already had too much to do. No senator present supported the idea.

This hearing was the first occasion when a senior official, Geithner, and the members of the Banking Committee could discuss regulatory reform in concrete terms. It was a reminder of the orneriness of senators, who take themselves awfully seriously, and a reminder too that the fate of regulatory reform remained far from clear. As the law firm of Davis Polk wrote in its memorandum about the white paper for its clients, "It is too early to predict with certainty which proposals are likely to be enacted and in what form." The ponderous process of legislating had barely begun.

CHAPTER EIGHT

A Rich Variety of Humanity

Always impatient, Barney Frank began 2009 thinking he could get an ambitious bill through the House by the summer. He knew that the Senate would move more slowly, but he didn't care about the Senate's timetable. "It's the old version of the House and the Senate," he explained. "We do most of it [the legislative work to produce a regulatory reform package], and they're the appeal body—it's a totally legitimate thing [for the House] to do."

By "appeal body," Frank meant the place interest groups traditionally turn to argue for changes in the House version of a bill. As this remark suggests, Frank viewed the Senate with disdain—"it's a dysfunctional body," he once observed, where individuals and minorities had too much influence over both substance and procedure.

But before he began work on a bill, he wanted to enact new versions of bills the House had passed in the previous session of Congress, but which died in the Senate. First up was the credit card legislation. Then in April the Financial Services Committee passed a new and tougher version of a bill to ban subprime mortgages and predatory lending practices that it first passed in November 2007. Both addressed what Frank perceived as a political problem: The huge bailouts for banks under TARP had created the impression that Congress cared more about them than about ordinary citizens. Frank wanted to pass bills that the banks disliked, and they detested both the credit card and subprime mortgage bills; both would cost them money. But Frank thought both were "good public policy," and passing them sent what Frank considered a positive signal. Voters had to see that banks were being held accountable for their sins before they would support reforms to "make sure it doesn't happen again"—"it" being the great financial crisis.

Impatient or not, however, there was no way Frank could accelerate the consideration of regulatory reform in the spring of 2009. Having deferred to the incoming administration's desire to write the first draft of reform legislation, he had to wait for its product. That meant first waiting for completion of the white paper, which came in June, then for the administration's drafts of actual legislation—"legislative language" in the argot of Capitol Hill—which would arrive in sections over the summer.

While he waited, Frank had to fend off an idea that caught on in some influential circles that spring to create a modern-day Pecora Commission. In the last days of the Herbert Hoover administration in early 1933, Ferdinand Pecora, a New York lawyer, was named chief counsel of the Senate Banking Committee, which asked him to conduct an investigation into the causes of the stock market crash and Great Depression that followed. Left largely to his own devices by members of the committee and making creative use of its subpoena power, Pecora led one of the great investigations in Senate history. It continued after Roosevelt became president. Pecora humiliated many of the titans of the financial world with blistering cross-examinations, and exposed shameless profiteering and tax evasion on Wall Street. The resulting public anger contributed to a political environment that helped FDR win congressional approval for the sweeping financial reforms of the New Deal.

In January 2009, the historian and biographer Ron Chernow wrote an op-ed piece for *The New York Times* urging Congress to create a modern-day equivalent of the Pecora Commission to investigate the causes of the financial crisis. "Our current stock market slump and housing bust can seem like natural calamities without identifiable culprits, creating free-floating anger in the land," Chernow wrote. "A public deeply disenchanted with our financial leadership is desperately searching for answers. The new Congress has a chance to lead the nation, step by step, through all the machinations that led to the present debacle and to shape wise legislation to prevent a recurrence."

This notion appealed to some liberals in Congress. Representative

John Larson of Connecticut, a member of the House Democratic leadership, and Senator Byron Dorgan of North Dakota, a senior Democrat, pushed for legislation establishing such a commission. Speaker Pelosi liked the idea too, to Frank's annoyance, and she made a public statement supporting it.

"So I called her," Frank recounted. "She said, Oh no, I knew we'd talk about it, but she said she just finds—she's all over the country—that there's an overwhelming insistence on it, it's a political necessity. I said fine, but it cannot be used as an excuse to hold off [on regulatory reform legislation]."

Pelosi's travels around the country typically took her to fundraising events where she met with potential donors, hardly a cross section of the American public. How she could divine an "overwhelming insistence on it" among the public was far from clear. Pecora was hardly a household name, and few living Americans remembered his investigation or understood its significance. There was no obvious public pressure for a new investigation of the crisis. But someone, or ones, had bent Pelosi's ear on this subject. Frank and other colleagues were used to her enthusiasms, realizing that they often came from the last person she talked to.

For Frank, a commission was a distraction, potentially a delaying tactic. At a meeting of the senior Democratic House leadership in late April, he told his colleagues that appointing an investigative commission was "a silly idea whose time has come." Silly, Frank thought, because the causes of the Great Crash were already well understood. For an explanation of the crisis he advised friends, colleagues, constituents, and reporters to read *Financial Shock*, a short book by Mark Zandi, chief economist of Moody's Analytics, whom Frank liked to describe as "an adviser to John McCain," which he was in the 2008 presidential campaign. Zandi's book argued that indiscriminate home loans by overaggressive mortgage brokers, sloppy securitization of mortgages by banks and investment houses, and woefully inadequate government regulation were the principal causes of the financial crisis. Frank agreed.

Frank persuaded Pelosi that if a bill authorizing creation of a commission was to move forward it should stipulate that the commission make its final report at the end of 2010, twenty months in the future. That would assure that the commission had no impact on the legislative process, which Frank intended to complete long before then.

Pelosi agreed, and so did the Senate. The Financial Crisis Inquiry Commission never got in his way.*

Frank's attitude toward a commission reflected his identity: He was a man of the House of Representatives. He played out his ambitions in the House, not on the national political stage. Yes, he was a staunchly partisan Democrat, and he hoped that good financial reform legislation would strengthen his party's position in the country. But Frank's professional interest was to legislate improvements in public policy. Legislating was, for him, an inside game, played on the peculiar terrain of Capitol Hill.

Frank did not share Ron Chernow's desire to help people understand whom to blame for the financial meltdown. Frank thought that was obvious—irresponsible financiers and anti-regulation Republicans were to blame. Mobilizing public opinion against rapacious bankers and lax regulators was not a priority for him. He had low expectations for the role of public opinion, especially on complex issues. Frank was more honest than most of his colleagues about the public, saying aloud what many of them felt but did not articulate: "The voters are no bargain either," as he put it on numerous occasions, usually when responding to criticism of politicians.

Frank was more interested in cultivating the Democratic members of the House Financial Services Committee—"my Democrats," he called them. He thought this was the most useful thing he could do while waiting for the administration's draft legislation. In early April Frank said, "The single biggest thing I spend my time doing is cultivating the members of my committee, going to their fundraisers. I've already done fundraisers this year for Mary Jo Kilroy [of Columbus, Ohio, a new member of Congress] and Steve Driehaus [of Cincinnati, also a new member] and Gwen Moore [of Milwaukee, a member since 2005]. . . . I'm committed to going to Chicago for Melissa [Bean]. I've promised Emanuel [Cleaver] I'll go to Kansas City."†

---

* When it completed its report at the end of 2010, its Republican members all refused to sign the document. It proved to be just another ineffectual enterprise riven by the partisan acrimony that colored so much of what now comes out of Washington.

† During the life of the 111th Congress, from January 2009 through December 2010, Frank would attend forty-four fundraisers for Democratic members of Financial Services. For several members he attended more than one. Most were held in Washington; for eleven of them he traveled, to Palm Beach, Florida, Denver, Chicago, and elsewhere.

Frank understood political egos and the need to feed them. He had a big one himself. "I have to be careful that there is not a reaction against my prominence," he said in April 2009. "I've been on the Sunday talk shows* five times this year, which is more than I usually am in two years combined, and I have a sixth one coming up. I have worked hard at getting along with the members but a certain amount of resentment if one individual appears to be getting too much credit is always a problem in this business. I have to especially be careful that the members don't feel that they are being portrayed as people who simply do what I want. . . . I spend a lot of time figuring out what it is that the other members want and need and that has always shaped what I've tried to put forward as chair."

Frank also relied on Jim Segel, his former student at Harvard, colleague in the Massachusetts legislature, and the manager of his first congressional campaign. Segel abandoned his own political ambitions after an unsuccessful campaign for state treasurer of Massachusetts. He worked in Boston as a lawyer and, briefly, an investment banker. When Democrats captured control of Congress in 2006 and Frank realized he was going to become chairman of the Financial Services Committee, he approached Segel about coming to work for him.

"I wanted him to be my Leo Diehl," Frank explained. Diehl was the Boston pol and lifelong friend whom Tip O'Neill brought to Washington when he was elected Democratic whip in 1970, his first job in the leadership. Diehl, confined to a wheelchair since he was a young man, stayed at O'Neill's side for sixteen years, including the ten years O'Neill served as speaker of the house. Diehl handled political assignments of all kinds, concentrating first on cultivating the voters and politicians of Massachusetts.

Frank asked Segel to keep an eye on Massachusetts, and wanted his help working with the Democrats on Financial Services. "Jimmy's good," Frank said that spring. "He goes and sees them." It was a revealing remark from a man who never much liked the interpersonal aspects of politics, the schmoozing and arm gripping and such. Frank did nuts and bolts; Segel did lubrication. He had an easy way with people. He made friends easily, and conveyed genuine interest in the

---

* *Meet the Press, Face the Nation, This Week, Fox News Sunday,* and CNN's *State of the Union* were the principal Sunday talk shows. Members of Congress covet appearances on them as indicators of their prominence. The audiences of all of them are small, but they include most members and most Washington reporters, the insiders who are normally the politicians' primary audience.

members Frank wanted him to cultivate. He kept in touch with their needs and desires, and kept Frank informed. Frank's Democrats were a complicated group, not easily managed. The aforementioned Paul Kanjorski of Pennsylvania, the second-ranking member, resented Frank's brains, fame, and seniority. The next two most senior members were difficult women: Maxine Waters of Los Angeles, and Carolyn Maloney of New York City. A handsome woman born in 1938, Waters was a formidable figure in Southern California politics. She won her first election, to the state Assembly, in 1976, and her first seat in Congress in 1990. She ran a kind of family political machine that printed and circulated a "sample ballot" of candidates and ballot initiatives that Waters endorsed for every election. The candidates mentioned had to pay for the privilege, as much as $25,000, and Waters's daughter Karen was paid hundreds of thousands of dollars to run this operation.

Though not an expert on financial issues, Waters was smart and tough, and relentless in her support for minority business and other black causes. She was willful and sometimes single-minded. Her chief of staff, Mikael Moore, was also her grandson. Frank said he liked Waters, but this was not a universal view among House Democrats, many of whom worried about her ethics.*

Maloney was vain, sometimes aggressive and not particularly bright. Frank found dealing with her difficult. He allowed her, as chairman of the Financial Services Subcommittee on Financial Institutions and Consumer Credit, to handle the credit card legislation, then was disappointed when she succumbed to lobbying by the big banks and delayed implementation of the new rules in the bill. The Senate version, ultimately adopted by the House, was tougher.

Next in seniority was one of the more interesting members of the House, Luis Gutierrez of Chicago. Of Puerto Rican ancestry, Gutierrez learned politics on the Chicago City Council, then came to Congress in 1993 when he was forty years old. He quickly made a name for himself by giving an outspoken interview on *60 Minutes* in which he committed a classic Washington gaffe: He made the mistake of telling the truth, and rather bluntly.

Gutierrez was one of 110 new members elected to the House in

---

* In 2010 Waters was the subject of an investigation by the House Ethics Committee because of her efforts to win TARP money for a Boston bank in which her husband owned stock. She was ultimately cleared—in 2012—of any wrongdoing.

1992. "I thought that there would just be this huge group of people all running to the same finish line," he told *60 Minutes*, "all of us saying, 'We're going to do campaign finance reform. We're going to eliminate the parking [reserved for members of Congress] at National Airport. The chauffeurs are gone, the perks and the privileges, the things that make us different.' Well, people take that stuff pretty personal here. They take it as a personal affront to themselves." Congress, Gutierrez continued, was "the belly of the beast. . . . It's a monster." He pleaded with the House Democratic leadership to make reforms and clean up their act. This was not what freshmen were supposed to do. "They told me to shut up," he recounted.

In his second year as a member, the House voted on NAFTA, the North American Free Trade Agreement. Gutierrez opposed it; he thought there should be more protections for both American and Mexican workers. He told *60 Minutes* about the phone calls he received from people who had raised money for his campaign: "It was, 'Luis, how you doing, buddy? How's everything going? . . . Luis, we need you to vote for the North American Free Trade Agreement [NAFTA]. I'd like you to vote for it. It's important. The president needs you.'

" 'Well, you know, I'm having some difficulty with that,' " Gutierrez quoted himself as saying.

" 'Well, I'm calling to tell you about my difficulty. I'm having a difficulty in raising money for your next fund-raiser, and it'd be a lot easier for me to make the phone calls and to be there for you because people love you, Luis. Don't take me wrong, they really believe in you. But this—you'd be amazed how many people are saying to me, "I just can't help Luis unless he votes [for NAFTA]." ' "

"And if anybody thinks that there wasn't an orchestrated, organized, coordinated effort on behalf of the White House and political operatives there to talk to your key fund-raisers," said Gutierrez, "then you're living in another world. People understand that in order to get elected to Congress, it costs a lot of money."

Gutierrez's punishment for being so outspoken was to be denied membership on any of the committees he wanted to join. "Let me suggest to you I'm not on the Banking Committee [later renamed Financial Services] because it was a committee I wished to serve on. I'm on the Banking Committee because there were five empty slots they couldn't fill," he said.

The *60 Minutes* interview caused him a lot of grief in the House. "It was a very difficult time. Many members shunned me, would not speak to me at all. People made fun of me." Then Republicans won control of Congress in 1994, for the first time in forty years. Gutierrez felt vindicated—the country really was fed up with the ways of Congress, and wanted change. But he realized that new members can't make change happen. So he stuck it out, learned how to get along, and stopped giving outspoken interviews. Sixteen years later he was the fourth-ranking member of the committee. Frank liked the fact that he learned a lot about the committee's work and often could make a serious contribution. "Gutierrez is impressive," he observed.

The fifth senior member of note was Mel Watt of North Carolina. Watt was a Yale-trained lawyer who represented Charlotte, North Carolina, the banking capital of the American South. He knew the committee's issues as well as any other member, and was one of the few Frank relied on consistently for help. Frank held him in high regard personally and substantively. Frank had good relations with all nine members of the Congressional Black Caucus serving on Financial Services, but Watt was Frank's closest ally in this group.

The senior members were all liberals, but further down the seniority pecking order the politics got more complicated. The influx of new Democrats in 2006 (thirty-one of them) and 2008 (twenty-one more) had altered the political coloration of the Democratic caucus in the House, and of the Democratic membership of Frank's committee. Six of the forty-one Democrats on Financial Services belonged to the Blue Dog caucus of relatively conservative Democrats, and sixteen had joined the centrist "New Democrat Coalition." Both groups wanted to separate themselves ideologically from their older, generally more liberal colleagues. Many represented competitive districts and worried about their ability to win reelection, an anxiety that tended to make them cautious. Jeanne Roslanowick, Frank's staff director, called them "the news and blues," and she tried to respect their concerns.

Several of the newer and younger members were unusually knowledgeable about the substance of the committee's work because of their prior careers. Jim Himes of Connecticut accumulated millions as a young partner at Goldman Sachs, then made his reputation in Fairfield County, Connecticut, as a promoter and developer of low-income housing for poor residents of Bridgeport. He won his seat in 2008. Walt Minnick of Boise, Idaho, was a graduate of Harvard's Business and Law Schools and a successful businessman. Alan Grayson of Palm Beach, Florida, was an eccentric character who had accumulated substantial wealth as a plaintiff's lawyer; he graduated summa cum laude from Harvard College in economics. Ed Perlmutter of Colorado, a trial lawyer, had extensive experience in Denver working with banks and banking issues. A popular and talented politician, he became one of Frank's favorites on the committee.

Frank was also partial to his colleague Michael Capuano from Massachusetts; Dennis Moore, a Blue Dog elder statesman from Kansas; and Brad Miller, an old-school liberal from North Carolina long interested in housing and consumer protection issues; Emanuel Cleaver, the former mayor of Kansas City, Missouri; and Bill Foster, a brilliant nuclear physicist who came to politics late in life after running Fermilab, a national research laboratory outside Chicago. In a special election, Foster won a Republican seat vacated by the former speaker, Dennis Hastert, then won reelection in 2008, accomplishments that impressed Frank and other senior Democrats.

But even the most talented members rarely take the time to bore deeply into complex issues like regulatory reform. The typical House member is spread thin. He or she belongs to one or two standing committees and as many as four subcommittees, each with its own specialized subject matter and schedule of meetings and hearings. And in a media age when members are expected to answer questions about any topic in the news, specialization can be risky. So real expertise is rare, even among the brightest members.

Frank's committee also included Democrats of no particular intellectual distinction or political skill, many of them products of the redistricting practices in America's state legislatures that had transformed the House in the previous three decades. States redraw the boundaries of their congressional districts after every national census, once a decade. California showed America's politicians how to do this job to achieve maximum partisan advantage in 1982, when a congressman named Phillip Burton made what he called "my contribution to modern art" by drawing a map of weirdly shaped districts that gave his Democrats a big advantage in the state—and nine more House seats than Republicans held. The map was adopted because Democrats then controlled the legislature and a Democrat was governor. Such gerrymandering has been common in American politics since the early nineteenth century, but Burton's accomplishment inspired both parties to maximize their advantages after the 1990 and 2000 censuses.*

---

* The gerrymander was named for an early governor of Massachusetts, Elbridge Gerry, who created misshapen districts for the state Senate in 1812.

By the beginning of the new century, a majority of House districts were decisively Democratic or Republican, creating reliably safe seats for at least 300 of the 435 members. Some of the Democrats' safe seats were the consequence of court decisions and Justice Department policies that encouraged the creation of districts likely to produce minority members, black and Latino—rulings that governed some states' redistricting decisions.* Other safe seats for both parties simply reflected partisan muscle in the redistricting process.

House members from safe seats—members who don't really worry about being reelected—can indulge their ideological instincts without much fear of political retribution. This has contributed significantly to the partisan warfare that has typified the House of Representatives since the 1980s. Members who feel no political need to court voters from the other party are also unlikely to seek legislative compromises with congressional colleagues from that party. (Senators, significantly, represent entire states, few of which outside the South are always safe for Republicans or Democrats.)

In the House, demonizing the opposition actually became easier and more common than collaborating and compromising. This behavior was encouraged by the fact that most members never developed personal relationships with colleagues from the other party. This was a side effect of the decisions by nearly all members to leave their families at home and commute to Washington for a workweek that was often no longer than three days, and rarely longer than four. When Chris Dodd's father, Tom, was a member of the House in the 1950s, he and most of his colleagues installed their families in homes in Washington and its suburbs. They socialized across party lines, while both Republican and Democratic wives got to know one another; their kids sometimes played on the same school teams. Members joined Washington-area country clubs and played golf together, also across party lines. By the twenty-first century, that way of life was extinct. Almost no members kept their families in Washington; those who played golf played it at home, not in Washington.

Members not worrying much about reelection can get by without doing much work or mastering many subjects. There is no easy way to

---

* Eight southern states' redistricting plans must be approved by the Department of Justice under the Voting Rights Act of 1965, which encouraged creation of black-majority districts in the South.

say how many safe-seat slackers sit in the House in any one Congress, but the number isn't small.

And like most human institutions, Congress includes a rich variety of humanity. There was a reminder of this in Frank's big hearing room on January 13, 2009, even before the new Congress had formally convened. Frank wanted to help members understand the financial crisis and called what would have been a hearing if the new Congress had been formally constituted; instead it was labeled a "meeting." One of the witnesses was Donald L. Kohn, then vice chairman of the Federal Reserve Board.

One member who questioned Kohn was William Lacy Clay Jr., an African American safe-seat member from Missouri. His predominantly black district was created in 1967 after the Supreme Court's one-man, one-vote ruling required many states to redraw district lines. The first person to represent it was Clay's father, William Lacy Clay Sr., whom the son succeeded in 2000, at the end of the elder Clay's sixteenth term in the House. Revealingly, the younger Clay had grown up in Silver Spring, Maryland, a Washington suburb, where his father moved his family when first elected to Congress in 1968. Once elected to the House, however, the son never moved his family to Washington. He won election easily, and reelection more easily. By 2009 he had won five elections, never with less than 70 percent of the vote.

When it came his turn to question Kohn, Clay wanted to ask about the hundreds of billions then being distributed to banks under the TARP program. "Let me just ask you some simple questions," Clay said. "Is this not taxpayer money?"

"Yes it is," Kohn replied.

"Then why can't we direct this [money] to the rescue of the taxpayers who are really on the front line of all of this?" Clay asked. "They are getting hit with the devaluing of their 401(k) [retirement accounts]. Some of them have lost 30 and 40 percent. Some of them are already retired and have lost quite a lot of value in that." He was referring to accounts invested in the stock and bond markets that had been clobbered in the Great Crash. "Would you entertain legislation," Clay continued, "that would actually help them and put some value back into those 401(k)'s and retirement plans?"

In other words, Clay was suggesting congressional action to put taxpayer money into the retirement accounts of people whose assets had lost value in the crash—a government bailout of private investors who had made the wrong bets. Someone who understood the vagaries of financial markets would not have made this suggestion. Nor was it a "serious" suggestion, in the sense that no member, even Clay, had actually proposed such legislation. But it was a startling reminder of the range of talent on Frank's committee.

CHAPTER NINE

Politics First

While Barney Frank waited for the Obama administration to provide the legislative language he needed to begin formal consideration of regulatory reform, he worried about politics. Release of the administration's white paper in mid-June provided targets for the interest groups that disliked its contents, and began to raise anxieties among his Democrats, including many of the news and blues. There were also anxieties on the left that worried Frank. The left was his natural home in the House Democratic caucus, and he wanted to be in its good graces.

He had been hearing from both sides all spring. "For example," he recounted, "I had a conversation with Gwen Moore [a liberal member from Milwaukee] in which it became clear that she was feeling some heat from the left and feared that we might be too corporate in our approach"—code language for being too respectful of the banks and their problems. Many liberals had "a formula" when it came to financial issues: Whatever pleases Wall Street has to be wrong. "There's such negativism in the public debate," Frank said—and a bit of a double standard too, he thought.

In the spring of 2009 he noted that liberals liked to complain that "these financial people have no sense of the public interest, all they think about is their shareholders. But then one of them puts the public interest to some extent ahead of his shareholders, Ken Lewis [then the president of Bank of America], and he's crucified." Frank was referring to Lewis's willingness to acquire Merrill Lynch at the height of the crisis even after he realized that its bad assets would cost Bank of America hundreds of millions to resolve. Many House liberals were attacking Lewis for betraying his stockholders. "Ken Lewis is now being attacked because he put the stability [of the financial system] ahead of the immediate interests of his shareholders. . . . Maybe it was a mistake, but it wasn't evil. . . . He was doing exactly what we said he ought to do. . . . It's a sign of the negativism. That could be seen as a patriotic gesture—I've said that [publicly], one of the few."

Frank thought he was penalized by many liberals for actually understanding—and talking about—these financial issues in their full complexity. There was, he agreed, a high degree of ignorance about the subject. "And the worst of it is ignorance when people don't know that they're ignorant. To be honest, I think I know more, and am more conscious of what I don't know, than almost everybody else [in the House]. Because I've worked at it. I've learned a lot about it." But being able to speak fluently about why, for example, helping the banks with TARP was the unavoidable price for preventing another Great Depression did not help Frank with the liberals who viscerally detested bailing out banks. He saw that it was easier to have a formulaic response to every question. "It's comfortable to have a formula."

Frank felt harassed by bloggers and commentators on the left who saw nefarious Wall Street plots at every turn, and seemed utterly pessimistic that he or anyone could impose meaningful new limits on the financial sector. One thorn that kept scratching him was a remark made in April by Senator Dick Durbin of Illinois.

Durbin wanted to give bankruptcy judges the power to compel mortgage lenders to amend the terms of mortgages for people who filed for personal bankruptcy, as a way to help them hold on to their homes. He was far from alone; the House had approved this idea, and it had considerable support in the Senate. But banks of all sizes mounted an aggressive lobbying campaign in the Senate to block it, and they succeeded. A discouraged Durbin told an Illinois radio station that "the banks—hard to believe in a time when we're facing a banking crisis that many of the banks created—are still the most powerful lobby on Capitol Hill. And they frankly own the place."

Frank was on Durbin's side of this issue, but rejected his explanation for what happened. "Durbin is wrong," he said. "The banks" were not a monolith, and the big banks had lost most of their political influence as a result of the crash, Frank thought. They did not own Congress. "Durbin lost it to the community banks and the credit unions," Frank said—the little guys in the industry, not the big financial institutions. "They're the ones with political clout. And they turned against him." Small banks argued that they had to be able to count on the long-term stability of the mortgages they held. Mortgages were assets—bankers hated the idea that judges could play with their value by changing their terms. They feared that if bankruptcy judges were free to rewrite them, more people would file for bankruptcy, and the housing market would be further destabilized. It wasn't the most persuasive of arguments, especially since bankruptcy judges already had the authority to modify mortgages on second homes or loans on boats, but it persuaded members of the Senate who feared the political clout of their small banks.

Of course big banks benefited too, but Frank noted the obvious hole in Durbin's contention. If banks were so powerful in Congress, why couldn't they block the recently passed credit card bill, which would cost them billions of dollars, and which they detested? "Here's the difference," he explained. "Credit unions and community banks don't issue credit cards.* Credit cards are big banks. So on credit cards they get knocked on their ass, bankruptcy they win. The difference was the community banks and the credit unions."

But the image of the all-powerful Wall Street institutions was entrenched, and journalists kept writing stories suggesting that Congress would be no match for them. That June, Frank was annoyed by a front-page article in *The New York Times* reporting previously unpublicized lobbying by the big financial institutions to limit new regulations, particularly for derivatives. The article had a dark, conspiratorial tone and implied that Wall Street could prevail in this round of regulatory reform as it had often prevailed in the past. "As a result of the lobbying efforts," the *Times* reported, "champions of broad-based regulation are concerned that proposals will be significantly limited by banking interests."

"Gretchen Morgenson [coauthor of this article] is just such a dreadfully inaccurate reporter," Frank complained. "She is so determined to

---

* Frank's statement was not entirely accurate. Some community banks did and do issue credit cards, but their share of the national credit card business is tiny.

be negative, she just gets it wrong." He was certain that the tables had turned against Wall Street, and that he would be able to pass tough legislation. "I am very good at reading this place," Frank said. "I am not a great wholesale politician [dealing with public opinion], I'm a very good retail politician [dealing with colleagues], I'm very political myself. I really can read not just my members but the other members. I haven't had a single Democratic member tell me, 'Jeez, don't be too tough on these guys [Wall Street].' "

That summer Roslanowick and her colleagues scheduled briefings to give committee Democrats opportunities to question the key regulatory officials from the Federal Reserve, the Securities and Exchange Commission, the Office of Comptroller of the Currency, and other relevant organizations. Roslanowick thought these meetings helped members, particularly the new ones, understand the issues, and let them feel as though they were participating directly in this historic reform effort. Many of the junior members "didn't yet know what these agencies do," Roslanowick said. The briefings couldn't fill all the gaps in their knowledge, but they could give a new member the sense that she or he was in the game, talking directly to the most important regulators. Frank sometimes forgot why they were holding these meetings, so she reminded him. "The other members don't have the access that Barney has, and they can feel a little marginalized," she said.

Frank decided to skip most of these sessions. "I would be a distraction," he said. The senior officials invited to brief the members "would tend to talk to me. . . . I think I'm a distorting presence when I'm there. They'll want to talk to me or ask me what do I think."

Frank made a more substantive gesture to half a dozen colleagues whom he admired and to whom he wanted to give a chance to participate more directly in the reform effort. He told Roslanowick he'd like to set up working groups to allow interested colleagues to work on the issues that would constitute the regulatory reform package—derivatives, the rating agencies that give letter grades to bonds, the systemic risk regulator, resolution authority to wind down failed institutions. Frank proposed an informal arrangement that would allow members who got involved to feel they were making a mark on the legislation. To the staff it just looked like more hand-holding and more paperwork, but they knew their role and went along. And they generally had a high regard for the members who participated: Ed Perlmutter of Colorado,

Bill Foster of Illinois, Jim Himes of Connecticut, and Mel Watt and Brad Miller of North Carolina. It was up to the committee staff to make them feel that their ideas would be taken seriously, something the best staff members knew how to do, especially for the brighter, more serious members. Most of the committee Democrats "are like deer in the headlights," one staff member confided. "They don't really understand the issues or what to do." For most of them, "participation on the committee is a passive process." These working group members were different.

Perlmutter, one who appreciated the opportunity to participate in a working group on derivatives, was one of Frank's staunchest admirers. "After he barks at you, he still listens, and he may change his position. Once you learn that, it's great. He's great."

The credit card bill was part of Frank's answer to anxious liberals who worried that they weren't being tough enough on banks. Another was the mortgage bill that the House also enacted in May that banned many forms of subprime mortgages and required lenders to confirm that a borrower had enough income to repay the loan. A third was legislation on executive compensation to require companies to allow stockholders to express their views of the remuneration they pay to senior executives, introduced in May and approved by the House in July. This "say on pay" provision was in fact unlikely to have much impact on the earnings of bankers, but Frank liked the way it sounded. His staff thought it was largely for show.

The most important answer to the nervous liberals, Frank decided that spring, would be the consumer protection provisions in the regulatory reform bill. Creating a new agency to protect consumers from financial abuses by private firms of many types would be the best way to do something for the voters at the expense of the financial institutions, Frank thought.

In its white paper published June 17, the administration announced its support for an independent Consumer Financial Protection Agency (CFPA).* This was the only entirely new regulator the administration would propose, and the only novel idea in the regulatory reform package. It would prove to be its most controversial element. The other ideas in the package had been bouncing around for a long time, as we have seen. The white paper generally reflected the same broad consen-

---

* This became the Consumer Financial Protection Bureau in the final legislation.

sus that was evident in the speeches given in March 2008 by Paulson and Obama.

The CFPA idea was first articulated by a Harvard Law School professor named Elizabeth Warren in an article for *Democracy*, a liberal journal with a circulation of five thousand. It appeared in the summer of 2007, long before the crash, but after the housing bubble began to lose air.

Warren was not a typical Washington policy wonk. In fact she had never held a job in Washington. Born (in 1949) and raised in Oklahoma City, she was a champion debater at age sixteen, then married at nineteen. She became a mother before finishing law school in 1976, and a professor of commercial law soon after that. She first joined the Harvard law faculty in 1992 and became the Leo Gottlieb Professor of Law, a distinguished senior appointment, in 1995.

She made herself an expert on the economic plight of the "disappearing" American middle class. She did extensive original research showing how the cost of credit, especially credit card debt, undermined middle-class standards of living, and she exposed the "tricks and traps" that the credit card companies used to jack up the costs of using their plastic substitute for money. In 2003, Warren and her daughter, Amelia Tyagi, published a best-selling book, *The Two-Income Trap: Why Middle-Class Mothers and Fathers Are Going Broke*. In 2009, Warren said, there were 50 million Americans who could not pay off their credit card debts, and carried balances from month to month. "They pay more in interest than they spend on clothes," she said.

Warren is a slim, handsome woman who wears her straight blond hair pulled back over her ears from a part near the center of her head. She looks at least a decade younger than her age, and she has extraordinary energy. She is no ivory-tower academic.* When she decided that credit cards were an important problem, she raised foundation support to try to launch a "clean card" with no tricks or traps. After extensive research she wrote a clean card contract offering straightforward credit terms without any legal gobbledygook. Then she tried to find a financial institution that would offer her card to the public. "They all told me that without the tricks and traps, they would have

---

* In 2012 she ran for the Senate from Massachusetts and defeated Republican incumbent Scott Brown.

to charge an interest rate on the clean card that would look like the highest rate in the market." No one would issue the card.

Warren concluded that only the government could fix the problem, the argument she made in *Democracy*. The country, she wrote, needed a "financial product safety commission," a play on the name of the Consumer Product Safety Commission, created under President Nixon in 1972 to keep unsafe consumer products off the market.

"It is impossible to buy a toaster that has a one-in-five chance of bursting into flames and burning down your house," Warren wrote. "But it is possible to refinance an existing home with a mortgage that has the same one-in-five chance of putting the family out on the street—and the mortgage won't even carry a disclosure of that fact to the homeowner. . . . It's impossible to change the price on a toaster once it has been purchased. But long after the papers have been signed, it is possible to triple the price of the credit used to finance the purchase of that appliance, even if the customer meets all the credit terms, in full and on time. Why are consumers . . . left at the mercy of their creditors?"

Only a new federal regulatory agency, Warren argued, could eliminate credit abuses. A financial product safety commission could "establish guidelines for consumer disclosure, collect and report data about the uses of different financial products, review new financial products for safety, and require modification of dangerous products before they can be marketed to the public." Such an agency could end price gouging by banks, payday lenders, credit card issuers, and other providers of credit, saving billions for more productive purposes.

Warren's idea began to accumulate supporters. Former senator John Edwards, a Democratic candidate for president, embraced it on the campaign trail. So did Senator Hillary Rodham Clinton. Obama did not mention it in his campaign, but he knew Warren personally and was intrigued by her idea, according to Michael Barr, the assistant secretary of the treasury who was one of the principal authors of the white paper. Barr, Neal Wolin, Diana Farrell, Cass Sunstein, and the others who participated in the brainstorming that produced the white paper decided that consumer protection should be one of the "core" elements of their proposal, as Wolin put it. This pleased Chris Dodd, who, as we've seen, thought from the outset that consumer protection had to be a central part of regulatory reform. At the beginning of 2009, Frank wasn't as sure.

Frank knew Warren; they had appeared together early in 2008 at a forum in Florida where she presented her idea for a new agency. At first Frank was skeptical. They rode together to the airport after the forum, and she used the opportunity to argue her case. "He was trapped in the car, and I'm relentless," she remembered.

Frank's first instinct was to allow state governments to provide more aggressive consumer protection. Was a new federal agency also needed? At the end of February, Frank was uncertain. "The extent to which we furnish consumer protection and whether or not we adopt the idea for a financial product safety commission" was still to be decided, he said. Just days after making that remark Frank met again with Warren in his home district office in Newton, outside Boston. She restated her case, and this time she felt she had won him over. "It was only a fifteen-minute meeting," she said. "He doesn't waste any time."

Once he embraced the agency idea, Frank became its insistent advocate, both on its merits and for the political benefits he thought it would bring. As he was often reminded by his friend Rahm Emanuel, public opinion polls consistently showed the high popularity of consumer protection. When, in June, both the American Bankers Association, largest of the bank lobbies, and the Chamber of Commerce, the voice of American business in Washington, both denounced the idea, it became even more attractive to Frank. By June he had become an enthusiastic supporter of what the white paper called a Consumer Financial Protection Agency.

On June 30 the Treasury delivered to the Financial Services Committee its proposed legislative language to create the CFPA. Frank, impatient as always, instructed the staff to put it through the Office of Legislative Counsel, an obscure but important House institution that is responsible for the form and language of new legislation. Frank wanted to introduce the administration bill as his own as quickly as possible. He did so on July 8. He announced publicly his intention to mark up the bill creating a CFPA—that is, to complete and act on a committee version of the bill—before the House began its summer vacation, known euphemistically as the August "district work period."

Setting this early deadline proved somewhat embarrassing. Frank soon had to abandon it. Too many of his Democrats on Financial Services had been shaken by intense lobbying, particularly from their hometown bankers, against the idea of a new consumer agency that would give them yet another regulator examining and potentially harassing them. "The bankers have a good line," said Perlmutter, who was hearing from his bankers in Colorado. "Why are we getting picked on first when we had so little to do with causing the crash?"

Jeanne Roslanowick thought Frank was being pressured by Rahm Emanuel to move quickly on consumer protection because it polled so well, though she wondered what the actual polling questions were, and how people answered. For Roslanowick, creating a new agency that could examine banks the way their regulators do and veto some of the products they might offer to the public was a bold initiative that raised serious practical questions. She told colleagues that "Barney doesn't want to hear them." She found him hardest to deal with when he was unwilling to hear staff out on policy arguments, or was doing something for what he considered good political reasons that she thought would lead to flawed policy.

She also thought Frank still wasn't used to Democratic colleagues who were markedly less liberal than he. Many of the news and blues nervous about the consumer agency had been elected by narrow margins, and some represented districts with Republican majorities. Roslanowick thought their nervousness reflected what they were hearing at home. "If what they were feeling back home and reading in their local papers suggested the public was crying for an independent consumer protection agency, they would be responding to that," she said.

An independent agency for consumer protection was not the only controversial item weighing on the news and blues that July, which Frank's staff seemed to understand better than he did. The moderate Democrats were nervous about the health care bill that was Topic A in the news media for most of the year, and also about the "cap and trade" energy bill meant to limit carbon emissions that would come to a final vote in the House on June 26. "The Blue Dogs and New Democrats [the two principal groups of moderates] are feeling slammed on health care and cap and trade by leadership," meaning Speaker Pelosi, Roslanowick said in mid-July. Both bills were shaping up as more liberal than the moderates would have preferred, but Pelosi pressured her caucus relentlessly to remain united behind both.

The proposed consumer agency became a tool the nervous members used to vent their anxieties. Kanjorski, the second-ranking Democrat on the committee, who had won reelection in 2008 by a scant 52–48 percent margin, and his aide Todd Harper, technically an employee of the Financial Services Committee but effectively Kanjorski's key assistant on financial issues, were fomenting trouble among other moderates who worried that the Consumer Financial Protection Agency idea was too radical. Kanjorski was quoted in press accounts questioning why Frank was moving so fast on the consumer agency. Frank and his staff blamed Harper, a man who loved the maneuvering that is always part of the congressional game, for encouraging or even organizing a protest against the CFPA plan at a briefing on it that committee staff had organized for Democratic members on July 15. Four or five members expressed reservations at the briefing. "I'm a 'No' at this point," announced Carolyn McCarthy of Long Island, New York, who won her seat in Congress with the notoriety she earned as the widow of a man killed by a deranged gunman in a mass shooting.

After the briefing, Frank said the next day, "Kanjorski and I had a very angry conversation. I told him Todd worked for the committee, and could lose his job." The next morning Frank and Kanjorski made peace.

Reluctantly at first, Frank had to accept that he could not ignore this unexpected uprising on the committee. Jim Segel and Roslanowick made sure he understood this by confronting their boss with their own concerns about Democratic members' attitudes. Frank asked why, if the members were unhappy, he hadn't heard it directly from them. Segel told his old friend that some of them found him arrogant, and had difficulty talking directly to him about their concerns. Some were afraid of him. "Afraid of me?" Frank asked dubiously. He did not appreciate the way his unequivocal self-confidence could intimidate colleagues who knew they didn't understand the issues as well as he did. When confronted by a colleague's concern he considered unwarranted, Frank's first instinct was to dismiss it, not to ask sympathetic questions or probe for more information. Those dismissals had an impact.

Once confronted this way by trusted aides, Frank quickly made adjustments. This was, Roslanowick and Segel both thought, one of his strengths. He could be stubborn and impatient, but he could also be flexible when he saw that he had to.

The day after his blowup with Kanjorski, Frank said he was hard at work putting down the rebellion. "I talked to people, I said, 'Look, it's complicated, I understand that.' " He reminded them of his earlier warnings that the banks might come after them over the consumer agency.

"You know, conflict avoidance is the most serious motivation of many members of Congress much of the time," Frank said. "So the banks are now mobilizing, going crazy about this [CFPA]. Some of my members are getting shaky. I've said to them, you've got to understand, if you kill this bill now, you'll get creamed. You'll get primary opponents. It will be the people against the banks, and the Democrats caved in again. So I think I've stemmed that tide. Jimmy Segel has told people [members] this is important to me personally. I have talked to a bunch of the members. I will get a good bill out, I believe."

"Important to me personally" was, Frank hoped, a winning argument that would produce the payoff he wanted to think he had earned from his colleagues by working so hard to help them, attend their fundraisers, and show them how good relations with him could be good for them politically. In other words, he hoped his attempt to mimic Lyndon Johnson's style as Democratic leader in the Senate six decades earlier was working.

If Frank felt he needed to show some patience and understanding to his colleagues, he felt no such compunction toward the lobbyists for the banks. During these difficult July days he walked into Roslanowick's office when she was being visited by Floyd Stoner, a popular figure who was the American Bankers Association's lobbyist for the House committee. Stoner was telling Roslanowick what the bankers hoped might end up in the legislation, and Barney cut him off. "I'm told we're in all-out war," Frank said, quoting what he'd heard Stoner and others from the banking industry had been saying about their opposition to the CFPA. "So what the hell do I care what you want in there?" Stoner, a Democrat himself who had enjoyed good relations with Frank, was taken aback.

A week after the spat with Kanjorski, Frank passed the word that he would not try to get committee approval of the consumer agency before the August recess began ten days later. The committee would take it up in the fall. But this was not a signal that he was prepared to give up the consumer agency, or lacked confidence in his ability to deliver a large and important bill. He made that clear in a July 27 speech to the National Press Club in Washington. He knew that C-SPAN broadcast Press Club speeches, so his would be noticed. He was in a feisty mood.

Frank never read a prepared speech, but he did rehearse his lines, often in personal conversations. On this occasion he had two large themes. First was the historical point he had been making in conversation and in public statements for months: This was the third great moment in American history for government to set rules for American capitalism that would insure its survival and long-term health. As Theodore Roosevelt and Woodrow Wilson had been first to do this early in the twentieth century and Roosevelt second in the 1930s, so this Congress and Barack Obama would do it now. "We have the responsibility as Democrats to come up with a system of rules to allow capitalism to thrive," Frank declared.

Frank had a message for the financial community: "I want them to work with us. They need to understand, when I talk about restricting leverage [borrowing], having a systemic risk regulator, curtailing the excesses in derivatives, some risk retention, protection of consumers in a single, effective agency—these are all going to happen. I can guarantee you that the votes are there—not because I want them, but because I have had a series of conversations with people, and I know that that's what is going to happen. And I know that if the financial community or people who believe in total deregulation, if they want to make that a national debate, I welcome it. They will lose that debate. . . . We will prove that the best thing you can do for capitalism is to have rules that give investors the confidence to get back in the system, that protects the great majority of decent people from abuses. . . .

"I invite the judgment of failure if we are unable to deliver," Frank said boldly. "And I will tell you, I am not politically inclined to take on responsibilities I don't think I can handle."

This sort of pronouncement from a senior member of Congress about the outcome of a still undecided and controversial issue is rarely heard in Washington. Just days after quelling a rebellion in his own ranks, Barney Frank had put down his marker.

CHAPTER TEN

An Impotent Minority

Democrats outnumbered Republicans 257 to 178 in the House of Representatives of the 111th Congress and 41–29 on the House Financial Services Committee, so the Republicans could not expect to have much influence on the regulatory reform legislation enacted in 2009 and 2010. In earlier eras, when party labels were less significant, members of a minority party in the House could often make a mark on the bills the House enacted, but by the first decade of the new century, bipartisan collaboration was thoroughly out of fashion. It rarely happened.

So Spencer Bachus of Jefferson County, Alabama, knew that despite his lofty status as the ranking Republican on the House Financial Services Committee, he and his Republican colleagues would not have much impact on the legislation that he knew was coming to reform financial regulations. He would have preferred to participate. He agreed that the Great Crash demonstrated the need for better regulation of the financial markets, including improved protections for consumers. And unlike many of his more fiery conservative colleagues, he actually believed in bipartisan legislating.

Bachus was personally conservative, but not a "movement conservative" like so many of his party's leaders in the House—politicians committed to a sternly conservative ideology on both social and economic issues implacably opposed to any tax increases and hostile to most government initiatives. Bachus was an easygoing, gentle sort, with an unfortunate inclination to sound dumb in public. He had trouble articulating, and could stumble when speaking extemporaneously. But he was actually an intelligent man who did a lot of reading on the issues he had to deal with, and a lot of talking with participants in the financial markets.

He employed a smart, knowledgeable right-hand man named Larry Lavender, a successful Alabama businessman and longtime personal friend who came to Washington in 2001 to work first as Bachus's staff director, then as the senior staff member of the Republican staff of Financial Services. Lavender's white handlebar mustache and sense of humor set him apart from the mass of interchangeable staff assistants on Capitol Hill. Lavender was viewed with deep suspicion by more conservative aides working for the House Republican leadership, who doubted his ideological purity. Ohio's John Boehner, the Republican leader, more than once suggested to Bachus that he find another staff director, but Bachus remained loyal to Lavender.

Lavender repaid that loyalty in kind. He loved telling stories about his friend the "lucky politician." One of his favorites was the story of Bachus's first campaign for the Alabama state Senate in 1982, when he was practicing law. One of Bachus's clients was the family of a child killed by a drunk driver, and he had worked on the family's behalf to toughen Alabama's laws on drunk driving. He went to see the state senator who represented Jefferson County to ask for his support. The state senator dismissed the idea, telling Bachus there was no chance the legislature would enact new laws on drunk driving. This experience got Bachus interested in running for the legislature himself. In 1982 he decided to challenge the man who had dismissed his concerns about drunk drivers.

Bachus, born in 1947, grew up like nearly everyone in Alabama of his generation—as a Democrat in what was then a one-party state. His opponent looked invulnerable to a primary challenge, so Bachus ran as a Republican. As the campaign got under way, the incumbent was arrested for drunk driving. In the ensuing scandal, the Democrats dumped him and anointed another candidate, and Bachus won the election.

Bachus became the chairman of the Alabama Republican Party in 1991. In 1992, after a court-ordered redistricting pushed a Democratic incumbent into a new congressional district that was predominantly

Republican, Bachus entered the race and won a seat in the House. After the 2000 Census the district was again redrawn, this time becoming one of the safest Republican House seats anywhere.

"They've done that all over the country," Bachus observed disapprovingly in an interview. "I mean, you've either got Democrat districts or Republican districts. You don't have any more people getting elected in the middle, very few. You fight over maybe fifty districts. . . . Once you have a very conservative district or a very liberal district, you have a tendency to have people on the extremes. . . . And the middle is eroded." Bachus was comfortable in the middle, but by 2009 he couldn't find it.

He had tried to work with Barney Frank in 2005 on a bill to ban most subprime mortgages, which he understood to be a serious threat to financial stability. He recalled having lunch with a Birmingham, Alabama, bank president that year who told him that "people are going to lose their shirts over this [subprime] stuff." Bachus understood that "there were tremendous gaps in the regulation [of mortgage lending]," and that fixing it would require "a comprehensive bill," which is what he proposed. Bachus thought that if it had passed in 2005, subprime lending would have dried up, and the Great Crash could have been avoided or at least made much less serious.

The conservatives who dominated the House Republican caucus did not share Bachus's views in 2005, and they helped kill his subprime bill. Bachus tried again in 2007, when Frank had assumed the chairmanship of Financial Services and decided to push a new bill curtailing subprimes. Bachus joined the effort, helping produce a rare bipartisan proposal. The House passed this bill easily with the votes of 227 Democrats and 64 Republicans, including Bachus. But 127 Republicans, including most members of the Republican Study Committee—the dominant faction of the House Republican caucus consisting of its most conservative members—voted no. Many of them did not forgive Bachus for collaborating with Frank on a bill imposing stiff new regulations on the mortgage industry. The RSC favored fewer, not more, government regulations.

Bachus's reputation with the RSC suffered again in 2008 when he decided to support the TARP bailout legislation. At one point during the tense days of September 2008, Bachus took part in a bipartisan meeting of House members and senators to work out the terms of TARP. He shocked others present, including Republican senators, by announcing, as Bachus recalled it, "I am under instructions that I can't negotiate." He repeated this several times, to make it clear that Boehner had instructed him not to negotiate for the House Republicans.

Bachus's problem with the conservative firebrands was based on a simple but profound disagreement: They often put partisan warfare ahead of all other considerations, and Bachus was never comfortable in that posture. He actually cared about policy outcomes—about legislating. The conservatives who dominated the caucus, he and his staff thought, cared more about "messaging"—political propaganda.

Bachus and his staff had seen e-mails sent by a senior aide to Boehner shortly after Boehner had embraced TARP in the meeting in Pelosi's office. "We need to rise above politics and show the American people we can work together," Boehner had said then, promising to work as long as necessary to pass the bank bailout that President Bush and his team were seeking. But immediately afterward Boehner's aide took a different view. His e-mail said the House Republicans would agree to attend meetings to negotiate a deal on TARP, but would never make a deal. "Then we'll blow this thing up." They would blame the bailout on the White House and Democrats: "We're going to let them have this turd," the e-mail said, according to someone who received it. Bachus was appalled.

In December 2008, when the House Republican Steering Committee designated the ranking Republicans on all the standing committees for the incoming 111th Congress, Boehner tried to replace Bachus as ranking Republican on Financial Services. Unlike the Democrats, who choose their committee leaders based primarily on seniority, the Republicans have adopted a more democratic system of selection based on a vote of the Steering Committee, which consists of all the party leaders and a sample of rank-and-file members.

Bachus impressed his colleagues as a rather passive figure, small of stature and soft of voice. But when challenged by Boehner he staged a fierce fight to save his position, exploiting the personal popularity he had won over his eight terms in the House. He won handily. "He walloped John Boehner," in the words of one proud Bachus ally.

But Bachus could never be entirely confident of his position. He knew he had to toe the party line and appease the conservatives to preserve it, a concern that often led him to "self-censor" or bite his tongue, according to his aides. He also had to accept several staff assistants assigned by Boehner's office to work on the minority staff of the committee.

Bachus's political insecurity was evident at the White House meeting of February 25, 2009, when Obama and his senior aides first discussed regulatory reform with Frank, Dodd, Shelby, and Bachus. The two Democrats and Shelby agreed then, as we have seen, that they could work together on a package of reforms, but Bachus did not commit himself. The one concern he expressed was about publicity for this meeting—he hoped there wouldn't be any.

In early 2009 the Republicans began debating what posture they should adopt on financial regulatory reform. At a meeting in Bachus's office that spring, they decided they should offer their own plan so they would have a response to whatever Obama and Frank came up with. From the outset this was a political exercise; its primary purpose was to enable Republicans to say they had an alternative to the Democrats' plan, which they knew was going to call for sweeping changes and stern new rules. They had no delusions about their ability to actually affect the legislation fundamentally. At best they thought they might be able to win a few votes on amendments in the committee markups of whatever bills Frank decided to bring to the floor.

The minority staff was assigned the job of writing a Republican proposal for regulatory reform. The proposal was designed primarily to try to show a united Republican front on the major regulatory issues, not to propose concrete new regulatory initiatives. A week before the White House released the administration white paper outlining its proposed reforms, the Republicans presented their own, briefer document at a news conference in the Radio-Television Gallery on the House side of the Capitol. They were obviously hoping to sneak into the spotlight ahead of Obama.

The Radio-TV Gallery is one of the artificial backdrops for a category of Washington events perhaps best described as attempts to get on television. The backdrop of the stage used over the years for thousands of news conferences and announcements is a painted library wall full of books. It looks quite real on camera, but there are no actual books. It's a small stage, but nine House Republicans crowded onto it for this event, including most of the senior members of Financial Services and two members of the leadership.

"Republicans are united today in introducing this plan," Bachus said proudly; it was "our blueprint for preventing [a recurrence of] what happened last year." Representative Shelley Moore Capito of West Virginia confessed the political purpose of the exercise: "It's important that we [Republicans] join the process of regulatory reform," she said.

Politics had shaped the substance of the plan. The Republicans realized that they had one club with which to whack the Democrats that ordinary Americans would like—a simple slogan: "No more bailouts." Any politician with an appreciation for public sentiment understood in 2009 that the bailouts promoted first by Paulson and Bernanke to respond to the Great Crash had no admirers in the general public, except perhaps from people who benefited directly from them. Pollsters for both parties had picked up the popular anger, aggravated of course by the absence of bailouts for the ordinary citizens who had been clobbered by the crash. Being against bailouts was about as controversial as supporting apple pie.

So the summary of the Republican plan released at the media event said near the outset: "The guiding principle of the Republican alternative can be summed up in one sentence: no more bailouts." The Republican plan would "put an end to ad hoc, improvised and unprincipled bailouts designed to spare big Wall Street firms and their creditors from the consequences of their mistakes." Each of the Republican members who spoke picked up this theme. No one mentioned the fact that the original bailouts were the idea of the Republican Bush administration, which had urged all House Republicans to support them (91 Republicans did so, 108 voted against). Nor did Bachus, deputy Republican leader Eric Cantor of Virginia, or Representative Judy Biggert of Illinois, who all spoke at the news conference, mention that they had voted for TARP and its bailouts in October 2008. These omissions were not surprising; the point was to use the club that was available, not to dwell on the past—territory that these politicians were eager to avoid.

The Republicans' plan was largely rhetorical. It "rejects the Democrats' call for a government-run economy that depends upon the omniscience and omnipotence of government regulators," their press release said, though no Democrat had issued such a call. The Republicans rejected the idea of a new resolution authority to dissolve failing financial firms, proposing instead to amend the bankruptcy laws and insist that failing firms formally go broke. This was an option that many financial experts, beginning in 2008 with Paulson and Bernanke, rejected as unworkable. But other, mostly conservative, experts liked the idea, and Republicans stuck with it throughout the debate over regulatory reform. Instead of a new systemic risk regulator, the concept that Frank and the administration embraced to prevent financial institutions from engaging in too risky behavior, the Republicans proposed a Market Stability and Capital Adequacy Board that would periodically publicize its assessments of risk taking in the financial sector, but have no power to regulate it.

The Republicans proposed creating a single bank regulator, and giving it the powers of existing regulatory agencies including the Federal Reserve Board and the Federal Deposit Insurance Corporation. They suggested strictly limiting the Fed's ability to provide assistance to banks and other firms in a crisis. They proposed privatizing Freddie Mac and Fannie Mae, the two giant entities effectively nationalized by Paulson in September 2008 that supported the national mortgage market by buying and securitizing home mortgages. But the Republicans did not spell out how they would perform this difficult act, and many Republican members who had ties to the real estate and home building industries opposed the idea. The Republicans also proposed changes in the rules governing ratings agencies that give report-card-like grades to financial institutions, national governments, and specific securities, such as Triple A bonds. Finally, the plan called for improved methods of resolving complaints against financial institutions from consumers, but had no equivalent to the Democrats' Consumer Financial Protection Agency.

Producing this plan proved to be a fruitless exercise. It got almost no attention from the major news media, and was soon forgotten. Republicans eventually forgot it themselves. It was the work of a powerless minority looking for ways to remain relevant in a hostile political environment.

But in one respect this public relations exercise was revealing: Even the conservatives who dominated the House Republican caucus were acknowledging that the regulation of financial institutions needed to be improved. As Congresswoman Capito had implied, Republicans could not afford the political risk of not participating in "the process of regulatory reform." Somehow, even people who were among the least disposed to increase federal regulations of the financial industry had accepted a political reality they didn't like, but couldn't avoid. Financial regulatory reform was coming.

CHAPTER ELEVEN

Peddling Influence

One cause of the rebellion that Frank had to put down in July 2009 was a lobbying campaign against an independent consumer protection agency launched by financial and business interests in June. The American Bankers Association, the National Auto Dealers Association, the U.S. Chamber of Commerce, the Mortgage Bankers Association, the American Financial Services Association (the trade association of the credit industry), and the scores of lobbyists who worked for them all joined this effort. In Washington, this was standard operating procedure; everyone in the game expected it. Interest groups exist to promote their own interests, and lobbying Congress is usually their first line of attack.

Lobbyists have long been members of the congressional family. If the news media constitute a Fourth Estate, a notion from nineteenth-century England that survived in modern America, then lobbyists are a Fifth. They are much more numerous than the journalists on Capitol Hill, and they have a lot more money. Money in the form of campaign contributions enhances their status and promotes their successes. Over the previous thirty years, financial interests and their lobbyists had an especially good record promoting deregulation of financial markets. They also won victories that went beyond deregulation, such as the Bankruptcy Act of 2005. This law, promoted by banks and credit card companies and opposed by every consumer group in the country, was enacted by large bipartisan majorities in the House and Senate. It made filing for personal bankruptcy more difficult, and required citizens who did file to pay off their credit card debts before they could pay child support or alimony. It followed intense lobbying and more than $40 million in financial industry campaign contributions to House and Senate candidates over the fifteen years that preceded the vote.

The escalating costs of election campaigns gave the financial sector incentives to contribute. Through direct donations and political action committees set up by individual firms, they gave both to individual members and to the two parties' campaign committees. The huge amounts they gave were a good measure of the degree to which American politics became a money game over the previous generation. Political action committees and individuals from the financial, insurance, and real estate industries donated $287 million to candidates for federal office—the House and Senate—in 2005–6, or "the 2006 election cycle" as it is known inside the Beltway. That was an average donation of more than $530,000 per member, though not every member got money. In 2007–8, when the total included contributions to presidential as well as congressional candidates, it rose to $501 million.

In the words of the Center for Responsive Politics, a nonprofit organization that monitors political donations, "the financial sector is far and away the largest source of campaign contributions to federal candidates and parties." This is why the Senate Banking and House Financial Services committees are called "money committees" in Washington. Their members have little trouble raising money for their reelection campaigns. Another watchdog group, the Public Campaign Action Fund, calculated that members of House Financial Services had received a total of $62.9 million from the financial sector during their political careers, through the spring of 2009—an average of $885,000 each.

But there is an ironic and revealing fact about these big numbers that is easily missed: For the prominent Wall Street institutions, they aren't big numbers at all. For example, according to the Center for Responsive Politics, Goldman Sachs, the investment bank, and its employees contributed nearly $20 million to political campaigns from 1989 to 2010. That sounds like a lot of money in a political context, but Goldman's profits over those two decades totaled more than $50 billion. Political contributions represented roughly .04 percent of Goldman Sachs's profits over those two decades. Seen in this light, $20 million is chump change.

Washington numbers and Wall Street numbers are radically different. When Lloyd Blankfein, the chairman of Goldman Sachs, testified before a congressional committee in 2009, the event featured a man who in a good year made more than $60 million talking to members whose government salaries were $174,000 each.* What do those contributions buy? The answer is rarely obvious and often ambiguous. The donors wouldn't give so much if they weren't convinced that the money helped them, but they don't always get what they want.

Four decades earlier, in 1971, Senator Russell Long of Louisiana observed in a debate on campaign finance that "the distinction between a campaign contribution and a bribe is almost a hairline's difference. You can hardly tell one from the other." But it wasn't simple bribery. Many special interests gave money to politicians with no guarantee of winning specific benefits in return. The financial sector's money went to both supporters and opponents of stronger regulations. Barney Frank and Chris Dodd both received large amounts. In 2007–8, Frank recorded financial sector donations of $1,041,298; Dodd received $6,081,836. Both insisted that accepting this money had no impact on their approach to regulatory reform, and in terms of specific issues, there is no evidence to the contrary. They both supported reforms that the big banks bitterly opposed.

On the other hand, Frank, Dodd, and virtually all of their colleagues declined to use the Great Crash of 2008 and the subsequent regulatory reform process to seek the breakup of America's big banks or any other fundamental alteration of the financial sector. Both men actively supported the bailout of the banks in 2008. As they began to consider regulatory reforms in 2009, both agreed it would be enough to put the financial sector under stricter new rules, without trying to undo the two decades of growth and concentration that had transformed American finance, making it the most profitable sector of the American economy.

In earlier eras real radicals could be found in Congress, men who

---

* Most members of Congress in 2009 had substantial private wealth, so did not have to live on $174,000 a year, but only a tiny number of members lived in the rarefied financial precincts occupied by Blankfein.

were ready, even eager, to enact harsh measures to impinge on the privileges of the rich, though they almost never enjoyed majority support. By 2009 such firebrands were all but extinct. The moderation shown now even by liberal Democrats surely was influenced by the political money game. Tony Coelho, a California congressman in the 1970s and 1980s who taught his party how to raise money from business interests, admitted that the need for this money "does affect legislation" by convincing members to avoid angering moneyed interests that may contribute to their campaigns. Under Coelho's tutelage, Democrats discovered in the 1980s that business interests would give them money, and they came to depend on PACs and corporate donors almost as heavily as Republicans did, and sometimes more so.

The senior Washington representative of one of the biggest Wall Street institutions admitted in a moment of candor that "the only reason we give them all money is, we want them to be reasonable! You want to defeat the craziness." If that really was the objective, then it was successful year after year. Of course, there was always room for argument about the meaning of a term like "craziness."

The one reliable reward for making campaign donations was access. Members of Congress accepted the proposition that someone who has given them money should be able to convey their views to the member or his or her staff. Members often argue that they give access to nondonors as well as contributors, but it isn't difficult to imagine who gets priority. What member's appointments secretary is going to put a nondonor ahead of someone who has been generous to the boss? The interest groups that regularly sought out meetings on Capitol Hill rarely had any trouble scheduling those meetings.

Nor did the prominent freelance lobbyists who hired out their services to special interests including the financial industry. They also gave substantial sums to members' campaigns to grease their relationships on Capitol Hill. In 2009–10, the Center for Responsive Politics calculated, the twenty-five most generous lobbyists gave more than $3.1 million in campaign contributions. This was a small fraction of all lobbyists' contributions. And their donations were limited by campaign finance laws, or they would have given more.

Money wasn't the lobbyists' and special interests' only advantage. Relationships were another. In the modern era, an extraordinary number of the people seeking appointments are former friends and colleagues of those they wanted to meet and influence. This was the effect of the revolving door that had carried thousands of former government officials into the ranks of Washington's lobbyists since the 1980s.

According to an analysis by the Center for Responsive Politics and Public Citizen, another watchdog group, financial institutions and organizations representing them retained the services of 1,447 former government employees to lobby Congress or federal agencies in 2009–10.* All of them had passed through that revolving door. Seventy-five were former members of the House and Senate, colleagues and often friends of those they tried to influence on behalf of their clients. This group included a former speaker of the house (Dennis Hastert, an Illinois Republican), two former Senate majority leaders (Bob Dole of Kansas and Trent Lott of Mississippi, both Republicans), and two House majority leaders (Dick Armey, a Texas Republican, and Richard Gephardt, a Missouri Democrat). All had become rich and successful Washington lobbyists after leaving Congress. They converted their public service into personal wealth.

Another 148 men and women who registered in those years to lobby on financial issues were former members of the staffs of the key committees or their members. Sixty-seven of them had worked for the House Financial Services and Senate Banking Committees; the other eighty-one had served on the personal staffs of members of those committees. In other words, to say that lobbyists were part of the family on Capitol Hill was not a metaphorical observation; it was literally true.

The representatives of the American Bankers Association, the Chamber of Commerce, and the others who banded together in June 2009 to fight the consumer agency idea had no trouble making their views known quickly and effectively to members. (The ABA was a leading employer of former members and staff as lobbyists; it retained the services of forty-nine ex-government officials.) They probably would have done fine without campaign contributions, which the member groups or their members all made. They probably didn't need those family ties either. Such groups have little trouble getting appointments on Capitol Hill because they can mobilize large mem-

---

* These calculations were made from disclosure forms that lobbyists and those who retain them are required to file by law and under House and Senate regulations.

berships and command respect from their member institutions, which typically can be found in every state and every congressional district. They were established political players.

In June 2009, the U.S. Chamber of Commerce announced "a sweeping national advocacy campaign encompassing advertising, education, political activities, new media, and grassroots organizing to defend and advance America's free enterprise values in the face of rapid government growth and attacks by anti-business activists." In other words, the Chamber was getting ready to campaign against the Democrats who had taken over Washington. To make clear its seriousness—or to intimidate members of Congress worried about its influence—the Chamber said this open-ended program "will be budgeted at tens of millions of dollars annually." This was the sort of thing that congressional offices noticed.

And the access these groups got involved more than just their perceived clout. The best lobbyists make themselves invaluable to members of Congress and their staffs by providing useful information, the coin of the realm on Capitol Hill. Of course the information can be tendentious, but a good lobbyist knows that playing the game without special pleading or one-sided arguments is usually the most effective approach. Only a dumb lobbyist will lie for a client in a way he or she knows will eventually be exposed. There are dumb lobbyists, of course, but good ones will always tell the person they are lobbying what arguments can be made against the position they are trying to promote and who is likely to make them.

This was a key to the popularity of the good lobbyists, like Floyd Stoner, who lobbied House Democrats for the American Bankers Association. Stoner, himself a Democrat, once worked for Congressman David Obey of Wisconsin, a leading House liberal. Jeanne Roslanowick first met him as a colleague, and maintained friendly relations when he became an ABA lobbyist.

Stoner's boss, Edward Yingling, president of the ABA and its chief lobbyist for twenty years before he became president in 2005, also had a Democratic background, and called himself a "bipartisan" Democrat. His father, Jack Yingling, had served as chief clerk—equivalent of today's staff director—of the Senate Banking Committee in the 1950s and 1960s, under two Democratic chairmen. His mother worked as a secretary to Congressman Wilbur Mills of Arkansas in the 1940s. So Yingling had tribal credentials on Capitol Hill, where he was well liked. A tall, slim, handsome man with white hair, Yingling was smart and easygoing. He had vaguely patrician manners perhaps acquired at Princeton, where he was a member of the class of 1970. And he knew how to take full advantage of the ABA's formidable intellectual resources.

The American Bankers Association was one of the largest trade associations in Washington, which became a city of trade associations beginning in the Nixon administration. In 2009 the ABA occupied four and a half floors of a big office building on Connecticut Avenue, across the street from the Mayflower Hotel. It had 370 employees. Among them were economists and policy analysts who could support Yingling, Stoner, and the ABA's other lobbyists—more than a dozen of them—with the kind of information and analysis that staffs on Capitol Hill craved. Their ability to produce both statistics and useful arguments contributed to their success.

The best lobbyists understood that they could often be most successful by concentrating on the details of a piece of legislation. Proponents of a bill could and usually did promote it as a glorious contribution to the public interest, but its impact on the real world would depend on the details of its provisions. This was precisely the situation with the proposed Consumer Financial Protection Agency, the only provision of the Obama administration's package of financial regulatory reforms that had broad popular appeal, and was reasonably easy to explain to ordinary citizens.

The obvious justification for a new agency was the huge contribution to the meltdown of 2008 made by unregulated financial products, particularly dubious home mortgages issued to millions of homeowners who couldn't afford them and often didn't understand their complicated terms. Most of those mortgages were issued by unregulated mortgage brokers. Under existing law the Federal Reserve Board had the legal authority to regulate them, but never chose to exercise it. Now, the Obama administration said, the country needed a new agency to police markets whose failure could have such devastating impact.

But the proposal sent to Congress went far beyond a new way to regulate the mortgage market. On the day the white paper was released, Obama described the CFPA as "a new and powerful agency charged with just one job: looking out for ordinary consumers. . . . This agency will have the power to set standards so that companies compete by offering innovative products that consumers actually want—and actually understand. Consumers will be provided information that is simple, transparent, and accurate. You'll be able to compare products and see what's best for you. The most unfair practices will be banned. Those ridiculous contracts with pages of fine print that no one can figure out—those things will be a thing of the past."

Obama's proposal was an example of the way a crisis can sometimes be exploited to achieve goals considered unreachable in ordinary times. In this case the goals belonged to a network of organizations that promoted consumer protections for years without great success. "We were used to losing," said Travis Plunkett, a Washington lobbyist for the Consumer Federation of America. The recently passed credit card bill was their first big victory in years; now Plunkett and his allies in the consumer movement hoped they could also promote Elizabeth Warren's idea for a new consumer protection agency into reality.

These self-styled "progressives" created a new group called Americans for Financial Reform to try to counter the lobbying of the industry groups that were trying to limit reforms. AFR was the offspring of several trade unions and consumer groups and quickly grew into an alliance of several hundred organizations around the country. This was an unusual show of energy and determination from the left, which for years had been outgunned on Capitol Hill by business interests. Announcing its existence in mid-June, the group said it would raise $5 million to lobby in Washington and organize grassroots agitation around the country. This sounded like a lot of money to the liberal groups involved, though $5 million hardly compared to the financial interests' spending on lobbying in 2009 and 2010, which totaled more than $750 million.

The pro-reform consumer groups had important allies in the administration, particularly Michael Barr, the University of Michigan law professor who had become assistant secretary of the treasury for financial institutions. Barr had worked for years on ways to help poor Americans get access to financial services, and he had strong views on the subject. In 2009 he was designated the chief drafter of the consumer section of the regulatory reform package.

The draft Barr and his colleagues produced startled Ed Yingling and the Bankers Association—it startled the entire conservative banking industry. Bankers had taken comfort from leaks during the spring indicating that the administration had abandoned the idea of reorganizing the patchwork of regulators that the banks had learned to deal with, instead adopting Frank's idea of imposing uniform rules on all the regulators and preserving all of them but one, the unpopular Office of Thrift Supervision. But the Consumer Financial Protection Agency proposal provided no comfort at all.

Barr's original draft would have extended the CFPA's authority to any company that used formal loan agreements to extend credit to its customers—auto dealers, for example. It would have authorized state governments to enforce their own consumer protection laws against banks and other financial firms, even if they were tougher than the proposed new federal law. This meant that a big national bank might have to operate under many different sets of regulations. The administration proposed that the new agency take over enforcement of all consumer laws, and conduct its own examinations of banks and other financial firms to insure that those laws were being observed. None of this had any appeal for the banks.

One provision in the administration's draft bill attracted particular criticism. This would have authorized the CFPA to create simple, straightforward versions of the most commonly used loan agreements—among them, mortgages, credit card agreements, and car loans. These became known as "plain vanilla" products. Lenders would have to offer their customers the opportunity to use these simple loan agreements, and would also have to explain the differences, including cost differences, between more exotic products and the plain vanilla ones.

"When the CFPA proposal came out," Yingling said in an interview, "there was a feeling that there was so much momentum behind it, it would be hard to fight. So somebody had to come out hard against this. We decided we should be the ones."

The ABA put out a statement on the day Obama released the white paper that reflected the bifurcated tactic Yingling had adopted, combining support for reform in general with opposition to the CFPA in particular. "Regulatory reform is badly needed and Congress should move this year to adopt such reforms," the ABA statement said. But an independent consumer protection agency was another matter altogether. The ABA saw the CFPA as "an enormous and unnecessary new federal bureaucracy that would harm the safety and soundness of insured depository institutions." Banks' safety and soundness—what traditional bank regulation was meant to guarantee—would be at risk because consumer agency inspectors could insist that banks stop offering profitable financial products, or could force them to make loans to risky borrowers in the name of equal access to credit. Yingling told *The Washington Post*, "The inclusion of the highly controversial Consumer Financial Protection Agency will undermine chances of enactment of needed reform."

This was a clever formulation, but more hope than prediction. As Yingling admitted in July, there was probably no stopping some kind of new consumer protection agency: "If you had to make a bet at this point I'd say yes, there will be a new agency, because President Obama, Barney Frank and Chris Dodd are all committed to it." But Yingling was an old hand who understood the vagaries of the legislative process. He knew he couldn't see around the next corner, and couldn't predict in July 2009 what would eventually be included in the regulatory reform bill that he did expect to pass. "We don't know where things are going to turn out." So he made a tactical decision to come out strongly against the proposed agency, in hopes that he and his members could at least limit a new agency's ability to make bankers' lives more complicated.

In his testimony on the CFPA to Frank's committee on June 24 (repeated to the Senate committee three weeks later), Yingling recited a litany of arguments against a new consumer agency, then played to what he knew was a soft spot for nearly every member—the small local banks in each of their districts. "Think of community banks, and credit unions also for that matter," Yingling said in his testimony. "These banks never made one sub-prime loan and they have the trust and support of their local consumers. As this committee has frequently noted, these community bankers are already overwhelmed with regulatory costs that are slowly but surely strangling them. Yet last week, these community banks found the Administration proposing a potentially massive new regulatory burden that will fall disproportionately on them"—the CFPA.

Yingling's tactic was to mobilize the community banks that belonged to the state affiliates of the ABA to lobby their own members of Congress. This effort had already begun; the anxieties that came to the surface inside the Financial Services Committee's Democratic caucus was evidence of its initial success.

But the lobbying campaign had a consequence that did not help the ABA. The organization's strong public criticism of the consumer agency infuriated Barney Frank—an anger that, as we have seen, was felt personally by Floyd Stoner, the ABA lobbyist whom Frank yelled at in Jeanne Roslanowick's office in July. As Frank recounted, he warned the bankers that if they succeeded in blocking committee approval of the CFPA, there would be a fight. "We'll have this debate . . . but you understand, the debate will be the people against the banks. If we have to fight back, we'll fight back by demonizing you."

Yingling considered Frank perhaps the smartest member of Congress on financial issues and "a great legislator." He did not want a fight with the chairman. But he calculated that an ABA campaign against the CFPA could force changes that would make it more acceptable to banks of all sizes even if it couldn't be stopped. From the outset, Yingling expected the final version of regulatory reform to be worked out in the Senate, not the House. He expected a bipartisan Senate bill, which meant, he thought, that Richard Shelby and his Republicans would ultimately make it friendlier to banks than a House version was likely to be.

Yingling was important, but he was not the only representative of banks who had strong views about regulatory reform. Camden Fine of Jefferson City, Missouri, was another, and his importance in the process was no less than Yingling's. Cam Fine's approach to the matter was very different.

Fine was the president of the Independent Community Bankers of America (ICBA), an organization of 5,300 smaller banks. A practical-minded midwesterner with an open, friendly face, Fine also had a Democratic background. His father was a personal friend of Harry Truman's, the most famous Missourian of the twentieth century. Fine worked for years in the Missouri state government, most prominently as the state's tax director—"the most unpopular job in the state." It taught him tact and the art of self-denigration. Later he became a small-town banker, running the Midwest Independent Bank in Jefferson City and the Mainstreet Bank of Ashland, Missouri, not far from Jefferson City. Fine became active in the ICBA, eventually serving on its national board of directors. The president of the association then recruited Fine as his successor. In 2003 Fine moved to Washington to take the job.

Fine had political experience. He had served on the school board and city council at home, had run a Democrat's unsuccessful campaign for Congress, and had toyed with the idea of running himself. He told his father he might like to run, "and my dad gave me some good advice: 'Son, it's better to be the best friend of a politician than to be the politician himself.' I always took that to heart." Now he had a field of 535 politicians—members of the House and Senate—to cultivate as potential friends on behalf of the ICBA.

There was overlapping membership in the ICBA and ABA, but most small banks belonged to Fine's organization, which was known as the trade association of hometown banks. The ABA's identity was more ambiguous, and Fine believed that the homogeneity of his membership made his job easier than Yingling's. "To be fair," Fine said in an interview, "Ed [Yingling] had a very, very difficult time. . . . Ed had to satisfy the behemoths on Wall Street at the same time he was trying to please the community banks. That was a very awkward position."

Beginning in 2007, when a weakening housing market and tightening credit heralded the beginning of the financial crisis, Fine tried to separate the community banks from the big boys in the minds of Washington politicians. "At that point," he recalled in an interview, "official Washington saw banks as all pretty much alike. But I realized this was a Wall Street centered crisis triggered by Wall Street and the shadow-banking industry.[*] The community banks around the country did not trigger this economic meltdown."

Fine's first objective was to plant the idea that community bankers did not deserve punishment for a crisis they did not cause. ICBA launched a public relations and lobbying campaign to try to explain this. Full-page ads were purchased in the three newspapers aimed at Capitol Hill,[†] op-eds were drafted for member bankers to place in their local papers, and ICBA officials aggressively sought interviews with reporters to make their pitch. Ads were taken out in financial publications and regional newspapers. "Our goal was to differentiate community banks from—the term we used was megabanks, the Wall Street megabanks. We made this about Main Street versus Wall Street."

Fine was delighted when, on January 27, 2009, Obama's new sec-

---

[*] "Shadow" banks were institutions such as mortgage brokers that performed the functions of banks but avoided government regulation.

[†] *Politico, Roll Call,* and *The Hill* are tabloids published when Congress is in session. They are a favorite advertising medium for special interests trying to influence the House and Senate.

retary of the treasury, Geithner, called him on the phone. It was Geithner's second day on the job, and he invited Fine to drop by the next day. "I don't routinely get calls from the secretary of the treasury," Fine said. A day later he was in the secretary's huge office on the second floor of the Treasury, looking out at the Ellipse and the Washington Monument, for a seventy-five-minute tête-à-tête with Geithner. Fine reviewed the ICBA's agenda for him, spelling out its desire to avoid blame for the Great Crash, and to avoid being unfairly punished in the reform process.

Fine recalled Geithner's words: " 'You're the very first meeting I've had as secretary of treasury, because I think community banks are important, and as president of the New York Fed, I was watching your campaigns in Washington and listening to your speeches and so forth, and I think you made some points.' " Said Fine, "That was kind of a big deal for ICBA."

Geithner promised Fine that regulatory reform legislation was coming, and Fine knew that "we had to make a decision: How were we going to posture ourselves for the legislation to come? . . . The gut reaction of the entire industry was, Of course we have to oppose, oppose, oppose, because it's going to mean more regulatory burden on us all. It's a disaster, we've got a bunch of liberals in government, the Democrats control everything. Seventy-five to 80 percent of my members are Republicans."

But Fine did not want to just oppose. First he had to persuade his ten-member executive committee to hold back. "I started to jawbone my ten members in April. I said look, there's going to be landmark legislation. You've got heavy Democratic majorities in both chambers, you've got a Democratic president. . . . Even if the Republicans were in charge, this is such a deep and horrendous economic crisis and financial crisis that this Congress cannot afford to do nothing. Something will happen. There will be a bill, and it will be sweeping in nature.

"I told the executive committee, we're going to take a calculated risk here. I can guarantee you that the Financial Services Roundtable, the ABA, the Financial Services Forum, the mortgage bankers, all of these other interest groups are going to oppose this thing tooth and nail, because it will be primarily focused on going after Wall Street."

But joining the big boys in a common front opposed to new reform proposals would be "the death of our industry," Fine said. "If we just joined up, our voice would be lost, and the community banks would just be road kill on the financial highway. Because we would have played right into the hands of Wall Street, and there were genuine issues that divided us." The challenge, he thought, was to try to influence the reform legislation so that it went after the real miscreants who caused the crash but left community banks alone, or even put them in an improved position.

"I said, Guys, look, Wall Street always has a seat at the table. They have the clout, they have the money, they have the influence, and they have nearly every main K Street lobby shop tied up, so they'll send swarms of lobbyists to Capitol Hill." This sentence is a wonderful example of Washington-speak. Fine meant that the big banks had retained most of the big lobbying firms, known collectively as K Street, where many of them were once located, to work against reforms.

"Jamie Dimon [CEO of JPMorgan Chase] gets invited regularly to the White House. Several other of the big Wall Street CEOs are regular guests at the White House. We're not. They can say 'oppose, oppose, oppose' and still have a seat at the table; we can't. If we say 'oppose, oppose, oppose,' not only do we not have a seat at the table, we don't have a voice in the debate, because we'll be subsumed by the big guys. We'll just be their little mouthpiece. We can't afford that path."

Fine persuaded his executive committee to approve his approach. When Frank and Dodd held hearings on the CFPA idea in June and July, Yingling testified at both, but neither Fine nor any other representative of the community bankers had anything to say. "Keep our powder dry" was the ICBA philosophy then, Fine explained. When Yingling invoked the community banks in his testimony, obviously hoping to burnish the ABA's position with the respectable aura of the hometown banks, Fine looked for ways to remind Frank and other members that the ICBA, not the ABA, spoke for those banks.

Frank understood what Fine was up to, and hoped to exploit the tension between the two banking organizations. He signaled this in the speech he gave to the National Press Club on July 27: "To the community banks, yes, they have been unfairly traduced, because they weren't the problem, but they have to be careful not to allow themselves to be used by some of their big, big brothers who would like to have them shelter them. We can set up a consumer protection agency that will respect the role of the community banks. They were not the perpetrators of the abuses, they will not be the subjects of the corrections, and they need to work with us to help us do that." This of course is just what Fine was telling his executive committee.

Frank was buttering up Fine and his members, and in a letter written a day or two later, Fine reciprocated in kind. "As we enter the August recess," he wrote to Frank, "I wanted to personally thank you and acknowledge your thoughtful leadership during [these] most critical times. I remain committed to working with you on behalf of the ICBA [on reform legislation] and meaningful consumer protection. I am deeply grateful for your recent comments to the National Press Club acknowledging the role of the community banks. ICBA strongly supports appropriate consumer protection and would not oppose the creation of a consumer regulatory structure that properly focuses efforts on those firms responsible for mistreatment and abuse of customers."

Flowery rhetoric of the kind employed in this exchange between Frank and Fine is as routine in Washington as political posturing or shameless self-promotion. But meaningful substance lay behind the words. Fine and Frank were warming up for some classic Washington deal making.

CHAPTER TWELVE

"We've Got an Opportunity Here"

Barney Frank and his staff worried that their inability to act on the consumer agency before the August district work period would allow the opponents of reform, especially hometown bankers, to turn members against the idea during their summer break. "The members don't want to spend August being lobbied on this," Frank said in mid-June. "They want to be able to spend August saying, Jeez, it's too late now, you should have come to me [sooner], it's already out of the House."

But Frank was wrong. Financial regulatory reform was largely forgotten during the August break, overtaken by a national debate on health care. Opponents of the Democrats' sweeping proposals to alter the system to provide health insurance to millions of uncovered Americans turned out for the town meetings of scores of House members, denouncing "Obamacare" and often creating a ruckus. The American political culture isn't good at multitasking. We tend to let the most controversial or dramatic topic of the moment take up nearly all the room for discussion and debate, and especially for news coverage. That is what happened in August 2009, when health care became Topics A, B, and C.

On August 25, Edward M. Kennedy succumbed to brain cancer at the age of seventy-seven. This development, long expected, had large implications for financial regulatory reform—not in Frank's House of Representatives, but in the Senate, where Chris Dodd was next in line to assume the chairmanship of Kennedy's committee on Health, Education, Labor and Pensions, the HELP committee. Frank was one of many politicians in Washington who expected Dodd to give up the chairmanship of Banking to take over HELP. (A senator can only be chairman of one major committee, so Dodd would have to choose.) In an interview in June, Frank said, "I think if Ted dies Dodd . . . will abandon the [Banking] committee altogether. I don't think there's any hesitation. . . . Somebody else can do a better job [on financial regulatory reform] starting from scratch."

Frank was wrong about this too. He had gotten impatient with Dodd, who hadn't made as much progress as Frank on writing a bill. But "somebody else" would have been Senator Tim Johnson of South Dakota, still far from fully recovered from his brain aneurysm, and always a reliable friend of the big banks. Johnson was next in seniority on Banking, and Senate Democrats, as we've seen, stuck religiously to seniority when appointing committee chairmen. Frank hoped that because of his health problems—he had difficulty speaking clearly, and he moved gingerly—Johnson would share the duties of chairman with one of Frank's favorites, Senator Jack Reed of Rhode Island, a former House colleague. Reed was liberal, bright, and hardworking—Frank's kind of member. But the idea of Johnson sharing power with Reed was probably a pipe dream. Johnson had shown no interest in it, and sharing power does not come naturally to senators.

When members of Congress gathered in Boston on August 29 for Kennedy's funeral, a rumor spread among those present that Dodd, who spoke eloquently at the funeral and served as a pallbearer, was going to take the chairmanship of HELP. Frank and Dave Smith of his staff, a former Kennedy employee, reported this "news" when they returned to Washington. But it too was wrong. There might have been a time when Dodd would have picked HELP over Banking, but that time had passed. The reason for this was political, not substantive. In Congress, politics almost always dominates substance.

Chris Dodd, who planned to run for reelection in sixteen months, was still in serious political trouble. His approval rating in Connecticut, according to a Quinnipiac University poll, had fallen to 33 percent in April, his lowest ever. Approval that low is a danger signal for any incumbent. For years before Dodd's run for president in 2007, he had been the most popular politician in the state, with approval ratings in the 60s. By July 2009, just before Kennedy died, it had inched back up to 42, but still, 52 percent of voters said they disapproved of Dodd's performance as their senator. Even more painful, only 35 percent said they considered Dodd "honest and trustworthy"; 55 percent did not. The poll included a hypothetical contest between Dodd and former congressman Rob Simmons, a potential opponent. Simmons led Dodd 48–39.

Dodd's unsuccessful presidential campaign and his rash decision to move his family to Iowa started his troubles. They were compounded by two articles on Dodd's real estate transactions. The first, in *Portfolio* magazine, in June 2008, disclosed that five years earlier Dodd had received mortgage loans on his houses in Washington and in Connecticut from Countrywide Financial, an increasingly notorious mortgage lender whose many subprime loans put the firm at the center of the housing meltdown. *Portfolio* revealed that Dodd's name was on a list of "friends of Angelo"—Angelo Mozilo, the Countrywide CEO—who received special attention from the firm as "VIPs."

Dodd denied he got any special break from Countrywide, and the interest rates on his mortgages seemed to confirm that. He told reporters—creatively if not convincingly—that he thought he was classified as a VIP because he was a loyal customer, not a senator. For months Dodd declined reporters' requests to provide more details about his mortgages, attracting more attention to the story, which played badly in Connecticut.*

Then seven months later, in February 2009, the *Hartford Courant* published a column by a former Republican legislator who suggested that what looked like a sweetheart deal had given Dodd ownership of a cottage in Ireland and ten acres of land. A subsequent *Courant* news story disclosed a complicated series of transactions that made Dodd owner of the property. Initially he had a partner, a Kansas City businessman who put up most of the original cost of the cottage. In an interview Dodd told the *Courant* that the businessman helped him when he was short of cash, but said he eventually paid the man a fair market price for full ownership of the property.

The *Courant*'s story on the purchase of the Irish cottage brought

---

* The Senate Ethics Committee investigated the Countrywide loans to Dodd and a second senator, and concluded that they did not seek or receive special breaks from the company. But the committee chastised Dodd for failing to see how it looked for a member of the Banking Committee to be put on a VIP list by Countrywide. "Once you became aware that your loans were in fact being handled through a program with the name 'V.I.P.' that should have raised red flags for you," the Ethics Committee wrote to Dodd in August 2009.

back the name of Edward R. Downe Jr., a Long Island socialite and former husband of Charlotte Ford, the auto heiress who was a long-time pal of Dodd's. As the *Courant* reported, it was Downe who, years earlier, had introduced Dodd to the Kansas City businessman who helped him buy the cottage.

Downe was a financier who pleaded guilty in 1992 to federal charges of tax and securities law violations, including insider trading that had earned him more than $3 million. After Downe pled guilty, Dodd stood by his friend. On the very last day of Bill Clinton's presidency in 2001, Dodd wrote a personal letter to Clinton seeking a presidential pardon for Downe. Clinton granted the pardon. Because of Dodd's intervention, the pardon request never went through the normal pardon procedures of the Department of Justice.

His relationship with Downe was an example of a side of Dodd that worried many of his friends and supporters in Washington and Connecticut. His gallivanting around Washington in the 1980s with Kennedy was another example. The handsome Irishman who could charm a doorknob could also be a serious legislator, but that wasn't all he could be.

For decades the charm and the legislative accomplishments helped keep him out of trouble. Before 2007, Dodd had very little experience with negative publicity, and when it grew worse in 2008 and 2009, he just hated it. The voters of Connecticut had always loved him, but suddenly, 55 percent of them did not consider him honest. He had been stung by criticism that he was an absentee chairman of the Banking Committee while he ran for president, and stung more sharply by the stories generated by the Countrywide and Irish cottage revelations. This was why Dodd decided to stay put in Banking.

The new staff director of the Banking Committee, Ed Silverman, had predicted this in an interview in June. Silverman, who spent the 1980s on Dodd's staff, then became a personal friend and advisor, had just returned to service as staff director in May. When the Obama White House hired away the previous director, Shawn Maher, Dodd had asked Silverman to find a successor. Silverman was then working as a strategist for RBS Greenwich Capital, a large bond-trading firm owned by the Royal Bank of Scotland. He tried to persuade Amy Friend to take the staff director's job, but she wanted to shape the regulatory reform legislation, not manage the committee. He could find no other strong candidate, and Dodd persuaded Silverman to take the job himself.

Dodd couldn't walk away from Banking, Silverman explained in mid-June, when he and everyone in the Senate knew that Kennedy was gravely ill and unlikely to return. "It would be politically disadvantageous to give up the Banking Committee in the midst of the biggest financial crisis in generations." Moving to HELP could be criticized as walking away from an opportunity to really help the voters of Connecticut who had been clobbered by the Great Crash. Dodd had had enough of being accused of neglecting his job as chairman of Banking.

On September 8, ten days after Kennedy's funeral, Dodd began calling colleagues to announce his decision: He would stay at Banking. The next day he went through one of Washington's rituals to make the announcement in front of television cameras. The Democrats held their weekly caucus lunch on September 9, and when it was over, Harry Reid and a few others would, as always, come out into the hallway just south of the Senate floor, under the Capitol's soaring ceilings, to talk to what was once "the press," but was now "the media."

The Capitol's hallways, with their floors of marble and ceramic tile, all echo, which exaggerates the noise of a crowd. These scrums after the caucus lunch had begun to attract quite a few cameras and reporters during the first year of Obama's contentious presidency. But the composition of the group was changing. The last newspaper reporter from a Connecticut paper assigned to Congress had been laid off by the *Connecticut Post* earlier in the year; no home state reporter covered Dodd in 2009. More than a dozen had covered him earlier in his career. Many of those in the hallway that day were young, and represented the three Capitol Hill tabloids, the cable news networks, and the trade press. For them, Dodd was just another name on the marquee.

The media's prominent role in today's congressional life reflected fundamental changes in American government and politics. The Senate before the era of the permanent campaign—in the 1960s and 1970s—was an inward-looking institution. Its members focused on legislation, and on their standing within their gentlemen's club. Few members actively curried favor with the news media; they spent more energy currying favor with one another. But the modern Congress was composed of political entrepreneurs who constantly cultivated public support, which meant playing to the cameras whenever they had the opportunity. This weekly gathering outside the caucus lunches was another chance to do that.

On this occasion Reid walked up to the microphones with two new chairmen and one old one, Dodd. The others were Tom Harkin of Iowa, who would assume the chairmanship of HELP, and Blanche

Lincoln of Arkansas, who would succeed Harkin as the chair of the Agriculture Committee. Among the HELP Democrats, Harkin ranked just behind Dodd in seniority; Lincoln ranked fifth on Agriculture, but the four ahead of her all had chairmanships of their own that they wanted to keep, so she was the most senior eligible candidate.

Reid spoke first, reiterating his support for the seniority system, a source of "stability and predictability" in the Senate. Seniority would be respected now, Reid said. "Senator Dodd had the opportunity to be chair of a number of committees," Reid continued. "To his credit, recognizing the amount of work ahead of him, he's decided to stay as chairman of the Banking Committee."

Dodd then explained that "I want to complete the job" of financial regulatory reform. This was best for "the voters of Connecticut." He added that he would also keep his promise to Kennedy "to fulfill the work left to be done on the health issue." Dodd also noted that he had spoken "a number of times" to Senator Shelby in the days since Kennedy's funeral. They had "a good working relationship," Dodd said, and they shared the goal of writing reform legislation "as comprehensively as we can." It remained an article of faith for Dodd that Shelby's cooperation was crucial to the enterprise.

Silverman was one of many aides who had come over to the Capitol for this ritual. When it had ended he looked pleased. He had wanted Dodd to stay at Banking. Silverman said his staff was close to finishing an "ideal version" of what regulatory reform could look like, a draft bill intended to both shape and provoke debate. The Banking Committee staff, led by Friend, had been working on it all summer. It would be ready in about a month, Silverman said, and would differ from the Obama administration's proposals on a number of important points. The administration had made too many concessions to what it considered political necessity, Silverman said. By contrast, Dodd wanted to offer a plan that would actually provide the best ways to confront the regulatory failings that had contributed to the Great Crash.

Silverman reported that during the summer, Shelby had hired several new aides with good credentials, people who knew the financial subjects and looked like they were serious about writing a comprehensive bill. This was another sign of Shelby's determination to collaborate, Silverman thought.

In a subsequent interview, Dodd gave a careful, detailed explanation of his decision to remain as chairman of Banking and try to push through a big regulatory reform bill.

"First of all the subject matter lends itself to resolution. Why do I say this? I say this respectfully of my colleagues, but this is the one subject matter that most members are willing to admit they don't know much about. Most people here think they'd be qualified to be secretary of state, secretary of defense, so when you bring something [proposed legislation] from the Foreign Relations Committee, the Armed Services Committee . . . there's no [senatorial] tentativeness, no reluctance to step up and offer your view." But the arcane financial issues were another matter. "In this committee, given the subject matter, if you're able to develop a consensus, the likelihood that you'll succeed I think is higher than most other committees [with] other subject matters. So that's the first reason I think we've got a chance."

Dodd was suggesting that if he could build bipartisan support for a bill in the Banking Committee, the full Senate would support it. That was why Shelby was so important to his calculations. "A lot [depends on] how you deal with people," Dodd said—perhaps his most important rule. "After Teddy's death, making this choice [of which chairmanship to take] . . . I went to talk to Shelby. Shelby and I have a very good relationship. He's very clear when he can work with me and when he cannot, for whatever reason. And if he can't, I will say, do you mind if I start working with some of the other [Republican] members? He has no problem with that whatsoever. So it is a wonderful way to deal with someone, when you actually know you can produce some results. . . . When I talked to him this summer about my choice [to remain chairman of Banking], he had a lot to do with the choice I made."

In conversation Dodd is not the most articulate man in Washington. His mind races ahead of his spoken words, so he doesn't always complete his thoughts. His next comments illustrated this tendency: "Basically I wanted to know whether I was dealing with sort of a rope-a-dope environment where there was a larger game going on here which is going to say 'no' and reap the benefits politically in 2010 with the elections, or whether we have a chance of doing something here. [Translation: Would the Republican leadership in the Senate, anxious to see Obama fail, block Shelby from agreeing on regulatory reform with Dodd?] And if we didn't have much of a chance of doing anything, then I might have reasonably made a different choice and said look, there are other matters, I can hold hearings on stuff that I passionately care about."

When Dodd asked Shelby directly if the Senate's Republican leadership, meaning Majority Leader Mitch McConnell of Kentucky, would ultimately order him not to make a deal with Dodd, Shelby avoided a specific answer. That would depend on the political context at the time, he said. Shelby could not commit McConnell to any position in advance. He also acknowledged that several of the Republicans on the Banking Committee might be hostile to a deal. But he wanted to try.

"Richard is serious about this," Dodd said several weeks after he decided to stick with the Banking Committee. "He understands this is one of those rare moments you get here. Most of the time we chew polenta—a little bit here, a little bit there. It's important, I don't minimize the importance of stuff [he meant the normal run of legislation], but you rarely get a chance—maybe once a generation—to deal with something that is very basic and very fundamental. We're in that kind of a moment now. . . . And Richard I think is very serious about doing something pretty fundamental here. And that had a lot to do with my decision to stay with this."

Dodd liked the fact that "there's so much attention being paid to health care and all these other issues, and you know the attention spans can only go so far, we're kind of under the radar screen on this." And he also felt ready to proceed. "I think we're kind of in the perfect moment here, where we've done a lot of work, there's a lot of understanding about these issues, and there's still a sense of enough urgency to it that I think people don't want to miss the moment to be a part of getting something done. . . . I hope to write this [reform bill] in a way that people [senators] will not want to go home to say, given the moment and opportunity to make our financial system more responsive to the needs of consumers, shareholders, depositors, and others, they said no." He thought a great many senators, faced with the horrific consequences of the Great Crash, would prefer to say yes.

"So all those are the reasons why I think we've got an opportunity here. It could easily blow apart because of something I can't predict at this juncture, but I think we're in fairly good shape as we're going forward."

This was a revealing glimpse of Dodd's mind at work. How to get something done was his principal concern. The importance of the substance was implied, not spelled out. Substance remained in the background, as it always would for Dodd. Tactics were his first consideration.

Dodd's analysis was correct in a way—there were reasons to be optimistic that the Senate would pass a big reform bill. But his analysis of how this would happen would prove utterly wrong.

CHAPTER THIRTEEN

In the Legislative Weeds

When Congress reconvened on September 8, 2009, Frank and his staff began an intense period of work and politicking on financial regulatory reform. For the next three months, the Financial Services Committee and then the whole House of Representatives would demonstrate how complicated, consequential legislation can be created.

Frank realized during the difficult July days when he put down the small rebellion among his Democrats over the new consumer agency that he was not going to be able to rely on the Obama administration to the extent he had hoped. "They're busy," Frank said in July, referring to the distractions created by legislative battles over health care and energy legislation. "And their political antennae are not so great"—a reference to the controversial provisions of the Treasury's legislation to create the Consumer Financial Protection Agency.

"The substance has problems," Jeanne Roslanowick said a fortnight after the administration draft arrived. "We need to dial back the proposal without appearing to abandon it or undermining the principles and key reforms." Roslanowick and Frank were both sensitive to accusations from the left that they were being too soft on the big banks.

As it became clear during July that the administration draft was creating too many political problems, Frank began to rethink his own position. "I really have to know what's in here," he told an aide in mid-July, referring to Treasury's legislative language. He called Elizabeth Warren to feel her out on the aspects of the Treasury's CFPA proposal that had provoked controversy, particularly the plain vanilla provision, and was relieved to discover that she thought it was a bad idea. Frank concluded that his committee would have to improve the administration's drafts.

"Barney must have said fifty times in the last few days, 'I'm writing this thing,' " Roslanowick said at the end of July. "He has taken ownership, he's in dealing mode, and this is more interesting for him. He's more focused now; he sees for himself the flaws in the administration's CFPA draft."

After thinking things over during his August break, Frank began to talk optimistically about the opportunity the administration's missteps had given him. He was going to disarm critics of the Treasury draft by dropping several provisions that he thought were ill-advised anyhow.

"The administration badly over-drafted the bill," he said in early September. "One of the things that's nice is that the attacks [from critics of the CFPA proposal] are almost all on things that we're not going to do. It is true that if you read their draft, it might be [concluded] that any retailer who extends credit to anybody would be covered [by the CFPA]. We don't intend to do this, it's only about financial products. If you have a store credit card that you use only in that store, you're not going to be covered. . . . Plain vanilla products, product standardization [as proposed in the Treasury draft]—we're not going to do any of that. And we are going to stress, which they didn't, that it will regulate the check cashers and the payday lenders, the nonbank competitors" of the community banks that were anxious about the consumer agency.

As often happened, Frank's formidable brain rushed ahead of his staff, skipping over details that might bog them down for days and jumping to optimistic conclusions before—in the opinion of Roslanowick and her colleagues—optimism was warranted. This was life with Barney Frank. It could drive them batty, but most of his staff seemed to enjoy the exhilaration of dealing with such a formidable figure, even when he exasperated them. And he did that often.

The August recess had given the staff a chance to get a head start on the drudge work of legislating: preparing analyses of provisions in the administration's drafts, explaining the choices Frank would have to make, and reporting on how various provisions could affect the interested parties, from individual companies and industries to the existing regulatory agencies and members of the committee. Frank may have said "I'm writing this thing," but as a practical matter he would write very little: His staff and experts from the executive branch would do all of the drafting, under his supervision. Occasionally he would propose a phrase or sentence.

Staff members had two distinct responsibilities when working on such a big bill. First, they had to hear out and sometimes seek out the opinions of every party that would be significantly affected by it. This meant, for example, hearing the complaints of the Federal Reserve Board and the Federal Deposit Insurance Corporation about the proposal to deprive them of their historic (if little used) consumer protection functions by transferring them to the new CFPA; hearing the banks' complaints about the consumer agency; hearing the investment banks protest against new rules on the derivatives markets that would cost them money; hearing the concerns of individual members of the committee, often pleading on behalf of specific constituents who disliked some aspect of the proposal; and more. Fulfilling this responsibility required thousands of meetings—literally thousands—many of them with the lobbyists who worked for banks, trade associations, individual corporations, consumer advocates, labor unions, and others who had a stake in regulatory reform.

Lobbying is a huge Washington industry. Because it isn't easy to define "lobbying," its true scope cannot be precisely measured. The officially reported expenditures on lobbying (required by law) disclose only the costs of the most direct forms of influence peddling, and they have risen to more than $3.5 billion a year. Year in and year out, the financial sector spends more on lobbying than any other industry. During 2009–10, the interests most concerned about financial regulatory reform—banks, insurance companies, mortgage banks and brokers, securities and investment firms, credit and finance companies, and credit unions—spent considerably more than $750 million on lobbying the government. Together those industries retained more than 2,700 individual lobbyists in 2009, and nearly as many in 2010.

Staff on Capitol Hill generally consider it part of their job to meet with lobbyists who ask for a meeting. After twenty-six years working on the staff of Financial Services, Jeanne Roslanowick had good relations with numerous lobbyists. She knew the phone numbers of many of them by heart. And she had total confidence in her own ability and that of her staff to consort with lobbyists without being corrupted or blinded by them. "Floyd Stoner [of the American Bankers Association] could take me out dancing every night of the week, and it wouldn't affect what I think or what I do," she said emphatically. No one who worked with her doubted the truth of that assertion.

In a democracy, Roslanowick thought, everyone has a right to petition their government, "and it's our job to listen to their concerns. And we do. And it's not corrupt to do so." Often it was helpful. Lobbyists "can explain the impact of our ideas on the real world," which helps avoid mistakes and unintended consequences. "Lobbyists help us understand if we are solving a problem effectively. You never want to rely on one source," she observed.

The staff's second responsibility was to weigh all the special pleading, and either make recommendations or offer choices to those who would make the final decisions. In this case, "those" were just one man, Barney Frank. Eventually other members would vote on specific elements in the legislation that the staff would write for Frank, but in this important period when it was being shaped, he alone would decide what was in, and what was out. Sometimes he would delegate particular topics to colleagues; on other occasions he would ask advice from a colleague and actually take it. But Frank had the power to make the choices, and the committee staff directed all of its reporting and analysis to him.

Staff did this in a blizzard of memoranda typically headed "Financial Services Committee Staff Memo" and written in the acronym-heavy jargon that was the shared language of Capitol Hill staff. These memos were addressed to "Barney" from staff members identified by their first names, with their telephone extensions in parentheses after each name so that Frank could pick up the phone to ask any of the authors a question. He did this regularly. In September and October 2009 many of these went to Frank to prod final decisions on the contents of the legislation.

The memoranda were written for a knowledgeable expert, not a layman. They told Frank where interest groups stood, what the relevant government agencies thought, and often what specific members of the committee preferred. They also reflected preferences Frank had already made clear in the many conversations he held, formally and informally, with the people who worked for him. A typical memo on the Consumer Financial Protection Agency, sent to Frank on October 7,

2009, began this way: "We are beginning to prepare the manager's amendment (MA) for mark-up of the CFPA bill. Highlighted below are major issues requiring your decision before we can complete the MA for the mark-up . . ."

The manager's amendment would contain the changes Frank [the "manager" of the bill] proposed to make to the language submitted at the end of June by the Obama administration. For example, it would include a list of "exclusions" enumerating the types of merchants whose business would not be regulated by the new agency. This memo said, "we [have] excluded from CFPA purview any merchant, retailer or seller of non-financial services that provides credit and other financial activities exclusively for the purpose of enabling its customers to purchase the goods and services it offers." There followed a more detailed enumeration of specifically excluded transactions, such as "student loans where the university or for-profit trade school makes the loan."

Many of the issues raised in these memoranda were mind-numbingly technical. One example: A staff memo of September 17, 2009, addressed the power of the new Financial Services Oversight Council, the body of existing regulators that Frank and the administration had agreed should perform the role of systemic risk regulator. The draft legislation provided by the Treasury considered how the new council might resolve disputes among existing regulators in specific circumstances. Here's a typical passage: "The Council's only specific interagency dispute resolution role is mediating disputes about the FRB's [that's the Federal Reserve Board's] exercise of backup enforcement authority for payment system supervision. . . . Should we pursue language to make the Council's dispute resolution role more concrete?"

Frank was proud of his ability to take on even such arcane matters, though he didn't always enjoy doing so. "I've learned an enormous amount of things I never wanted to know," he quipped.

And Roslanowick was proud of her team's ability to give Frank the information he needed to make decisions about the legislation. Twenty professionals, nearly all hired by her, shared the work. During these months in the fall of 2009 they got used to six- or seven-day work-weeks, long hours, endless meetings, late nights of writing. Without their contributions, no legislation could ever have been enacted. Yet what they did got no attention from the news media, and very little recognition from members of the committee, though the serious members certainly understood their importance.

The idea that staff work should be essentially invisible was deeply rooted in the culture of Capitol Hill. Any advertisement of the real role of staff could undermine the image that members of the House and Senate worked hard to project. Members share a compulsion to appear knowledgeable, judicious, even wise, and of course, influential. But apart from a handful of committee chairmen and members of the leadership, the actual power of a member of Congress is considerably less than most voters probably assume. This is especially true in the House, where one member acting alone cannot accomplish anything. Senate rules empower individual members, so they can occasionally make a personal difference, but that is quite rare.

This reality conflicts with members' desire to be seen as active agents who are taking care of business for the folks at home. But members can compensate for the reality of their relative impotence as legislators. Comforted by the thought that most voters wouldn't understand the arcane details of the legislative process in any event, they can concentrate on two objectives that everyone can understand.

The first is "constituent service," which usually consists of intervening with executive branch agencies to help voters solve problems they're having with "the government." The most common examples involve payments from the Social Security Administration, whose benefits support more than 50 million Americans. The Veterans Administration is another federal agency that can easily frustrate its constituents, who often turn to their congressman or senator for help. Most federal agencies maintain teams of dedicated civil servants to respond to queries from members of Congress who write on behalf of citizens who have a problem. Because Congress provides the money to run those agencies, they are generally responsive. Members quickly learn that nothing is more useful at the next election than a reputation for providing good constituent service. Of course, the actual work of constituent service is done by employees of the member—staff.

The second tactic members use to try to advertise their effectiveness in Washington is to "bring home the bacon." For many years this was a common practice, most often pursued through earmarks, or directed appropriations of funds for named projects, that members worked to arrange for their home states or districts. All those Shelby centers at Alabama's universities were classic examples. The lobbying scandal set off by the case of Jack Abramoff, who ended up in jail for his misdeeds, put a spotlight on earmarks that resulted in a radical diminution of their number and size in the 110th and 111th Congresses (2007 to 2011), but they never disappeared entirely.

When Congress takes on a big issue like financial regulatory reform, the members of the committees principally responsible for the legislation like to feel that they play an important role. But unless Frank decided to defer to a colleague on a particular issue, which he did only rarely, the members had less influence on the legislative product than did members of the committee staff.

They were an impressive group, many with years of experience with the issues being debated. Dave Smith, the chief economist, once supervised the budget of the city of New York, and was a longtime aide to Edward M. Kennedy in the Senate. He was the senior member of the team. Lawranne Stewart was the egghead of the group. She had the title of deputy counsel of the committee. A lawyer and former banker, she spent thirteen years as a staff attorney for the Federal Reserve Board and four years at the Treasury Department during the Clinton administration before joining the Democratic committee staff in 2001. Roslanowick considered her a brilliant lawyer who understood the most complicated issues. Michael Beresik was a veteran of the Senate Banking Committee staff and the Clinton-era Treasury Department, where he was a deputy assistant secretary. He also worked as a lobbyist for H&R Block, the tax preparation service. He joined the Financial Services Committee staff in 2007. Andrew Miller, another lawyer, had just come to the staff at the beginning of 2009. After several years in private practice working on exotic financial products, Miller spent eight years as a senior attorney at the Federal Reserve, then two years as a vice president and deputy general counsel of Fannie Mae, the Federal National Mortgage Association. He became one of Roslanowick's favorites because of his quick mind and capacity for learning the political as well as substantive parts of his new job.

Roslanowick had developed strong ideas about the staff's responsibilities, particularly its obligations to the chairman or, when her Democrats were in the minority, the ranking member. The way she describes these duties illuminates the mind-set of a senior congressional aide who was a potentate in her own world.

The first obligation, she thought, was to provide "coherent and comprehensive information regarding the positions of all relevant stakeholders—the administration, the regulatory agencies, other members, the Senate, state officials and regulators, companies, trade associations, advocacy groups, think tanks—and staff's own analysis and assessment of the legitimacy of the concerns voiced. All this should be informed by staff's own views of the right policy direction based on their experience and substantive expertise, and their view of the political realities. . . . In effect, it's our responsibility to get him [Frank] all the relevant facts, the value judgments, and the premises on which they're based—everything necessary for a fully informed decision."

The staff also has to evaluate the concerns expressed to them by interested parties—to separate the phony cries of alarm from legitimate questions. "Folks can come in with an endless array of 'major concerns'—it's our job to ferret out what cuts to the bone or comes close. . . .

"Some of this information and perspective comes to us naturally—companies' trade associations, advocates, constituents ask to share their views and we open our doors to anyone who wants to do that. . . . And we are, of course, routinely in touch with administration agencies, members' offices, etc., on a day-to-day basis. . . . When perspectives aren't volunteered, it's our responsibility to reach out to those who may have a legitimate interest and perspective, and bring their views into the calculus." Roslanowick wanted to be sure not just that they had found the best ways to deal with individual issues, but also "whether the overall balance works both as a policy and political matter."

Doing your duty to the boss "feels more like an art than a science to me," Roslanowick said. "I find there is an element to all this that is intuitive or instinctive and hard to describe. You can imagine how one could easily get overwhelmed by the sheer volume of information and competing views—how do you decide what's important, what matters, etc.? How do you find the balance? Particularly given the fact that, for everyone who comes in with ten well-paid lawyers, we might have two or three staff to put in the room. . . . I have people making $150,000 a year negotiating with people making $800,000, $900,000, and they are almost always better than the people they're negotiating with. The demands of their clients require industry representatives to view the world through a particular prism that narrows their vision. The caliber of the staff makes such a difference here—having staff with substantive expertise, sharp minds and good intuition who are not ideologically bound but who like to leave their minds free to think about good policy. They are enthusiastic about what government at its best is designed to do.

"Staff at their best know or learn how to read people and situations and perspectives, how to read between the lines, and whom to trust—and how to discriminate between talking points and real issues. Cross-examination skills are very useful here, but at bottom it's people talking honestly and forthrightly to others with differing views and trying to do the right thing. . . . Equally important is having staff who work well together, and who can communicate effectively with both allies and opponents—you can't learn if you can't listen and communicate. We talked and talked and thought and thought, and talked and thought again—with each other and everyone we could think of."

Andrew Miller, who was new to the Hill in 2009 and realized he had a lot to learn, developed his own rules for good staff work. "You have to put everything in front of him [Frank]," Miller concluded. "Barney needs to know what everyone thinks about every choice he has to make. You can't censor the news."

Miller also learned that he had to be both forthcoming and utterly straight when responding to suggestions for particular changes in the legislation. "You can't just say, 'That's a dumb idea' " when an interested party—outside interest group, government regulator, whoever—makes a proposal. "You have to say, 'That's a dumb idea—how do you want me to present it to Barney?' " When the suggestion comes from a member or a member's staff, "you have to be more diplomatic. You have to be quick on your feet so you can explain what might be controversial about a suggestion they are making, and explain the implications of their idea for Barney"—explaining who might be angered by the proposal, or disadvantaged if it were adopted.

In the fall of 2009 Miller discovered how hard he could work. "I have never been busier in my life," he said. He saw little of his four children for three months. "I consider those months the high point of my career," Miller said. They were "tense, difficult, challenging, but all in all a very positive experience."

To make it a positive experience, of course, something concrete had to be accomplished. First, regulatory reform had to be formulated and then enacted in the House of Representatives.

CHAPTER FOURTEEN

Making Sausage

During the hectic final months of 2009, the House of Representatives converted the concept of "financial regulatory reform" into an enormous piece of legislation called the Wall Street Reform and Consumer Protection Act (H.R. 4173). When published by the Government Printing Office, it filled a paperback book 2,223 pages long. Something big had happened.

Every such bill represents a kind of miracle of American democracy. Ideas and interests collide, a path of least resistance is discovered, the House or Senate—and eventually, both—enact. In the history of the republic this has happened thousands of times. Some new laws have little palpable effect; others make large changes in American life. Every successful legislative enterprise vindicates the founding fathers' optimism that the elected officials of a representative government can actually govern a vast nation. When the republic was launched nearly two and a half centuries ago, this was a radical idea. At various times since, it has seemed quite ridiculous. But periodically, the founders' vision has been fulfilled; the system they invented has worked.

Even when some success is achieved, the legislative process can be ugly. This is what Otto von Bismarck, the German statesman, had in mind when he made his famous remark that "Laws are like sausages, it is better not to see them being made." Perhaps not seeing the messy procedural details was "better" by the standards of polite society in

Bismarck's nineteenth-century Prussia. But it can also be both educational and entertaining to sneak behind the curtain and watch the
slicing and dicing that produces the sausage.

There is one unavoidable fact about legislating in a democratic
system: No single person, faction, or interest can get everything it
wants. Legislating inevitably means compromising, except in the rare
circumstances when consensus is so strong that one dominant view
can prevail with ease. Such a consensus, for example, allows resolu-
tions saluting Veterans Day to pass the House and Senate year after
year with no dissent. But few real issues have the kind of support that
Veterans Day enjoys.

So when Barney Frank turned his attention to solving the political problems raised by the proposed Consumer Financial Protection
Agency, he knew he would have to make compromises. This instinct
comes naturally to Frank; he had internalized the idea that compromise was inevitable when he was still a member of the Massachusetts
legislature. He skipped quickly to more sophisticated questions: How
little compromise could he get away with? And with whom should he
try to compromise first?

Frank tried to answer the first of those questions on September 25,
when he released a new "discussion draft" of the CFPA legislation
that his staff had written with help from the Obama administration.
It included the changes Frank had decided to make to the administration's CFPA proposal to pacify his committee Democrats, including
limits on the CFPA's authority. Frank had persuaded the administration to publicly accept these changes.

With whom should he try to strike a deal first? Frank's answer to
that one was simple: Camden Fine, president of the Independent Community Bankers of America. Fine's decision not to join the big banks
in immediate, all-out opposition to the proposed consumer agency
had been a calculated risk that, as we've seen, Frank appreciated. That
was why he sent a positive signal to Fine in his Press Club speech at the
end of July. And Frank was delighted when Fine wrote him the letter
praising that speech—Fine's own signal, which made it clear that he
had understood Frank's.

By late September, Frank was ready to try to make a deal. He asked
Roslanowick to invite Fine for a meeting.

"I got a call from Jeanne," Fine recalled later. "She asked me to
come over, the chairman wanted to meet with me." Fine went to the

meeting by himself. Frank was accompanied by Roslanowick, Michael Beresik, and Jim Segel.

"Barney started to talk very fast: 'There's going to be a bill, and either you're going to have to get on the bus or be run over by it.' I said I didn't necessarily agree. At that point he said, 'My staff says you're really worried about this consumer agency.' And I said, 'Yes, I think it's totally unnecessary for the regulated part of the industry [he meant banks, as opposed to the other financial institutions, mortgage brokers and the like whom Fine blamed for causing the Great Crash]. If you want to create a consumer agency for the shadow-banking sector go at it.' " Fine repeated the banker's usual argument: "The bank regulators already have consumer divisions, we don't need another consumer division . . . to be shoved down our throats, we're up to our eyeballs in that stuff, and have been for years."

"And then came a turning point," said Fine. "Barney turned to his staff and said, 'Jeanne, could you and the others please leave me alone with Cam? I just want to talk with Mr. Fine.' They were surprised, filed out of the room, and Barney says: 'Okay, Cam, it's just you and me, what's it going to take to at least—I don't expect you to support the consumer agency in public, but what's it going to take to get you to be neutral, just not say anything?'

" 'Well, Mr. Chairman, that's going to take a lot!' I said first of all, 'We can't have examination forces from this bureau coming into our banks. They just can't take another one. They already have external auditors, they have the FDIC or the Fed or the OCC [Comptroller of the Currency] coming in, they get compliance exams now, they have IT [information technology] exams, they have safety and soundness exams—hell, these banks only have twenty or thirty employees, and they're being eaten alive by exams.' "

The two men began to discuss the idea of limiting the jurisdiction of the new agency's examiners to larger banks. After some back-and-forth, they settled on a standard: The CFPA's supervisory authority would extend only to banks whose assets exceeded $10 billion, a number the Federal Reserve had already suggested marked the line between small and big banks. (The assets of the biggest banks are measured in trillions of dollars.) "I'm okay with that standard," Fine said. He knew, but did not volunteer at that moment, that of the 5,300 institutions that belonged to the ICBA, just four had assets of greater than $10 billion. Frank understood, but also did not say, that the issue on which he was compromising only involved who would enforce the CFPA's new rules at the smaller banks—the rules the new agency wrote would apply to banks of all sizes. Frank's compromise was to allow the traditional regulators to do the enforcing at the smaller banks most of the time.

In that meeting with Fine, he began with another proposal. As Fine remembered it, Frank said, "What if there was a CFPA examiner with the FDIC, riding along in the car, so to speak?" Fine didn't like that idea: "I think that's still too much, that's dangerous," he remembered saying.

Frank had still another idea: What if there was a random sampling system that would put a CFPA person on the regulatory team, but they wouldn't have supervisory authority, they'd have to yield to the regulator in charge, they could make suggestions, and the prudential regulator would have to consider the suggestions? And the law could require that the CFPA person take into account any objections offered by the prudential regulator? Fine said this arrangement could be workable.

Frank impressed Fine by talking with apparent candor about the politics of his committee. As Fine remembered it, Frank said, "Here's my problem, Cam. I've got some pretty radical guys on the left on my committee, and they're not going to like this. They're purists, and they don't want any compromise at all. I've got to do enough to satisfy them while at the same time satisfying the right as well." Fine said he understood this reality.

Then Fine asked Frank about his secret weapon, "the Gutierrez amendment." The ICBA had persuaded Luis Gutierrez, the once outspoken Chicago congressman, to introduce a proposal that would change the formula by which banks were assessed to support the Federal Deposit Insurance Corporation's bailout fund, so that big banks would pay more and small ones less. This is the fund the FDIC uses to finance its insurance of all the assets in regulated banks whenever an FDIC-insured bank fails. Historically the assessment was based on the deposits held by a bank.

The ICBA thought it should be based on total assets, not just deposits. The big banks held relatively fewer deposits and much larger assets from sources other than their customers' bank accounts. So basing the assessment on all assets would shift more of the insurance premium burden to the big banks. Fine pointed out that small banks were paying 32 percent of the total FDIC assessments, though they held just 19 percent of total bank liabilities. Frank agreed that this seemed unfair,

Fine recalled. He also told Fine that the big banks "have about as much credibility around here as Ahmadinejad [the president of Iran]," a line Fine gleefully reported to his board of directors.

Frank told Fine he would allow the Gutierrez amendment to go forward if Sheila Bair, the director of the FDIC, approved the idea. Fine already knew she was sympathetic. The change would save community banks about $1.5 billion a year—more than 30 percent of what they were paying in FDIC assessments. This was money that went "straight to their bottom lines," as Fine put it. Rarely is a Washington lobbyist able to deliver such a cash benefit to his clients as Fine would with this change in the FDIC assessments.

"So we go back and forth, back and forth, and we finally agreed to a deal," Fine recalled. "Barney to me is the consummate [politician]— I mean he's just brilliant, I think. I have great respect for Barney Frank whether I agree or disagree with him on issues. . . . And he said, 'Will you keep your association at least neutral [on the new consumer agency]? I'm not asking you to come out in support, but will you just stay silent and keep neutral?' . . . I said I can make that work, we've got a deal. We shook hands actually, I reached across the desk and shook his hand."

Fine rushed back to his office and wrote an e-mail to his board. With characteristic enthusiasm for his own accomplishment, Fine put this headline on his message: "ULTRA SECRET—BURN BEFORE READING—EYES ONLY—DO NOT SHARE OR DISSEMINATE TO ANYONE!" After warning that any leak could be disastrous, Fine recounted his meeting with Frank. Then, using the language that many Washington operators consider English, he concluded:

"The bottom line is that I think at the end of the day we can work a deal that pretty much gets our banks out from under the CFPA rock, but hangs the megabanks out there. . . . The take-away is that ICBA is the player on the House financial reform legislation and the other financial trades [trade associations—he was referring primarily to the American Bankers Association] are not. This is a very unusual position for ICBA. . . . We are on the inside, and the other guys are wondering what is happening."

"A few days later," Fine recalled, "we bumped into each other, both of us going to the same fundraiser at a Capitol Hill townhouse, and I said, 'Oh, hi, Chairman,' and he said, 'Cam, I've got this thing done on my side, will you keep your side of the bargain?' I said, 'I shook your hand, I'll keep my side of the bargain.' And I did."

This was the first big deal made on the path to what would become, nine months later, the Dodd-Frank bill, and it made an important difference. Frank had neutralized one of the most influential interests in the game, one whose sway with members he feared—the community bankers. He had done this shrewdly, without giving up anything he considered vital to the reform effort generally or the consumer agency specifically. He had made Fine a partner, and their partnership proved invaluable over the months ahead.

Though the Frank-Fine deal was one of the most important made during the odyssey of financial regulatory reform, the world at large knew nothing about it. The meeting between the two men on September 25 was never reported anywhere in the news media. The small number of people who knew about it kept the secret. This happened again and again in the months that followed. Most of the important, backstage events that made Dodd-Frank possible happened out of public view and remained there.

Even the Gutierrez amendment was treated as a stealth event by the news media. It got no attention from any important news outlet, even when it was approved by the Financial Services Committee on November 19 by a voice vote, with no recorded opposition. Ultimately it became part of the final Dodd-Frank bill. It cost the big banks big bucks—at least $1.4 billion in increased dues for the FDIC in its first year in force, every dollar of which was saved by a small bank whose assessment went down.

Jeanne Roslanowick worried about the Consumer Financial Protection Agency. She was concerned that it had become a lightning rod for criticism from many directions that would distract attention from the elements of the reform package that she considered more important: the new systemic risk regulator and the resolution authority to enable regulators to put failing financial firms out of business in an orderly fashion.

She was upset with the Treasury Department's draft, which she thought had been largely responsible for the uprising among news and blues nervous about the new consumer agency. Michael Barr, the assistant secretary of the Treasury primarily responsible for the

On February 25, 2009, President Obama invited this group to discuss financial regulatory reform. Sen. Chris Dodd sits at Obama's right, next to him is Sen. Richard Shelby, Shawn Maher (arms crossed), Secretary of the Treasury Timothy Geithner (back to camera), White House chief of staff Rahm Emanuel (back to camera), Lawrence Summers, Phil Schiliro, Rep. Spencer Bachus, and Rep. Barney Frank. Maher and Schiliro worked in the White House office of legislative affairs as the president's lobbyists on Capitol Hill. Dodd had insisted the White House invite Shelby, ranking Republican on the Banking Committee, to demonstrate its interest in a bipartisan bill.

The dramatic meeting in Speaker Nancy Pelosi's conference room on September 18, 2009, where Secretary of the Treasury Hank Paulson (the bald, clean-shaven man opposite Pelosi) warned of imminent catastrophe. "If we don't act in a very huge way, you can expect another Great Depression, and this is going to be worse," he told the group. It included House and Senate leaders, Ben Bernanke of the Federal Reserve (with the beard) and Chris Cox of the Securities and Exchange Commission, to Paulson's left. Barney Frank sits on Bernanke's right; Chris Dodd on Cox's left.

Mr. Chairman—Barney Frank holds forth from the top row of members' seats in the House Financial Services Committee. Frank became chairman in January 2007, and he loved the job.

The chairman and the ranking member—Chris Dodd and Richard Shelby—of the Senate Banking Committee. The two had a cordial relationship, dined together often, with their wives, and spent many hours working on a bipartisan version of regulatory reform legislation, an effort that came to naught. Democratic staff blamed the man sitting behind them, William Duhnke, Republican staff director of Banking, for complicating the senators' negotiations.

Timothy Geithner, Obama's boyish secretary of the treasury, testifies to the House Financial Services Committee. Geithner's tenure got off to a rocky start when the Senate committee considering his nomination discovered that he had failed to pay taxes for a nanny who looked after his children. But by the spring of 2009 he had established considerable authority by his forceful testimony and ability to answer members' questions.

Freshman senators Mark Warner of Virginia (left), a Democrat, and Bob Corker of Tennessee, a Republican, hit it off when they first met at President Obama's inauguration in January 2009. Both members of the Banking Committee, they decided to collaborate on financial regulatory reform, an unusual bipartisan team. Here they are giving a television interview outside the U.S. Capitol.

Sheila Bair, a Kansas Republican who once worked for Senator Bob Dole, became chairman of the Federal Deposit Insurance Corporation (FDIC) in 2006. Her political skills and personal charm made her a favorite among members of both parties. She had considerable authority on Capitol Hill. When the Republican leader of the Senate charged that Dodd's reform bill would perpetuate "bailouts" of big banks, Bair boldly contradicted him.

Paul Volcker, chairman of the Federal Reserve Board of Governors from 1979 to 1987, was eighty-two years old when he gave testimony to the Senate Banking Committee on the "Volcker rule" to ban banks from making risky investments with their own capital. Volcker had enormous influence during the debate on financial regulatory reform. Senator Warner called him "the hundred and first senator."

Mitch McConnell (left), Kentucky senator and minority leader of the Senate, and John Boehner. Boehner stayed in the background during the legislative struggles over financial regulatory reform, but McConnell gave himself a leading role. He looked for ways to please Wall Street bankers who began to give substantially more money to Republican causes in 2009–2010 than they had in prior years, but also told them that it was politically impossible to try to block financial regulatory reform.

Jonathan Miller (left), one of Dodd's favorite members of the Banking Committee staff and an expert on housing and consumer issues, talks with Mark Oesterle, Republican counsel to Banking and a longtime aide to Shelby. They are outside the Russell Senate Office Building. These were two of the most influential aides on Capitol Hill.

Chris Dodd (left); Ed Silverman, staff director of the Banking Committee; and Jonathan Miller sit on the floor of the Russell Senate Office Building, outside Dodd's office, on a Saturday morning. They were waiting for a Capitol police officer to let them into Dodd's office. Weekend work was normal during the months the financial reform bill was being written.

Elizabeth Warren, Barney Frank, and Travis Plunkett, of the Consumer Federation of America, talk to reporters in the meeting room of the House Financial Services Committee. Warren, a Harvard Law School professor, came up with the idea for a new Consumer Financial Protection Agency, and promoted it vigorously. She had to persuade Frank that it was a good idea, but when she did he became its avid advocate. Plunkett was an important lobbyist for the CFPA,

representing his organization and the ad hoc group created by labor unions and other liberal groups to promote a consumer agency, Americans for Financial Reform.

Julie Chon (left), the derivatives expert on the staff of the Senate Banking Committee, explaining Dodd-Frank at the French Foreign Ministry in Paris. Dealing with foreigners was part of Chon's job, and foreign experts helped her understand how derivatives markets might be better regulated.

Amy Friend, chief counsel of the Senate Banking Committee, talks with Dodd and Senator Carl Levin of Michigan (right) just outside the Senate chamber during the floor debate on Dodd's financial reform bill. Friend, usually with a stack of documents, was often at Dodd's side.

Neal Wolin, deputy secretary of the treasury, was instrumental in finding compromises with difficult members of both House and Senate on issues that had to be resolved before Dodd-Frank could be enacted. Wolin was the only senior official at Treasury with extensive experience in the private sector. He had run the insurance companies of the Hartford Group between stints in Washington.

Edward L. Yingling was the president of the American Bankers Association during the deliberations on Dodd-Frank. The son of a former chief clerk of the Senate Banking Committee who worked for years as an ABA lobbyist on Capitol Hill, he calculated that Barney Frank would pass a tough bill in the House that would then be moderated in the Senate, where a bipartisan approach was likely. Yingling warned his members that the banks would be on the defensive, even if events played out as he expected them to. But they did not, and Yingling ultimately was outmaneuvered by Camden Fine, in effect a rival who was president of the Independent Community Bankers, a trade association of small banks.

Camden Fine won more for his members than any other lobbyist working on the bill. His members were exempted from some examinations by the new Consumer Financial Protection Bureau, and saved $1.5 billion from a change in the way assessments were levied by the Federal Deposit Insurance Corporation, so big banks would contribute much more.

Neal Wolin (left) talks with Michael Barr, assistant secretary of the treasury for financial institutions, and Diana Farrell of the National Economic Council, in front of the White House. These were the Obama administration's three key actors on financial regulatory reform.

Representative Maxine Waters, a Los Angeles Democrat, was a leader of the Congressional Black Caucus faction on the House Financial Services Committee. She led the boycott by the committee's ten African American members of the final committee votes on Barney Frank's financial regulatory reform bill, which she organized to pressure the Obama administration to do more for minority-owned businesses suffering in the Great Recession.

Lloyd Blankfein, the CEO of Goldman Sachs, testifies on April 27, 2010, before the Senate Permanent Subcommittee on Investigations, chaired by Senator Carl Levin, Democrat from Michigan. Blankfein and half a dozen colleagues from Goldman Sachs were lambasted by senators from both parties during a long day of testimony. Senator John McCain, the Arizona Republican, told Blankfein there was "no doubt" that his firm had behaved "unethically."

Spencer Bachus, the senior Republican on the House Financial Services Committee, addresses the conference committee that worked out the differences between the House and Senate bills. Frank and Paul Kanjorski of Pennsylvania sit to Bachus's right. Andrew Miller of Frank's staff sits behind Bachus, reading a document.

Frank and Dodd shake hands at dawn on June 14, 2010, after signing the conference report that melded their two bills into the legislation that had just been named "Dodd-Frank." The woman behind Dodd is Jeanne Roslanowick, staff director of Frank's committee.

President Obama signs the Dodd-Frank bill into law at a ceremony in Washington. Dodd and Frank are behind Obama's left shoulder. All the others were members of the House and Senate. Blanche Lincoln, Democratic senator from Arkansas, is third from the left. Tim Johnson, Democratic senator from South Dakota, is at the far right.

draft, was not one of her favorites. She understood why his draft had alarmed bankers and their allies—she thought it was too aggressively anti-bank. She opposed playing to the popular anger displayed in the AIG bonus controversy. "You play to the anger at your peril," she said. "You can play to it, but then it's a savage beast."

She was struck by Barr's failure to understand the limits of the administration's power once the legislative process was under way. When the controversy over his draft of the CFPA legislation erupted, Barr asked her, "How do we deal with areas of disagreement?" She replied, "*We* don't." Congress was now performing its role, she explained, and the administration would have to stand aside on issues that required political trade-offs. "He didn't like that one bit."

But she also understood that her boss had embraced this new agency, so she did too. She just hoped the final version would be sensible.

Once he'd made the deal with Fine, Frank was eager to mark up "the consumer piece," as he called it. But he needed to be sure that his decision "to pull the fangs that the administration put in there" by moderating the scope of the consumer agency could win broad Democratic support, especially from the liberals who were most enthusiastic about the CFPA. He did this with help from Elizabeth Warren.

Frank invited Warren to a meeting where he reviewed the concessions he had agreed to make to Cam Fine with Brad Miller of North Carolina, one of Frank's favorites on the committee and one of its most liberal members, who was particularly interested in consumer protection. Roslanowick recalled the meeting.

"Barney went through it rapid-fire, the way he does," explaining what he had offered to Fine, particularly the compromise on examination and enforcement, "which was complicated." Roslanowick had brought two of her senior staff, Beresik and Miller, to help explain how limiting the role of the new agency's inspectors in examinations of the small banks could placate Fine's members without meaningfully jeopardizing the CFPA's ability to police abuses, even by the small banks. Frank explained that the new agency would be able to investigate any complaints against banks of all sizes, and the rules it wrote would apply to all institutions. Brad Miller was so impressed that he agreed to cosponsor the amendment that would codify the Frank-Fine deal as a provision of the new law. His cosponsor would be Dennis Moore, a Blue Dog moderate from Kansas and another Frank favorite on the committee.

Warren thought Frank's explanation of the deal was masterful and she endorsed it. She said later this meeting had given her a new appreciation for the legislative process. That meeting showed "how it really works," she said.

After consulting with dozens of colleagues, Frank was optimistic that only one or two of the committee's Democrats would vote against the independent consumer agency. "We'll lose Walt Minnick," he said in early October, speaking of the first-term congressman from Idaho who had won his seat in 2008 in a district that John McCain carried against Obama with 60 percent of the vote. Minnick won barely more than 50 percent. "He's got the worst district," Frank said. A former timber industry executive, Minnick cast himself as a conservative and independent Democrat, and expressed reservations about the consumer agency from the beginning. "And I'm not sure about Travis [Childers]," Frank said—another conservative Democrat, from Mississippi. The other thirty-nine Democrats on the committee all supported the agency.

Frank was struck by the evolution of the two parties since he was a young man. In the 1960s and 1970s the leading conservatives in Congress were southern Democrats, including Childers's predecessors from Mississippi, and some of the most effective liberals in Congress were Republicans from the Northeast and Midwest. But now, every Democrat in the House was more liberal than every Republican. Conservative Democrats were rare; liberal Republicans were an extinct species. "If you're a Democrat from the South today, you are a *Democrat*. You do believe there's a positive role for government," Frank said. Of course there weren't many Democrats from the South left in the House. But the existence of a strong Democratic consensus, even with the divisions between, for example, Black Caucus liberals and Blue Dog moderates, made it easier for Frank to sell his view of financial reform to his Democratic colleagues.

The deal he struck with Fine "buys us a lot," Frank said, by neutralizing the community banks. "And then you know, people [Democratic members] don't want to be anti-consumer. And I think some of them don't want to go against me." He referred back to his personal bible: "That chapter in [Robert] Caro about Lyndon [Johnson] as minority leader*—there's a very simple pattern. People think, well you [mem-

---

* *Master of the Senate: The Years of Lyndon Johnson* by Robert A. Caro.

bers of Congress] trade everything. No, you don't do that. Whenever people ask you to do something, people whose votes you are ultimately going to need, you do it. You give them a real vested interest in being your friend. You be as helpful to them as possible, for nothing. So that when you go to them [for support on a particular issue], it's not just that you're trading with them in a crass sense. They have an understanding that this is a very important relationship. So you build one-sided relationships, you do favors for people all the time, so they are invested in being your friend."

To build those relationships in the fall of 2009, Frank called dozens of meetings of his Democrats, including a series of formal meetings with experts and Obama administration officials. He was deliberately flattering the members, of course, trying to make them feel like active participants in the legislative process. The crowded schedule this produced for the Democrats on the committee became a topic for wisecracks and jokes among them.

Emanuel Cleaver of Missouri, the first black mayor of Kansas City before he was elected to the House in 2004, captured the spirit of October 2009—a particularly hectic month—in a handwritten note to Jim Segel, Frank's chief political aide, who had cultivated good personal relations with many of the committee Democrats:

Dear Jimmy,

The members of the financial services committee are in desperate need of your help. As you may know, our committee is the most active of the standing panels in the House. In fact, we are probably the hardest working committee on the planet.

You can help. We need you to tire Barney out and the committee is willing to raise money (within the ethics requirements) for you to go out several nights a week and stay late. In our committee it is generally understood that free time is what we can get if the chairman is tired. How about movies, dinner, concerts, roller derby, whatever. . . . We'll pay.

Jimmy we need your help. . . . And for you to know what is right and not do it is as bad as doing wrong. It's up to you. —E

On October 14, 2009, the Financial Services Committee convened to begin marking up the regulatory reform legislation—working out a version of the bill that could be sent on to the House floor. Once Frank had hoped to do this in June, then in July, but the delay was both predictable and traditional. Congress only works quickly in extreme emergencies. And to old hands, the pace of action this time was hardly slow. Getting such a huge bill ready for action over a period of less than four months was extraordinary.

Even some of the participants in the process thought it had been rushed. One of those was Segel, who had been at his boss's side as most of the final deals were made. "This is only a markup," he said, reassuring himself. There would be time after the committee reported out a bill and before the full House acted on it to fix whatever needed fixing.

The first item of the bill to be considered covered the most complicated, opaque issue of financial regulatory reform, derivatives.* These are the financial contracts whose price depends on, or is derived from, some underlying asset or assets—the price of oil, for example, or the value of a euro measured in Japanese yen. As described earlier, AIG's traders had nearly destroyed the company by selling derivatives that guaranteed the value of mortgage-backed bonds that collapsed in the Great Crash.

The government had rejected the idea of regulating derivatives in a notorious episode in 1998, when a woman named Brooksley Born, a smart lawyer who was then the chairman of the Commodity Futures Trading Commission, suggested that it was time to regulate the burgeoning derivatives market. Derivatives were becoming an increasingly popular means for companies and investors to hedge risks, and also to gamble on future price movements of commodities, currencies, interest rates, stocks, and bonds. Born thought the market was too big and too risky to be left in the dark—which is where it was operating, out of the view of the public and all government regulators.

Bill Clinton had appointed Born to the CFTC. Clinton also appointed Robert Rubin to be secretary of the treasury, Arthur Levitt to be chairman of the Securities and Exchange Commission, and Alan Greenspan to his second term as chairman of the Federal Reserve Board. All three of them thought Born's suggestion was misguided, so it went nowhere. A few years later the investor Warren Buffett spoke ominously of derivatives as "financial weapons of mass destruction . . . that are potentially lethal." In 2008, the Great Crash con-

---

* Gillian Tett's *Fool's Gold* (2009) is an excellent primer on derivatives.

firmed the accuracy of Buffett's warning and made Brooksley Born
something of a prophet.

Regulating derivatives in some fashion was part of the broad consensus on the need for regulatory reform. This was tricky, not least
because derivatives were such a lucrative business for the firms that
created and traded them, mostly the big banks. They lobbied intently
to try to save their derivatives business and preserve its profitability.
They had to operate in a virtual intellectual vacuum on Capitol Hill,
where there weren't half a dozen members of the House and Senate
who really understood this esoteric topic. Even among the sophisticated staff, deep understanding of derivatives was rare. Lobbyists
would try to exploit this ignorance.

Frank's interest in the derivatives issues was primarily political. His first goal was to make a peaceful compromise with Collin
Peterson, the chairman of the House Agriculture Committee, whose
jurisdiction included the Commodity Futures Trading Commission
that would, Frank knew, have to share responsibility with the SEC
(overseen by Frank's committee) for any new regulation of derivatives.
Frank instructed his staff to work with Peterson's to come up with a
joint position that both chairmen could embrace.

Peterson and Frank were odd bedfellows. The chairman of the
Agriculture Committee was a gregarious character with a friendly,
weather-beaten face who grew up on a Minnesota farm. He was one of
the most conservative Democrats in the House, a founder of the Blue
Dog Coalition of moderates. He played country music in a band called
Collin and the Establishment. He began 2009 trying to throw his
weight around on the derivatives issue, as we have seen, but Frank and
Speaker Pelosi convinced him that collaboration with Frank would be
the best way to proceed.

Both men thought derivatives were a good issue to exploit politically,
because the natural opposition to any reforms, and particularly to any
attempt to force traders to trade in the open and use exchanges to do
business, would come from bankers and big financial institutions, the
new villains of American politics. The big traders of derivatives liked
to trade confidentially because secrecy eliminated open competition
and made comparative shopping difficult or impossible. Forcing trades
onto exchanges or into the open would increase competition, lower
prices, and dent the big traders' earnings.

"Barney is going to tack to the left on derivatives," one of his senior aides said in July, "to show that he is tough on the big guys." Tacking to the left meant opting for more vigorous regulation.

At the same time, farmers—Peterson's primary constituency—were among the customers for derivatives who were anxious to preserve their ability to hedge, for example, the price of wheat or corn the way airlines hedged the price of jet fuel, or multinational corporations hedged the value of the dollar against foreign currencies. These were all "end users" whose use of derivatives did not pose great risks to the financial system, and who wanted to preserve their ability to buy derivatives contracts in a new regulatory environment. Peterson and Frank were both willing to try to make this possible. At the same time, Peterson and many of his colleagues on the Agriculture Committee suspected that speculators used derivatives to distort the prices of commodities like wheat, corn, and oil, and they hoped to limit this speculation.

The staff negotiations produced a joint "concept paper" that both chairmen released at a news conference on July 29. Neither tried to hide his satisfaction that they had come to an agreement. The consensus they had achieved, Frank said, defied "the expectations of many and the hopes of some." Peterson made clear their shared political calculation: "We want to err on the side of too much regulation rather than too little," he said. According to aides who worked on the deal, neither chairman fully understood the derivatives market at the time.

"In some cases we're being tougher than the administration [in its draft legislation] on derivatives," Frank said soon afterward. That was what mattered to him.

Staff still had to spend weeks converting their concept paper into legislation. Their meetings were held out of public view. This could often be the most important part of the legislative process, where practical decisions were made that could have a big impact when enacted into law. Members never participated in those technical conversations. They relied on their aides to respect whatever instructions they had given. The instructions were invariably broad and vague, so much was always left to the staff's creativity and discretion.

"This notion that members of Congress are power-hungry—absolutely the opposite," Frank observed. "Most members like to duck tough issues."

Staff produced a new draft bill that was released on October 2. On October 6, Frank presided over a hearing on derivatives and learned that the regulators, particularly Gary Gensler of the Commodity Futures Trading Commission, considered the new draft too weak. He began discussing alternatives with the staff.

At the end of that week Frank traveled to Colorado for two fund-raisers hosted by Ed Perlmutter, a colleague on the Financial Services Committee whom the chairman was eager to help. He returned on October 13, the day before the markup was to begin, with consideration of the derivatives section, and met at noon with Roslanowick, Lawranne Stewart, and Peter Roberson. Stewart and Roberson were the aides working on derivatives. They took Frank through the derivatives "title" section by section. It was, Roberson said later, the first time the chairman had tried to wrap his mind around all of the issues.

While they were meeting Frank took a phone call from Secretary Geithner, who wanted to convince him to include a provision requiring that derivatives contracts between financial institutions or between speculators and institutions be traded on exchanges, the equivalent of the New York Stock Exchange or the Chicago Mercantile Exchange, and make several other small changes. Frank and his staff saw Geithner's requests as ways to toughen the bill, and Frank readily agreed to them.

The change would be good politically, he told the staff. They all realized that Frank continued to worry about criticism from the left—liberal bloggers, *The New York Times* editorial page, and the consumer groups. Looking tough on derivatives was a good reply to all of them, Frank felt, and requiring exchange trading was a visible sign of toughness. That evening the Democrats on the committee caucused to discuss the markup beginning the next day, and Frank explained his plan to propose a new provision on exchange trading.

And so on the morning of October 14 the committee finally got down to work on the most significant piece of legislation it had considered since the 1930s. A citizen who stumbled into Room 2129 on the ground floor of the Rayburn Building that day would have seen no clue that something momentous was happening. When Frank gaveled the meeting to order there were perhaps ten committee members in the cavernous room. The strongest visual image greeting that visitor would have been four long, ascending rows, fifty feet from end to end and curved slightly, of oversized executive desk chairs covered in black leather. They were lined up behind four rows of benchlike, mahogany work surfaces that served as desks for the members—when they were present. In the center of the top row sat the chairman, wearing a white button-down shirt and a blue-and-white repp tie. His gray suit jacket was draped across his overstuffed chair. He was businesslike and relaxed, though the dark circles under his eyes hinted at the strains of his life that fall. So did his volatile weight, which could vary by thirty or forty pounds over a few months, but was up to around 250 pounds on this occasion.

During the course of the day the committee considered thirty amendments. Twenty-one of them were adopted by acclamation or voice vote. Those requiring a roll call vote were held over until the next morning and voted on one after another.

The most important change proposed on the first day was Frank's own amendment to require mandatory use of exchanges. Several Republicans expressed surprise that the chairman had changed his position on mandatory exchange trading, but no voices were raised. The Republicans voted no on almost everything proposed by Democrats, but nothing favored by Frank was in any danger. The day passed without a whiff of drama. Never were more than two dozen of the committee's seventy-one members present at the same time.

The second day of markup began in a similarly benign atmosphere. The first order of business was roll call votes on half a dozen amendments held over from the previous day. In markups, most amendments are usually dealt with by voice votes that leave no record of how members voted. But when either side wants to force a recorded vote—a tactic often intended to try to embarrass members and create fodder for the next election—members can ask for one, and if 20 percent of those present support the idea, under committee rules the chairman must agree. Committees typically schedule roll call votes in bunches, so members can vote on a number of them at the same time. This allows them to save time. They can avoid accusations from future opponents that they had shirked their duty by failing to participate in committee votes—a charge that has been used effectively in television commercials against some incumbent members—without sitting for hours in a markup in case a roll call vote is called. In other words, if they show up for the roll call votes, they can continue to shirk their duty by mostly staying away from markups without creating the appearance that they are shirking their duty.

When six amendments had been dealt with, the committee voted on the entire derivatives title. It carried easily, by a vote of 43–26. A lone Republican (Congressman Walter Jones of North Carolina, one of a tiny number of independent-minded mavericks in the Republican caucus) voted "Aye," as did every Democrat, affirming Frank's confidence that all his members were remaining loyal to him.

Next on the agenda was H.R. 3126. Every bill is numbered when introduced—this was the 3,126th bill to be offered in the 111th Congress. Most bills are introduced just for show, with no expectation they will be enacted or even voted on, which is why the numbers get so big. H.R. stands for House of Representatives. Frank and his staff decided that each title of the big bill the administration drafted should be handled as a separate bill. This one was named the Consumer Financial Protection Agency Act of 2009.

Finally, a big, controversial, well-publicized piece of the reform package was being debated. But once again, an inexperienced visitor would not have realized the significance of the moment. For the first several hours of the markup, a calm decorum continued to prevail. Amendments were offered and debated—ultimately forty-seven in all. Many were adopted by voice vote.

The committee considered seven amendments on the second day of the markup, a Thursday. It then adjourned for the congressional weekend. The committee reconvened on Tuesday morning, when the debate on amendments continued. Frank took mischievous pleasure in embracing one that was offered by Randy Neugebauer of Texas, a conservative Republican, who proposed spelling out explicitly that the CFPA would not have the authority to require lenders to offer plain vanilla products. Republicans had seized on this issue when the administration released its draft, decrying it as a Big Brother–like attempt to put the government between merchants and customers.

Neugebauer, a homebuilder and real estate developer from Lubbock and not the brightest Republican member of the committee, seemed to think his amendment was a clever way to embarrass Frank, but the chairman surprised him. The amendment was, he observed, unnecessary, because after his own "de-fanging" of the administration's original bill, it no longer contained any reference to plain vanilla offerings. So, Frank said, Neugebauer's proposal was "redundant and useful"—useful because sometimes, "redundancy is reassuring to people." With Frank's approval, the amendment was approved unanimously, by voice vote.

The markup proceeded in an orderly fashion for several hours. Then suddenly the mood changed. Spencer Bachus, the ranking Republican, changed it.

Bachus's difficult position in his own party was on display in this markup. He yielded the ranking member's seat, next to the chairman on the top row, to Jeb Hensarling of Dallas, one of the most outspoken conservatives in the House. Frank thought that the House Republican leadership had forced Bachus to give Hensarling and Scott Garrett of New Jersey, another outspoken conservative, prominent roles in the committee. Both were the ranking Republicans on Financial Services subcommittees. But Bachus insisted that enhancing their roles was his own idea, obviously intended to strengthen his position in the Republican caucus, which was considerably more conservative than Bachus was.

During deliberations on the consumer protection agency, Bachus tried to show some sympathy for consumers. While most of his Republican colleagues were simply lambasting the idea of a new agency, Bachus observed, "I think that we all agree that consumer protection is terribly important, and that there was a failure of consumer protection over the last several years." Rules intended to protect consumers needed to be better enforced, he added. But he also embraced his colleagues' rejection of a new agency.

Late in the afternoon of the third long day of businesslike, well-mannered discussion of amendments, Steven Driehaus, a freshman Democrat from Cincinnati, observed that Republicans "were nowhere to be found when sub-prime mortgages were thriving in the United States" in the years before the Great Crash. There was a crisis in the country, he said, and the Republican-controlled Congress "failed to do anything about it." Bachus took umbrage. "When I was subcommittee chairman of Financial Institutions," he said in typically awkward syntax, "I proposed to the majority a sub-prime lending proposal." What he meant was, he had proposed to certain Democrats—who were in the majority when Bachus spoke, but in the minority when Bachus took that initiative in 2006—that they try to work out a bill that would limit subprime lending. Bachus was indignant at Driehaus's remark because in fact he had been worried about subprime loans and the foreclosures they seemed to be causing and did try, albeit ineffectually, to do something about them. "I think even the chairman," Bachus went on, referring to Frank, who was one of the Democrats he had approached in 2006, "would acknowledge that I never received a response to that offering."

That remark set off Frank, who, unlike Driehaus, knew this history and rejected Bachus's "distortion" of it. "Remember," Frank said with evident emotion, "he is talking about the years when the Republicans controlled the House. . . . He was the chairman of the subcommittee of jurisdiction [that is, the Financial Institutions subcommittee that had jurisdiction over mortgage lending rules]. He could have brought the bill up if he wanted to. . . . He decided not to bring up a bill. . . . I think what happened was, the Republican [House] leadership didn't want it. . . . We were the minority; we didn't control what was going on."

Frank then decided to embarrass Bachus more bluntly. He recalled that there actually was bipartisan collaboration on a subprime mortgage bill in 2007, after Democrats won control of the House and Frank ascended to the committee chairmanship. "We did work together" on that measure, Frank said. "The gentleman [Bachus] voted for the bill and helped us with the bill in 2007. But he has publicly acknowledged he was then criticized by many members of his own party for supporting us." When Frank again brought up a subprime lending bill in 2009, he said, "we were not able to work together." Bachus lost his appetite for defying his conservative colleagues who did not want a bill.

This catfight went on for about ten minutes. It had nothing to do with the business at hand—the consumer title. In their very different ways both men showed real emotion. They had both lived through the years of irresponsibility when government policy and the practices of private lenders and securitizers encouraged the housing bubble that exploded so destructively in 2007–8. Bachus understood Republican complicity in these events; Republicans ran the government, including the Federal Reserve Board, during the years when the seeds of disaster were sown. And Frank knew that Democrats' hands were not clean either; they too had encouraged subprime lending and expanding home ownership to lower-income Americans. But Frank was indignant that Bachus would try to blame him for the failure to bring a subprime bill before the House in 2006.

In fact there was room for a great deal of blame, and guilt too. Congress, like the rest of the government, had supported and encouraged the mortgage lending that contributed so much to the disaster in 2008. And Congress had acquiesced to the deregulation that made the worst predatory lending possible, and also the most irresponsible speculation on housing and commercial real estate. Characteristically, members of Congress generally did not step forward to confess their complicity in this national tragedy. Most never seemed to consider the possibility that they shared responsibility for what had happened, at least not publicly.

Under the rules of the House, a committee markup is arguably the most democratic moment in the legislative process. In a markup any member can offer an amendment to the pending legislation and get a vote on it. Not even the powerful committee chairman can block a member from doing this. Senior staff members often observe that this is the only setting in which the House operates like the Senate, where members sometimes have the right to offer amendments when a bill is being debated on the floor. There is no comparable right in the House, because—largely for practical reasons, given its 435 members, compared to the Senate's 100—the House allows its Rules Committee to decide which amendments can be offered on the floor. The Rules Committee acts as an agent of the House leadership, so it can maintain legislative discipline for the speaker and majority leader.

There is no mechanism for maintaining comparable discipline in House committees. The only limitation on the right to offer amendments in a markup is time. Chairmen do have the authority to move to end a markup session, and if approved by a majority of committee members, the markup will end. This prevents the minority party from delaying action on a bill indefinitely, the way the Senate minority can.

The freedom to introduce amendments led to Frank's only embarrassing defeat during the markup of the consumer title of the reform bill—officially, "Title IV—Consumer Financial Protection Agency Act." Embarrassment came over an amendment introduced on October 22 by John Campbell of Orange County, California.

Before coming to Congress, Campbell was a Saturn and then a Saab dealer for twenty-five years. Even as a member of the House he collected rent on six properties he owned that housed auto showrooms and body shops. According to his financial disclosure form, made vague by House rules that allow members to report their income and assets in broad ranges, the rent from his auto properties fell somewhere between $600,000 and $6 million a year. When the CFPA was being debated in the committee, Campbell offered an amendment to exclude car dealers from the new agency's purview. This quickly became known as "the auto dealers' carve-out" on Capitol Hill, where there is a reflexive predilection for such terminology.

Campbell's colleagues did not make an issue of his apparent conflict of interest in the matter. Nor did they mention the $170,000 in campaign contributions that he had raised from auto dealers during his political career—most of his colleagues knew nothing about that money. Members never criticize a colleague's fundraising, the congressional version of "people who live in glass houses . . ."

Curiously, Campbell himself had earlier recognized a potential conflict based on his association with the auto industry. When the House voted on bailouts for General Motors and Chrysler, Campbell voted "present," an unusual gesture meant to acknowledge his desire not to cross any ethical lines. He showed no such compunction about offering the amendment to strip the CFPA of any authority over auto dealers. When asked about this by his hometown newspaper, Campbell said excluding dealers from CFPA oversight gave them no direct financial benefit, just spared them a regulatory headache. "All this is trying to do is save them from needless regulation. It's not like it's a tax credit, not like it's stimulus money."

And what about the political contributions? Campbell said the suggestion that he shouldn't vote on a matter because he had accepted money from donors who had a stake in the outcome was "absolutely absurd." If such a rule applied, he said, "every one of us [in Congress] would be exempted from voting on nearly everything we vote on."

On the day when he introduced the amendment, Campbell gave the impression that he hadn't written it himself. When Mel Watt of California asked him specific questions about one detail of the proposal, Campbell couldn't provide a clear answer. This was hardly surprising. Members almost never personally write the amendments they offer; either they are prepared by staff in consultation with "legislative counsel," the team of lawyers employed by the House to perform this function, or they are written by interest groups or their lobbyists. Introducing amendments for others is common practice in Congress. Lobbyists are always looking for sponsors of amendments they have drafted.

In this case the National Automobile Dealers Association waged a ferocious lobbying campaign, bringing about five hundred dealers from around the country to Washington in September to prod their members to protect them from the CFPA. Their argument was simple. "It makes sense to exclude dealers. Dealers had absolutely nothing to do with the credit crisis," as one NADA official put it.

Of course this was not a criterion used by those who drafted the reform bill, particularly its consumer protection provisions. Elizabeth Warren had proposed creating a consumer agency more than a year before the Great Crash. She and other consumer advocates had long criticized the gimmicks some car dealers used to direct their customers to subprime car loans whose originators would pay the dealers a finder's fee, and which left the customer paying a lot more for his car than he would have with a straightforward loan.

But in the fall of 2009, there was little appetite in Congress for a proposal that upset car dealers, as Frank acknowledged in the discussion of Campbell's amendment. Car dealers enjoy a special status in America's communities. As Dave Smith put it, there's a Buick dealer in every town in America, and he often buys the uniforms for the Little League. Moreover, in 2009 the dealers were a wounded tribe. Both Chrysler and General Motors, teetering on the edge of bankruptcy before the government bailed them out, had moved to close hundreds of dealerships around the country, provoking yelps of pain from those who were affected. Frank discovered that black-owned dealerships were particularly persuasive with his Black Caucus members. Once the dealers made a stink about being subjected to the CFPA, many members were ready to dump the idea just to show their sympathy for the dealers' plight.

The scene when Campbell's amendment came up for a roll call vote was revealing. The "top row," the senior Democrats on the committee, all opposed the amendment, but as the committee clerk calling the roll moved down to the third and fourth rows, where the newer members elected in 2006 and 2008 sat, the fruits of the auto dealers' lobbying began to appear. On the lower rows "Ayes"—a dozen of them—outnumbered "Nays." Soon it was clear that with unanimous Republican support and the votes of at least twelve Democrats, Campbell's amendment would pass. Once that was obvious, five of the Democrats who initially stood with Frank asked to change their votes to "Aye." The final tally was forty-seven votes for the amendment, twenty-one against.

"I knew I couldn't win that one," Frank said later. "What I have found to be the irresistible force of American politics are the natural grassroots networks. You cannot create one. They are the natural networks of people who are engaged in activity that's very important to them, generally economically, and if they see a threat, you cannot beat them." He was talking about the auto dealers.

The vote on the Campbell amendment came near the end of deliberations on the CFPA. Republicans still had more amendments to offer, all intended to vitiate the new agency in one way or another, but after three days of debate on CFPA amendments, committee Democrats had voted to terminate the discussion. Bachus said he was "disappointed."

A vote on the entire consumer title followed soon afterward. Frank's efforts to keep his Democrats in line were rewarded: The committee approved the legislation by a vote of 39–29. As Frank expected, he lost just two Democrats, Minnick and Childers. And he got the vote of one Republican, Mike Castle of Delaware, a former governor of his state and one of the last of the moderate northeastern Republicans.*

Perhaps most gratifying to Frank, who remained anxious about his standing with the left, was the reaction from Elizabeth Warren. "Everybody told me," Warren said to reporters right after the vote, "that the banks always win. 'Quit now because they always win.' But they didn't win today."

This was the last day during the markup when the press seats in the hearing room were full. There were more provisions to complete, but none that brought any drama. The most consequential sections of the legislation, creating the new resolution authority to allow regulators to put failing financial firms out of business and setting up the new council of regulators with extraordinary power to tell firms when they needed more capital, or had to cease certain behavior, passed without fanfare or excitement. The committee embraced an amendment offered by Paul Kanjorski authorizing regulators to break up big firms if they thought this would eliminate a serious risk to the financial system, an unprecedented power. Republicans voted against all of these provisions, but to no effect. Except for Campbell's amendment exempting the auto dealers from CFPA examination, the Republicans remained essentially irrelevant throughout this process.

In November, after weeks of work, the committee approached the end of the markup. Frank planned a final vote on the bill on November 19, the day before the Thanksgiving recess was to begin. But then, unexpectedly, his ten Black Caucus members asked him to postpone the vote. Frank felt he had to comply.

---

* Castle ran for the Republican nomination for a Senate seat in 2010. A right-wing opponent supported by the Tea Party defeated him.

In Congress, multiple story lines are always proceeding simultaneously—there is no avoiding the constant clash of priorities that can yank members' attention first this way, then that. This postponed vote was a classic example of what can happen when story lines collide.

On November 4, members of the Black Caucus, forty-two strong in the 111th Congress, held an unpublicized meeting with a group of African American businessmen who enumerated the woes they faced in the worst American economy since the Depression. The meeting alarmed the members who attended, who decided they had to do more for the businesspeople they represented, first by demanding more help from the Obama administration for minority-owned businesses clobbered by the downturn.

Several senior members of the caucus turned to Frank for help. "I was flattered," Frank said later. He immediately got on the phone to his pal Rahm Emanuel, President Obama's chief of staff, and told him the administration had to help. But key administration officials, including Geithner, were traveling at the time, and it took days to arrange appropriate meetings. Frank invited his Black Caucus members and Barbara Lee of California, chairman of the caucus in the 111th Congress, to meet for a discussion of what might be done.

Frank convened this group at 8 p.m. on November 16 in the Financial Services Committee's hearing room. He boasted afterward that nothing leaked out of this meeting, which was never reported by the news media. Frank was taken aback by what he heard that night. "They are really shaken by the reaction they are getting in the community," he recounted. "Mel Watt [Frank's most important Black Caucus ally on his committee] said, 'We're going to lose the black middle class, everything we've gained in the last fifteen years is at risk.' " That remark from the usually unflappable Watt shook Frank. He began discussing possible initiatives that might help threatened businesses.

Maxine Waters, the senior black member of Financial Services, wanted to exploit leverage she thought was created by their ten votes on Frank's committee. They could threaten to scuttle one of the administration's highest priorities, financial regulatory reform, unless they got satisfaction, she suggested. Frank hated that idea, but agreed to postpone the final vote on the bill while he tried to help the black members win something from the administration.

The pressure on Frank led to an unusual meeting in his office with Lloyd Blankfein, the president of Goldman Sachs, on November 19. This was not one of Frank's finest nor one of his favorite moments.

The Black Caucus, it turned out, had some specific firms in mind when it complained about the plight of black businesses. One was Inner City Broadcasting, owned by Percy Sutton and his family. Sutton was a famous Harlem politician and former president of the borough of Manhattan in New York City. He was an early mentor to Congressman Charles Rangel of Harlem, the most influential member of the Black Caucus in 2009, when he was chairman of the House Ways and Means Committee. (Rangel was forced out of that position in an ethics scandal in 2010.)

Sutton's firm owned seventeen radio stations that catered to black listeners. It was the biggest minority-owned broadcasting company in the country. In 2009, when advertising revenue for radio stations sank like a stone, Inner City faced extreme financial difficulties. It had outstanding debts of about $230 million to at least two big financial firms, GE Capital and Goldman Sachs. Sutton's friends in the Black Caucus sought to help him by convincing both the Obama administration and Frank to pressure GE and Goldman Sachs to renegotiate their loans to Inner City.

Politicians trying to influence big corporations is not something either side is usually inclined to publicize. In most circumstances, neither group wants to advertise the seeking or granting of favors. Both can look unsavory. But both are quite common.

The fact that Frank summoned Blankfein to his office to ask this favor was never publicly disclosed. *The New York Times* did report on the Black Caucus's effort to help Sutton. The story quoted Frank saying he had contacted "public and private companies" on Inner City's behalf, but did not mention the meeting with Blankfein. Frank was obviously uncomfortable when asked about it later. "I just said [to Blankfein], 'I hope you can do something.' I never got into anything specific," Frank said. He called GE as well. Not surprisingly, given the implicit power Frank held over both companies as the author of reform legislation that could affect them profoundly, they did agree to renegotiate their loans to Inner City.

When the House reconvened after Thanksgiving, Frank scheduled final committee action on the last section of the regulatory reform package for 10:15 on the morning of December 2. He kept talking to his Black Caucus colleagues, and kept trying to help them win specific benefits for minority businesses from the Obama administration. But he never got a firm commitment that they would appear on the 2nd and vote for the bill. He also kept talking, and had his staff keep talking as well, with the other Democrats on the committee. He was confident that not one would vote against the bill—Minnick and Childers had told Segel they would cast "Aye" votes. Since the committee had thirty-two Democrats in addition to the ten Black Caucus members and Republicans had just twenty-nine, Frank would have enough votes to approve regulatory reform even if the black members stayed away. The only danger was if they came to the hearing room and voted against the bill. Frank was confident that they wouldn't go that far.

As ten o'clock approached on the day of the vote, Frank asked Jeanne Roslanowick to go to the meeting room on the second floor of the Rayburn Building where the ten Black Caucus members of Financial Services were meeting to find out what they intended to do. He hoped they might still show up and vote. Roslanowick knocked on the door of the meeting room; Maxine Waters's chief of staff, Mikael Moore, who was also her grandson, opened it. When he recognized Roslanowick, he looked alarmed.

The chairman, she said, wanted to know if the group meeting inside had any "recommendation" for him. "Give me a minute," Moore replied, then closed the door in her face. She waited several minutes (it was now nearly 10 a.m.), and knocked once more. Moore opened the door and again asked for "a minute." More waiting. Finally Roslanowick opened the door herself and walked into the room. She approached Maxine Waters and asked what she should tell the chairman. "We don't know yet," Waters replied. Roslanowick then looked at Mel Watt, Frank's closest ally in this group, and someone she admired. "We won't be there" for the vote, Watt said. This was the good news she was hoping for. As long as they stayed on the second floor, the bill would be approved.

At 10:15 Frank called for the vote. Lois Richerson, the clerk of the committee, who sat at what was ordinarily the witness table down at floor level, facing Frank, called out the members' names in order of their seniority, Democrats first. The Republican seats were nearly all filled, but there were ten empty chairs sprinkled throughout the Democratic benches—the seats of the black members of the committee. Richerson called each of their names too, but never got a reply. When everyone present had voted, the clerk's assistant handed her a piece of paper with the final tally, and she read, "Mr. Chairman, on that vote, the aye's are thirty one and the no's are twenty seven." The ninth and final installment of the reform package, creating the systemic risk regulator and the new resolution regime to put failing financial firms out of business, had been approved.

"When that vote was over," Roslanowick recalled, "I got this smile I don't usually get" from Frank. He hurriedly whacked his gavel and announced, "The bill is passed." Now staff would combine all the elements the committee had approved since October into one huge bill that was ready for final action on the floor of the House of Representatives.

Well, nearly ready. One potentially important issue was still hanging out, in the argot of Capitol Hill. It had to be dealt with before the bill could be considered by the full House. This issue had a one-word name that only a few members ever really understood: preemption.

Preemption is the name given to a long-standing fact of life in the banking business: Under a variety of statutes and court rulings, federal rules and regulations for national banks that operate in more than one state generally took precedence over—preempted—state laws and regulators. This did not mean that national banks were immune from state laws, but it did give precedence to federal laws and rules. The boundaries had shifted many times over the years with different regulators' rulings and court decisions.

The Obama administration's draft legislation proposed that state legislatures and attorneys general "should have the ability to adopt and enforce stricter laws for [financial] institutions of all types." States should be empowered to enforce federal as well as state laws. And the new rules to be written by the Consumer Financial Protection Agency, the administration proposed, "would serve as a floor, not a ceiling"— a starting point for regulation, not the maximum regulation allowed.

Though the subject matter was arcane, the proposal was in fact quite radical. Under it, national banks would have to comply with the consumer protection laws of fifty different states and the federal government, with no guarantee that all those laws would be consistent with each other. For the biggest national banks with branches in most states of the union, this posed big challenges. All of the changes in preemption law in recent times had made their lives easier; now the administration wanted to make them more complicated. The American Bankers Association came out strongly against the idea.

Frank liked the original administration proposal. He thought federal bank regulators had taken preemption too far, denying the most progressive state governments the opportunity to give their residents meaningful protections against financial chicanery. "I would like as little preemption as I can get by with politically, but I don't know how much that is," Frank said in an interview at the end of July 2009. Building support for greater states' rights in consumer protection "depends upon the consumer groups' lobbying and the [state] attorneys general." If they could persuade enough members, changes in the rules would be possible.

But the banks did a better lobbying job on preemption than those who might have favored a change. The banks' most important success came with the New Democrat Coalition in the House, the caucus of sixty-eight moderate members who cast themselves as pragmatic, pro-business Democrats in a Bill Clinton mold. The "New Dems," as they called themselves, discovered the financial benefits of making friends on Wall Street. They raised millions of dollars for their campaigns from financial industry donors, whom they actively cultivated.

Melissa Bean of suburban Chicago was a leader of the group, and an active member of the Financial Services Committee. The reported contributions to her campaign mirrored those of other New Dem leaders. In the 2009–10 election cycle, for example, she raised a third of her campaign cash, or $756,000, from the employees and political action committees of financial firms, banks, and insurance companies. On the subject of preemption, Bean cast herself as a friend of the national banks. She argued her case in practical terms: "Fifty different sets of rules cannot be efficient." Liberal critics saw this as carrying the banks' water, but Bean and her colleagues said it was only common sense.

Frank decided that he had to placate Bean and the other New Dems on this issue. Sixteen New Dems served on the committee, the largest single faction, and their support for the reform package, particularly the consumer agency, still had to be solidified. Jim Segel, who was always counting votes for Frank, came to the conclusion in late September that to keep New Dems in line behind the CFPA, "there will have to be some accommodation on preemption." Frank knew he would have to accept more of the status quo than he wanted to.

In fact Bean and her New Dem colleagues were willing to modify the status quo somewhat and restore what the cognoscenti called "the Barnett standard," a reference to a 1996 Supreme Court case. The court ruled that states had the authority to regulate the activities of national banks within their borders only when "doing so does not prevent or significantly interfere with the national bank's exercise of its powers." This ambiguous standard—what does "significantly interfere" mean?—was the law of the land until 2004 when the Comptroller of the Currency, the principal regulator of national banks, ruled that state regulators could not take any action that "prevents, impairs or conditions the ability of a national bank to engage in the business of banking." The Obama administration considered this language too broad, and Frank agreed. Bean also agreed that it could be modified. The question was, how?

An extraordinary amount of time and energy was expended on this issue in the fall of 2009. The key player for Bean was J. D. Grom, her bright, hardworking legislative director, whom she had brought to Washington from Illinois when she first came to the House in 2005. Grom spent hours with Andrew Miller of the Financial Services Committee staff talking about preemption. Grom understood the issue more thoroughly than his boss—not an unusual situation—and he kept pushing for a version of preemption that would cause the least disruption for the big banks. As his assigned interlocutor, Miller was impressed by Grom's knowledge, and by his determination.

Frank, who liked Bean, told her he would try to work out a compromise with her "on the way to the floor," meaning in the days between final committee action on the bill and floor debate. Miller's job was to explore how a deal might be made, but he wasn't expected to make it.

Bean understood the delicacy of Frank's position as the markup of the consumer title drew near. Grom, with help from banking lawyers working with the ABA and the Office of the Comptroller of the Currency, had written an amendment they thought would restore the Barnett standard while generally preserving preemption pretty much in its current form. But, Bean said, "certain progressives on the committee" threatened to vote against the CFPA if Bean's amendment was part of it. Bean said she and the other New Dems wanted the CFPA to be approved, "so I worked it out with the chairman" that there would be a floor vote on her amendment before final passage instead of a showdown in the committee markup.

The situation was a little more nuanced than Bean's account suggested. Frank and Roslanowick were trying to keep all the Democratic factions on board. They wanted to avoid the impression that Bean was getting her way, knowing this would upset liberals on the committee and outside it.

Frank, characteristically, had his eye on the main objective—getting the bill to the floor. He preferred to make as few concessions to the moderates and the banks as possible. He also realized that Bean might prevail in committee if she offered her amendment, so he asked Mel Watt to work on a compromise with her. This was not a good choice; Bean and Watt had difficult personal relations, and they did not find a compromise. Luckily for Frank, his problem was postponed when Bean had to miss the markup session because of illness in her family. Her absence allowed Frank to temporize, hoping that a deal could be struck before the floor vote.

But once the bill left his committee, Frank no longer had complete control over it—the House leadership took over. Speaker Pelosi and Steny Hoyer of Maryland, the majority leader, had left regulatory reform entirely in Frank's hands until it was voted out of the committee, but then they insisted on a role. The Obama administration wanted to kibitz as well. Bean decided to go ahead with the amendment Grom had been working on.

The leadership controlled the Rules Committee, which in turn controls the circumstances under which every bill is debated on the floor, including which amendments offered by members are brought to a vote. This power over amendments severely limits the legislative prerogatives of every member of the House. A member may have a brilliant idea for how to improve a particular bill, but without the Rules Committee's approval, it will never even be considered.

In the early days of December 2009, the leadership wanted to move briskly, hoping to get the financial reform bill enacted before the Christmas break. So Rules, as the committee was known, had to decide quickly which of more than a hundred amendments offered by members would be brought up for a vote. Bean's aide, Grom, met with Rules Committee staff early on, and learned that they were disinclined to recommend a vote on Bean's amendment on preemption. Grom also heard that both the White House and Treasury wanted to block a vote on the amendment.

Frank and his staff tried to head off the problem by offering a compromise version of the preemption language that Mel Watt had helped draft, but Grom told Bean it wasn't adequate, and they rejected it. Bean then submitted her version that Grom had been working on for weeks. This was the version that Treasury and the White House wanted to block entirely.

"When we heard those rumors [of administration opposition]," Bean explained, "we pulled our troops together—we rarely do it as New Dems—and said, We've got to take down [defeat] the rule, because we're not being taken seriously." In other words, Bean and her New Dem colleagues saw an insult to their man- and womanhood, so they would threaten to try to block floor consideration of the entire bill by defeating "the rule" that the Rules Committee would pass that described the duration and form of the debate, and designated which amendments would be voted on. In House proceedings, the rule for a bill must be approved before the bill itself can be considered. This lack of respect was especially painful for, in Bean's words, "a group of folks [the New Dems] who were the biggest champions" of regulatory reform. "To be left out wasn't acceptable," Bean said. "So we pulled together. We found out we had the votes to take down the rule and we said so."

It had not escaped their attention that the Black Caucus's boycott bore fruit just days after its members refused to vote on final passage in committee. On December 8, Frank announced that he would modify the bill to allocate $3 billion to mortgage relief for people who lost their jobs in the recession, and $1 billion to allow cities to buy foreclosed properties and use them for public purposes. Maxine Waters took obvious pleasure in trumpeting this "victory." If the Black Caucus could throw its weight around successfully, the New Dems could use their clout too. They reported their intention to "take down the rule" to Steny Hoyer, who paid special attention to the Blue Dogs and New Democrats. Hoyer then set off an alarm, instructing everyone involved to find a solution to this problem before the reform bill got blocked on the floor.

The first idea was to gather staff to work out a deal; the principals' aides were summoned to Speaker Pelosi's office with officials from Treasury. Bean's chief of staff told Roslanowick that "my boss cannot have a loss on this." But no agreement was reached. Bean ultimately agreed to negotiate with Neal Wolin, the deputy secretary of the treasury, and Michael Barr, the assistant secretary. J. D. Grom was present, as were several Treasury officials and Andrew Miller. Frank himself stayed away. He was counting on others to solve this problem.

Talks dragged on. After more than two hours, Bean said, "we were still four words apart." Hoyer was exasperated. "Just take what you've gotten," he urged her, but in Bean's eyes, she was still being asked to yield too much. Hoyer threatened to take the bill to the floor without her amendment; Bean said do what you want to do, but we will vote against the rule. "We didn't blink," she said. "Frankly, we had the cards at that point." Hoyer believed she had the votes to kill the rule.

"This had become symbolic," Bean said. "When I had gone to the floor [of the House] earlier that day, I had people coming up to me who weren't even Blue Dogs or New Dems saying, 'We're with you.' Because a lot of moderates were feeling excluded from the process." She was referring to moderate anxieties about health care and cap and trade energy legislation that the leadership had pushed through the House already, leaving some moderates feeling politically vulnerable.

Bean and Grom eventually returned to the room where Wolin was waiting. The final disagreement was over the words to be used to summarize the Barnett standard in the bill. The Financial Services Committee had approved a Watt amendment that said state regulators could not do anything that "prevents or significantly interferes with" a national bank's business. Bean said the national banks deserved more protection. Wolin proposed a two-word addition: State regulators should take no action that "prevents, significantly interferes with or materially impairs" the national bank's business. "Materially impairs" was meant to provide the extra protection Bean sought.

On its face, this didn't look like much. Both words were vague and hard to define. But Bean had the wit to realize that together with the earlier, modest concessions Wolin had offered, she had won enough to declare victory. This was easier for her because her insistence on a long day of negotiations had created a sensation for the tribe of reporters covering the story, not to mention an obvious headache for Hoyer and Pelosi, who seemed to be so eager to mollify her. Some reporters wrote that the entire bill was in jeopardy because of Bean's demands. For a moment, the world was waiting on Melissa Bean.

"We're satisfied that we came to a good place on this," Bean told reporters at the end of her very long day.

Only one step remained before the reform package could come before the full House of Representatives. The Committee on Rules had to formally decide which of the 238 amendments that members had offered would be debated and voted on when the legislation reached the floor of the House.

CHAPTER FIFTEEN

Looking for a Path

The presumption that the Senate Banking Committee would write a bipartisan regulatory reform bill guided both its chairman, Chris Dodd, and its chief counsel, Amy Friend, for all of 2009. Their interest in a bipartisan deal was purely practical. They doubted it would be possible to get a major reform bill through the Senate by relying only on Democratic support, even in a Senate with sixty Democrats. Dodd had an impressive legislative record over three decades in the Senate, and every success shared one attribute: "I've always had a Republican partner," as Dodd put it, "every time." In his experience, it just wasn't possible to enact a big, important bill on a partisan vote.

"When you put something into the legislative process," Friend observed, "you never know how it's going to turn out." This was inevitably true. No member could control the fate of a bill once it got to the floor of the Senate, where any amendment could be offered and passed. She thought the best way to head off crippling amendments was to start with and stick with a strong bipartisan majority of supporters who could band together to defeat all bad amendments. "We want to have senators invested in the product so it is their [bill] as well as ours," Friend said. "When you go to the floor there are no rules. It's really a scary place to be. A bill that comes to the floor with strong bipartisan support will discourage a lot of mischievous amendments."

In April 2009, Friend had briefed William Duhnke, the Republican staff director, and Mark Oesterle, Friend's Republican counterpart as senior substantive expert, on the Dodd team's early ideas about what a regulatory reform package should contain.

Duhnke, a former Navy pilot, had no background in financial issues. He had worked on the staff of the Senate Intelligence Committee when Richard Shelby was its chairman (1997–2001), then moved to Banking. A tall, white-haired man with an athlete's build who wore small, rimless eyeglasses, he was a sharp-elbowed partisan who had a military officer's bearing and a quick wit. "He sees the world through the prism of his military training," said a longtime Democratic colleague. "We [Democrats] are the enemy." The atmosphere on the committee staff changed when Duhnke replaced Kathleen Casey, who had been the Republican staff director for most of the four years that Shelby was chairman of Banking (2003–7). Democratic staff remembered Casey as easy to work with and relaxed, a description none would apply to Duhnke. The Democrats also paid attention when Duhnke fired a popular Republican colleague, Peggy Kuhn, who had worked well across party lines.

Oesterle, like Duhnke an attorney, had spent his entire career with Shelby, and was an expert on financial issues. He had strong views about the need to do more research into the causes of the Great Crash, a position Shelby adopted in some of his public statements. He spoke often of the contrast between earlier eras when senators did the hard work of figuring out big issues, and the modern era when they usually relied on staff to do the work.

A cautious operator, Friend put nothing in writing when she first briefed Duhnke and Oesterle. She gave them an oral presentation. It covered a lot of territory, including a consolidation of existing bank regulators into a single new agency; provisions on consumer protection; a new council of regulators to oversee all large financial institutions; new rules on the amount of capital financial institutions had to maintain; and a new way to put failing firms out of business. She remembered Oesterle's reaction: "Wow. You're really going to do all that? . . . That's really ambitious." They asked some questions, then asked for more time to react.

Friend waited several weeks, wondering what was happening. Finally Duhnke and Oesterle presented a list of fifty-three questions about the presentation she had given them. She responded with questions of her own: "Do you want to answer them with us? Do you want to go on this exploration together? Or do we have to answer them before you join?" She never got any answers. That should have been a warning.

In mid-June the Obama administration's white paper was released, followed over the summer by its draft legislative language. "We spent days and days working through" the Treasury's proposals with the Republican staff, Friend said. "We worked through the summer, taking a break in August. We realized that without putting something on paper, we could talk until we were blue in the face without results. So in September we gave them a document, to which they said—well, nothing much." The document was a detailed description of what they proposed to include in the bill. The Republican staff did not react to it.

Ed Silverman recounted what happened next: "After three weeks of waiting for them to respond, Senator Dodd went to Senator Shelby and said, 'We're waiting for a response.' Then I think Shelby told his people, Sit down with these [Dodd] people."

Duhnke and Oesterle told Silverman, he said, that "they were not going to make a counteroffer, but they were going to ask questions. We had a couple of sessions with them, and it was clear to me that the questions were not going anywhere. They were philosophical questions, they weren't questions designed to produce a counteroffer. It wasn't a negotiation.

"And then, after our third session, I was pretty much told that the Republicans had caucused, and to a man they could not accept a bill that had any version of an independent consumer protection agency," Silverman recounted. "Then Dodd and Shelby talked a couple more times, because we really wanted to be clear on what we were being told." And Shelby told Dodd that he would not negotiate further on the legislation unless Dodd agreed to "take the independent consumer agency off the table."

"That was a nonstarter," as Dodd put it later. "It's not a negotiation where you're taking off the table a critical issue to the president, one that many of us felt was important."

Silverman considered Shelby's demand an affront to Dodd. "I can't imagine any senator who would agree to something like that." Shelby wanted Dodd to abandon a critical piece of the legislation simply because the minority party, with only thirty-nine votes, demanded it, Silverman concluded.

Dodd and his aides decided "this was probably being driven more by the Republican leadership than it was by Senator Shelby," as Silverman put it. A key bit of evidence had reached them via Jonathan Miller, a senior member of the Banking Committee staff and its resident expert on consumer issues.

A personal friend of Miller's was the CEO of a major company who attended an event organized by the Business Roundtable, the trade association of big business in Washington. Senator Mitch McConnell of Kentucky, the Republican leader in the Senate, addressed the gathering. McConnell was an avid fundraiser for the National Republican Senatorial Committee, which helped pay for the GOP's Senate campaigns. He hoped someday soon to be the Senate majority leader. Democrats' desire to impose new regulations on Wall Street created a fundraising opportunity that McConnell appeared eager to exploit. According to Miller, his friend the CEO—whom he declined to identify—"was appalled" by McConnell's remarks. "It was all politics. 'We're going to beat this financial reform for you'—all of it politics, no policy. McConnell assumed he was among friends."

This anecdote on top of the remarks Shelby and his staff made to Dodd, Silverman and Friend persuaded them that further negotiation on the consumer agency at this stage would be fruitless. "So Dodd finally told us we had to draft a bill," Friend recalled. She and her colleagues spent October drafting. She communicated with Dodd verbally and with decision memos that asked him to make choices when she saw several options for dealing with specific subjects.

For Friend this was a labor of love. She had developed strong views about regulation of the financial sector in her ten years as a lawyer for the Comptroller of the Currency. She believed in good regulation, and considered the Great Crash embarrassing evidence of how badly the regulators had done their job.

She was particularly offended by the fact that three of the regulators competed with each other for "customers," because many banks could shop for the regulator they thought would be most congenial. National banks could become savings banks to avoid supervision by the OCC, which was a tougher regulator than the Office of Thrift Supervision (OTS), regulator of the savings and loan associations. State banks could choose to be regulated by the Federal Deposit Insurance Corporation (FDIC), or by the Federal Reserve Board. National banks could switch their charters and become state banks, regulated by the Fed or the FDIC. OCC and OTS both charged fees to the banks they regulated; the Fed and FDIC did not—another stimulant to shopping for a regulator. If a big bank moved, say, from OCC to OTS, the OCC suffered significant financial consequences. Friend remembered hearing the comptroller himself warning the staff that losing a big bank to a rival regulator would cause big problems.

"I don't think there's another country in the world that has anything like our system," Friend said. "We've got fifty state regulators [supervising state-chartered community banks], and we have four federal banking regulators, and we have a credit union regulator, and on top of that we have market regulators, the SEC and the CFTC. We have a lot."

"This seemed like fertile ground," she explained. "We knew for instance that OTS was viewed as a regulator that was particularly tolerant," a risky situation. Friend noted that under international banking rules, a firm like AIG, not subject to U.S. bank regulators because it wasn't a traditional bank, could only operate in Europe if it had a "consolidated regulator." It got one by buying an American savings and loan, making OTS its regulator. AIG could then open the most important branch of its derivatives business—the one that almost destroyed the company, and the global financial system—in London. OTS never figured out what AIG Financial Products, the unit doing the derivatives business, was up to. Derivatives lay well outside OTS's area of expertise.

Friend's most radical recommendation, which Dodd accepted, was to propose one federal regulator for banks, a new Financial Institutions Regulatory Administration. It would bring together the regulatory functions of the four existing bank regulators.

Dodd did not propose merging the SEC and CFTC, as many academic and legal experts urged, nor did his draft bill propose to touch the politically powerful credit unions. "We were looking at consolidation only in the banking space," as Friend put it, speaking Washingtonese. As we have seen, both Frank and the Obama administration (acting on Frank's advice) had rejected a single bank regulator as politically and substantively impractical, but Dodd "wanted to be bold," as he put it. "This is no time for timidity," he announced at a news conference presenting his "discussion draft." The proposed single bank regulator was intended to be a symbol of Dodd's boldness. It got most of the media attention when the Dodd bill was introduced.

"The staff produced a Herculean effort," Silverman recounted proudly four days after the discussion draft was released. "I don't know how they did it. Because I can tell you, there's 1,100-something pages, and I drafted not one word of it. My role was basically to bring them sandwiches on Saturday." He also made tentative judgment calls on positions the staff wanted to be sure Dodd approved. "If there were medium-level calls to be made—should we include this, should we not include this, should we go in this direction—knowing Dodd and with my relationship with him, I was comfortable doing that. And if there were calls I thought had to be elevated to him, then I called him. We spoke over the weekend three or four times on issues I did not feel comfortable making the ultimate call on. . . . The staff was here till midnight, and they were in here all weekend. They did a final run-through on Monday with the Senate's legislative counsel, page by page of this thing. And we got this bill out on Tuesday."

The final version incorporated a number of ideas from other Democrats on the Banking Committee that Friend had included to build support for the draft. For example, she included derivatives provisions that were the work of Jack Reed of Rhode Island and his key aide, Kara Stein; and proposals for the resolution of failing firms produced by Mark Warner of Virginia and his aide Nathan Steinwald.

Some of Dodd's provisions angered interested parties. Cam Fine of the Community Bankers immediately denounced Dodd's treatment of state bank supervision. The regulators who would give up staff and responsibilities to the new, single regulator all howled. Yingling of the Bankers Association also attacked the single agency idea. Frank reiterated his view that there was no need to create a single regulator, and good political reasons to avoid the fights this would provoke. The single regulator got little public support from any affected party, though academic experts applauded it.

But the similarities between the Dodd plan and the House and Treasury versions were larger and more substantial than the differences. Dodd's bill reflected the consensus position on what needed to be done. It called for a systemic risk regulator (Dodd's was similar to Frank's council of regulators, also intended to diminish the role of the unpopular Federal Reserve), new resolution authority to allow regulators to put failing firms out of business, regulation of derivatives markets, better regulation of the ratings agencies, government registration of hedge funds, and a new consumer protection agency.

This was a first draft; Dodd wasn't committed to it. "If I were king for a day," he explained, "this [the new arrangements described in his draft] is what it would look like." He knew he was never going to be king. The point was to put down a marker, a starting point. "I called it a discussion draft," Dodd said. "I never intended it to be a final product." This was part of his philosophy of legislating. "To get to an end point [to pass a bill, in other words], you have to plant a flag, get reactions, then you have to move [that is, compromise], and you get to a product that is hopefully what you want. If you start here [he gestured to the middle], you're never going to get here [he gestured to a place on the edge]."

Dodd had not abandoned the goal of writing a bipartisan bill. He remembered the credit card bill earlier in the year, when unanimous Republican rejection in the Banking Committee was followed by intense negotiations and a good, bipartisan deal when the legislation reached the Senate floor. He still believed that his best shot at success would be a Dodd-Shelby bill that could win votes from both parties.

Dodd called a meeting of the Banking Committee for November 19 to begin marking up his bill. Nine days from introduction to markup was a provocative schedule; he knew a real markup was unlikely to begin so quickly. But after dawdling for months, Dodd wanted to get going. To emphasize that point, he called every Republican member of the Banking Committee to tell them he wanted to work together on a bipartisan bill. On the morning of November 19 he sent a copy of his draft bill with a personal note to each member of the committee, reiterating his desire to collaborate.

To celebrate what he hoped would be a momentous occasion, Dodd asked the staff to reserve the mammoth caucus room on the second floor of the Russell Building, the original Senate office building, which opened in 1909. In a city of grand interior spaces, Russell's caucus room is one of the grandest: a vast marble enclosure in the Beaux Arts style measuring seventy-four by fifty-four feet, under an elaborately decorated thirty-foot ceiling. The room is lined with Corinthian columns and pilasters and lit by four enormous crystal chandeliers. This space has been the stage for numerous national dramas, including the Army-McCarthy hearings of 1954, the Watergate hearings of 1973–74, and the confirmation hearings for Clarence Thomas in 1991. Both John F. Kennedy and Robert F. Kennedy announced their presidential candidacies in the caucus room. After the death of Edward M. Kennedy, Dodd proposed and the Senate agreed to formally name it the Kennedy Caucus Room. Dodd hoped the grandeur of the setting might contribute to a historic achievement, which was the goal he had in mind.

He cracked his gavel against a piece of mahogany shortly after 10 a.m. on November 19 to announce the beginning of the meeting. The room was flooded in electric light for television cameras, but the networks had not responded to Dodd's attempt to create a historic occasion. Just C-SPAN sent cameras. The two long tables reserved for reporters had many empty seats, as did the public gallery. Only the seats for Senate staff were full, at least sixty men and women in rows behind the long table covered in wine-red felt where the senators sat. The absent cameras and empty seats were reminders of how small the audience was for the esoteric business of regulatory reform.

Dodd announced an ambitious schedule: He wanted senators to submit amendments in just six days, so a proper markup could begin in early December. "We've got to move," he said, while also insisting that "my intention here is not to jam anybody, or have them feel they have a gun at their head." This was an unusually important bill, Dodd said. "We have to do it carefully, and do it right."

He then introduced his proposals in a spirited speech that trumpeted Dodd's populist ambitions: "American families are suffering through the worst economic crisis since the Great Depression," he said. "Millions have lost their jobs, their homes, their retirement security—and their faith in our markets. They watch some of the people and institutions that caused this mess collect million dollar bonuses and receive billion dollar bailouts. They find themselves unable to find jobs, unable to find credit. And they wonder: who is looking out for them?" One answer, Dodd said, would be the new Consumer Financial Protection Agency, which would have "one mission: standing up for consumers."

He invoked the Kennedys: "[This is] the kind of moment the brothers whose name this room now bears confronted throughout their careers in this body. Then, as now, the status quo was simply unacceptable—and inaction not an option. Failure to take strong action to reform our system would be an act of legislative negligence. We cannot, and will not, protect a broken status quo."

Dodd read his speech without spectacles—a clue that he, like many other victims of senatorial vanity, wore contact lenses. Then he turned the floor over to Shelby, another victim, who also read without glasses, and whose hair, considerably sparser than Dodd's white mane, was still a deep chestnut brown in his seventy-sixth year—a triumph of chemistry. Shelby read his opening remarks in a halting, eyes-to-the-paper manner, conveying the impression that he wasn't familiar with the text—the usual clue that a member is presenting the work of his staff.

From the opening lines, Shelby's remarks were startling—particularly to Friend, her colleague Ed Silverman, and Dodd. All three thought they had worked hard to collaborate with Shelby and his staff. Dodd and his wife, Jackie, had gone out to dinner with the Shelbys several times to cultivate their personal relationship, which Dodd thought had been excellent. None of this seemed to influence Shelby as he read a withering critique, denouncing Dodd's bill and ridiculing the process that produced it.

He began with a complaint that the Banking Committee had failed to launch a modern version of the Pecora investigation that took two years to establish the causes of the 1929 stock market crash. "I believed that the American people deserved a full accounting of what happened. I also believed that such an accounting would be absolutely necessary to lay a foundation for any future legislation." But "ultimately," Shelby noted acidly, "Chairman Dodd chose not to pursue a Committee-led investigation." A bill like the one Dodd had introduced "should be supported by an exhaustive factual record, and then be thoroughly scrutinized in its own right," Shelby said. "I am afraid that this bill fails both tests.

"For example, AIG was at the epicenter of the crisis. One would think that this Committee would have gathered all of the relevant data associated with the activities within AIG's Financial Products Division and interviewed everyone that had anything to do with that debacle. . . . One would think we would have done this, but one would be wrong." This began a long list of items related to the Great Crash that Shelby said should have been exhaustively investigated but weren't.

As he continued this indictment of the committee's negligence, Friend, sitting just a few feet behind Shelby, began to shake her head. On this day she was wearing a dark pink sweater over a black dress, and she was easy to spot. Silverman too had a troubled expression. Dodd kept his head down and made notes as Shelby spoke. In a listless, slightly hoarse voice, Shelby read on. When he finished a long list of items the committee had not thoroughly investigated, Shelby said: "Mr. Chairman, I will repeat, probably for the last time knowing your determination to proceed, that this Committee has not done the necessary work to even begin discussing changes of this magnitude."

This was a put-down that tested the limits of senatorial decorum. Shelby cultivated the image of a nice guy; Dodd thought he really was one. But with these words he accused Dodd of serious dereliction of his duty as chairman.

"Our hope was that the Dodd proposal would provide a base bill that could be amended and then agreed upon," Shelby said, using the royal "we" favored by many senators. "We have concluded that the bill requires a complete rewrite and we intend to offer a substitute at the appropriate time." The absence of an adequate factual basis for legislation would not deter him from presenting his own bill.* Only at the very end of his speech did his tone change.

He would be "opposing this legislation," Shelby said, "not because we disagree on its ends, but rather on its means. For this reason I remain hopeful that we may yet find some common ground. As has been my custom over the years, I remain open to discussions on every aspect of this bill."

These concluding bromides could not take the sting out of all that preceded them—"the eighteen-minute tirade," Friend later dubbed it. She and Silverman were livid, but Dodd had the self-discipline to stick to his game plan despite Shelby's slap in the face. When Shelby had finished, Dodd flashed his winning grin: "I thank you for your endorsement of the bill," he said, provoking general laughter and puncturing the tense atmosphere created by Shelby's remarks. Even Friend grinned.

One after another, senators took up Dodd's offer to make an opening statement. When Frank did something similar in his House committee, every speaker had to respect a tight time limit. In the Senate the clock is rarely a factor; members can drone on. In the first two hours of this meeting, the pace was businesslike. Eight members spoke after Dodd and Shelby, four from each party. None was unreservedly enthusiastic about Dodd's draft, and many had reservations, including Democrats.

Several pleaded with Dodd to work out a bipartisan deal that could enjoy broad support on the Senate floor. One was Michael Bennet, the newly appointed young Democrat from Colorado. Another was Evan Bayh, a moderate Democrat from Indiana. Many seemed unprepared for the speedy timetable Dodd had announced.

---

*   Shelby never introduced a bill of his own; there never was a Republican substitute.

One of the most outspoken was Bob Corker of Tennessee, who had worked with Dodd on the TARP legislation despite opposition to it from many of his Republican colleagues, and who liked the way the chairman ran the Banking Committee. "This has been one of the few places in the Senate where I actually feel like a senator," Corker said, praising both Dodd and Shelby for respecting the views of even junior members. But he was sharply critical of the bill Dodd had introduced. If the Dodd draft were enacted, he warned, the result would be "pandemonium." He wanted to restart the drafting process from scratch to achieve a bipartisan consensus.

Both Dodd and Shelby had lunchtime appointments, and senators had to vote on the floor soon after noon, so the hearing was adjourned for nearly three hours. During the break Friend ran into Shelby just off the Senate floor. She decided to let him see how she felt about his statement. "Senator," she said, "how could you?"

"Oh, that's just politics," she remembered him replying. Friend didn't think so. "It was really shocking to all of us," she recalled, that Shelby would say what he did after she and her colleagues had spent so much time with his staff going over their ideas and intentions, and Dodd had tried so assiduously to include him in the process.

Dodd decided to attribute Shelby's nasty comments to his aides, and perhaps to McConnell. Dodd thought it was obvious from Shelby's presentation that he was reading words written by somebody else. So the eighteen-minute tirade, he thought, was "more a reflection of staff work than coming from him."* Dodd knew, from his staff and from his own experience, that Duhnke was a sharp-edged partisan who had no apparent enthusiasm for bipartisan collaboration. But Dodd was not going to let staff interference get in the way of the deal he was seeking.

When he got back to the Kennedy Caucus Room after that midday break on November 19, Dodd startled Friend and Silverman with an entirely new idea for how to proceed. He didn't ask their advice or approval, he told them what he had already started to do: create bipartisan teams of committee members who could work out compromise positions on some of the most vexing and contentious issues. He'd

---

* Republican staff told their Democratic colleagues later that Shelby had gone over the speech before he read it, and even asked if it were too tough to deliver. Its authors, Duhnke and Oesterle, said it was not, and Shelby went ahead with it.

begun speaking to colleagues about this idea during the break, and it looked hopeful, he told his two aides. He would not be deterred by Shelby's decision to read that statement dumping all over his draft bill.

Dodd told Silverman and Friend he wanted to recruit Shelby himself to work on the contentious issue of consumer protection. In his eighteen-minute speech Shelby had said, "We share the goal of enhancing consumer protection, we do not yet agree on the means to achieve it." That was an opening Dodd wanted to exploit.

Dodd wanted to use two of the most eager and serious-minded members of the committee, Mark Warner of Virginia and Corker. These two had a budding relationship based on a mutual desire to get beyond partisan warfare. They had previously begun working together on regulatory reform issues in an unusual form of bipartisan collaboration. Warner, a successful governor of Virginia known for his moderate approach to issues before coming to the Senate in 2009, accumulated a fortune of $200 million before entering politics, and thought he understood financial markets. He wanted to make a mark on this bill. He also had a long-standing relationship with Dodd: As a student in the 1980s he had been hired as Dodd's personal driver, and had looked up to him ever since. Corker, a successful contractor and real estate developer worth at least $20 million, became mayor of Chattanooga in 2001 and a senator in 2007. He built what he considered a good working relationship with Dodd during the 2008 financial crisis and hoped to play a meaningful role in writing the reform bill. Warner and Corker and their staffs had organized a series of seminars with outside experts to discuss the regulatory reform issues. Both were ambitious junior senators eager to have more influence than is usually accorded to newcomers.

Dodd also wanted help from Jack Reed of Rhode Island, a workhorse much admired inside the Senate and little known outside it. A graduate of West Point and an outspoken liberal on domestic issues, Reed and his talented Banking Committee staff assistant Kara Stein had already drafted a bill to regulate derivatives markets. Dodd wanted Reed to work on derivatives with Judd Gregg of New Hampshire, the newest member of Banking. Like Corker, Gregg had volunteered to help Dodd get the TARP bailout bill through the Senate the previous fall. He saw himself as an expert on financial markets, and he too was interested in derivatives. Dodd saw a natural partnership.

Finally, Dodd wanted to recruit Chuck Schumer of New York and

Mike Crapo of Idaho. He considered both practical-minded and interested in results. He wanted them to explore a set of issues that liberals hoped would be part of financial regulatory reform that fell under the heading of corporate governance. The idea was to require corporations to be more responsive to their stockholders, particularly on issues of remuneration for top executives—"say on pay." Many of the experts who had studied the Great Crash blamed Wall Street firms' incentive schemes that seemed to reward their executives for risk taking rather than long-term success. Frank included a "say on pay" provision in the House bill, requiring companies to consult stockholders about their compensation policies, and Dodd was interested in something similar.

After presenting this novel idea to Silverman and Friend, Dodd presided over three more hours of the opening statements. All included reservations about aspects of Dodd's draft bill; the Republicans were hostile to it. But Dodd would not show any sign of discouragement. "I sense a lot more common interest on at least 70% of the issues here," he said when the last senator had spoken. But he also abandoned the timetable he had announced when the hearing began eight hours earlier, "in light of all the commitments made to really roll up our sleeves and go to work."

Shelby also decided to change his tone. Perhaps he had been taken aback by Friend's pointed "How could you?" His closing remarks were upbeat. He agreed that there might already be agreement on 70 percent of the issues. "We've got a lot of the concepts we've got to work out, but I think we can do it," he said at the end of the afternoon. "We can do it, we've shown it in other things [on other issues], and this is the time to do it. . . . We should be putting together the most important piece of legislation to come before this committee in eighty years. We're going to try hard to work with you to do a good bill." No mention this time of inadequate preparation or knowledge to write a bill.

Over the next two days, Dodd lined up the seven senators he wanted to work on the bipartisan working groups. This task was made easier by the fact that the Senate stayed in session for the next two days, Friday and Saturday, debating the cloture motion to end debate on health care reform legislation and bring it to a vote.

Cloture was the dominant issue in the modern Senate, because sixty votes were needed to cut off debate and force a vote on any pending legislation. As partisan warfare intensified over the previous generation, cloture votes became something they had never been in earlier

Senate history—commonplace events, demanded by the minority party on all kinds of legislation.

To organize his working groups, Dodd exploited the fact that all his colleagues were milling about the Senate floor during those two days. As the health care cloture vote approached early Saturday evening, he passed the word to all Banking Committee members that there would be a special committee meeting right after the vote in Room S116, the meeting room of the Foreign Relations Committee on the first floor of the Capitol, a few steps from the floor. Nearly every member showed up. Dodd announced that he had asked these four teams to get to work on new versions of the key provisions of the bill. He said he couldn't promise to embrace whatever they came up with, but he expected to achieve a bipartisan consensus. Dodd was pleased by the positive reaction his new idea received.

An hour later, as he arrived at Johnny's Half Shell, a popular restaurant at the foot of Capitol Hill, for a late supper, Dodd's cell phone rang. It was Corker, and he had, as Dodd recalled it, a brief message. "I can't tell you his exact words because that would be profane. All I heard was his voice saying 'F-ing brilliant, just f-ing brilliant.' "

It's difficult to argue with Corker's evaluation. Dodd had managed to launch a bipartisan project to look for consensus on a regulatory reform package. It wouldn't be his "ideal world" draft, but he was ready to abandon it. By abruptly changing course, Dodd revived the process. The only losers, he thought, were Duhnke and Oesterle, "who were thrown off balance because all of a sudden there was a possibility of the center of gravity moving to places other than where it is traditionally in such matters." In other words, their boss, Shelby, would not be the only important Republican in the process. If McConnell's intention really was to sabotage the bill, Dodd had outmaneuvered him too, at least temporarily.

Dodd believed in the importance of personal contact. He didn't want any senator to feel left out. "I made a point of calling everybody [on the committee] and telling them I want everybody to be involved in this thing. I said, I'm just setting up working groups, it doesn't mean no one else can work on these things. I did it based on who was interested. As long as people know they're invited and you call them. So much of what we deal with in life is because people feel as though they haven't been talked to. . . . When you talk to people you minimize some of those problems that could emerge."

On November 30, during Congress's Thanksgiving recess, Senator Shelby traveled to Oxford, England, to give a speech at the Oxford Union, the renowned undergraduate debating society. The invitation to give this speech had delighted Shelby. He loved England, and he loved the idea of this son of a steelworker from Alabama at the Oxford Union. He worked hard on the speech he would give there, consulting his wife and a number of outside advisors as well as his Senate staff.

He called the speech "Protecting Taxpayers from Private Losses." It was a serious analysis. Shelby reviewed the government bailouts of American financial institutions, deplored most of them, then proposed remedial steps to prevent the need for more bailouts in the future. He proposed stiffer oversight—something that sounded like a systemic risk regulator—to identify problems before they developed into crises; a new resolution regime to dissolve failing financial firms; new rules to compel institutions to hold more capital in reserve; and increased over-sight for the biggest firms. He explicitly endorsed the idea of "living wills" for financial institutions—a requirement that each firm prepare in advance for its own liquidation, in case it got into serious trouble. All these ideas were consistent with the proposals made already by Treasury, Dodd, and Frank. The only missing element was consumer protection, which Shelby did not mention. "It was a great speech," Dodd said. "I could have given that speech myself." Amy Friend called it "completely enlightened."

In the course of just eleven days, Shelby went from the nasty eighteen-minute diatribe to this statesmanlike performance at the Oxford Union. Dodd and his people were certain that Shelby hadn't written the diatribe, and when they read the Oxford speech, they allowed themselves to hope that it was a serious expression of his real views. Maybe the diatribe really was "just politics." Dodd would pro-ceed as though it was, and would continue pushing for a bipartisan bill he could take to the floor of the Senate.

CHAPTER SIXTEEN

The House Acts

The inner workings of the United States Congress are difficult to explain, and difficult for citizens to grasp, which contributes to the gulf that historically has separated Congress from the people who choose its members. Like any legislative body, the House and Senate have had to develop rules and customs to enable them to function. Many are peculiar; some appear undemocratic. Sometimes it's easy to blame those rules and customs for the mess in Washington.

Every two years, new members are elected to the House and Senate who have promised to clean up that mess. Then they arrive in the Capitol and discover that the mess isn't exactly what they had imagined and campaigned against, and that cleaning it up won't be easy. There always is a mess, though the degree of messiness varies quite widely in different historical periods. A significant portion of the mess is deeply rooted in the histories of the House and Senate. Often there's a good explanation for why some unappealing traditions survive. The Committee on Rules of the House of Representatives exemplifies this phenomenon.

As the traffic cop for the House, the Rules Committee decides what bills will reach the floor for possible enactment; how long the debate will be on each bill that makes it to the floor; how the time for debate will be shared; and what amendments will get a vote. These powers have been exercised by Rules since 1890, when Thomas Brackett Reed of Maine, a progressive Republican and ally of Theodore Roosevelt's, simultaneously held the jobs of speaker and chairman of the Rules Committee, and used the combination to impose (with his colleagues' support) a new order—known as Reed's Rules—on the House.

The idea that the speaker, leader of the majority party, should control the flow of legislation to the floor and the terms of debate went out of fashion twenty years later. For most of the twentieth century, the Rules Committee exercised its vast power autonomously. For decades it was dominated by conservatives, particularly southerners who traditionally enjoyed long tenure—and thus acquired much seniority—in the House. But in 1975, the vast new Democratic majority elected in the Watergate landslide of 1974 restored control over Rules to the speaker, who was given the right to name all Democratic members of the committee, subject to the approval of the entire Democratic caucus. Republicans later adopted the same procedure. This meant that Rules was effectively controlled by the leadership, since the leaders could count on the loyalty of those they appointed to the committee—and could replace them if they slipped into disloyalty.

Control by leadership meant that even in a democracy, legislating was not an entirely democratic enterprise. Every member did not have an equal chance to pass or amend legislation; many in the minority had no chance at all once a bill got to the floor. Leaders, elected by their party caucus, could decide arbitrarily whose bill or whose amendment came to the floor, and under what circumstances. Both parties' leaders have taken full advantage of this power when they controlled the House.

Speaker Pelosi's control was exercised through Louise Slaughter, a feisty liberal from western New York state who never lost the drawl of her native Kentucky, where she was born in 1929. Slaughter was the chairman of Rules for Pelosi; she did what she was told.

A Rules Committee hearing is one of Washington's least-known rituals. The meetings are never televised, and there are no seats in the room for the general public. There are only three dozen leather-cushioned, high-backed chairs for anyone other than the twelve members of the committee, and they are used by staff, members of the House interested in the day's proceedings, and reporters, though rarely do more than a few journalists show up. The committee almost never makes news.

The committee's quarters are tucked under the eaves of the Capitol on its third floor. The compact meeting room has arched ceilings and small windows that look east toward the original Library of Congress building and its copper dome. Portraits of past chairmen decorate the walls, as they do in most committee rooms. The dozen members of Rules sit at a semicircular, raised mahogany dais. The witness for the day's hearing—typically the chairman and ranking minority member of the committee whose bill is being considered—sit at an oval table covered with glass that faces the members.

After lunch on December 8, 2009, committee staff filled the water glasses at each member's seat and stacked the bills to be considered in front of them. One was the brand-new print of the regulatory reform bill, which was the size of a big-city telephone directory and carried a new title: "H.R. 4173, The Wall Street Reform and Consumer Protection Act of 2009." The name had come from Pelosi's staff, which liked to concoct politically appealing names for bills. According to a Pelosi aide, opinion polling had demonstrated the political efficacy of naming "the hated villain"—Wall Street—in the title of the bill. Frank had been offered several options, and he picked this one.

After the committee considered several other items, Frank's bill became the pending business in late afternoon. Frank introduced it, explaining that Financial Services had combined nine bills into this one monster* at the request of the Senate. "Madame Chair," Frank said, "this is a bill that we have been working on for a very long time. . . . We have had more than fifty hours of markups and hundreds of amendments." He noted the bill's bipartisan origins in the many ideas first suggested by Hank Paulson, the last Republican treasury secretary, that were included in the bill.

But the elected Republicans in the House weren't interested in bipartisanship. They just wanted to block Frank's bill. On this same day, December 8, Republican House leaders had invited about a hundred lobbyists representing the financial industry to a 4 p.m. meeting in the Capitol Visitor Center to plead for help. "The message was, Frank and the Democratic majority are ruining America, ruining capitalism, and [you should] stand up for yourselves," a lobbyist who attended the meeting told *Roll Call*, the Capitol Hill newspaper. "They

---

* From the outset, Dodd wanted to keep all elements of regulatory reform in a single package that would require just one cloture vote on the Senate floor. Senate cloture votes, ending debate and leading to a final vote, are the functional equivalent of a Rules Committee rule in the House.

said, 'Look, you all oppose this bill, but only a few of you have come out publicly.' "

John Boehner, the Republican leader, and Eric Cantor, the whip, asked the lobbyists for help from their Democratic contacts who might know if the Blue Dogs or the Black Caucus Democrats could be induced to block the bill. This was an unusual gathering that would have remained a secret had not a few of those present leaked word of it to a reporter.

Republican opposition to the bill was on display that afternoon in the Rules Committee. The four Republican members of Rules and Spencer Bachus, who was invited as ranking Republican on Financial Services to speak about the proposed rule, knew they would have no substantive impact. The outcome was preordained. That was the norm in the Rules Committee, which produced no surprises.

But for many years, partisan sniping had been part of most legislative undertakings in the House, and Rules Committee meetings were no exception. The Republicans, who often agreed in advance on talking points, had decided on this occasion to talk about "government overreach," "jobs," and "bailouts"—slogans they obviously hoped had some political appeal. Bachus spoke after Frank and led the way: "We believe this bill is a massive overreach," he said. "It contains a bailout fund." Bailout had become, for both parties, a dirty word, and Republicans were determined to attach it to Frank's bill.

Frank was eager to reply: "There is a fund there [in the bill—part of the provision creating the new resolution authority to put failing firms out of business]," he said. "It says explicitly in several places that the fund [can] be used only in conjunction with institutions that have been consigned to death. And it is for paying the expenses of winding them down, and some authority to pay some of the creditors. But it is very clear. And if the gentleman from Alabama thinks there is something in the bill that allows money to go to keep institutions going [in other words, to bail out failing firms], I will be glad to look at that language and knock it out." Bachus did not reply.

Pete Sessions of Texas, a conservative Republican member of Rules, was the designated spokesman on jobs. He cited "a study" showing that the Frank bill "will cost 450,000 jobs." Whose study or how it was done he did not explain. Frank replied acidly that the Great Crash had destroyed millions of jobs, and his bill would hopefully prevent the next crash from happening.

Just after 5 p.m. Chairwoman Slaughter brought up the rule that staff had written in advance for the committee's consideration. It called for three hours of general debate on the bill, two hours to be controlled by Frank and Bachus, and another hour to be divided equally between the Agriculture and Energy and Commerce committees, controlled by their chairmen and ranking members. This allocation reflected the fact that the bill included provisions that touched on the jurisdiction of Agriculture (derivatives trading) and Energy and Commerce (consumer protection).

Three hours of debate on a bill with such a broad impact on the financial world—three hours to be shared by 435 members of the House—wasn't much, obviously. If every member got a minute to "debate" the bill, that would require more than seven hours. But this is how the House of Representatives works. The discipline imposed by the Rules Committee allowed the House to consider and pass nearly twice as many bills as the Senate does in each Congress.

The notion that three hours is enough is based on the assumption that the House Financial Services Committee had already done a thorough job of preparing the bill, weighing the impact of its provisions, considering alternatives, and choosing the best ones. This is certainly possible, and in the past actually happened. But in an era when members are more interested in politics than policy, this was not the case. As we have seen, the debate on the bill's provisions in the House committee was sharply partisan and far from exhaustive.

The most careful consideration of the bill was done first inside the Obama administration, and then by the Democratic staff of the House Financial Services Committee. With a few exceptions, members had neither the interest nor the knowledge to immerse themselves in the details of the bill or study how its provisions might work. They deferred to their experts: the staff, and the chairman.

On December 9 the Rules Committee convened again on the subject of H.R. 4173, this time to consider the 238 amendments that members had offered to the bill. Some of them would be ruled "in order" when the bill came to the floor. The committee's job—at least in theory—was to decide which ones.

At a hearing of this kind, members are invited to explain their amendments and make a brief argument for them. Rules Committee members are free to debate any topic that arises—there is an anarchic quality to the discussion. For example, the first amendments offered at this session came from Luis Gutierrez of Illinois. One proposed constraints on "payday lenders," the businesses that make loans to people awaiting their next paycheck, often for very high interest rates. Alcee Hastings, a South Florida Democrat and member of Rules, took this opportunity to defend the payday lending industry. "You have well in excess of 20 million American families who use payday loans annually because they have pressing short-term credit needs," Hastings declared, as though reading a press release from the payday lenders.

Hastings is a unique member of Congress, the only one to have been impeached by the Senate. He achieved this honor when he was a U.S. District Court judge accused of taking a $150,000 bribe and then committing perjury. He was removed from office by the impeachment vote in 1989, but three years later voters in Florida's 23rd Congressional District elected him to the House, and reelected him every two years since. Hastings's remarks on payday lenders went on for several minutes; no one paid much attention.

Most of the real Rules Committee work was done in pre-meetings of committee staff—about thirty strong—and the men and women who worked for Pelosi and the majority leader, Steny Hoyer, and the majority whip, James Clyburn of South Carolina. When a bill like Frank's was under consideration, his staff would also be invited. So would representatives of other interested members or groups like the New Dems or Blue Dogs.

In this case, participants in the pre-meeting went through each of the 238 proffered amendments, wrote brief commentaries explaining the import of each one, and discussed the pros and cons of ruling them "in order." The group also considered special requests to allow or deny votes on particular amendments from the administration, Frank, and other interested parties.

Frank favored allowing numerous amendments to be offered. He believed in giving legislators the chance to legislate. And he had promised several colleagues that he would support giving their proposals a vote. Frank had told Walt Minnick of Idaho that he would support a vote on an amendment Frank ardently opposed, to drop the Consumer Financial Protection Agency from the bill. Frank encouraged Minnick only because he was confident he had the votes to defeat him.

Pelosi and her staff generally discouraged amendments. "Leadership is very amendment-averse," Frank explained, "mainly to avoid having members vote." Amendments can be written to embarrass the members who vote on them. Future opponents can make attack ads on the basis of a vote on one obscure amendment that no one really understands. Pelosi's reluctance to allow amendments was a classic expression of the insecurity that had tormented Democrats since the 1980 election, when Ronald Reagan first scared the stuffing out of them.

Frank never shared that insecurity. "The rule that I have for my staff is, if a member wants something, the default position is yes. And if it's no, then let's see if we can get it to yes," he said on the day the Rules Committee was beginning to consider amendments. "I was going through the amendments today, and somebody said, Well, so-and-so's amendment really doesn't do anything. And I got angry. I said it does do something, it makes someone happy, the member. And yes, it does do some harm if we say no."

In the end the staff agreed on thirty-six amendments that would be ruled in order, meaning they would get a vote. In the three years of Pelosi's speakership, this was an unprecedented number. When the health care reform bill came to a vote, for example, just one amendment was allowed, a Republican motion gutting the bill. The larger number this time reflected Frank's personal influence on Pelosi and the process. Republicans were hardly pleased with the outcome, however, since most of their proposed amendments were rejected—a typical expression of the majority's power to control what would happen on the House floor.

The in-order amendments were mostly technical changes, Republican efforts to undo parts of the bill, or were noncontroversial. Several involved changes to the derivatives provisions to make them less onerous for companies that use derivatives to hedge risks. The most troublesome for the bill's supporters was Minnick's proposal to kill the CFPA. The leadership's team of whips—members who worked under Clyburn and Hoyer to count heads on every issue before it came to a vote—established that once Melissa Bean and her New Dem colleagues were satisfied with the preemption compromise and would support the CFPA, Minnick had no chance of winning. So the decision was made to rule his amendment in order.

The second-day session of the Rules Committee ended at 8:45 p.m. Revealingly, the committee never actually cast a vote on any of the amendments. Staff effectively made the decisions, guided by the leadership. About seven additional hours of debate time were allocated to debate the thirty-six approved amendments. "Floor action" could now begin.

"Action" is a misleading term, however. Floor debate in the House is invariably disappointing. In the modern age it consists mostly of partisan finger-pointing. Occasionally real give-and-take occurs, but that is an exception. Eloquence is equally rare. When dominated by partisan politics, the legislative process rarely produces policy consensus or even a clear statement of policy alternatives. If defeating your political enemy is what is most important, then writing effective, intelligent legislation will inevitably decline in importance. The rules of procedure also minimize the possibilities for drama. Nothing can happen quickly or efficiently. As mentioned earlier, the first step is a debate on the rule. The full House has to approve a rule before it can go into effect. So an hour was set aside to debate the allocation of time and other provisions of the rule for H.R. 4173.

But there was one more wrinkle. The Rules Committee had only presented the draft rule that morning, having completed it late the previous night. Under the rules of the House (Clause 6(a) of Rule XIII), the body cannot consider a rule on the same day that it is delivered by the Rules Committee unless two-thirds of all members vote to do so. However, this provision can be waived by a majority vote. The Rules Committee sent Florida's Hastings to the floor to seek such a waiver, so that the rule for debate on the bill could be taken up at once. By tradition, an hour would be set aside to debate this waiver, and once the waiver was approved, another hour would be devoted to debate on the rule itself.

Consideration of H.R. 4173 finally began shortly before 7 p.m. on December 9, when the Rules Committee was still meeting to consider the amendments. Nighttime sessions were rare, and generally got less attention from the news media, but this didn't bother the House leadership. On the contrary, leadership aides were nervous about the Democrats' ability to use the debate to political advantage. Alexis Covey-Brandt, a senior aide to Majority Leader Hoyer, told Frank's staff she expected "the messaging from Republicans would be better than the Democrats." Republicans would just harp on "bailouts" and more government spending, she predicted, arguments from which they were "getting more mileage" than Democrats, whose bill was complicated and not easily explained.

This was another example of the gaping inferiority complex many Democrats felt in the face of concerted Republican propaganda, an insecurity that was nearly three decades old. Frank disagreed with the pessimistic view. He thought being against Wall Street and in favor of consumer protection was a fine political position, and he was eager to defend it.

Seven p.m. was an unusual time to begin consideration of a major bill, and the vast hall that is the home of the House was mostly empty. This is the chamber seen by large numbers of Americans once a year when they watch the president's State of the Union address on television. Its patterned carpet in peacock blue and gold reflects the electric light that was installed in the mid-twentieth century in place of the skylights that lit the House chamber for the first 120 years of its existence. No more than three dozen members were on the floor, and most of the seats in the galleries—balconies on the southern, western, and northern sides of the hall—were unoccupied when Ed Perlmutter of Colorado began to speak on behalf of the rule. He gave a calm, businesslike presentation, outlining the bill's provisions and defending its importance. The bill, not the rule, was his real subject.

"The legislation before us is the most significant reform to our financial system since the New Deal of the 1930s," he said. "We cannot afford another collapse as we had last fall. It cost this nation trillions of dollars and millions of jobs, and is no longer acceptable. We need to repair and restore the system so that confidence is restored."

The Republicans stuck to their talking points. An early speaker was Tom Price of Georgia, a medical doctor and chairman of the Republican Study Committee, the largest grouping of the most conservative House Republicans. "This ought to be called the 'unending bailout authority, credit-restricting, and permanent job loss act,' " Price said. "It not only doesn't solve the problem of government bailouts . . . it makes them permanent, putting us into a permanent political economy, politicians picking winners and losers." Democrats, he said, "want a government takeover of our economy and our financial services area." Price offered no evidence for these contentions, he just declared them as apparent matters of fact.

Price was not shy about his own ideology: "If we conclude as a society that we are here because of a failure of free-market capitalism and a failure of deregulation, then our kids and our grandkids will lose, because all of the solutions will harm free-market capitalism, depress the economy, and increase regulation, which will destroy jobs and destroy our economy." Alan Greenspan, Hank Paulson, and any number of Republican economists had concluded that the Great Crash did indeed represent a failure of the free market to police itself, but Price was having none of it.

Price's colleague Jeb Hensarling of Texas also took up the talking points. He rejected Perlmutter's assertion that the bill would end bailouts of financial firms. "Why do they have a bailout fund if you're not going to bail people out?" he asked. "My wife and I started a college fund for our children, and the reason we are having a college fund is because we intend to send our children to college." This bit of rhetorical wizardry seemed to please Hensarling.

The youthful-looking Texan, a leader of House conservatives, once worked for a Dallas hedge fund drumming up new clients. He clearly enjoyed the partisan repartee, and didn't worry much about factual accuracy. "This is a job-killing bill," he announced. "It is a bill that creates a huge Federal bureaucracy to ban and ration credit." This was his interpretation of the consumer agency, which in fact had neither mission, and as envisaged in the bill would be modest in size compared to most federal agencies. "I mean, this is the group of people [the Democrats] who have brought us double-digit unemployment, the worst unemployment in a generation. I would just ask my friends on the other side of the aisle, how many more jobs have to be lost under your plan? Small business needs credit. You're going to crush it."

And Perlmutter enjoyed the opportunity to reply: "I just want to respond to my two colleagues [Price and Hensarling] from the Financial Services Committee. After all the hearings we had, after all the witnesses that we heard from, it's almost as if they forgot everything they heard. The wild west mentality that permeated Wall Street permeated the investment community and the banking system and brought this country to its knees last fall. And as a consequence, trillions of dollars of wealth were lost, and millions of jobs have been lost, and it was based on a belief within the Bush administration and the Republican Congress that participated with it that you don't need regulation, these markets will take care of themselves."

When it was his turn to speak, Frank had even more fun ridiculing the Republicans. "Mr. Speaker," he began, respecting the House tradition that all remarks from the floor are directed to whoever is presiding at the time,* "few people in this House, or in the country,

---

* The speaker rarely presides, and only on historic occasions. Usually the job of presiding is shared by junior members of the House. A House parliamentarian is constantly at the presiding officer's side to explain how the job is done.

apparently recognize the enormous significance of January 21, 2009 [the first full day of Barack Obama's presidency]. That is apparently the day on which a number of extraordinary things happened. It's the day on which bailouts began. . . . Bailouts, you may think, started under George Bush—the bailout of General Motors, of AIG, of Chrysler, and the TARP bill [all of which occurred in late 2008, when Bush was still president]. No, apparently, they started on January 21, 2009. . . .

"That was also the day in which we had one of the worst outbreaks of illness in American history—mass amnesia on the part of the Republican Party, who forgot everything that had happened before," Frank continued. Republicans, he said, reminded him of the Bourbons who were restored to the French throne after the French Revolution: "It was said of them that they had forgotten nothing because they learned nothing. That's my Republican colleagues. They have learned absolutely nothing from the fact that a total absence of regulation caused this enormous financial crisis." He reminded his colleagues, "every single bailout now going on in America started under the Bush administration."

His Republican colleagues' "ideologically driven opposition to any regulation of derivatives, of sub-prime mortgages, of excessive leverage by banks" had produced a disaster, Frank said. Nevertheless, "that's [still] their answer: Leave it to the market, because if you try to regulate, you will kill the economy." The substitute bill that Republicans had released several days earlier and would presumably offer at the end of this debate, Frank said, "proudly does zero" to try to prevent a future crisis comparable to the Great Crash of 2008 by improving oversight and regulation the way his bill did.

As to the "bailout fund" in his bill, Frank repeated what he'd said in reply to Bachus at the Rules Committee meeting—yes, there was a fund, but it could only be used to "put an institution to death." His bill radically curtailed the legal authority the Fed had exploited to bail out Bear Stearns and AIG, so under his bill no government money could be used to prop up a failing institution. "There is no bailout," in his bill, Frank said again. "That institution has died."

This remained the tenor of the debate when the subject being discussed shifted from the rule to the bill itself. The blame game took precedence over all else: Republicans sought to blame Democrats for presiding over "a bailout nation"; Democrats blamed the Republican Congresses of 1995–2007 and the Bush administration for regulatory failings that caused the Great Crash.

The issues at hand could fairly be called momentous: The Frank bill created a new regulatory structure that would transform the financial marketplace. It addressed problems that had contributed to a disaster that created the worst economic conditions in the United States in seven decades. But during this unusual night session, the public galleries remained nearly empty; the Press Gallery (the balcony on the east side of the hall) never had more than half a dozen occupants; and the number of members on the floor never exceeded about forty. A dozen staff members sat at tables set among the leather-upholstered chairs of members. A visitor from Denver or Dubuque would have had no inkling that historic legislation was being debated.

The debate on the rule drew to a close shortly after 8 p.m. "Mr. Speaker," intoned Perlmutter, speaking with parliamentary authority, like an old hand and not the second-term, junior member he was, "I yield back the balance of my time, and I move the previous question on the resolution." The speaker pro tempore (the temporary chair) called for a voice vote. "The ayes appear to have it," he announced.

David Dreier of California, the ranking Republican on Rules who had been managing the Republican side of the debate, rose to his feet: "Mr. Speaker," he said, "on that I demand the yeas and nays." This meant he wanted a formal recorded vote, a request he was entitled to make, and that the speaker pro tempore was bound to respect. He called for the recorded vote. Bells in every clock on the House side of the Capitol and throughout the three House office buildings sounded twice, summoning members to the floor to cast their votes.

The bells had an effect the legislation itself could not match: They drew a crowd. Over the next fifteen minutes, more than four hundred of the House's 435 members came to the floor. Some took their credit-card-like voting cards out of their wallets, pushed them into the "Aye" or "Nay" slots on machines around the floor, and left. But most lingered to schmooze. The atmosphere was transformed. The place was full of men and women talking loudly, backslapping, grabbing each others' arms, laughing and teasing. Several were in tuxedos, on their way to black-tie affairs. From the Press Gallery above it looked like a convention of traveling salesmen or some similarly gregarious breed. But all this socializing occurred in two distinct groups. Republicans gathered on the south side of the hall, Democrats on the north. The two had almost nothing to do with each other.

Recorded votes draw a crowd because members are anxious about their attendance records. These too can be exploited for negative television commercials. No one wants to be depicted as a "no-show congressman." There is no easy way for the voters at home to know that their representative has skipped the debate on the Frank bill—attendance is not taken at big debates. But whether or not a congressman voted on the rule for the Frank bill is a matter of public record. In this case, just twenty-two of the 435 House members missed the vote—and it was a meaningless procedural vote. The rule was easily approved, as everyone knew it would be, 235–177.

As quickly as the noisy crowd had assembled, it dissolved. At about 8:30 the speaker pro tempore struck his mallet three times and declared that the House had become "the Committee of the Whole House on the State of the Union for the consideration of the bill, H.R. 4173." The floor was again mostly empty, as were the galleries.

Moving into the committee of the whole, as it is commonly known, is a standard parliamentary move. It simplifies the rules in ways that can expedite the debate. All bills are considered on this basis before the formal action of the House that can turn them into laws. At last, the formal debate on H.R. 4173 was under way. But the quality of the discussion did not improve.

At 8:50 p.m., an hour when the House is rarely in session, Frank stood at a long table on the Democratic side of the aisle and made another speech for his bill into one of the large black microphones that swing back and forth on long metal arms. He again teased the Republicans for criticizing provisions they claimed were in the bill creating a "bailout fund" and a "credit czar" who would control the allocation of bank credit. Neither, Frank noted accurately, was in his bill, but he knew they would be attacked anyhow, because those were the Republican talking points. "There will be a certain amount of fantasy tonight on the floor of the House as they [the Republicans] lament the existence of things that are not here," Frank said, patting the telephone-book-sized bill that lay on the table before him.

To offer his opening speech in the debate, Bachus walked down into the well of the house and put his text on a podium from which he could look out at the entire body. He had decided to make a philosophical address. He began this way: "Mr. Chairman [the presiding officer of the committee of the whole is chairman, not speaker pro tempore], this is a great country, and I think we are all proud of our country. It is no small tribute to our country that people all over the world dream about coming to America. Our forefathers, they were either born here or they dreamed of coming to America.

"America is not just a country; it's an idea, and that idea is about the individual. That's the basis of our country. It's not about the government. It's about the individual, it's about the citizen, it's about freedom, it's about choice.

"Mr. Chairman, the problem with this bill . . . is that it goes right to the heart and strikes a wound against the character of our country. It's the character and the culture of this legislation that is so wrong."

Taking a philosophical approach allowed Bachus to emphasize aspects of his personal political creed that he knew would please his conservative colleagues who were suspicious of him. He could also avoid discussing practical issues like whether the Great Crash had demonstrated the need for more and better regulation of the financial sector, a topic he never mentioned.

"Can we not agree on one thing, that it is time that we allow people in this country to succeed, and we allow them to fail?" he asked as he ended his remarks. "Let's not use the crisis that we have experienced this past year to create the calamity of a government-managed country where the individual, where freedom, where choice is a thing of the past."

The debate continued in this pattern; a Democrat spoke, then a Republican. Remarks from both sides of the aisle became predictable. The Democrats often began with praise for Frank, then defended the bill as a necessary antidote to the excesses that the Great Crash had revealed. Republicans stuck to their talking points—bailouts, big government overreach, jobs—some with a touch of moderation, many with no hint of it. In this sort of debate, there is very little actual debating. The two sides generally talked right past one another, often without reacting to or even hearing the other side's arguments.

Much of the Republican rhetoric was proudly immoderate. Dan Burton of Indiana was an exemplar: "My Democrat* colleagues have moved to take over the auto industry, the health industry, the energy industry, and . . . now they're doing it with the banking industry and the financial institutions of this country. Now, when the government

---

* Calling his political opponents "Democrat colleagues" and not the commonly used "Democratic" was a calculated insult used by many conservative Republican members.

takes over the private sector, that's socialism. And if you don't believe it, look it up in the dictionary." But there was no provision in the bill to "take over" the financial industry.

Lamar Smith, a Texas Republican who was not a member of the Financial Services Committee, announced that "as we have investigated the causes of the financial crisis, one conclusion has become clear. What caused the financial crisis of 2008 was government intervention in the economy." The subprime lenders and borrowers? The Wall Street bankers? Bear Stearns and AIG? Not mentioned by Smith.

Chris Lee of western New York joined in: "This bill creates . . . a new credit czar, who will limit consumer choices, ration credit and increase the cost of doing business. It's outrageous that we want to give this new credit czar virtually unchecked authority to restrict financial product choices for businesses and consumers at a time when this economy is in dire straits." This was apparently a reference to the director of the consumer agency, who in the initial Obama administration proposal could have ordered the use of plain vanilla financial products—a provision Frank had dropped from the bill weeks earlier. And rationing credit had never been mentioned by any of the bill's authors or supporters.

A more detailed statement of the immoderate position came from a member of Financial Services, Michele Bachmann of Minnesota. At the time she was a little-known member who had not yet decided to run for president.

She said in the debate, "Madam Chair, last July an economist from Arizona State University had determined that since the inception of 'Bailout Nation' in September of 2008, the Federal Government has taken ownership or control of eighteen percent of our economy. And if President Obama gets his way and takes over the health care industry, that's another eighteen percent of our economy, or forty-eight percent. [Somehow, eighteen plus eighteen came to forty-eight.] Then, if President Obama and former Vice President Al Gore have their way and cause electricity rates to necessarily skyrocket by taking over the energy industry and imposing a national energy tax, that would mean the government takeover of another eight percent of the economy for a total of fifty-four percent [now forty-eight plus eight equaled fifty-four].

"As harmful to freedom as these bills are, they don't hold a candle to the government takeover and control of every financial transaction of the financial industry. And why? Because when government controls credit, when government rations credit and bails out its politically well-connected friends, that's gangster government at its worst, and that throws a net of government control over every financial transaction entered into in this country. Some experts say that is government control of another 15 percent of the economy for a total of 69 percent. This is nothing less than stunning."

These comments were all examples of a new reality in Washington. Daniel Patrick Moynihan, the professor, author, and four-term Democratic senator from New York who died in 2003, often observed that "everyone is entitled to his own opinion, but not [to] his own facts," which once seemed like a simple statement of common sense. But in the era of unrestrained partisan warfare, politicians have often made up their own facts—as Burton, Lee, Smith, and Bachmann did in this debate—with apparent impunity. Of course, without an agreed set of facts, meaningful debate is impossible.

Most Democrats who participated in the floor debate stuck to their own talking points and ignored the comments of their Republican colleagues. Several did reply to the accusation that the bill constituted socialism. One was David Scott of Georgia, one of the Black Caucus members of Financial Services: "Oftentimes, when we've had great debates and when people get heated up in the call of the debate, when there's nothing else to argue, when there is no other point, you can always rely on 'it's socialism' or 'it's communism.' No. What this is is good old Americanism. This is the most severe financial crisis since the Depression, and it requires this Congress to step forward with the intelligence and the sober mindedness to respond. This isn't socialism."

Scoring political points was as important to the Democrats as to the Republicans. Rhetorical flourishes were favored by both sides over calm, reasoned debate. For example, John Boccieri of Ohio, a first-term Democratic member, offered a holiday season theme in his brief remarks: "Mr. Chairman, in this season of yule tidings, gift gifting, and silver and gold, just what are my colleagues on the Republican side attempting to give Americans with their opposition to this bill?

"My colleagues who oppose this bill would rather give gold to the corporate execs at Goldman Sachs rather than put a little silver and gold under the Christmas tree of ordinary Americans. Bah humbug.

"My friends on the other side of the aisle would rather stand with corporate executives and their thousand dollar suits than stand with those who are in the unemployment line. Bah humbug.

"They'd rather bail out the big banks on Wall Street than help Americans try to keep their homes on Main Street. Bah humbug." Boccieri was indulging in political spin; his assertions weren't facts either.

The general debate on the bill neared an end after midnight. Frank walked down into the well of the House to make his concluding remarks. He emphasized the differences between his bill and the Republican substitute, which would be offered the next day as an amendment that supplanted the entire piece of legislation. It was a modest proposal that offered little new regulation or consumer protection. The Republicans proposed a new chapter to the bankruptcy code to deal with failing financial firms, but no compulsory dissolution of failing institutions, and no significant new rules for derivatives trades. Their bill had no equivalent of the Financial Services Oversight Council—the systemic risk regulator empowered to police and restrict risky behavior by big firms—that was a central element of Frank's bill.

Frank first responded to "misstatements that we've heard," seizing specifically on the oft-repeated Republican criticism that his bill would damage small businesses and thus cost jobs. With evident satisfaction, he reminded the House of the fact that the Independent Community Bankers of America—the bankers of small businesses everywhere—supported his bill. He loved being able to exploit the deal he had struck with Cam Fine three months earlier.

The Republican substitute, Frank said, "is very small because it does nothing to retard the kind of activity that got us in trouble. It does not stop over-leveraging [excessive borrowing by financial institutions], it does not stop unregulated derivatives trading, it does not stop credit default swaps without anything to back them up, it does not stop any sub-prime lending abuses. So yes, that's their view, and they're very clear: Leave it to the private market. We say the private market always does better with sensible regulation."

When Frank spoke there were three other Democrats and four Republicans on the floor, plus about a dozen staff. Just one person sat in the Press Gallery, the author of this book, and a couple of dozen spectators were sprinkled around the public galleries. The three hours of general debate ended as they began, without the slightest drama or excitement.

At two o'clock in the afternoon of December 10, the House reconvened to consider amendments to the bill. But first, two more votes were necessary. The first vote was on a second waiver of the rule requiring a two-day wait between Rules Committee action and floor consideration of a bill, this time for the rule on consideration of amendments. One hour was taken up with that, though again, members talked mostly about the bill itself, not the waiver. A second hour was devoted to debating the rule on amendments, which stipulated how they would be considered, for how long and in what order. Yet again, the discussion was mostly about the bill. Some Republicans used the opportunity to complain about amendments they had offered that the Rules Committee (really the leadership, as we have seen) refused to make in order. Roll call votes, each taking fifteen to twenty minutes, were tallied on both of these measures; both got virtually unanimous Democratic support; no Republican voted for either one.

At 4:25 p.m. the full House, sitting again as the committee of the whole, began to consider the amendments that had been approved, or ruled in order. A five-minute rule was in effect for most of them, so they were speedily dispatched. For the next six hours, amendments were considered. Many were technical and were enacted by voice vote. A few made substantive changes in the bill. One was the Bean compromise on preemption, included in Frank's manager's amendment, though its true significance was far from clear. Frank and the Obama administration both thought it was essentially meaningless.

Scott Murphy, a New York Democrat, offered an amendment favored by the National Association of Manufacturers and many big corporations that allowed somewhat more room for customized derivatives that they used to hedge commercial risks. Some liberals thought the Murphy amendment significantly compromised the bill, but this too was far from clear. Frank proposed an amendment to try to strengthen regulators' hands when dealing with such derivatives, but it was defeated. In both votes, New Dems and Blue Dogs mostly voted with the big companies that wanted the changes that Murphy proposed and opposed Frank's, a reminder that the liberal house leadership could not always count on their moderates' votes. But Frank insisted that the defeats he suffered were relatively minor. The House adjourned after 10 p.m., the second late session in a row.

The most important amendment, Minnick's attempt to abolish the CFPA, came up on Friday morning, December 11, the last day of the debate. Minnick proposed creating a new council of regulators with twelve members to oversee consumer protection efforts by every existing regulatory agency. In addition, the regulators would have to create new divisions of consumer protection. Minnick said this was a better idea than creating a new agency that would have to share responsibility for overseeing financial institutions with the traditional regulators. His critics, including Frank, said it was a bureaucratic monstrosity that wouldn't work.

The key moment in the debate on the Minnick amendment came when Melissa Bean of Illinois rose to speak. To pass, the Minnick amendment would need the support of a large minority of the New Dems. Bean and Minnick were friendly colleagues, and had worked together on the New Democrats' task force on financial regulation, but after winning her language change on the preemption issue, she had no interest in sabotaging the new consumer agency. The CFPA would be a good thing, she insisted when she spoke against Minnick's amendment in the debate. It would have "the expertise, resources, and mission to update consumer financial protection laws and protect our constituents from abusive and unfair financial products and services. . . . I urge my colleagues to oppose this amendment and support this historic underlying legislation and the CFPA it creates."

On the recorded vote, thirty-three Democrats voted with Minnick to replace the new consumer agency with his council of regulators, but a narrow majority of the sixty-eight New Dems voted with Bean and Frank to save the CFPA. The final tally, after every Republican who voted supported Minnick, was 208 in favor of his amendment, and 223 against. The big banks and the Chamber of Commerce had spent millions to try to kill the consumer agency, and Frank (and Camden Fine) had beaten them, at least for a time.

The final chapter of this melodrama began just before 2 p.m. on December 11—a Friday, when members were more than eager to be gone, back to their districts for the holidays. Under the rules of the House since 1995, the last step in the process was a Republican "motion to recommit with instructions," a final chance for the minority to make a statement explaining its opposition to the bill and offering some alternative to it. This took the form of a motion that would, if approved, send a pending bill back to the committee from which it came with instructions about how to change it. For years, the party in control had made it difficult for the minority to get floor votes on its amendments; the motion to recommit was a legislative crumb that majorities offered instead. No one ever expected a motion to recommit to be passed. The idea was "to have a record vote upon the program of the minority," in the words of Frederick H. Gillett, a Massachusetts Republican who was speaker of the house from 1919 to 1925.

But in this case the House Republican leadership decided not to bother with a "program" of its own. The Rules Committee had allowed the Republicans' substitute bill to come up for a vote; it was defeated easily by the unanimous votes of Democrats. The Republican leadership then decided to draft a motion to recommit for messaging purposes—that is, to make more political propaganda. So instead of recommendations for how the bill could be improved, which the Republicans on Financial Services had already prepared in their substitute bill, the motion's instructions were simple: "Strike all after the enacting clause"—kill the substantive provisions in the 1,300-page bill—and replace them with a 247-word substitute with a single purpose: the termination of "the authorities provided under section 101(a) of the Emergency Economic Stabilization Act of 2008"—the Troubled Asset Relief Program, or TARP—on December 31.

TARP had become a dirty word in American politics. In the popular imagination, the acronym stood for the bailouts of the big banks. John Boehner, the Republican leader, Spencer Bachus, and eighty-nine other House Republicans had voted for TARP in October 2008 at the urging of George W. Bush and Hank Paulson, but that was now forgotten, ancient history. In Republican rhetoric, TARP had become a Democratic program.

The Republican leadership chose Charles Dent of Pennsylvania to introduce the motion to recommit. The Republicans on Financial Services disliked the idea of discarding their substitute bill and proposing simply to kill TARP instead. Frank said later that he had asked Bachus why this had happened: "He said, 'Beats me. I told them that was stupid.' " "Them" was the Republican leaders who had proposed this idea.

When it was again his turn to speak, Frank eagerly made rhetorical use of this unexpected development: "For those who might have believed that when the Republicans . . . offered a substitute that they said that was a better way to regulate, for those who might have believed that somebody meant that, here's the proof that it was all a sham," he said. "The gentleman from Pennsylvania [Dent] I think forgot to mention . . . that the recommit motion kills all regulatory reform—dead, gone. There's no regulatory reform."

Frank consumed the last five minutes of time available. The chair called for a vote on the motion to recommit, which the Democrats easily defeated. Then at 2:20 p.m. the speaker pro tempore announced the final vote: "The question is on the passage of the bill." Once again members trooped to the floor with their electronic voting cards. An excited buzz on the floor as the members assembled was the first clear sign since the debate began that something big was afoot.

When a vote is under way, the results are projected onto the wall above the speaker's dais showing both the votes of individual members and a running total of "yeas" and "Nays." Many members watched closely as the total of "Aye" votes approached 218, the magic number in a House of 435 members. When the tally hit 219, applause broke out on the Democratic side, with all eyes directed at Frank. The chairman, obviously delighted, took a grand bow, then gestured toward Roslanowick, Beresik, Miller, and other members of his staff who were standing at their places behind the long table amid the members' seats. The Democratic members gave more applause to them. The staff then gave a bow of thanks. This was unusual—Roslanowick said later she couldn't remember another example of such an acknowledgment to staff. But it was surely earned—there would have been no bill if members had been required to produce it by themselves.

When all present had voted, the final tally was 223 "Ayes," 202 "Nays." Frank had lost twenty-seven Democrats, mostly from conservative districts, but his bill had been enacted. Colleagues approached him to offer congratulations and pat him on the back; Frank beamed.

His big job was done, but there remained rituals to perform. Much of what passes for events on Capitol Hill are really shows put on for the television cameras, and one such had been prepared by Pelosi's staff for this moment of victory. The setting was the Rayburn Room, a large space a few steps from the floor of the House named for Sam Rayburn of Texas, the Democratic speaker from 1940 to 1961 except for four years in the 1940s when Republicans controlled the House. A few minutes after the final vote, Pelosi and Frank arrived together in the Rayburn Room. Frank looked exhausted. His shirttail was untucked and visible under his jacket, his pants legs were falling down around his shoes like downed sails on a yacht, his eyes were bloodshot, but colleagues in the room were eager to hug him and clap him on the back. Henry Waxman of California whispered too loudly, "tuck in your shirt!" Seven television cameras and two dozen reporters awaited them, an audience the speaker's staff anticipated and was eager to exploit.

Pelosi's staff had found Sue Chapman of Staten Island, New York, a woman who lost her house after being persuaded—"tricked," in her words—to take out a variable rate mortgage she couldn't afford or understand, and put her in front of the cameras as an example of the human suffering the Democrats would now prevent with their new regulatory reform law. This gimmick was a flop—no network put Chapman on the air, and her appearance felt forced and artificial. Pelosi's Democrats had little talent for messaging, and chronically envied Republicans' ability to do propaganda more effectively.

This event quickly deteriorated into a classic example of the way Congress can do things for its own reasons that appear silly or worse to ordinary citizens. Pelosi had invited eight Democratic members to participate in this media event misnamed a news conference. None of the eight made any news; instead they scored political points and heaped praise on one another. It all felt like a missed opportunity.

There was one genuine moment when Frank spoke about the role of his staff: "I don't think the American people understand what a bargain they get with the people who work on our staffs, who are so talented and hard-working and could make a great deal more money elsewhere but really put in very, very long hours under difficult circumstances." Many of them were in the Rayburn Room to hear these words.

News accounts in the next day's papers emphasized the compromises Frank had had to make to get the mammoth bill through the House: on preemption of state laws, on the exemption for auto dealers, on the administration's original desire to require lenders to offer plain vanilla products. These all reflected a moderate strain among House Democrats that prevailed in the end.

Frank considered himself a proponent of moderation too, despite his reputation as an outspoken liberal. None of these compromises bothered him, because none was really significant. Frank was pleased that "I have a sense of what's important and what isn't important, and am perfectly willing to trade off the unimportant."

The same news stories reported the conventional wisdom of the time that the House bill was destined to be watered down in the Senate, where Dodd and Shelby were still working on a bipartisan version. *The Washington Post* quoted Ed Yingling of the American Bankers Association: "'There is a possibility of getting a bipartisan bill in the Senate, but it will entail compromise. I think it [the House bill] would have to be modified significantly."

Frank shared this view. "I am pessimistic that we can get the whole thing," he said in December. The consumer agency was especially vulnerable to Senate machinations, he thought.

Revealingly, Frank had little personal contact with senators, and no inside information of his own. He relied on regular conversations between Jeanne Roslanowick and Ed Silverman for intelligence on what was happening in "the other body," as House members often called the Senate. Frank and Dodd had friendly personal relations and agreed on most political questions, and they were wrestling with exactly the same regulatory reform issues, but they had not spoken directly to one another in weeks. "Chris resents it if I get involved" in Senate deliberations, Frank said, so he had to keep his distance. This was typical of Congress, where the two bodies generally have little to do with each other, despite the fact that for anything to be accomplished, they must eventually act in concert. "I think Chris has tried his best, I'll see what happens," Frank said.

CHAPTER SEVENTEEN

Searching for Consensus

Typically, the Senate had fallen far behind the House. By December, when Frank was celebrating passage of his bill, Dodd had nothing concrete to show for the year's efforts. This did not alarm him. He felt he understood the rhythms of his institution, which was almost always slower-moving than the House, and he had long anticipated that it would be the end of 2009 or early 2010 before financial regulatory reform would move to a front burner in the Senate. In a conversation in October he spoke of a window of opportunity that he thought would remain open for the subsequent three or four months.

Dodd was prescient. He did make significant progress in the subsequent four months, and seven months later he won Senate approval for a bill. The story of how that happened is a rich tale of political maneuvering, intrigue, and hard work over endless hours by talented staff—a classic example of how the Senate can accomplish something substantial when the gods are smiling on "the world's greatest deliberative body," as senators like to call their institution.

The four working groups that Dodd had created after the Shelby tirade on November 19 provided a vehicle for renewed involvement by Shelby and his staff, which Shelby agreed to after his return from England in early December. Friend reported in mid-December that "there have been a lot of meetings." Dodd and Shelby talked several times, as did their staffs. The two also met with Senators Warner and Corker—the working group on resolution authority—and with Senators Gregg and Reed, who were considering derivatives regulation. Staff members who participated memorialized these meetings on paper that then bounced back and forth between the two offices. "Shelby keeps saying, let's keep working to get an agreement," Friend reported.

"We're meeting, we're back talking, we had a little estrangement," Shelby said in a conversation on December 16. "I'm about to go meet with Senator Dodd, again. We are honestly making progress. . . . We will probably make a joint statement before we leave here [for the Christmas break]. . . . We hope maybe toward the end of January to have crystallized a bipartisan agreement."

Just six days later Shelby switched signals once again. He came to a December 22 meeting with Dodd, Silverman, and Friend with his senior aides, Oesterle and Duhnke, carrying a list of items "on which we are still far apart." Dodd had hoped to use this meeting "to try to tie down agreements on issues he thought were close to being settled," in Friend's words, but Shelby wanted to read this list. Dodd and his aides were convinced that, like the tirade speech, the list had been written by Duhnke and Oesterle, and they were exasperated by it. Shelby said again and again that a good bill should do X or Y or Z, "but our bill doesn't do that."

Friend interrupted Shelby several times, insisting that his list misrepresented their positions. His presentation "seemed to take us backwards," Friend said. "I was flabbergasted, and I'm not very good at hiding my emotions." Shelby reacted by tacking once again, insisting that he still wanted to come to an agreement.

The next day, December 23, all eight senators involved in the working groups and their aides had a good meeting. According to Friend's notes from that occasion, Shelby said at one point, "Let's get this done by spring." Afterward Shelby invited Silverman and Friend to come to his office for a glass of holiday eggnog, which he described as "a peace offering." Friend recalled, "It was incredibly nice and friendly, and he said again that he wanted to agree on a bill." Later that day Shelby and Dodd jointly issued an upbeat press release: "For the last few weeks we, and other members of the Banking Committee, have been engaged in serious negotiations. . . . These talks have been extremely productive. . . . We hope to resolve the remaining issues before we reconvene in January," after the holiday break.

If Dodd's legislative method was to smother his colleagues with kindness and consideration, Shelby's was to be unpredictable. "He'll drive [his colleagues] crazy," explained his old friend from Alabama Mike House, a Washington lobbyist. "They can't figure out where he is. He won't deal, he won't deal, he won't deal—and suddenly he's dealing. That's what makes him such a good legislator."

Dodd was distracted by the final stages of the Senate debate on health care reform, which finally came to a vote just after 7 a.m. on Christmas Eve—a vote scheduled for an early hour to allow senators time to get home for the holiday. This bill had been Dodd's principal preoccupation all year, and his largest responsibility since his friend Ted Kennedy had left the Senate in May because of his cancerous brain tumor. Dodd and many colleagues had Kennedy on their minds when the Senate passed the health care reform he had championed for many years by a party-line vote of 60–39. Dodd considered the vote one of the great events of his Senate career, and an apt memorial to his pal. Democrats since Harry Truman had tried to assure health insurance for Americans, and they had finally succeeded.

Like most other senators, Dodd left the Capitol that morning for Reagan National Airport, headed home to Connecticut. But Dodd's plane was late, and he had time to kill. He asked the aide who was driving him to stop at Arlington National Cemetery so he could visit Ted Kennedy's grave. On the way there he got a call on his cell phone from President Obama. The president thanked him for his help with the health care bill—another reminder that he had been part of something historic.

"I knew Teddy's grave was there near his brothers," said Dodd. "So I got up to President Kennedy's grave. . . . Then I could look down and see where Teddy was off on the right. . . . I was looking out over the city."

This is perhaps the capital city's finest view. From the Kennedy gravesite one can look back across the Potomac River to the Lincoln Memorial, the Washington Monument, and, in the far distance, the dome of the Capitol, lined up in a row. "It was cold, there was snow on the ground, an incredible morning," Dodd said. "There was a haze on the city and the sun coming up."

And Dodd asked himself a difficult question. "Do you really want to do this again?" He meant, did he, at age sixty-five, and five months after surgery for prostate cancer, really want to run for a sixth term in the Senate? Did he want to devote the coming year to fundraising and campaigning, then serve into his seventies for yet another term? "Maybe it was the place, maybe it was being tired, maybe it was the wrong time to ask the question," Dodd said later. "But I remember answering the question that morning, and it was a relief."

The answer was "No, I really don't want to spend seven more years doing this." It was an answer that grew out of Dodd's personal frustrations with the ways the Senate had changed, and with the unexpected difficulties he confronted when trying to persuade his constituents that he still deserved their support. And once he said that no to himself, "I didn't look back for a single second. I mean it really was the right decision."

One factor that influenced him, Dodd said when he told this story later, was the realization that he would have a much better chance of winning approval for a financial regulatory reform bill if he were not a candidate for reelection. He explained this in classic senatorial terms: "I can't imagine that John Cornyn [the Texas senator who was chairman of the National Republican Senatorial Committee, charged with helping Republicans defeat Democratic incumbents] was going to let me, as a candidate in 2010 and chairing the Banking Committee, get away with writing a bill and getting the credit for it politically without making it a lot harder for people to work with me." In other words, at a moment when Republicans thought they might be able to win control of the Senate, and when Dodd looked like a vulnerable Democratic incumbent, the pressure would be on his Republican colleagues on Banking not to help him produce a reform bill. The imperatives of partisan warfare would overtake any sense of responsibility to reform the financial system—these were the values of the modern Senate.

"I might have robotically kept on moving through all of this, you know, going to the fundraisers and trying to do all this [campaign] stuff. And even if I hadn't been banged around a lot and in deep political trouble, it would have been hard to get the bill done. In a sense, you're given moments. Would I like to stay? Really no. If you asked me, would you stay a couple more years and do this bill? Yeah, I'd do that. But the six and seven"—the number of years he'd have to stay at the job, if he ran for reelection and won—"really just were daunting to me. So in a sense I was given a gift."

He admitted that bowing out wasn't a thought that came naturally to a politician with a healthy self-regard and an unblemished record of electoral victories over thirty-five years. "I don't think I thought of that [giving up], believe me, for those [previous] two years that I was getting the articles every Friday and Saturday [stories from Connecticut newspapers clipped by his staff], reading some columnist kicking the crap out of me, accusing me of all sorts of things—it was not pleasant, believe me. And then the phone calls stop. And the people look at you without looking directly in your eye." And then a particularly painful memory: "I remember being at a UConn basketball game and some guy just flipping me the bird. I didn't know what he was doing at first—just glowering. I never in thirty-five years had that happen to me before." Being unpopular was no fun.

Much else had changed in Dodd's world over those thirty-five years. He entered one kind of Congress, and now served in something very different. He had a longer view than most others, because he could remember his father's Congress of the 1950s, and the cross-party fraternizing of that era. As recently as the 1960s, members of the House and Senate got just three paid trips home per year. Soon after Dodd arrived in the House in 1975, that number was raised to forty, an early warning of what was to come. Today there are no limits on the number of paid trips home that a member can take.

Ed Silverman had been Dodd's chief of staff in the late 1980s. He recalled that Dodd in those days often ate lunch in the senators' dining room in the Capitol where only members were welcome. "Many days sixty senators had lunch there," socialized with each other, talked frankly without any staff in the room, Silverman recalled. "Now I don't think anyone eats lunch there." By 2009, most of the close friends Dodd had made had left the Senate. He felt quite lonely.

The atmosphere on Capitol Hill had changed radically. Dodd particularly regretted the transformation of the Republican Party during his years in Washington, which he thought began with Ronald Reagan's presidency in 1981, which was also Dodd's first year in the Senate. He lamented "that decision to really go after government" that began with Reagan's inaugural address, which included one of his most famous lines: "Government is not the solution to our problem, government is the problem." That, said Dodd, was the beginning of the end of Republicans who believed in governing and cared about the quality of government. He mourned their disappearance.

Partisan warfare intensified in the 1980s. His Democrats were partly to blame, especially with their emphasis on redistricting House seats to try to assure as many safe ones as possible, Dodd acknowledged. Safe House seats meant more partisan combat. "If I could change one thing, it would be how districts are drawn," he said. The Senate was a healthier environment than the House, Dodd believed, because many fewer of its members could assume they would win reelection. Entire states were more diverse than individual House districts. Representing a diverse state encouraged pragmatic moderation.

The character of the House changed fundamentally after Republicans won control in 1994, Dodd said. Newt Gingrich of Georgia, the new speaker in 1995, came to prominence by denouncing the alleged corruption of his political rivals, and he believed in the efficacy of all-out political war. Over time, many of the Republicans who cut their political teeth in Gingrich's House moved on to the Senate. "The House is the farm system for the Senate," Dodd observed, "so we have become more like the House"—more partisan, less collegial, less congenial, and for Dodd, a lot less fun.

By 2009 there were eighteen Republican senators who had learned their congressional politics in Gingrich's House. Few of them shared Dodd's view of the Senate as a place to collaborate with colleagues regardless of party. Even inside the Democratic caucus, Dodd perceived a disheartening change. "There used to be raucous debates in caucuses about various issues, but you never read about them, they were private. Now you've got whole press conferences [given by senators] to announce what they said inside the caucus meeting. The very purpose of having a closed-door session is so you can have a real debate. Now you get very cautious about expressing your views even in . . . those meetings." The debates Dodd remembered were about policy; now most of the heated discussion was about politics. Dodd was dismayed by the fact that many Democratic caucus sessions were devoted to discussions of fundraising and partisan warfare. Pragmatic moderation was what "made the place work," he thought, but now "everything works against" that moderation.

Dodd hated what money had done to Congress. "We're actually shrinking the pool of people who think about doing this [running for the Senate]," he said, and a disproportionate number of those who do think about it are rich. Too many good people would never dream of running because the money required was out of their reach. Dodd perceived a palpable decline in the quality of senators in the age of big money: "The quality isn't what it was." Nearly two-thirds of his colleagues at the time had personal wealth of more than a million dollars. Because some were enormously rich, the average wealth of all one hundred senators was $13.2 million.

Dodd's first campaigns for the Senate cost about a million dollars. Planning a 2012 race, he thought he would need "somewhere around $5 million." He still had debts from his hapless campaign for president in 2011. The prospect of raising all that money "really is daunting," he said.

But Dodd's biggest frustration was his inability to communicate effectively with his voters. He blamed changes in the news media for this. The fact that no Connecticut newspaper or television station had a reporter in Washington meant that no one had the job of reporting what Dodd was doing. For most of his career, he knew that his votes and his speeches would get special attention in the Connecticut papers, because their Washington reporters focused on the doings of the Connecticut delegation. So voters who cared could follow their members, keep an eye on them. Now no one reported regularly on Chris Dodd for the citizens of Connecticut. Public policy and the deliberations of Congress were no longer considered a big story—in Connecticut, or, most of the time, in the country.

When his father was a Connecticut senator in the 1960s, Dodd said, Tom Dodd would come to a Lions Club dinner in the town of Ansonia, say, and find five hundred people waiting to hear from him. "He'd have a clear shot at an influential group of people. He could explain his votes and positions on big issues, and make a real impression." Now, said Dodd, if he went to the same dinner, there might be fifty people present—the Lions Club wasn't what it used to be. They were likely to be people who followed the news on their favorite, ideologically compatible cable channel, and they had set opinions already. "They would not be waiting to hear an explanation from me." Dodd worried that "the whole notion of representative government has been eroded. I'm not sure where this is all going to end up."

This was of course a self-serving analysis. Dodd had been wounded by the collapse of his public support that opinion polls had documented over the previous two years, and like most politicians, he preferred to blame others, not himself, for his travails. Just as he had never wanted to acknowledge his father's ethical transgressions, he also avoided for months taking responsibility for his transactions with Countrywide, or for the consequences of his foolish decision to move his family to

Iowa in 2007. But even if his political problems were largely of his own making, his analysis of how the Senate was changing was accurate. The conditions he described made it much easier for him to give up his seat than it would have been ten or fifteen years earlier. This was not the Senate Dodd had fallen in love with; leaving it would not be so hard.

Dodd announced his decision from the front steps of his home in East Haddam, Connecticut, on January 6, surrounded by family: "None of us is irreplaceable. None of us are indispensable. . . . In the long sweep of American history, there are moments for each elected public servant to step aside and let someone else step up. This is my moment to step aside."

The Hartford Courant, the state's most important newspaper and a source of much criticism of Dodd in recent years, reacted generously. "He's a major league political player, a lion in his own right, a workhorse who managed four major pieces of legislation last year alone, a partisan who could nonetheless reach across the aisle, a lawmaker good at the inside game," the *Courant* editorialized. "He has occasionally disappointed, yes; but on balance he's delivered. For four decades, Connecticut and the nation have benefited from Mr. Dodd's work in Washington."

For Dodd's staff on the Banking Committee, this was sad but also welcome news. Two months earlier, discussing the grim polls from Connecticut, Ed Silverman had wondered aloud, "Has the Connecticut electorate just written him off?" Silverman was obviously afraid that this was exactly what had happened. So he was relieved that his friend and boss had found a graceful exit from his political difficulties, and could concentrate on one last legislative challenge, financial regulatory reform.

Amy Friend hoped that the affection many senators felt for Dodd, Republicans and Democrats, could now be exploited to advance regulatory reform. And without the demands of a reelection campaign, Dodd would have more time to work on the issue. On the day after his retirement announcement, she said she felt a new optimism that they would get a good bill through the Senate. McConnell and the Republicans had an incentive to try to frustrate Dodd's efforts as long as he was a candidate for reelection, she said, but now that motivation "is gone." She continued to believe that Republicans would ultimately come down on the side of a bill. "Do they really want to be the party identified with protecting Wall Street?" she asked. She thought not.

But not everyone agreed. In that same month of January 2010, a seventeen-page memorandum began circulating among Republicans in Washington that suggested ways to oppose financial regulatory reform without incurring political liabilities. This document was written by Frank Luntz, an entrepreneurial Republican pollster who had long advised Newt Gingrich on effective political terminology.

Luntz's findings and advice had colored American politics for two decades, though his work was controversial and not always reliable. His polling and focus groups had helped Gingrich formulate a famous essay, "Language, a Key Mechanism of Control," which was distributed in the early 1990s to hundreds of Republican candidates by GOPAC, Gingrich's political action committee. The memo advised Republicans to describe themselves and their plans with "optimistic, positive words" like active, humane, moral, fair, passionate, principled, tough, and courage. Democrats and their policies should be described with words like decay, betray, cheat, corrupt, disgrace, liberal, incompetent, pathetic, taxes, and traitors. None of this had any connection to facts, obviously; it was all a matter of labels.

In 2009 Luntz had advised Republicans to describe the Obama health insurance reforms as a "government takeover of health care"—something it wasn't, but a slogan that the GOP embraced and many Americans came to believe, judging by opinion polls.

House Republicans used the "government takeover" rhetoric in the December 2009 floor debate on Frank's regulatory reform bill, as we have seen, even before this Luntz memo appeared. The new memo was based on polling and focus groups done after the House passed Frank's bill. Luntz's work was expensive, but the sponsorship of this memo was never disclosed, and Luntz refused to discuss it. The Obama administration assumed it was done for the Republican National Committee but had no evidence of this. Whoever sponsored it, the memo's clear purpose was to rationalize opposition to financial regulatory reform. It offered no new ideas for how to prevent future financial crises, even as it gave this stern warning to its audience—obviously Republican members of Congress. (The underlining, capitalization, and boldface type are from the original document):

"<u>You must acknowledge the need for reform that insures this</u> [financial crisis] <u>NEVER happens again</u>. Despite the different perspectives [voters held] on the causes of the crash, there is an agreement that the crisis must be addressed—that changes must be made so the mistakes that led to this point are never repeated. <u>The status quo is not an option</u>. The system failed us—all of us—and the causes of the failure **must** be corrected."

But the closest Luntz came to a concrete policy recommendation appeared under his favorite heading, "Words That Work." The words he proposed that Republicans use were these:

"We don't need more laws. We need better enforcement of current laws. We don't need more bureaucrats. We need the people in charge to do their jobs as they were meant to be done. We don't need layers and layers of additional federal bureaucracy. What we need is to instill accountability, responsibility and effective oversight to what is being done already."

In other words, the status quo that was, earlier in the memo, "not an option," turned out to be the only option—no new laws or regulations, no new agencies or regulators, just a more effective version of what had been tried already.

To defend this do-nothing position, Luntz wrote, Republicans could depend on voters' distrust of all government programs and officials. He offered these additional "Words That Work":

"If there is one thing we can all agree on, it's that the bad decisions and harmful policies by Washington bureaucrats that in many ways led to the economic crash must never be repeated." This, wrote Luntz, "is your critical advantage. Washington incompetence is the common ground on which you can build support."

The Republicans' most potent verbal weapon, Luntz wrote, was the word "bailouts." "Frankly, the single best way to kill any legislation is to link it to the Big Bank Bailout"—the bailouts orchestrated by George Bush's government and embraced by Republican leaders of both houses of Congress, of course, but Luntz didn't care about that detail. The truth was irrelevant. "You must be an agent of change," he told Republican politicians, because the pain inflicted by the crisis "is real and omnipresent." But the change they should favor is to demand "government accountability," never mentioning Wall Street, banks, or mortgage brokers. "It is important to ask some basic questions: What government regulator lost their job for their hand in the crisis? What government policies were changed? What laws were repealed? The obvious answer is **none**."

Of course the Frank bill, the implicit target of Luntz's memo, actually would cause some regulators to lose their jobs and would change many government policies and existing laws, but no matter—the argument was the thing. The cynicism was breathtaking. Here was a vivid example of a powerful phenomenon that had become common in American politics: creating an alternative reality for a political purpose. Such "realities" are designed to cater to popular prejudices, whether or not they are rooted in facts. Luntz and like-minded manipulators called them "perceptions." Their use had become a hallmark of the partisan warfare in Congress, especially among the Gingrich brand of Republicans. And for Luntz this game was second nature. He once told Nicholas Lemann of *The New Yorker,* "Perception is reality. In fact, perception is more real than reality."

Democratic pollsters ridiculed Luntz's memo, arguing that in their surveys, Luntz's "words that work" in fact didn't work, and that public opinion strongly supported new regulation of the financial markets. Polls taken by news organizations and independent polling organizations confirmed this conclusion.* Celinda Lake, a Democratic pollster, wrote a memo to "progressives" that mimicked Luntz's style. She argued that Democrats should welcome a fight over financial reform. "Our opponents are defending the rigged, unfair system we have now. Never forget this. Emphasize early and often that the status quo is unacceptable and the other side wants to keep us going in the wrong direction—the same direction that got us into this economic crisis. Force the other side to defend the status quo, and we win," she wrote.

Dodd and his aides agreed that the politics of the issue favored them. Dodd said repeatedly in conversations from mid-2009 onward that he was certain that a significant number of his Republican colleagues wanted to be on the side of reform, not least because quite a few told him so personally—and privately.

On January 19, Democrats lost their sixty-seat majority in the Senate. Scott Brown, a Massachusetts state legislator, won the special election to fill Kennedy's seat. Brown, a charming, good-looking moderate who crisscrossed the state in his pickup truck preaching common sense and exploiting Tea Party enthusiasm, was the first Republican to

---

* For example, a poll by the Pew Center for the People and the Press in March 2010 found that voters favored "stricter regulation of financial institutions" 61–31 percent.

win a Massachusetts seat in the Senate in thirty-eight years. This was a jolt to Senate Democrats and to Obama.

Two days later, President Obama made a brief speech at the White House on the subject of financial regulatory reform. Since October, Obama had been toying with the idea of publicly embracing a suggestion from Paul Volcker, the legendary former chairman of the Federal Reserve, to try to ban banks from making investments in financial markets using their own capital, a practice known as proprietary trading. Obama had decided he wanted to do this in December, and had telephoned Dodd to tell him so. "He didn't have the secretary of the treasury call me, the president called me himself," Dodd recounted. "That's not normally what happens." The phone call persuaded Dodd that Obama was serious about this idea, which hadn't been part of the original administration white paper or its draft legislation.

After the phone call, Dodd said, he discussed the issue "as a general matter" with colleagues, including Republicans, and without mentioning the phone call from Obama. "The reception was pretty good"; even some Republicans were interested. Dodd was pleased, and decided that some limits on, or ban of, proprietary trading should be part of his effort to come up with a bipartisan bill.

But before he could start that process, Brown won in Massachusetts and Dodd was summoned to the White House for the January 21 media event. So was Frank. They found Paul Volcker there too. The three of them were to be part of the backdrop when Obama formally embraced what the White House political operation had dubbed the "Volcker rule." Obama described it as a way to "strengthen the financial system while preventing future crises."

"We simply cannot accept a system in which . . . banks can place huge, risky bets that are subsidized by taxpayers. . . . And we cannot accept a system in which shareholders make money on these operations if the bank wins but taxpayers foot the bill if the bank loses," Obama said. *The New York Times* headline the next day was just what the White House wanted: "Taking a Populist Stance, Obama Takes on Banks." This was widely seen as a response to the Democrats' humiliating defeat in Massachusetts.

Dodd played the part of the good soldier, but with considerable caution. He put out a statement after the White House event expressing his agreement that "taxpayers should not be underwriting the risky activities" of banks and the holding companies that owned them.

"Companies that choose to take such risks should do so on their own dime and not in a way that threatens the stability of our economy," he said. But he was cool about Obama's specific suggestion: "I look forward to studying the President's proposal and will give it careful consideration as the Committee moves forward on financial reform," Dodd said.

Dodd was angry, and his anger had nothing to do with the substantive idea of limiting or banning risky trading by government-insured banks. "My problem wasn't the issue, it was the idea that it would be introduced the day after the Massachusetts election," Dodd explained a few days later, "and that it was the subject of a major press conference, with the lining up down there [he meant he, Frank, and Volcker serving as props at the White House media event]. . . . Why? What was the point, at that moment? Things were moving pretty well, I had the issue [of banks' proprietary trading] on the table, we were talking about it a little bit, but all of a sudden it looked as though it was something other than what it was."

What it looked like was an attempt by Obama to score political points by bashing the banks in response to Scott Brown's victory. "I don't think it gains anything politically," Dodd said. "It looked as though the motivations behind it were completely contrary to what we were trying to achieve"—partisan political point scoring just when Dodd thought a bipartisan deal was within reach. "It looked like it was presented in panic," said Ed Silverman of the Banking Committee staff—"because it was."

Dodd worried that the political hands at the White House were more interested in scoring those political points than in getting a bill. He understood the temptation to play politics. Goldman Sachs had just reported earnings of $13.4 billion for 2009, the biggest annual profit in Goldman's history. All the major banks were again paying large bonuses to their executives because—thanks to government intervention—they had done so well in 2009, infuriating their many critics. But Dodd felt there was no time for political maneuvers. He had announced his retirement, and had to get moving on a bill right away—"a consensus bill" with bipartisan support. If the White House succumbed to the temptation to score debating points, Republicans would respond in kind and the bill would die—this was Dodd's fear.

Dodd took the temperature of Republican and Democratic Banking Committee members. He was relieved to discover that Obama's embrace of the Volcker rule had not changed the generally positive atmosphere. "The members still seem to want a bill," Friend reported at the end of January.

On February 4, Shelby came to Dodd's office with Duhnke and Oesterle to meet with Dodd, Silverman, and Amy Friend. It was an upbeat session. Shelby read a prepared document on consumer protection that contained significant concessions to Dodd's position, though not enough yet to satisfy him. For the first time, Friend said afterward, "I heard Shelby say, 'I want to make a deal.' " He told his two aides to work out the details. But later that afternoon, when Friend, Silverman, and Jonathan Miller, one of Dodd's favorite staff members, sat down with Duhnke and Oesterle, the optimism evaporated. Duhnke, Friend recalled, said, "Okay, it's yes or no." He was demanding that she accept Shelby's latest position on consumer protection, which did not create the independent agency Dodd sought.

"Is that what you call a negotiation?" Friend replied. Yes, she recalled Duhnke saying, "That's what negotiation is—yes or no." Duhnke said Shelby would "never accept an independent consumer agency," according to Friend's notes. "He seemed very anxious to get out of the meeting, because I don't think he thought it was going anywhere. Oesterle came back a little while later by himself to make more of an impassioned plea. I think he genuinely was searching for something." Oesterle made several suggestions, "but it was nowhere near enough."

So the most basic method for working out deals—asking staff to find ways to bridge differences—wasn't going to work. "This place functions because you get talented, bright people who can pick up on where you're coming from and provide the kind of knowledge and expertise, and be creative enough" to work out a deal, Dodd explained. The best staff can figure out "How do we get as close to that idea you have without giving up on it, and simultaneously being able to move far enough to bring along the other side." But this only works, he added, "if you have someone on the other side who has a similar capacity." Duhnke and Oesterle never acted as though they were committed to making a deal on a bipartisan bill. "You've got to have staff on the other side that can not only represent the interests of their member, but also [know] how to negotiate in a legislative context," Dodd said. "If everything is a 'No,' it's very difficult to find the common ground—if you're not thinking about it, and working at it."

Dodd was describing how the legislative process actually works.

Members can come up with ideas, but it requires those "talented, bright people" on the staff to convert them into actual legislation. Members conceptualize, usually at a high altitude; staff bring their conceptions down to earth, and also to life—when the process works.

Weren't Duhnke and Oesterle following orders from Shelby? Dodd agreed that it was hard to imagine they were freelancing, though on occasion the two of them surprised Dodd's staff by criticizing their boss undiplomatically. But, for Dodd, it was also hard to reject all of Shelby's reassurances as insincere window dressing.

On February 5, Dodd cried uncle. He issued a statement announcing that he and Shelby "have reached an impasse." Expressing the hope that "we will ultimately have a consensus package," Dodd said, "It is time to move the process forward. I have instructed my staff to begin drafting legislation to present to the committee later this month." He promised to include in this new draft the proposals that the bipartisan working groups had agreed on "over the past two months." He complimented "the good work that has been done to this point by Senator Shelby and the other Banking Committee members who have worked so hard in this process." This was the Dodd method at work: burn no bridges, continue always to be open to making deals and generous with praise for the other side. Dodd decided on this course of action himself, and "there was no Plan B" at the time, as Friend said later. "It was exasperation" that prompted this move.

And then it snowed. A blizzard began on Friday the 5th, the day Dodd announced the impasse with Shelby, and continued for two days, dumping thirty inches of snow on Washington. After a two-day respite, another huge storm produced another twenty inches. Wags called the first "Snowmageddon," and the second "Snoverkill." Washington had never seen anything like it.

Dodd did not even try to cover the half mile distance from his Capitol Hill townhouse to his office in the Russell Building until Tuesday. Then he had to call the Capitol Police to ask for a four-wheel-drive escort. Characteristically, he arrived at work wanting to do something to advance the legislative process. But he had lost his Republican negotiating partner, and now the city was shut down by snow—what could he do?

CHAPTER EIGHTEEN

More Tactical Maneuvers

B ob Corker, a Republican and the junior senator from Tennessee, had also managed to get to the office on that snowy Tuesday. As a first-term senator and a member of the minority, his suite on the ground floor of the Dirksen Senate Office Building was not as grand as Dodd's in the Russell Building. This was one of the many reminders of his junior status, a status that could annoy Corker, who was impatient with many of the Senate's rituals. He was impatient generally, and eager to get things done.

Most of the junior Republicans in the Senate were former members of the House, longtime politicians and veteran partisan warriors. Corker was none of those. A self-made businessman, his only elected office before winning a Senate seat was one four-year term as the mayor of Chattanooga. He also served for nineteen months as the state of Tennessee's commissioner of finance, in charge of the state's money. That was a job of doing, not talking, and he loved it—"a great opportunity for a business guy," he said.

Corker is a small man with a handsome face, a thinning white mane, and the body language of someone carrying a lot of pent-up energy. He is a conservative fellow with pro-business inclinations, but he was not remotely a "movement conservative," the label adopted by the true believers of the right who had taken over the congressional Republican Party since Gingrich had led it to victory in 1994. In his way, in fact, he was a bit of a bleeding heart.

In the early 1980s, before he was thirty, Corker had gone to Haiti on a church mission to help poor Haitians, and was moved by the experience. Back home he launched a nonprofit organization to improve living conditions in Chattanooga's poor black neighborhoods. It built a dental clinic and set up a fund to help residents fix up their houses. "I met some guys who had graduated from Chattanooga High School, as I did," Corker recounted, "who lived in the most godawful thing I'd ever seen . . . a little shotgun place, the windows were broken out . . . and the toilet was just a hole in the floor. The stench was tremendous." He became a civic activist and worked with the Urban League, Memorial Hospital, and the Boys Club.

Corker loved being mayor, a job that made him feel "more whole" than ever in his life. He found himself choking up in public when people thanked him for things he had done. "The impact you can have is just incredible." These were not the sentiments of an anti-government, right-wing Republican.

In 1994 Corker decided to run for the Republican nomination for an open Senate seat. He lost badly to Bill Frist, heir to a hospital company fortune and distinguished heart surgeon, who easily won the Senate race that fall. But Corker made a good impression on Frist, and when he decided ten years later that he would retire from the Senate, he encouraged Corker to run again for the job. Corker decided to do so in 2006.

In a competitive Republican primary against two former members of the House, Corker recast himself as a staunch conservative, for the first time adopting a strong anti-abortion position. After winning that primary he was heavily favored to defeat the Democratic candidate, Congressman Harold Ford Jr., a bright and charismatic young African American. Ford belonged to a family of Tennessee politicians with more than a few skeletons in its closets. No black candidate had ever won statewide office in Tennessee, and the local experts doubted that the boyish Ford, then thirty-six, would be the first. But he ran a surprisingly effective race in what was shaping up as a Democratic year, and Corker stumbled. By the end of September Ford had a clear lead in the polls, and Corker's campaign was in disarray.

Frist and Mitch McConnell, the Republican leader in the Senate, decided to intervene. They asked Tom Ingram, then chief of staff to Lamar Alexander, the senior senator from Tennessee and a popular former governor, to take over Corker's campaign. Ingram, an experienced Tennessee pol who loved electoral competition, became Corker's campaign manager on September 29.

Ingram interviewed every member of the campaign staff and discovered that no one was really in charge. "There were a lot of things wrong, and not much right except that he had won the primary," Ingram recalled. With less than six weeks before election day, Ingram hired a new campaign team, moved the headquarters from Chattanooga to Nashville, and set out on a new path.

Ingram realized that Corker was responsible for what had gone wrong—"the buck stops at the top," as he put it. "But I give Bob a lot of credit for being willing to make a change, which was a significant one that late in the game. Not many candidates have that agility."

Tom Griscom, then executive editor of the *Chattanooga Times Free Press* and a friend of Corker's, wrote a column recounting what happened next: "Mr. Corker, Mr. Ingram and the newly formed campaign team faced a choice: Either reconstruct Bob Corker's image or take apart the positive impression [voters had developed] of Rep. Ford. They knew both could not be accomplished with limited time and money, so the decision was to deconstruct Rep. Ford."

The anti-Ford campaign they ran featured television commercials critical of Ford's father, his predecessor in the House, who was indicted for bank fraud, disciplined by his Democratic colleagues, but ultimately acquitted at trial. In 2006 the senior Ford was a registered Washington lobbyist, fodder for those commercials.

The most controversial anti-Ford commercial of the campaign was sponsored not by the Corker campaign, but by the Republican National Committee. In it an actress playing the part of a dumb blonde said she met Ford, then a bachelor, "at the Playboy party." The ad ended with her winking into the camera and saying, "Harold, call me." Corker and Ingram both insisted they had no role in creating this commercial and did not approve its use. Corker publicly called for it to be taken off the air. The RNC first said it could not pull the ad, but a day later it stopped running after both Democrats and Republicans had denounced it as racist.

The commercial had an effect. An independent poll taken days before the election indicated that it swayed a significant number of votes to Corker. The Ford camp never accepted Corker's protests that he knew nothing about the preparation and distribution of the commercial.

On election day Corker won by 3 percent, or fifty thousand votes. He was the only Republican who won a Senate seat for the first time in 2006.

Asked later what he had learned about Corker by running his campaign, Ingram replied with a list of attributes: "tenacious, persistent, questioning—he wanted to test every idea and understand it before we went forward with it, and there wasn't a lot of time for that in a campaign. He was committed; he worked very hard. He was going to put out whatever it took to get there"—to win.

It was those qualities of tenacity and persistent curiosity that impressed Chris Dodd about Corker—and Dodd was not alone. Corker arrived in the Senate under a bit of a cloud because of the way he defeated Ford, and his first reactions to the life of a senator were skeptical. When he realized how difficult it would be to have any impact as a freshman member of what had become, in 2007, the minority caucus, he worried that he had made a wrong career move. But he buckled down, did his homework, and built a reputation as a serious person who learned issues for himself—an uncommon attribute in the Senate.

Dodd had been a strong Harold Ford supporter and had no prior connection to Corker, but knew his reputation as an innovative mayor of Chattanooga. "He was creative on housing, and hardworking," Dodd recalled. "He struck me as interesting." On the Banking Committee, Corker "was very good, did his homework. He was thoughtful." Then, at the height of the financial crisis in the fall of 2008, when Shelby decided to oppose the TARP bailout and Dodd was looking for Republican partners to push it through the Senate, Corker volunteered to help. Dodd found him a useful, energetic ally. They collaborated again when General Motors and Chrysler came to Washington looking for bailouts. Corker took an active role in the hearings Dodd held on the auto companies' request, and for a time worked with the chairman to try to find a bipartisan agreement on the bailout.

In December 2008, "we almost got a deal done," Dodd recounted. He and Corker negotiated a package that tried to accommodate the interests of bondholders in GM and Chrysler, the United Auto Workers Union, and the two companies. When they seemed on the verge of success, Corker told Dodd he needed to leave their meeting to tell his colleagues about the agreement they were negotiating. "I urged Bob to stay in the room," Dodd said, until they had finalized a deal—fearing that Corker's Republican colleagues would force him to abandon the talks if he gave them a chance to do so. But Corker insisted on reporting to the Republican caucus. Just as Dodd predicted, he never returned. "It just got scuttled," Dodd said.

At President Obama's inauguration in January, Corker was seated next to an even more junior senator, Mark Warner of Virginia, just sworn in days earlier. The two hit it off. Warner visited Corker in his office for a longer chat. They realized that they had a lot in common. Both defined themselves as businessmen who had gone into politics with the intention of improving the world. Neither was interested in partisan warfare. Both were self-made multimillionaires.

Like Corker, Warner shunned ideological combat and political gamesmanship. As governor of Virginia from 2002 to 2006, he built a reputation as a practical, nonpartisan executive. His successes made him extremely popular. For a time he flirted with running for the Democratic nomination for president in 2008, but saw that there was no room for him in that contest, and decided to run for the Senate instead. In November 2008, he smothered his Republican opponent by a margin of nearly two to one.

Early in 2009 Corker and Warner decided to collaborate. They asked their staffs to organize a series of seminars on financial regulatory reform for interested senators and staff members to which they jointly invited outside experts to make presentations and answer questions. These sessions were well attended by staff and as many as ten senators, mostly nonmembers of the Banking Committee interested in the subject. They met with a wide range of people, from Alan Greenspan to Sheila Bair of the FDIC and Rodgin Cohen, the senior partner of Sullivan & Cromwell in New York and the country's most prominent banking lawyer. Warner and Corker traveled to New York together to talk to Wall Street executives.

This partnership was highly unusual. Both senators reported that their staffs had difficulty adjusting to the idea that they were supposed to work collegially with each other, across the partisan divide that had become a chasm in recent years. "It took the famous beer summit to deal with that," Warner recalled later with a grin. In the summer of 2009 he and Corker took their aides to Johnny's Half Shell for beers and peacemaking. It worked. Eventually, Warner's principal Banking Committee aide, Nathan Steinwald, and Corker's, Courtney Geduldig, became both effective collaborators and fast friends.

Warner considered Dodd a kind of political big brother, having first driven his car twenty-six years earlier, and as a senator tried to stay in close touch with him, never hiding his eagerness to play a role and get involved in substance. On that snowbound Tuesday, February 9, he too made it to the office, and paid a call on his mentor and friend to commiserate about the impasse with Shelby and to make a suggestion. He and Corker, Warner told Dodd, were working well together on systemic risk regulation and resolution authority. Unlike Dodd and Shelby and their staffs, Warner and Corker and their aides seemed committed to making a deal, and were close to doing so. Why not, Warner asked Dodd, encourage the two of them to try to work through the other contentious issues together, in hopes of achieving a broader agreement?

This was a bold initiative by an impatient junior senator, one that was never publicly revealed, so never known to other senators. Dodd was intrigued. He appreciated the talents of both Warner and Corker, and he was eager to find a new path to an acceptable compromise. But turning the quest over to his junior colleague who once drove him around Washington was not what Dodd had in mind. He told Warner that the chairman ought to be leading the effort to make a deal, so he would approach Corker himself. Warner was disappointed, but understood that Dodd held all the cards. Seniority mattered.

That evening, Dodd called Corker and said he would like to discuss possible collaboration. They agreed to meet the next day. "I really believed I needed to have a Republican sponsor at some point if I could get one," Dodd said later. He realized that Corker wasn't the sort of senior partner he had in mind, but perhaps he would do.

Corker was thrilled. He held Dodd in high regard, and was flattered by Dodd's proposal. The two men and their aides began substantive talks that same afternoon.

After agreeing with Dodd to keep their arrangement "low-key," Corker could not resist publicizing it. Early the next morning, he went on CNBC, the business news channel, to disclose what he and Dodd were doing. "He went off on his own," Friend said. Corker told CNBC, "The Dodd and Shelby teams reached impasse on Friday and began drafting their own bills, which obviously leads toward a legislative train wreck. So yesterday, with all the snow that was happening, Senator Dodd and I decided to try to do what we can to craft a bill that will receive bipartisan support. I notified Republican leadership yesterday afternoon of my decision. We sat down together late in the afternoon, our two staffs did, in a conference to begin working . . . [on] those things in financial regulation that need to be dealt with."

Steve Liesman, a CNBC anchor, asked Corker, "Are you stepping forward here and sort of replacing Senator Shelby when it comes to the negotiations on the Republican side?"

"Well," Corker replied, "I'm just one senator and I certainly would never say I'm going to replace Senator Shelby, somebody I respect and like a lot. But I am stepping forward as a Republican senator and saying this is a piece of legislation that needs to be passed. There are issues that need to be addressed." Corker's impatience won out over political caution. As he said on CNBC, "I have expressed my dissatisfaction pretty strongly with the way things have been going." He really did believe there were important regulatory reform issues "that need to be dealt with."

Dodd followed Corker's CNBC appearance with a press release of his own that praised Corker as "a serious thinker. . . . I am more optimistic than I have been in several weeks that we can develop a consensus bill."

Friend liked this new Corker gambit. She also liked Courtney Geduldig, who would be her partner in the negotiations. From their first meeting on that snowy afternoon, Friend said, negotiations with Geduldig were businesslike, and promising.

Corker had a hard time containing his enthusiasm. Suddenly, the news media's spotlight shone on this junior senator, and he loved it. But he also understood the risks of his initiative, especially with his elders in the Republican caucus. After giving interviews to television networks and print reporters that Thursday, Corker put out his own formal statement to emphasize his regard for more senior Republicans: "I called both Republican Leader Mitch McConnell and Banking Committee Ranking Member Richard Shelby about my decision. I greatly respect both men, and I appreciate the cordial conversations I had with them yesterday. I hope to make it clear that I am stepping forward purely as one Republican senator who believes this is a piece of legislation that needs to be passed and is willing to see if it is possible to do it in a bipartisan way."

Corker's statement was a revealing indication of how the Senate had changed after years of partisan warfare and party discipline. Once, a senator was a potentate in his own right, in most matters a free agent who could build his own alliances and pursue his own goals with colleagues in either party. But in the modern era every senator was subject to party discipline, and they all knew it. So, for example, if Shelby was ever to achieve his goal and become the senior Republican on the Appropriations Committee, he would need the support of his Republican colleagues, beginning with the elected leadership. If Corker were to realize his considerable ambitions, he would need the blessings of Republicans with more seniority. After barely three years in the Senate, Corker was still a parvenu who was expected to show respect for his elders. Despite his diplomatic words, however, Corker really had stepped out of line. Shelby was angry, which he conveyed in a chilly telephone call. Shelby's aides, Duhnke and Oesterle, made it clear to Corker's staff that their boss's initiative was unwelcome. Relations between the staffs, already strained, became much worse. The Democratic staff working with Geduldig were upset with the nasty way Duhnke and Oesterle dealt with her after the Dodd-Corker partnership was announced.

In that first substantive discussion with Dodd and his aides on the 10th, Corker proposed that they set aside what had been the most controversial subject, a consumer protection agency, and concentrate first on issues on which he hoped compromises would be easier to find. First on his list were regulation of systemic risk and a new legal authority for winding down failing financial firms—the issues that he and Warner had been working on for months. But he was ready to take on the other contentious issues too. He needed more staff help, and assigned several people from his Senate office to help Geduldig. He also hired some temporary help.

The Banking Committee staff and this new Corker team soon fell into a routine of long hours and hard work, exchanging proposals, discussing alternatives, consulting experts, and working toward a big bill covering all the topics that Frank had included in the House bill and Dodd had put into his November 2009 draft.

A fortnight after launching their new partnership, Dodd and Corker traveled together as members of the Committee on Foreign Relations to Central America for five days of consultations with local leaders. Central America had been one of Dodd's priorities since the Reagan administration, and he had made Latin America a specialty in his long service on Foreign Relations. Corker was a relatively new member of that committee, but it was so unpopular with the new breed of conservative Republican senator that he was quickly acquiring seniority.

The community of lobbyists trying to influence the regulatory reform bill was transfixed by this spectacle, wondering what Dodd and Corker might cook up as they flew from El Salvador to Nicaragua to Honduras. Geithner was so worried that Dodd would yield too much to Corker in pursuit of bipartisan concord that he contemplated making a quick unannounced visit to Central America himself to talk to the two travelers. Dodd was angry when he heard about this, and the treasury secretary stayed home.

In fact the two senators had only general conversations about financial regulation on their trip. As Friend explained, "It was naive to think that two senators, without staff, would try to work out the bill." Senators don't work out complex legislation without extensive staff support. She was surprised that the senior officials at Treasury didn't know how the Senate did its business.

By early March the Dodd and Corker teams were making real headway. They were close to agreement on most of the big issues: the systemic risk regulator, the resolution authority to wind down failing financial firms, reorganization of existing bank regulators and new regulations of hedge funds, mortgages, and more. The lobbyists following the bill began to buzz about what was going on; many were surprised that this odd couple was actually making progress.

Corker proposed an intriguing solution to the problem that had bedeviled the Shelby-Dodd negotiations, the status of consumer protection under the new legislation. Dodd insisted on four principles: There had to be a new organization with an independent director or chairman nominated by the president and confirmed by the Senate; it had to have a dedicated source of revenue not subject to the annual congressional appropriation process; the organization had to be given the authority to write rules for businesses that provided credit to consumers; and it had to have the authority to enforce those rules at financial firms not supervised by the traditional bank regulators—the so-called nonbank sector. Corker said he understood the four principles and was willing to work with them.

Corker's novel idea was to create an autonomous division of the Federal Reserve called the Consumer Financial Protection Bureau. It would be funded by a fixed percentage of the Fed's annual earnings, which came from its trading activities and were substantial enough to guarantee hundreds of millions of dollars a year for this CFPB. Its director could act independently of the Fed's Board of Governors, and would be appointed by the president and confirmed by the Senate.

It would have the rule-writing authority that Dodd sought, but the rules it wrote would be subject to a veto by a majority vote of a special committee of traditional bank regulators—a way to be sure that regulators charged with protecting the "safety and soundness" of the institutions they supervised could limit the reach of the CFPB if they thought its proposed rules would jeopardize the safety of banks. This "veto" power had become the principal bone of contention for Republicans. Corker also wanted to limit the bureau's jurisdiction in the nonbank sector to firms writing and financing mortgages. He insisted on excluding payday lenders.

The powers of this CFPB became, unusually, the subject of direct negotiations among four senators: Dodd, Shelby, Corker, and Judd Gregg of New Hampshire. The four kept hashing out details in impromptu meetings on and just off the Senate floor in the first days of March. No staff participated—the unusual part. During these talks Shelby seemed to accept the idea of an autonomous consumer bureau that was awfully close to the independent consumer agency he had flatly rejected, though with circumscribed powers. Dodd reported the results of this negotiation to Friend by handing her a napkin on which the details were jotted down. The four senators never did have a piece of paper that formalized their understanding. Dodd liked to quote Kennedy on the subject of complex negotiations: "Nothing is agreed to until everything is agreed to." In Dodd's view they did not yet have a deal.

Dodd liked Corker's idea of putting consumer protection in an autonomous agency under the roof of the Fed. He thought this was a clever way to achieve a meaningful, effectively autonomous consumer agency without accepting the totally independent Consumer Financial Protection Agency the administration had requested and the House had approved. It was actually an improvement on the independent agency in one important respect: its automatic funding. If the Fed supported the CFPB by a percentage formula of its profits, a future Congress hostile to consumer protection would be unable to squeeze it in the annual appropriations process. That is just what had happened, for example, to the Securities and Exchange Commission during the era of financial deregulation, when deregulating Republicans controlled Congress; the SEC's enforcement budget was sharply reduced, so it had fewer people and resources to police the securities markets.

But Dodd would only accept Corker's idea if he could sell it to his

Democratic colleagues on the Banking Committee. He invited them all to a meeting on March 4 in his conference room on the fourth floor of the Russell Building. Dodd was fond of what he called his "big conference room," though it wasn't really so big. The mahogany table could barely accommodate all thirteen Democratic members of the committee. Ten of them showed up that day. But members wanted their staff in the room as well, so a dozen men and women had to find one of the few additional chairs, sit on a sofa in the back of the room, or stand.

Dodd sat at the head of the table in what looked like a judge's chair upholstered in tufted black leather. From that perch he could see a long wall of photographs of himself and others from throughout his career—"grip and grin" photos recording his meetings with presidents, potentates, and colleagues. The opposite wall was dominated by a large portrait of Tom Dodd, his father, that hung above the mantel of a no longer operational fireplace. Further along the same wall were framed letters and pens from all the presidents since Reagan, the letters thanking Dodd for his work on bills that those presidents had signed with numerous pens, including the ones sent to Dodd as souvenirs. It was a dark room under a high ceiling—seventeen feet high, the standard size in the Russell Building.

As always, Dodd tried to accommodate his colleagues, inviting everyone to speak. Warner spoke up on behalf of a bipartisan bill, reviewing the progress he and Corker had made on systemic risk regulation and resolution authority. Jack Reed of Rhode Island described the progress he and Gregg had made on derivatives, but said key differences remained. Jeff Merkley, the liberal freshman from Oregon, was opposed to putting the consumer bureau inside the Fed, an arrangement he said would be hard to sell in Oregon, where voters were nervous about the Federal Reserve Board. Robert Menendez of New Jersey warned of the political dangers of "creating a fig leaf"— a consumer agency too weak to be meaningful. "It has to be truly independent," he said, according to Friend's notes of the session. Daniel Akaka of Hawaii said he wanted to be sure the bill held all financial advisors to the same high, "fiduciary" standard to act only in the best interests of their clients. In other words, it was a typical meeting of senators, each pursuing his own interests, often without reference to the interests of others.

For Dodd, the important part of the session was a report from one staff member, Jonathan Miller. Miller had worked on Capitol Hill since 1987, the first ten years for various House members, and on the Banking Committee staff for a dozen years. He was proudly a liberal whose first interest was in promoting low-income housing. He was the committee staff member closest to the national consumer groups that were lobbying for enhanced consumer protection in the regulatory reform bill, and he had kept them informed about Dodd's negotiations with Corker. Dodd asked Miller to brief the members on those negotiations and the reactions of the consumer groups.

Miller explained that they had accepted Corker's position to limit the new agency's reach over nonbank financial institutions to those involved in mortgages. He explained the idea of a regulators' veto over proposed CFPB regulations that might undermine the safety and soundness of banks. These concessions had an important tactical purpose—to protect the consumer agency when the bill came to the floor of the Senate. Senators, like House members, had been lobbied heavily by bankers, other businesses, and business groups who disliked the consumer agency. Dodd feared that an amendment gutting the agency—something like the Minnick amendment in the House—might win enough Democratic votes to pass unless he had a comprehensive bipartisan deal in advance of floor action.

This was a familiar gambit in the Senate. When a deal of this kind is struck, the parties agree to defend it by voting against any amendments offered on the floor that would undermine it. Corker had agreed to this approach on the consumer agency, Miller reported. "So the issue was, was this deal we'd reached with Corker worth getting?" Miller had discussed this with "the consumer community," he told the senators, and "came to the conclusion that it was worth the deal . . . to create the foundation of something that would really be significant." He compared it to the original Social Security Act of 1935, which excluded agricultural workers from coverage to win the votes of southern senators. (In the South, most agricultural workers then were black.) "This was the analogy we used," Miller said. "The deal was okay. The nonbank exclusion was the worst of it, but we decided it was tolerable."

Dodd made it clear that he agreed with Miller. For Dodd the key was bipartisan support; without it, passing a bill would be extremely difficult, or impossible. He watched his colleagues carefully. None denounced the tentative deal. "It wasn't warmly embraced, and we were putting forward the best case we could for it," he said later, but he was satisfied that he could keep trying with Corker without losing a significant number of Democrats. The liberals worried him most, and he was pleased when Sherrod Brown of Ohio, a leading liberal voice, told reporters after the meeting, "I think we're going generally in the right direction."

But the talks with Corker were not going in the right direction. Just as they seemed on the verge of success, Corker began to backpedal. Friend learned that Shelby had reentered the negotiations through a series of meetings Corker was holding with him, Gregg, and Mike Crapo of Idaho to review his negotiations with Dodd. This did not surprise her. She knew Shelby resented Corker's initiative, and she expected him to undermine Corker if he could. She concluded that Corker was feeling intense pressure from Shelby and probably Mitch McConnell as well. "Corker was growing increasingly nervous with us about the stands he was taking," Friend recalled. "He was changing his mind about things."

Dodd was determined to hold a markup session of the Banking Committee to consider a final bill before the Easter recess, which was scheduled to begin at the end of March. He hoped to bring a bill to the floor in April, before regulatory reform got lost in the predictable election year logjam that would make legislating in the summer nearly impossible. A third of the Senate and the entire House would be running again in November—for members of Congress, the ultimate distraction.

Dodd felt he had to force his talks with Corker to a conclusion. The two scheduled a meeting for the afternoon of March 10. Jack Reed and Gregg were also invited. For Dodd, the purpose of the meeting was to wrap up a final deal. He wanted to learn definitively if Corker and Gregg were ready to complete the package being negotiated, and if so, which other Republicans they would bring along. Dodd assumed he might lose a few Democrats on the CFPB issue, he said, so he had to be sure there was compensatory support from enough Republicans to assure final success.

Gregg backed out of the meeting. Dodd's staff thought Shelby and McConnell were pressuring him not to join a deal. Now Corker could offer no Republican ally who would support a Dodd-Corker package, though he kept insisting that he would ultimately win the support of many of his colleagues. Dodd didn't believe it.

"I knew I had to cut losses at that point," Dodd said later. "I was looking at a train wreck."

He agonized. "It was hours in his office talking about this and what he should do," Friend recounted later. "It was a very painful thing for him to bring this to a close, to approach Corker and say I have to move on. . . . It was clear Corker couldn't deliver. He just couldn't bring along any members."

On March 11, Dodd told Corker he had to move ahead with his own bill. It would, Dodd said, include many of the compromises he and Corker had agreed to. He also told Corker that his new bill would be tougher on the financial industry than Corker would like, because without Republican support, he needed now to be sure he would have unanimous Democratic support, and some of his liberal colleagues were wavering. But he couldn't wait any longer, Dodd said. The committee would hold a markup on March 22.

For Corker this was a body blow. "I never expected it," he said in a conversation a week later. He obviously thought Dodd had not adequately rewarded "the risk" he took when he signed on for negotiations a month earlier. Told that Dodd felt he had no choice, since Corker could not bring along any other Republicans, he replied defensively, "I never told anybody I was representing all Republicans. I'm only one Republican." He acknowledged that Gregg had backed out of that meeting, but wouldn't accept that as a justification for ending the negotiations. Then he admitted that "the issue was really Shelby. . . . I think Gregg was reticent to step out ahead of Shelby."

Corker could not let go of his disappointment. Instead he called a news conference to announce it, and reiterate it, and then repeat again how sorry he was that Dodd had decided to stop talking and mark up a bill. Corker graciously praised Dodd and his staff for making possible an exciting month of meaty collaboration—a unique experience in his twenty-six months in the Senate and an example of "the Senate working the way the Senate is supposed to work."

"I have enjoyed this immensely," Corker said. "I think what's happened over the last thirty days between the two of us and our staffs is what we came here in the Senate to do. We've laughed. We have debated. And we've gotten to the five-yard line. . . . This probably doesn't play so well to my Republican base in Tennessee, but I consider Chris Dodd to be my friend. I consider his staff to be standup people who are great to negotiate with." He rejected a reporter's suggestion that the negotiations had broken down. "We're going to continue to try to work through things." A bipartisan bill was still possible. After an hour Corker was told he had to vacate the room, so he ended by saying, "If we cannot do this in a bipartisan way—and I still have hope that we will—we can't do anything anymore in the United States Senate. We hopefully will get this done."

Dodd shared Corker's appreciation for what they had been through together. It was the kind of collaboration that he had often engaged in earlier in his career, before partisanship became so important in the Senate, and he missed it. He was especially grateful for the work done by Courtney Geduldig, who had collaborated so well with Friend and the other Banking Committee staff. Dodd sent her a handwritten thank-you note.

Because so much drafting of legislative language had gone into the Corker negotiations, Friend and her colleagues were able to produce a new bill relatively quickly. Dodd introduced it at a news conference on March 15, just four days after he ended the negotiations with Corker. Dodd announced his intention to mark up the bill in the Banking Committee beginning a week later, on March 22. This tight schedule suggested an aggressive use of the chairman's powers.

The new bill, more than 1,300 pages long, did reflect the Dodd-Corker negotiations. Its consumer agency was housed in the Federal Reserve, as Corker had suggested, but was given broader powers over nonbank financial firms than Corker favored. The resolution authority Dodd included to put failing financial firms out of business would be financed by a $50 billion fund to be raised in advance from those firms, another idea Corker had supported. Dodd abandoned his original notion of creating a single new regulatory agency for all banks, instead accepting the Frank position that the old structure of regulatory agencies should be preserved, with one exception: The Office of Thrift Supervision, widely seen as the least effective of the existing regulators, would be merged into the Office of the Comptroller of the Currency. Dodd proposed a council of regulators chaired by the secretary of the treasury—similar to the council in Frank's bill—that would play the role of systemic risk regulator, the most powerful new regulatory tool created by this legislation. The council would vote on any proposal to put a failing firm out of business. Dodd also included a version of the Volcker rule, limiting banks' ability to engage in risky financial trades with their own capital. Corker had not signed off on this idea.

The White House and Barney Frank both welcomed Dodd's new version, suggesting that he had remained loyal to the consensus that had brought together the key Democrats in this process. The Treasury Department had worked with the Dodd staff on the bill, and knew what was in it. Elizabeth Warren, the liberal Harvard Law School professor who originated the idea of an independent consumer protection agency, issued a strong statement in Dodd's defense: "Despite the banks' ferocious lobbying for business as usual, Chairman Dodd took an important step today by advancing new laws to prevent the next crisis. We're now heading toward a series of votes in which the choice will be clear: families or banks," she said.

The day Dodd's bill was announced the big financial interests made no effort to hide their confidence that they would win some of those votes on the floor of the Senate. Lobbyists and executives both expressed the hope that Dodd would continue to favor a bipartisan bill in the end—a bill that would be gentler on the big banks. Dodd seemed to offer some support to this view at the news conference he held to introduce his bill: "I don't have standing with me today bipartisan support at this podium," Dodd said, but "at any stage in the development of a bill, you can develop that consensus." Shelby, Corker, and other Republicans made comments to the same effect.

And Dodd did more than talk about it. He met with Corker on the 17th to reiterate his interest in continuing to collaborate; the same afternoon he had a glass of wine with Shelby on a balcony outside the window of his Russell Building office. Dodd still hoped and even expected that Shelby would make another attempt to find a package they could agree on before a bill reached the Senate floor, as he had with the credit card bill a year earlier.

But first, Dodd had to get a bill reported out of the Banking Committee. He sent out a notice to all members to file any amendments they wanted to be considered by 1:30 p.m. on Friday the 19th. This set off a mad scramble in the offices of committee members to complete work on their amendments. Dodd joked with his aides that there would be hundreds of them—he suggested a pool to see who could come up with the best prediction of exactly how many. Dodd guessed 401. He won the pool.

This stage of the legislative process can be hectic and complicated. Typically, the committee staff, representing the chairman, will look at all the proposed amendments with an eye out for proposals they might want to support. Those they like can be incorporated into a "manager's amendment," a catchall proposal sponsored by the chairman that usually includes amendments to the pending bill that the chairman himself has decided to embrace. Friend and her colleagues were in the midst of this process, and were working with the Corker staff in hopes of agreeing on some of his amendments, when they got word that Shelby had requested both Corker and the staff to drop the idea of incorporating any Republican proposals into the manager's amendment. This was Friend's first indication that something unusual was about to happen.

Corker recounted what occurred next: "I got a call at 11:30 in the morning on Friday, before the Monday markup, and it was Richard [Shelby]. All the amendments were due at two [1:30 actually]. All the senators were leaving town. He said, 'Bob, I've been thinking that we shouldn't offer any amendments in the markup.' And I could hear his staff talking to him in the background. And I said, 'You're kidding me!' We'd been working all week . . . with his [Shelby's] staff. . . . We had a ton of amendment ideas. . . . We had amendments we were doing with Warner, joint amendments. We had amendments we were working with Shelby on . . . Gregg too. . . . The staff was working until four in the morning."

To Corker's amazement, Shelby had decided, apparently for tactical reasons, to let Dodd report his bill out of committee on a party-line vote, without making any attempt to improve it with amendments. Shelby himself had said publicly that he and Dodd agreed on 85–90 percent of the bill; Corker also thought they were close to a bipartisan deal. But now Shelby was pulling the rug out from under his efforts.

"I said, Senator, with all due respect, we're filing amendments."

In the context of the modern Senate and particularly of its disciplined Republican caucus, Corker's was a defiant act. It was the culmination of a series of spats between Corker and his staff with Shelby's two principal aides, Duhnke and Oesterle, and at least one public confrontation between Corker and Shelby, apparently set off by a Corker complaint about the behavior of Duhnke and Oesterle.

Courtney Geduldig, Corker's Banking aide, was at the center of the storm over amendments, because all of her colleagues working for the other Republicans on the committee were looking to her for a cue. If she filed Corker's amendments, they would have to file the amendments their bosses had approved. On that Friday, Geduldig recalled, "everybody else was scrambling to get theirs done." And the process wasn't simple; committee rules required that fifty copies of any amendment be filed.

When Corker made his decision to defy Shelby and file his amendments, Geduldig and the staff members working for the other Republicans were all waiting in Bill Duhnke's office. When they learned of Corker's decision, Geduldig said, "everyone sprints out of there, runs to their offices. People were down in Printing and Graphics [a Senate office] on every copier in the building and in their office space, trying to get amendments copied and filed on time. . . . The [Banking Committee hearing] room was filled with stacks of paper everywhere. . . . People were just screaming at each other across the room. It was true and utter chaos."

Both Dodd and Corker joined the exodus of senators from Washington that Friday. In the evening, Corker called Dodd, then in Connecticut, from his mansion in Nashville. The chairman was "in a jovial mood," Corker recounted later. "He said Bob, we're going to have a helluva markup, we're going to get this bill fixed, it's going to be a great process. . . . So I said great, we're ready to go, we're excited."

Twenty-four hours later, Dodd called Corker. "And he said 'Bob, I got a call from Richard,' " Corker said. " 'And Richard thinks we're better off if we don't have a markup, if we don't do any amendments.' " Corker again expressed amazement. In his recounting, Dodd had an explanation of Shelby's reasoning: If there were a markup, "what's going to happen is, a lot of you-alls' [meaning Republicans'] amendments probably won't pass, and it'll just harden the two sides against each other." Dodd told Corker this would happen because his liberal members wouldn't support Republican amendments. "But we'll have a different cast of characters on the floor," meaning the entire Senate, both Republicans and Democrats. Corker quoted Dodd as saying, "I'm beginning to think that's a good idea, I think we shouldn't have a markup."

Dodd was still hoping that he and Shelby could strike a deal. He thought he understood another reason why Shelby didn't want a proper markup. "There was zero consensus on their side," Dodd said later. "They just couldn't agree on anything." This was confirmed by the amendments Republicans did file, which reflected no coherent view of the issues. After reading through all of them, Friend concluded that Shelby had no hope of developing a unified Republican position (which he never did). Even amendments offered by Shelby's staff sometimes contradicted each other, Friend said. A markup session that revealed all these differences could have embarrassed Shelby.

On Sunday afternoon Corker realized that he was virtually alone on the Republican side; he decided he would have to yield to Shelby's desires. One rebel could not force a proper markup without the cooperation of others. Corker called Dodd again and agreed to withhold his amendments when the committee met the next day. "Dodd committed to me that after the bill got out of the committee we could fix it," Corker said. "Now that's a loose deal, and I wasn't born yesterday, and it's not near like having a committee markup," but he did believe that Dodd still wanted a bipartisan compromise, so he would keep working on one.

That Sunday, March 21, has a small place in the history books, but not because of the machinations on the Senate Banking Committee. Just before eleven o'clock that night, the House (like the Senate, rushing to finish pending business before the spring recess) approved final passage of health care reform legislation. For President Obama and the Democrats this was an exhilarating turn of events. After Scott Brown's January victory in the special Senate election in Massachusetts, which deprived Democrats of a filibuster-proof, sixty-seat majority in the Senate, the year-long crusade for health insurance reform initially appeared doomed. Some of Obama's senior advisors urged him to abandon it and instead seek more modest changes. But Obama and the Democratic congressional leaders, Harry Reid in the Senate and Speaker Nancy Pelosi in the House, all wanted to try to enact the bill. So its passage by a vote of 219–212 on the evening of March 21 was a big victory for them. After the vote Obama exulted: "Tonight, at a time when the pundits said it was no longer possible, we rose above the weight of our politics. . . . We proved we are still a people capable of doing big things and tackling our biggest challenges."

The House vote altered the political mood in Washington, especially on Capitol Hill. Mood is one of the mystery ingredients in the legislative process. At any particular moment, the mood depends on politics, or perceptions of politics. A popular president riding a wave of successes is much harder to beat in Congress than a controversial one who isn't having much luck enacting a program. Fear is at play here—the fear of the members who consider themselves politically vulnerable. Generally speaking, the fearful like to be on the winning side. This calculus was evident in that health care vote, when thirty-four House Democrats voted against Obama and their party leaders. But that wasn't enough to beat them; their seven-vote margin of victory, oddly but indisputably, changed the mood.

"Suddenly the Democrats were feeling really good," Amy Friend observed. "People had been feeling so upset when Scott Brown won—it was 'the end of the Democratic Party' and so on. But after the health care bill passed, everybody [every Democrat like her, in other words] was feeling fantastic, and feeling, 'We're on a roll!'

"It seemed like the mood had shifted among Republicans as well," she added. Humiliating Obama had been the Republicans' first priority, and they too thought Brown's election had improved their chances of beating the health care legislation. McConnell had been particularly upset, and obviously frustrated by his inability to block the bill.

The Banking Committee convened on the day after the House vote. The committee's hearing room—a bland, wood-paneled hall far less imposing than the Russell Building caucus room that Dodd had used to introduce his first draft bill in November—had been reconfigured for the occasion. Ordinarily the members sat at a U-shaped dais at the south end of the large room, but for the markup, tables had been set up in a square where the public ordinarily sat so the members could look at each other. Staff crowded into seats behind the dais. Reporters sat at long tables on the east and west sides of the room. Though word had leaked out during the morning that both parties had decided not to offer any amendments—so the markup was likely to be anticlimactic—the television cameras were already in place. The room was brightly lit to accommodate them.

Dodd and Shelby both read upbeat opening statements, contributing to a sense that this had become a ritualistic event that was obscuring more serious business going on—or anticipated—somewhere offstage. Said Dodd, "We will not fail. We will have reform this year."

Shelby seemed to agree: "I do not view today's markup as the end of the road, but rather just another step in the process. . . . I remain optimistic that we can, over time, reach an agreement that will garner broad bipartisan support. I just don't believe we are there yet. . . . I pledge to the Chairman and my colleagues that I will continue to work with them as this bill approaches floor consideration in hopes of reaching a broad consensus." The tone of these remarks differed starkly from Shelby's eighteen-minute tirade of four months earlier.

The committee then quickly disposed of its business. All ten Republicans voted no; all thirteen Democrats said "Aye." As soon as the clerk announced the vote, Dodd whacked his gavel and adjourned the meeting. In just twenty-one minutes, the Banking Committee had reported out the most sweeping piece of legislation that it had considered since the 1930s.

Corker sat in his chair and stewed. "To not have a meaningful markup on a bill that was that technical, and had that kind of effect on our country's financial system, to me was absolutely one of the most irresponsible things I have ever seen happen," he said later. "There wasn't a drop of blood in my face. I just couldn't believe what was happening."

As the meeting was breaking up, Dodd approached Corker and asked him to join "Dick Shelby and me" to talk to reporters in the hall. Dodd asked if Corker would like to say something to the reporters. "I said you don't want to hear what I would have to say, okay?" But he and his pal Mark Warner did stand next to Shelby and Dodd.

Dodd said the event "brings us a step closer." A prolonged debate would have hardened positions on both sides, he added. "This allows us to buy some time, if you will, to work on the product we need to present to our colleagues as a whole."

Shelby concurred. "We're not going to the floor polarized; we're going to the floor right now in the spirit of trying to work a consensus bill, a meaningful, substantive bill that I've said all along that we need."

Then Corker decided to say something too: "It is pretty unbelievable that after two years of hearings on arguably the biggest issue facing our panel in decades, the committee has passed a 1,300-page bill in a twenty-one-minute, partisan markup. I don't know how you can call that anything but dysfunctional." Then he said he hoped "we can still get to a bipartisan bill before we get to the [Senate] floor."

Corker was right—the way Dodd and Shelby handled the markup certainly was evidence of dysfunction. The civics book expectation would be that a Senate committee confronted by such an important piece of legislation would actually work on it, figure out its implications, consider arguments from interested parties. As Corker pointed out, "a committee markup actually causes members to understand what's in a bill." There seemed little risk of such understanding in this case. Only a few members of the committee had dug into the bill's provisions; most never had the opportunity or took the time to try to wrap their minds around its many complicated provisions. A party-line vote sending Dodd's bill to the floor without any discussion or debate was an evasion of legislative responsibility.

But Dodd and Shelby were right too, if their objective was to agree on a meaningful bill. Because the Senate was dysfunctional, only a backroom deal between them could produce such an agreement. The Republican membership of Banking was deeply divided between a minority of more practical-minded members who wanted to pass a bill—including Corker, Gregg, Crapo, Robert Bennett of Utah, and perhaps Kay Bailey Hutchison of Texas—and conservatives who never showed any interest in reaching an agreement: Jim DeMint of South Carolina, a right-wing ideologue; David Vitter of Louisiana, also a staunch conservative; Jim Bunning of Kentucky, the former baseball player and a man of strong views but limited intellect; and Mike Johanns of Nebraska, a new senator with no experience in the subject matter of the Banking Committee. Shelby knew he could never get them all to agree on a regulatory reform bill that any Democrats would support. He was also right to fear that if a markup went forward, his most conservative members would offer weakening amendments that Democrats would fiercely oppose and defeat, aggravating partisan animosities and complicating Shelby's job.

But he thought, at least on the days when he was seriously considering a deal, that a bill blessed by both him and Dodd would attract support from senators in both parties, and probably command a strong majority on the floor. As we've seen, in a conversation a year earlier, when he said forcefully that the financial system needed a new regulatory regime, Shelby talked hopefully about the prospects for a good bill: "I'm optimistic," he said then, "if Senator Dodd and a lot of us [Republicans] stay together."

The Obama administration officials following the bill had produced a mountain of paper to prepare for the committee markup, including analyses of nearly every amendment that a Republican senator had proposed. Many of them were in the Banking Committee hearing room when the markup convened, or in offices of the committee staff across the hall. When the bill was approved without a single amendment, they could not hide their glee. In the hallway outside the hearing room they celebrated with grins and high fives. The prospect of a Democratic bill unsullied by Republican amendments delighted Wolin, Barr, and their colleagues.

But Dodd feared that a Democratic bill that attracted no Republican support could easily die in the face of a filibuster. Even if it could have passed, Dodd preferred a bipartisan version. He believed that such a significant bill ought to have support from both sides of the aisle to make it more legitimate, and to give it a longer life. Dodd knew that this year's bill could be the subject of next year's modifications. In Washington, nothing is permanent. A partisan bill passed when the Democrats had an unusually big advantage would be vulnerable in the inevitable future Senate when they were weaker or outnumbered.

President Obama had summoned Dodd and Frank to the White House on March 24, two days after the Banking Committee's pro forma markup and three days after Obama's big health care victory, ostensibly to plan strategy for the final stages of the legislative process, but really to put pressure on Dodd to wrap up the bill. Obama liked the version the Banking Committee had approved, and had no interest in diluting it to win more Republican votes. Frank agreed, and thought the new mood after the health care vote had "put the wind at our backs." Obama told Dodd, "We have the whip hand here, don't give up anything important," as Frank remembered the conversation.

This meeting annoyed Dodd, though he agreed with Obama that the health care vote had helped their cause. Dodd still wanted to avoid bullying the Republicans if he could. He thought Obama did not fully appreciate the culture of the Senate (where he had served himself, but for just four years) or the benefits of bipartisanship, if it were possible. "They've got to give me some room here," he told Friend, who rode with him in the car back from the White House.

On the same day, March 24, Corker gave a speech at the Chamber of Commerce's Palladian headquarters across Lafayette Park from the White House. Corker defied senatorial etiquette and criticized his Republican colleagues on Banking, who "made a very, very large mistake" by withholding their amendments at the markup. He even took a rhetorical shot at Shelby. "It would have been better," he said, "had Senator Shelby been negotiating a bipartisan bill last September, October, November. I think we could have already had a bipartisan bill passed if that did occur. It didn't occur."

Corker noted the change in mood since health care reform had passed. Democrats, he said "are emboldened, the testosterone and other juices are flowing." And at least some Republicans were nervous about opposing a reform bill, and Corker warned that some would probably vote for the bill. "It's going to be very, very difficult—very difficult—to get 41 [Republican] members to hold [the line against the bill], especially if many of [its] provisions address concerns that everyday people on Main Street have." Ultimately, he predicted, the bill would pass.

Judd Gregg of New Hampshire agreed. He said on the same day that there was "a one hundred percent chance" that a bill would pass.

Soon after that meeting with Obama, Dodd, Shelby, and their staffs resumed negotiations. Dodd and Friend were determined to keep trying, despite the frustrating results of their efforts thus far. Negotiations continued into April. Dodd and Shelby spent more hours together; the staffs again exchanged pieces of paper and ideas. "We gave a bunch," Friend said, meaning they made substantial concessions. "We were serious. . . . I remember Oesterle saying once, 'Wow, we didn't expect anything like this.' We still held out hope. And I think that they [Shelby and his staff] were working in earnest."

But Dodd and Shelby had come to this moment—their final attempt to find a deal—with different needs and ambitions. Dodd's thirty-five-year career in Congress would end in nine months. This was his last chance to leave his mark on an important bill, and he was determined not to miss it. Shelby, by contrast, had conflicting missions. Certainly part of him would have loved to put his name on a historic bill that would make the financial system safer. He had been signaling this to Dodd for more than a year. But his ambition to be the senior Republican on the Appropriations Committee was perhaps even stronger, and he wanted to remain in the good graces of Mitch McConnell and the rest of the Republican caucus.* Dodd was ready to give everything he could for a bill; Shelby had no comparable determination.

In this last round of negotiations Shelby told Dodd and Friend more than once that "he was getting hammered in his caucus," as Friend remembered it. The biggest obstacle to agreement was the proposed consumer agency or bureau, which the Chamber of Commerce continued to denounce in an expensive advertising campaign. Many Republican senators accepted the Chamber's argument that a new consumer

---

* Shelby fulfilled this ambition in January 2013.

agency would be a menace to American business. Friend came to wonder if Shelby would ever be able to strike a deal on consumer protection that would satisfy his caucus "and still be acceptable to us."

Dodd also understood after the markup episode that a deal might never arrive. So at the same time he agreed to once again try talking with Shelby, he initiated another tactic that ultimately proved more important. He told Friend and Silverman that they and their colleagues should establish close working relations with the staffs of three Republicans: Scott Brown, the new man from Massachusetts; and the two senators from Maine, Olympia Snowe and Susan Collins. Dodd wanted to make sure those three offices knew exactly what was happening with the bill, and were invited to express views about the legislation. Dodd said he would personally stay in close touch with all three senators as well.

Dodd liked both of the women from Maine, who were known for not liking each other, and also for being the two most moderate members of the Republican caucus. Brown, elected from an overwhelmingly Democratic state, was trying to put himself in the same moderate category, with an eye to the reelection race he would face in 2012. Dodd knew from his conversations with all three that they were open to voting for cloture on a regulatory reform bill—the vote requiring sixty senators' support to cut off a filibuster against the legislation—and also to supporting final passage of a strong bill.

"So much of this place is about relationships and how you treat people," Dodd said. "I made a point every day, either I or Eddie [Silverman] or someone in the office was in touch with someone on their staffs, if not member to member: Here's what's going on, here's what we're going through. Not that that meant they were going to be for the bill because of that. But it made it a hell of a lot easier."

In late March Dodd was still hoping for a bipartisan deal that would pass easily, but he also knew he had a good chance of pushing a bill through the Senate with the bare minimum of Republican votes he would need to cut off a filibuster—just one, if he got the support of all fifty-nine Democrats, though that was not guaranteed. But in all likelihood, two or three Republicans would be enough to provide the sixtieth vote required under Senate rules to get a final vote on a bill.

Dodd and Harry Reid, the majority leader, agreed that it was time to set a deadline. Reid wanted to bring the bill up in mid-April, perhaps in the third week. Dodd agreed.

CHAPTER NINETEEN

On the Senate Floor at Last

On April 8, 2010, when Dodd and his team were trying one last time to strike a deal with Shelby and his staff, Senator Mitch McConnell and his colleague John Cornyn of Texas traveled to New York for several unannounced fundraising events. Cornyn was the chairman of the National Republican Senatorial Committee (NRSC), the fundraising arm of the Senate Republican leadership. McConnell and Cornyn were optimistic about electing more Republicans to the Senate in November, and were trying to raise tens of millions of dollars to improve their chances.

McConnell and his House counterpart, John Boehner, hoped to win Wall Street back from the Democrats, who for several years until 2009 took in more money than Republicans from the financial sector. Now the GOP was trying to persuade Wall Street that Republicans were their natural allies, and thanks in part to the Democrats' efforts to enact new financial regulations, they were having some success. By that April, Republicans were getting nearly 60 percent of those dollars.

McConnell and Cornyn went to New York in search of more of that money. Their cover was blown by a Fox Business News reporter who disclosed some details of their visit on April 12. "About 25 Wall Street executives, many of them hedge fund managers, sat down for a private meeting Thursday afternoon" with McConnell and Cornyn, Fox reported. The two senators heard complaints about the Frank bill passed by the House and the Dodd version pending in the Senate. McConnell and Cornyn said they couldn't just oppose Dodd's bill without offering something of their own, and explained "how financial executives might help prevent some of its least market-friendly aspects from becoming law by electing more Republicans." And they passed the hat.

This was one of several fundraisers the two senators held during that quick visit to New York. In the days around their trip, Wall Street executives gave more than $150,000 to the NRSC. Three of those donations were for $30,400, the legal maximum one individual could contribute to a campaign committee. The hunting expedition to New York was a success.

McConnell seemed embarrassed about this episode after Fox Business News made it public. He avoided answering questions about the event for days afterward, and denied that he had discussed killing Dodd's bill with the financiers he met. He told Candy Crowley of CNN, "I don't know anybody in the Senate who thinks we ought not to pass a bill. The question is, what's it going to look like?" Then on April 13, McConnell delivered a harsh denunciation of Dodd's bill on the floor of the Senate:

"If there's one thing Americans agree on when it comes to financial reform, it's this: never again should taxpayers be expected to bail out Wall Street from its own mistakes. . . . And that's why we must not pass the financial reform bill that's about to hit the floor. The fact is, this bill wouldn't solve the problems that led to the financial crisis. It would make them worse. . . . This bill not only allows for taxpayer-funded bailouts of Wall Street banks; it institutionalizes them."

McConnell sounded as though he were channeling Frank Luntz, the Republican pollster who wrote the pamphlet advising Republicans on how to kill any new legislation by "link[ing] it to the Big Bank Bailout." (The capitalization was Luntz's.)

The Obama administration reacted swiftly. Neal Wolin, the deputy secretary of the treasury, said McConnell had misrepresented the Dodd bill. "There are no more taxpayer-funded bailouts, period." Dodd and his staff agreed. They had written the bill to insure that failing financial firms would be put out of business, and healthy ones would have to write their own "living will" to show how they would wind themselves down if they got into serious financial trouble.

But McConnell was undeterred by facts. He returned to the well of the Senate the next morning with another speech, repeating the charge that the bill deliberately perpetuated bailouts. "It does this first of all," McConnell said, "by creating a new permanent bailout fund— a prepaid $50 billion bailout fund, the very existence of which would of course immediately signal to everyone that the government is ready to bail out large banks."

The $50 billion fund in the latest version of Dodd's bill would actually have been raised from the big financial institutions, to cover the costs of resolving or winding down failing firms in a future crisis. Dodd added the fund to his bill at the request of Senator Corker. Dodd had no such fund in his original version of the bill. The $50 billion fund in the latest version could not be used to salvage a failing firm the way government money had bailed out Bear Stearns or AIG. This fund could only be used to put a firm out of business by providing the working capital needed to do so. In this second speech, McConnell went on with a litany of complaints about "bailout" provisions in the bill that didn't exist or that he misinterpreted.

Then he added a new accusation: This bill was partisan. "It has been reported," McConnell said without specifying where, "that the Democrat chairman of the Banking Committee backed out of bipartisan negotiations under pressure from the White House, [which] plans to take the same approach on financial reform that it took on health care—put together a partisan bill, then jam it through on a strictly partisan basis."

When Dodd heard these charges, he came to the floor to respond angrily. "After listening to some of the rhetoric of the last 24 hours," he said, referring euphemistically to McConnell's two speeches, "I wonder if we are in not only the same chamber in the same city but on the same planet when it comes to the efforts that have been made to try and reach bipartisan agreement to deal with financial reform."

Regulatory reform was a deadly serious topic, Dodd said. Millions had lost their jobs, their homes, and their retirement savings in the Great Crash. The financial system barely avoided "a total meltdown." So "playing politics with this issue is dangerous indeed. Unfortunately, the talking points deployed by the Wall Street lobbyists [he was referring to the Luntz memo], in an effort to protect the status quo, leave my constituents and many Americans vulnerable to yet another economic crisis. Those arguments are littered with falsehoods—outright falsehoods—that I regret to say are now being repeated by people who should know better and, frankly, do know better." Dodd was accusing McConnell of knowingly lying to the Senate and the country.

"This morning," Dodd continued, "I wish to set the record straight. I wish to start by attacking one of the wildest and, frankly, most dishonest objections to this legislation, which is the notion that it is somehow a partisan document. I consider the minority leader [McConnell] and the ranking member of the Banking Committee [Shelby] to be good friends. They are patriots, with whom I have worked over many years on many issues. Senator Shelby and I have been working together for over a year on these issues, and I cannot, for the life of me, understand how anyone can claim with a straight face that what I have tried to achieve on this bill is a partisan effort. I have spent the last year seeking bipartisan consensus."

Dodd reviewed his efforts, dating back to the meetings with President Obama and administration officials to which he insisted Shelby be invited, and including his bipartisan working groups, his negotiations with Shelby and Corker, and the changes he made in his bill to accommodate Republican ideas. The bipartisan talks that McConnell said he had "backed out of" were still going on, of course. Dodd then reviewed the contents of his bill in some detail, refuting McConnell's descriptions of it with the facts of what it contained.

He noted the similarities between McConnell's speeches and Luntz's recommended language. Just crying "bailout" was wrong, Dodd said: "It is a naked political strategy. If it succeeds and this legislation goes down, and another crisis sinks the American economy, then the next recession and all of the damage it will bring to the working families of this country will have happened for the sake of that false talking point. . . . The American people deserve better from us in this chamber."

Dodd came to the close of this unusually blunt speech from a senior senator:

"The door is still open. We are not yet on the floor debating this bill. I will have meetings with Senator Shelby and others. My patience is running out. I have extended the hand, and I have written provisions in the bill to accommodate various interests. I will not continue doing this if all I am getting from the other side is a suggestion that this is a partisan effort. We have been through it [partisan warfare] over and over on the floor for the last year and a half. I think the American people are sick of it. They want to see us work together to achieve results that benefit them, not some political party, or narrow ideology, and certainly not the narrow interests on Wall Street."

The speech reflected Dodd's liberation from the normal restraints on senatorial outspokenness. He wasn't running for reelection, and he really wanted to pass this bill. So he dropped his usual diplomatic approach and said just what he was thinking. He revealed his frustration with an institution that no longer beguiled him.

The next morning, April 15, Dodd read an article in *The Wall Street Journal* that made him angrier still. "Republican leaders," the story began, "are struggling to maintain a unified opposition to the White House's financial-regulation revamp, which is emerging as the next big test of the GOP's ability to counter the administration's agenda." This was just what Dodd hoped to avoid—turning his bill into a bone of contention between Republican senators and Obama. The *Journal* reported that McConnell was circulating a letter "committing all 41 GOP senators" to support a filibuster to block Dodd's bill from coming to a vote.

Dodd saw himself as a traditionalist; he had refused to support liberal colleagues who wanted to try to change Senate rules to weaken the filibuster, arguing that the rule provided important protection for the minority's rights. But he also opposed using it to prevent the Senate from debating the biggest issues—and especially the last big issue of his career, financial regulatory reform. So he went back to the Senate floor for the second day running to make an even angrier speech. He accused McConnell of carrying the water of the Wall Street banks that did not want to pay into the $50 billion fund that Corker had recommended the bill contain, contriving the "bailout" argument for this purpose.

"This legislation incorporates Republican ideas and Democratic ideas," Dodd said, "and it definitely includes one idea that we all agree on: ending taxpayer bailouts." Want proof? "Just ask Sheila Bair, the chairperson of the Federal Deposit Insurance Corporation, the organization that comes in and puts an end to failing banks," Dodd said, referring to the FDIC's authority to close down any failing bank. Bair, he noted, "is also a Republican," a former aide to Senator Robert Dole of Kansas, and who was appointed to the FDIC job by George W. Bush. Dodd quoted an interview with Bair published just that morning in *American Banker*. Its reporter had asked her if the Dodd bill would "perpetuate bailouts."

Dodd read her answer: " 'The status quo is bailouts. That's what we have now. If you don't do anything, you're going to keep having bailouts.' "

"Nothing," Dodd observed, "is what we will have if members deny having this bill come onto the floor." He returned to Bair's remarks: "It [Dodd's bill] makes bailouts impossible," she said, "and it should. We worked really hard to squeeze bailout language out of this bill. The construct [of the bill] is that you can't bail out an individual institution, you just can't do it."

There was no better ally for Dodd than Bair, who had cultivated good relations with members of both parties in the House and Senate during her four years on the job, and was widely admired. Frank and his staff had consulted her extensively when writing their version of the bill, and Dodd, Friend, and their colleagues had done the same, so she was entitled to say "we worked really hard" on the legislation.

Dodd was particularly agitated about the letter McConnell was circulating among Republicans: "I just don't want to believe that 41 of my colleagues here—many of whom have worked with me on this bill—are going to sign on to a commitment that they won't allow this bill even to be debated and discussed unless I agree to their provisions. I've never seen anything like that in my 30 years here. I've got to ask myself, why did I go through this process, agreeing to so much of what they [Republican colleagues] are offering, and there's not a single political vote to show for it . . . even [for] debating the bill. Why in the world would you go through what I just did to end up at this particular point?"

He was especially upset, aides said, with Corker, who had signed the letter. How, Dodd wondered, could someone who had done so much for the bill join this crude attempt to block it?

Dodd's emotions got the best of him; he couldn't stop talking. He was trying to shame McConnell and the Republicans who were supporting him—not an easy task.

"I know my friends on the other side of the aisle are faced with a difficult choice between supporting their party leadership [McConnell] and participating in this complicated, difficult debate. And I'm not naive. I know that's a hard place to be. But if we can't act like United States Senators for the sake of this issue, for the sake of legislation whose success or failure has such an enormous impact on the very survival of our middle class and our economy as we know it, then why are we even here?"

The Republicans had an answer to Dodd's complaints, though not one he found persuasive. Senator Cornyn of Texas revealed it on April 14. Republicans had to stick together, Cornyn said, because "that represents the best negotiating position we have. Otherwise there's no incentive for the majority to talk to us." In other words, forty-one united Republicans would force Dodd to make more concessions, particularly on the consumer agency.

Cornyn was revealing McConnell's real strategy. As he'd told those Wall Street bankers on his trip to New York, it was politically impossible to be seen to oppose the bill without offering an alternative, but it was possible, even desirable, to try to satisfy the business world's complaints by eliminating or weakening the proposed consumer agency.

There was another explanation for McConnell's behavior, for which Dodd had no sympathy: The Republican leader saw himself as a key participant in a political struggle against President Obama. He gave this away six months later when he said, "The single most important thing we want to achieve is for President Obama to be a one-term president." In McConnell's view, that meant denying Obama big victories.*

Months after the debate on the Dodd bill, McConnell made this confession to a reporter: "We worked very hard to keep our fingerprints off of these [Democratic] proposals, because we thought—correctly, I think—that the only way the American people would know that a great debate was going on was if the measures were not bipartisan. When you hang the 'bipartisan' tag on something, the perception is that differences have been worked out, and there's a broad agreement that that's the way forward." McConnell wanted none of that.

In making these comments, McConnell implied that presidents are more important than Congress. So refusing to cooperate with this Democratic president took precedence over legislating. The preeminence of presidents had been a widely accepted proposition for half a century or more, despite the founders' clear expectation that Congress would be the most influential branch of government. McConnell did not see his job as protecting the Senate's prerogatives or trying to help solve the country's problems. He ruled out bipartisanship because the

---

* McConnell said this to Major Garrett of *National Journal* in October 2010. He also said he would be willing to "meet President Obama half way" to make compromises, but he never hid his desire to prevent Obama from winning politically useful victories. Nor, in the case of financial regulatory reform, did he ever suggest a definition of "half way." He never made his own proposal or supported a specific alternative.

term itself implied a truce in, or even an end to, the partisan war. McConnell was no peacemaker.

But nor was he a dictator. To get the signatures of all forty-one Republicans on a letter attacking the Dodd bill, he had to change its wording. Susan Collins of Maine had declined to commit herself to supporting a filibuster, so he had to drop that idea. In the end it took several days to reach agreement on the text. When McConnell finally released it on Friday the 16th of April, it did not mention a filibuster. Its key paragraph said, "We are united in our opposition to the partisan legislation reported by the Senate Banking Committee. As currently constructed, this bill allows for endless taxpayer bailouts of Wall Street and establishes new and unlimited regulatory powers that will stifle small businesses and community banks."

As Sheila Bair had explained, the bill did not allow for bailouts. Nor did it cover most small businesses. And Cam Fine's Independent Community Bankers of America supported it. McConnell was blustering. The truth was that he knew that his caucus was shaky—that's why it had taken several rewrites to produce the letter, and why the threat of a filibuster disappeared. He was trying to push Dodd to make more concessions, particularly on the consumer agency. "We encourage you to take a bipartisan and inclusive approach," the letter—addressed to Harry Reid—said, "rather than the partisan path you chose on health care."

The ever-changing political environment had turned against McConnell at this moment. The mood change on Capitol Hill initiated by the health care vote was reinforced by a sequence of events that seemed to be playing into the hands of the supporters of financial reform.

First came two hearings in early April of the Senate Permanent Subcommittee on Investigations. The first was devoted to the collapse of Washington Mutual, a big savings and loan with branches all over the country that issued thousands of subprime mortgages. The subcommittee's chairman was Carl Levin of Michigan, an old-fashioned liberal who had served in the Senate since 1979. Levin had strong opinions about the Great Crash and what to do in response to it. Dodd complained good-naturedly that Levin was bombarding him with proposed amendments to the regulatory reform legislation.

That was Dodd's responsibility, and Levin could only make suggestions. But as chairman of Permanent Investigations, a subcommittee of the Committee on Homeland Security and Government Operations, he could at least try to influence his colleagues and public opinion. This venerable Senate institution dated back to the early 1950s, when Senator Joseph McCarthy of Wisconsin was its chairman. McCarthy used it to conduct his witch hunt of alleged communists in government. John McClellan of Arkansas, the chairman from 1955 to 1972, used the committee to pursue the Teamsters Union and a succession of its leaders. When financial markets collapsed in 2008, Levin asked the committee's talented staff to launch an investigation into what had happened. It produced a stinging 635-page report lambasting the ethics of Wall Street and the negligent failure of government regulators to do their jobs.

Levin's report was released on April 12, the day before McConnell first attacked Dodd's bill on the floor of the Senate. Levin was joined by his ranking Republican colleague, Tom Coburn of Oklahoma, in an unusual demonstration of old-fashioned bipartisanship on a controversial issue. Coburn endorsed the report, which concluded that the Great Crash "was not a natural disaster, but the result of high risk, complex financial products; undisclosed conflicts of interest [of big banks]; and the failure of regulators, the credit rating agencies, and the market itself to rein in the excesses of Wall Street."

On the 13th and the 15th Levin and Coburn held hearings into the failure of Washington Mutual, which had written its subprime mortgages without regard for borrowers' ability to repay the loans. Government regulators put WaMu out of business in September 2008—the largest bank failure in American history. At the hearings, former risk officers at the firm testified that they warned their bosses repeatedly about reckless lending, to no avail. On the 15th, a hearing into the Office of Thrift Supervision, WaMu's regulator, exposed egregious failures to regulate the bank's irresponsible behavior, and a proclivity by the OTS to worry more about protecting its turf than protecting the financial system.

Then on the 16th the Securities and Exchange Commission announced fraud charges against Goldman Sachs, a startling development. The SEC accused Goldman of allowing a hedge fund operator, John Paulson, to help select the mortgage-backed securities that the investment bank packaged in a complicated investment product called Abacus 2007-AC1. This was a "collateralized debt obligation," a pool of bonds, loans, and other assets—in this case, mortgage-backed securities consisting of subprime home loans. In early 2007, Paulson wanted to take a "short" position in such an asset, so he could benefit if its value went down. He thought the housing bubble was about to burst.

Goldman peddled the Abacus product to big investors, mostly banks, without telling them that Paulson had helped select the securities that were in it and hoped it would soon lose most of its value. Instead, the SEC charged, Goldman told potential buyers that a well-known, independent firm called ACA had selected the Abacus securities. The institutions that bought them ultimately lost more than a billion dollars. Paulson made a billion-dollar profit.

Levin had first raised the issue of a possible conflict of interest in Goldman's trading of mortgage-backed securities at a hearing of the Permanent Investigations Subcommittee a year earlier. But the SEC's enforcement action was unexpected; it stunned Goldman Sachs and sent a shiver through Wall Street.

There is no evidence that this sequence of events added any senators to the list of supporters of Dodd's bill, but it surely changed the conventional wisdom about the state of play in the Senate. This was nicely captured by Stacy Kaper, the reporter covering regulatory reform issues for *American Banker*, who wrote at the end of that week that the suit against Goldman and Levin's WaMu hearings had one clear result: "The political pressure to enact financial reform intensified."

The Obama administration sought to reinforce the idea that momentum was building in support of a strong bill, with or without a bipartisan consensus. In his weekly radio address on the 17th, Obama called out McConnell and Cornyn for their recent trip to New York, where, he said, they talked to "Wall Street executives about how to block progress on this issue. Lo and behold, when he returned to Washington, the Senate Republican leader came out against the common-sense reforms we've proposed." Obama said he hoped for a bipartisan deal, but then talked tough: "This is certain: One way or another, we will move forward. . . . We will hold Wall Street accountable."

Then on the 22nd, Obama traveled to New York City and addressed an audience composed in part of Wall Street executives, including Lloyd Blankfein of Goldman Sachs. The White House advertised this appearance as evidence of Obama's personal involvement in the final effort to push the bill through the Senate, and he used the occasion to criticize McConnell's use of the Luntz talking points: "We've seen misleading arguments and attacks that are designed not to improve the bill but to weaken or to kill it. We've seen a bipartisan process buckle under the weight of these withering [lobbying] forces." Administration officials told reporters they felt the wind at their backs—the politics were going their way.

On the day Obama spoke in New York, Goldman Sachs reported its first-quarter earnings: a staggering $3.29 billion. The firm said it had reserved $5.5 billion for compensation and benefits for its employees. Such numbers accentuated the new political atmosphere that looked more and more favorable for a tough reform bill.

But first the bill had to get to the floor of the Senate. As we've seen, McConnell's letter signed by all forty-one Republicans agitated Dodd. He issued a response: "If this bill does not represent a bi-partisan effort, I don't know what does. . . . Let's not engage in nonsense." He released a "fact sheet" consisting of press reports that described how hard he had worked to create a bipartisan bill. One quoted Shelby as saying that on the evening of April 14—soon after McConnell's second denunciation of Dodd's bill on the floor—he and Dodd "had 'the best meeting we've had in weeks.'"

This was true. Serious talks between the Dodd and Shelby teams had resumed just as McConnell and Dodd were getting into their public spat, and they continued for most of the second half of April. Both sides "were negotiating in good faith," Friend thought. Shelby sounded hopeful on April 21: "I'm more optimistic than I've ever been," he told reporters that day. "I think we can put a bill together pretty soon." On the same day, Dodd said, "We're getting closer." Then he added his standard caveat: "Nothing is done until everything is done." His language was cautionary: "Closer" wasn't necessarily "close," and he was determined that if Shelby refused to yield on an independent consumer bureau, he would make no deal in the end.

Dodd's caution was justified. Soon after Shelby's declaration of optimism, the negotiations began to falter. Friend described the situation: "I could see, increasingly in these meetings, Shelby was having trouble with his own caucus, mostly on the consumer issue. I think we could have reached agreement on everything else." Democrats' positions were hardening too—liberals were emboldened by the new mood. "It seemed to me," Friend said, "that things had moved too far in our caucus, and too far in their caucus, to bridge the gap. . . . Earlier it might have been possible."

Harry Reid was determined to proceed with the bill, and announced that it would be considered the following Monday, April 26. But it takes an affirmative vote of the Senate to bring up a bill, and when Reid moved to do that, his motion failed 57–41. Not that fifty-seven voted against considering the bill—they voted "Aye." But under the rules, a three-fifths vote is needed both to bring up a bill, then to begin debate on it. The minority can block consideration of any piece of legislation with just forty-one votes. This is the substance of Rule XXII, the foundation of the filibuster.

In recent years both parties resorted to filibusters so often that they came to be seen as an established, fundamental aspect of Senate procedure. But this was not the case. Rule XXII was adopted in 1917, after five senators—"a little band of willful men," President Woodrow Wilson called them—held up Senate action on legislation to arm merchant ships as part of the just begun war effort by engaging in unlimited debate on the issue. This was possible because of a mistake the Senate had made in 1805 when it adopted changes in its rules that eliminated a provision allowing a majority of senators to "move the previous question," or seek a vote on the pending business. (This is still a provision of the House rules.) Only decades later, and on rare occasions, did senators begin to take advantage of this anomaly by demanding unlimited debates. Rule XXII said two-thirds of the Senate could cut off a filibuster. Sixty years later, in 1975, the Senate changed this to three-fifths, or sixty senators.

Use of unlimited debate was rare, so motions to cut off debate and vote on the pending business were rare too. As recently as the Congress of 1969–70, fewer than fifteen cloture motions were filed in the Senate. Even in the 1980s, the first decade of partisan warfare, cloture motions never exceeded sixty in one Congress, or two-year period. In the 1990s and early 2000s, successive Senates invoked cloture between sixty-two and eighty times over two-year periods. But beginning in 2007–8, after the Democrats had regained control of the Senate, the number of cloture motions shot up, to 139 in the 110th Congress (2007–8) and 137 in the 111th (2009–10).

McConnell had adopted the threat of a filibuster as a basic tactic. He demanded cloture votes routinely on bills and nominations of executive branch officials. Harry Reid responded by sometimes invoking cloture preemptively when a bill or nomination first arrived on the floor. The Senate began to operate on the assumption that nothing contentious could win approval without a supermajority of sixty votes, a new impediment to legislative action.

Traditionalists like Dodd who thought there was a place for a rule that protected the rights of minorities to prolong debate found it increasingly difficult to defend this fundamental change. Some of the newer Democratic members talked of changing the rule, but that would be difficult—it would actually require sixty-seven votes.* So the Senate was broken, with no prospect of an effective repair.

On April 26, McConnell was able to hold his Republicans together; forty of them (and one Democrat) voted against Reid's motion to proceed to take up Dodd's bill.† On the 27th, Reid tried again, with the same result.

Dodd and Shelby announced on the floor on the 27th that they had agreed to drop the $50 billion fund that Corker had originally asked for. Dodd said he and Shelby had nearly reached a final agreement on the "too big to fail" issue—how failing firms would be dissolved—and expressed the hope that their deal would allow debate on the entire measure to begin.

But the big event of April 27 was not the second unsuccessful cloture vote. Senator Levin and the Permanent Investigations Subcommittee seized the spotlight with a hearing devoted to Goldman Sachs, in particular, the Abacus deal. Months before the SEC complaint about the firm's activities, Levin's staff had discovered Abacus in a mountain of Goldman Sachs e-mails and documents that the committee had subpoenaed. Staff investigators and then their bosses, Levin and the other members of the committee, believed Goldman had behaved at least unethically, if not illegally.

The subcommittee summoned as witnesses for this hearing seven past and present Goldman Sachs employees, including Lloyd Blankfein, the chairman. The hearing room was crowded with television

---

* When the Senate changed the "cloture" rule in 1975, reducing the number of senators needed to end debate and call up a bill for a final vote from 67 to 60, it did not alter Rule XXIII, requiring a two-thirds vote, or 67 senators, to formally change the rules. Similarly, in 2013, the Senate majority voted to make just 51 votes necessary to confirm a presidential nominee for executive branch positions and all judgeships below the Supreme Court, but again left Rule XXIII unchanged. The new standard for confirmations was a ruling by the chair, supported by a majority, and not a change in the underlying rule, so could be altered in the future by another majority vote. Yes, the Senate's procedures are difficult to understand or explain.
† The lone Democrat was Ben Nelson of Nebraska, who was trying to win a concession from Dodd on a technical issue that his wealthiest constituent, Warren Buffett of Berkshire Hathaway, cared about. Nelson was a Berkshire Hathaway stockholder, a fact that did not deter him from trying to help the company.

cameras, photographers, and reporters. The show—and it was a show—began at ten in the morning with what *The Wall Street Journal* described as "all the trappings of a Capitol Hill perp walk," the opportunity that police and prosecutors often create for photographers to take the picture of a newly arrested suspect.

In this case the committee allowed perhaps two dozen photographers to surround the first group of witnesses—four Goldman men— and fire away for several minutes. While they clicked their shutters, four protesters dressed in convict stripes walked around the hearing room. They wore masks with the faces of Blankfein and Fabrice Tourré, one of the first panel of witnesses, a thirty-one-year-old, French-born banker who had become notorious for referring to himself in e-mails the committee had released as "Fabulous Fab."

The hearing began with a tough opening statement from Levin, who accused Goldman Sachs of unethical behavior and lying. "The evidence," Levin said, "shows that Goldman repeatedly put its own interests and profits ahead of the interests of its clients and our communities." Before a long day of questioning ended eleven hours later, both Democratic and Republican senators had denounced Goldman Sachs and its behavior. No senator came to the firm's defense. Some of the toughest rhetoric came from Republicans, particularly John McCain. "There's no doubt" that Goldman's behavior was "unethical," McCain told Blankfein.

The bankers were universally more articulate and more careful users of the English language than the senators, several of whom had difficulty following the complex financial transactions under discussion, even as they denounced them. But despite their verbal skills, the bankers all remained stubbornly oblivious to the impact their explanations had on the senators present and the wider audience watching the televised hearing. As Jon Tester of Montana put it at one point, "it seems like we're speaking a different language here." It certainly did. The senators and the bankers talked past each other for eleven hours, neither finding a way to see the world through the other's eyes.

The Goldman Sachs men kept trying to explain what it meant to be a "market maker," as Goldman was. Its role was to help clients buy and sell what they wanted to buy and sell. The firm created and sold complex financial instruments to knowledgeable and sophisticated investors who knew what they were doing, the bankers said again and again.

But, the senators protested, the firm was simultaneously selling products to clients and making bets with the firm's own money that those products were going to decline in value. How could you sell something and then take a position based on the belief that the thing you sold was going to go bad? How could that be proper? For example, Coburn of Oklahoma, the ranking Republican on the subcommittee, suggested that Goldman "was making proprietary trades that were contrary to the financial interests of their clients and customers."

The Goldman men insisted that what it did within its own [proprietary] trading account was irrelevant to its market making. "I don't think our clients care or [that] they should care," Blankfein said at one point.

The internal e-mails the committee had acquired revealed the unvarnished attitudes of bankers whose only real concern was making money—not a pretty sight. One e-mail referred to a product the firm was actively selling as "a shitty deal." Levin challenged one of the bankers: "You didn't tell them you thought it was a 'shitty deal'? . . . [Yet] you knew it was a 'shitty deal.' . . . Should Goldman Sachs be trying to sell a 'shitty deal'?"

The e-mails also revealed the bankers' excitement when their bets paid off. "It is unsettling," said Susan Collins of Maine, "to read e-mails of Goldman executives celebrating the collapse of the housing market when the reality for millions of Americans is lost homes and disappearing jobs."

The events in Congress that get the most public attention are usually hearings like this one, where powerful people are embarrassed and humiliated for all to see. This is a modern American equivalent of the Roman circuses that featured gladiators who eviscerated one another before cheering crowds. In the modern era few members of the House or Senate and few committee staffs knew how to organize and run such hearings effectively, but on rare occasions they could still occur.

The timing of this one was particularly fortuitous—and, Levin and his staff insisted credibly, entirely coincidental. The hearing culminated eighteen months of work by the subcommittee staff; neither senators nor staff had known that the SEC would sue Goldman for fraud just a fortnight before their big hearing, or that the financial regulatory reform legislation would be the pending business on the floor of the Senate the day the hearing occurred. Thanks to those two coincidences, Levin's hearing got extensive coverage on television and in the newspapers. It was a Grade A media event.

The attention it got compounded McConnell's political problem. With even his own Republicans joining in the bashing of Goldman Sachs at the Permanent Subcommittee on Investigations' hearing—and many of them calling for new regulations on investment banks—the never strong rationale for a Republican filibuster to block Dodd's bill simply dissolved. This became clear the next day, April 28, just after 7 a.m., during a segment on NBC's *Today* show—not usually a venue for policy discussions about investment banking. The show began with a long (for television) report on the previous day's hearing and then a joint interview with Levin and Collins. Noting that Collins had said that new rules were needed for Wall Street, Matt Lauer, the interviewer, said he perceived "an irony. . . . For the second time yesterday, Republicans [including Collins] blocked further debate on this financial reform bill. How can you say in one room, 'We have a major problem here,' and how can Republicans say in another room, 'But we don't want to debate it openly on the floor of the Senate right now'?"

After the second time Lauer pressed her on this point, Collins signaled her true intentions: "I'm sure there will be open debate on the Senate floor. . . . I'm confident that we can get there. We do need reform." Later in the morning she joined her colleagues in voting against cloture for the third time. Then everything changed.

Shelby brought the first news of the change to Dodd. After that third cloture vote, the two met alone in Dodd's office. Shelby announced that their efforts to negotiate a comprehensive bipartisan deal would have to be abandoned. He hoped they could formalize the agreement they had reached on the "too big to fail" issues, including killing off the $50 billion fund, but that would have to be the end of it. He confided that several members of the Republican caucus had signaled their unwillingness to vote against cloture again. It's time to move on, Shelby said.

Later that day, after a caucus of Senate Republicans, the minority leader's office passed the word that there would be no further attempts to block the beginning of debate; the cloture fight had ended. At 6:15 p.m. Harry Reid asked for unanimous consent to call up the bill. No senator complained. The bill was the pending business of the Senate.

The Republicans' decision to cave "suggested that they saw political peril in being depicted as impeding tougher rules for Wall Street," *The New York Times* reported the next day. There were practical considerations as well: Reid had announced his decision to have cots installed in the Senate cloakrooms to accommodate members during an all-night session that he proposed to call to keep voting on the cloture motion. Until then, Reid had allowed (as he usually did) the Republicans to enjoy the benefit of a filibuster without having to hold the floor and keep speaking.

That was the old-fashioned understanding of a filibuster—endless debate. But for a decade or more, the majority party had allowed the minority to block floor action just by threatening a filibuster, as the Republicans had on the three cloture votes that week. This is not what the founders had in mind for the Senate, but then, the founders failed to foresee most of the ways Congress proved to be dysfunctional in the early twenty-first century.

CHAPTER TWENTY

Staff Warfare

While Dodd maneuvered his bill toward the Senate floor in April, his aides were engaged in a difficult negotiation over one regulatory reform issue that had unusual characteristics: It involved a gigantic marketplace that put trillions of dollars, at least theoretically, at risk; it directly threatened the earnings of the big banks and scared the financial vice presidents of American corporations; it provoked an intense turf battle between two executive branch agencies and the congressional committees that oversaw them; and it was utterly opaque. This was the question of how to regulate the complicated financial instruments called derivatives.

Neither Dodd nor Shelby had mastered this arcane subject. Nor had most members of their staffs. Nor had nearly all members of the Senate, for whom the derivatives market was as remote as Mars. Yet it really mattered to a lot of people, as Julie Chon found out.

Chon, the Banking Committee staff person responsible for derivatives, had an unusual personal history. As a sophomore at Cornell, she was elected the student member of the university's board of trustees. As a trustee she was exposed to the world of high finance, which intrigued her. After graduating in 1998 she took a job with Chase Securities, later acquired by J.P. Morgan. Later she worked for Salomon Brothers, the investment bank then a part of the Citigroup. Her principal interest in school was public policy, but the banks paid well, and allowed her to live in London for a time and learn a great deal about the money business—including derivatives.

In 2004, after six years as a banker, she decided it was time to try public service in Washington. This was a presidential election year. "My thinking was, as an outsider—I didn't have any contacts in Washington—there is usually staff turnover in big presidential years, so it would increase the chances of an unknown like me with no contacts or sponsors to get my foot in the door." It wasn't so easy. Eventually she volunteered for John Kerry's presidential campaign and befriended two of Kerry's speechwriters, who helped her find a job at the Democratic Senatorial Campaign Committee. Seven months later she was hired by the Democratic Policy Committee, which provided substantive staff work for Democratic senators and their offices. In this job she could exploit her experience in the financial world.

When Democrats won control of the Senate in the 2006 midterm elections, Chon was hired onto the staff of the Banking Committee. Her patron was Shawn Maher, the new staff director of the committee and Dodd's principal aide—the man who brought Amy Friend to the staff of Banking. Chon and Maher had gotten to know each other at weekly meetings organized by the Policy Committee staff. As the distress in the financial markets became steadily more ominous through 2007 and 2008, Chon's expertise became more valuable; Maher gave her more and more responsibility. She was surprised to find herself writing speeches for Dodd and influencing the stands he took. "We developed Senator Dodd's positions," as she put it.

In early September, as the titans of Wall Street scrambled to cooperate with government officials to wrestle with the fast deteriorating financial crisis, Chon got nervous; this was not a routine market event. On the night the Fed decided it had to rescue AIG, Chon was working out at the fancy gym she belonged to in the Ritz-Carlton Hotel on 22nd Street in Washington's West End—the one luxury she allowed herself. At the end of her workout she looked at her cell phone for the first time in ninety minutes and saw messages from Maher reporting the AIG bailout. "As soon as I saw that I really thought the world was coming to an end," she said later. "There's a huge window at the gym that looks down on an Exxon gas station, I thought maybe I should go into that gas station and buy as much water as possible, in case this whole country turns into a riot zone." She didn't buy the water that night, but friends from church stocked her home with water and food.

Chon realized that the crash would change the world profoundly. In her new world of the Senate, it would create conditions favorable for reforming the system that would have been unthinkable before the crisis. The vote on TARP was, she thought, an early and auspicious sign. She was on the floor on October 1, 2008, sitting in the staff section at the rear of the chamber, when the Senate voted to support Paulson's request for $700 billion to bail out banks. "That was such a dramatic, solemn moment!" she recalled. "All the senators took their seats and voted from their desks, seated. . . . you could hear a pin drop." The Senate, as we've seen, approved the bailout by a vote of 74–25.

She thought of that vote later when former Wall Street colleagues and other bankers protested vigorously against the reforms she was working on for Dodd. "I wish all of those people could appreciate the unusual and fortunate circumstance of two Democratic chairs of the House and Senate banking committees [Frank and Dodd] agreeing to support a Republican administration in a time of crisis. That is the proudest thing that I affiliate myself with in my time in Washington, is that moment of bipartisan sacrifice."

Chon's responsibilities on the committee staff centered on international financial issues, but as work progressed on regulatory reform, she realized she would be pressed into duty on some aspect of it. In August 2009, Silverman asked her to take responsibility for the section covering derivatives. She was no expert, but now she would have to master the subject.

"We were very organized in Dodd world," she said, referring to Dodd's staff with a moniker widely used on Capitol Hill. No member of the Senate lived or acted alone. As Richard Lugar, the longtime senator from Indiana liked to quip, the Senate consisted of "a hundred carrier task forces," the Navy's combination of a nuclear-powered supercarrier with a gaggle of destroyers, cruisers, submarines, supply ships, and other vessels that accompany American carriers on deployments in the world's oceans. Lugar was referring to the modern senator's entourage of aides, which considerably increased his or her firepower.

When the administration's derivatives proposal arrived in August, Chon began to organize a series of briefings. She lined up sessions with the Federal Reserve Bank of New York, the SEC, the CFTC, the Fed in Washington, and the Treasury. "I wanted to do these at a time that would be convenient for the Shelbys," she said. "But they said,

'We're not going to be available until September.' But the orders we'd gotten in Dodd world, internally, were to get cracking, don't waste August! So I told the Shelbys we'd have to go ahead by ourselves, we can't take a four-week break." The briefings went on through August.

"As soon as we returned after Labor Day weekend," Chon recounted, "I was bombarded with lobbying requests. That's when it all started, the whole lobbying onslaught. Literally every single business day, sometimes starting as early as 8:30 in the morning, sometimes going as late as seven at night, every half hour or hour increments were scheduled with lobbying requests. I was obliged to hear them out and take their views into account. We generally gave everyone an opportunity to make their case to us."

Chon was the target of a concerted lobbying effort orchestrated by the five big banks that controlled most derivatives trading. With their support and encouragement, the Chamber of Commerce, National Association of Manufacturers, Business Roundtable, and other business groups had created the Coalition for Derivatives End-Users, a group of companies that used derivatives to hedge their risks and the trade associations that represented them. Banking lobbyists told reporters they hoped corporate voices would be persuasive at a time when the big banks' reputations were tattered. The coalition argued that banks and companies should be allowed to make private derivatives deals without the world knowing what they were. This was the way it had been done for years; it allowed banks to charge big fees for derivatives without ever revealing them. But the companies were comfortable with the status quo, and happily made this case to members of Congress and their staffs, and to the Obama administration.

We had no role in the crisis, coalition members said repeatedly, and we need to preserve the existing derivatives markets to hedge against risks that could damage us and the economy. So they opposed mandatory use of transparent exchanges that would make most derivatives deals public, including their cost. Instead they suggested voluntary clearing of derivatives contracts, which meant the parties could clear them on an open exchange only when they wanted to.

This was a high-powered lobbying campaign, and it was an educational experience, which included this classic tale of Washington lobbying. "The in-house lobbyist for one of the big banks called," Chon remembered. " 'Can we meet with you on Friday, we'd like to talk about derivatives.' I said sure. We set up a time. A day later I got an e-mail from a lobbying firm. 'Hi, I'm working with a new client,' it was the same bank, 'I'd like to bring them in to talk to you about derivatives on Friday.' I called him on the telephone, and I said I've already got a meeting set up with them on Friday. And he said, What time? and I said, One-thirty, and he said, Can we do it at two? And I said, Okay, do you want to move the meeting to two? And he said, No, I want to have a separate meeting with you and them at two.' I said I'm sorry, I don't understand the point of that. Are you saying the same people will stay in the room, me, them, and then you'll come in at two? And he said, 'Yeah.'

"I didn't do it, I kept the original meeting. Later other people told me it was because he wanted to get credit for setting up that meeting. I didn't realize that, but that's what it was." She was learning that a large part of lobbying activity is really make-work to justify lobbyists' big fees.

This lobbying campaign was a response to the Obama administration's initial proposals on derivatives. The Treasury plan was tough; it called for mandatory trading of virtually all derivatives on public exchanges, maximizing the transparency of these trades, most of which had always been secret and invisible. But the administration's proposal had no natural constituency, and no lobbyists were supporting it. "If there's no political constituency behind a policy," Chon observed, "that policy is going nowhere."

By contrast, the banks and end users, located in every state, were taken seriously by Senate offices—they were an effective constituency. "You could see why people in Congress could be convinced that that was the way to regulate derivatives, because that was the only view we were hearing in September," she said.

In October, on a trip to Turkey for the annual meeting of the International Monetary Fund and the World Bank, Chon happened to sit next to Pierre Cardon, a senior official at the Bank for International Settlements (BIS) in Basel. It was a coincidence that helped transform Chon's view of derivatives.

The BIS is home to the Basel Committee on Banking Supervision, the body responsible for trying to coordinate bank regulations among the rich countries. Cardon was involved in this effort. He and Chon spent nearly eight hours together in that airplane, talking about derivatives—an eye-opening conversation. Cardon showed her a detailed report from the BIS on derivatives, and discussed why they could be so risky. He gave her the names of other Europeans who would be at the IMF meetings who could help her understand what others were thinking about derivatives regulation. She followed up in Turkey, found these people, and realized that there was an emerging international consensus in favor of stiff new regulation of the financial sector generally, and the derivatives market specifically. One of the people she met was Stephen Cecchetti, an American and former economics professor at Brandeis University, who "had been writing about the dangers of the unregulated derivatives markets for years," Chon said.

The meetings she attended in Turkey and the contacts she made there helped her realize that "there was quite a bit of academic research to back up the policy ideas that were being floated around for reg reform," especially the need for systemic risk regulators and new controls on derivatives. In Washington Shelby's staff had complained of a shortage of good research and hard facts, but "here I was in Istanbul and I see all of this great research work being presented."

When she got back to Washington, Chon followed up on the contacts she had made in Turkey. She invited Cecchetti to come to Washington to meet with Senate staff and explain the European view of what should be done, but he declined, saying it was inappropriate for a Basel employee to lobby in Washington. He did agree to talk to some staff colleagues on the telephone. Chon looked for other "validators" in America who could help her convince colleagues of the need for tough regulation. She found two.

The first was Steve Eisman, the hedge fund operator memorialized in Michael Lewis's book *The Big Short* for his decision to bet against the housing market near the height of the bubble. He made hundreds of millions of dollars on this bet, and honed his image as a skeptical contrarian who, in Lewis's words, "refused to be buffaloed by other people's gobbledygook," especially Wall Street's. Chon talked to Eisman on the phone to see if he would help her. He was outspoken. "There are two things that you must accomplish" with financial reform legislation, he told her. "Number one, you have to create a CFPA to protect consumers. . . . And number two, you have to have a tough derivatives bill. If you don't have both, you might as well not show up for work, it's going to be pointless."

Chon brought Eisman to Washington in October to meet with the staffs of Banking Committee members, Republicans and Democrats.

Eisman said derivatives had played a big, damaging role in the Great Crash. He argued eloquently for strong regulation. When one Shelby aide asked why it would have been wrong to let AIG go under in September 2008, Eisman had a blunt reply. As Chon remembered it, he said: "How can I explain this to you in English? There was a global freakathon going on. And when there are freakathons, you don't just let the world collapse." Her colleagues "hadn't dealt with someone like him," Chon said. She thought Eisman was terrific.

The second validator Chon found was suggested to her by Barbara Novick, vice chairman of the huge New York investment management firm BlackRock, and a fellow Cornell graduate with whom Chon had become friends. Novick suggested her colleague Nigel Bolton, part of a BlackRock team hired by the New York Fed to help wind down AIG's inventory of credit default swaps, the derivatives that played a big role in the crash. Bolton briefed senators and staff. "Dodd loved him," Chon recalled. He gave a just-the-facts presentation with his English accent about how sloppy AIG Financial Products had been, and how reckless.

October was the month when Dodd's team wrote the first version of his bill, the "discussion draft" that he released on November 10. It contained a strong section on derivatives, empowering the regulators—the SEC and CFTC—to force most trades onto exchanges, and to require participants in private, over-the-counter derivatives trades to post collateral to guarantee them. But Chon knew this was just an early draft.

She then watched the House produce what she considered weak provisions in its bill. She was troubled that the Treasury Department seemed satisfied with them, and hoped to do better. But the subject was finessed in Dodd's second draft bill, released in March, because Jack Reed of Rhode Island and Judd Gregg of New Hampshire—the original bipartisan working group on derivatives—were still trying to find a common position. Dodd announced that he would wait for them. So in the days before Dodd's bill was to go to the floor, the issue remained open.

But the Banking Committee alone could not resolve the derivatives issue. As in the House, two committees had to share responsibility for it. In the House, Frank and Collin Peterson of Minnesota, chairman of Agriculture, worked things out amicably through their staffs and agreed on the derivatives provisions included in the House bill. Things had not gone as smoothly in the Senate.

The basic arrangement was the same: The Banking Committee oversaw the Securities and Exchange Commission, while the Agriculture Committee had jurisdiction over the Commodity Futures Trading Commission. But the relationships were more complicated. The chairman of the Senate Agriculture Committee, Blanche Lincoln of Arkansas, had assumed the job just seven months earlier, at the time Dodd decided to remain chairman of Banking rather than replace Ted Kennedy on the HELP committee.

This was a big break for Lincoln, who ascended to an important chairmanship near the end of her second term in the Senate—a journey that had taken Dodd twenty-six years and five terms. It also threw her into an important role in the debate over financial regulatory reform, a subject in which she had no background or expertise. The daughter of a farmer, Lincoln had spent most of her adult life on Capitol Hill, as an aide in the House, then a House member, then a senator. When elected to the Senate in 1998 at thirty-eight, she was the youngest woman ever to win a Senate seat.

As chairman Lincoln got to hire the principal committee staff. As staff director she chose young Robert Holifield, an Arkansan who had worked for her for years, and had spent 2007–9 as a senior staff person at the CFTC, his first professional exposure to futures markets. To work on the regulatory reform issues, Holifield engaged Patrick McCarty, a bright, knowledgeable lawyer with extensive experience in the realm of financial markets and derivatives. He was a former general counsel of the CFTC, and in 2009 was working at the SEC. He had tried unsuccessfully to get the Senate Banking Committee to take him on to help with regulatory reform.

The Senate Agriculture Committee had a history of bipartisan collaboration. Its members all represented farm states, and shared an interest in defending the government's generous farm programs against periodic attempts by other members to reduce them. As the new chairman, Lincoln sought to collaborate with her ranking Republican, Saxby Chambliss of Georgia. Chambliss was a southern conservative with a nasty reputation stemming from his campaign against Max Cleland, the triple amputee Vietnam veteran elected to the Senate in 1996, whom Chambliss defeated in 2002. In that campaign Chambliss challenged Cleland's patriotism and ran an ad featuring photographs of Cleland, Saddam Hussein, and Osama bin Laden, suggesting Cleland was helping the other two. Two Republican senators and Vietnam veterans, John McCain and Chuck Hagel of Nebraska, sharply criticized the Chambliss campaign. The Georgian had worked hard in the Senate to overcome that first impression, with some success.

Initially, Lincoln and Chambliss agreed to work together on the derivatives issue to come up with a bipartisan Agriculture Committee proposal. Staffs produced such a document, and the two senators talked about releasing it publicly in mid-April. Robert Holifield shared it with Gary Gensler of the CFTC, his old boss, and Gensler told him it was too weak. The next day, Michael Barr, the assistant secretary of the treasury who kept close track of the debates on the Hill, and his boss, Tim Geithner, came to the same conclusion. They considered the Lincoln-Chambliss draft much too soft on the derivatives dealers, requiring too little transparency in the marketplace, too little exchange trading, and too little posting of collateral in risky trades. Barr told the Agriculture Committee staff that "we couldn't support it."

All spring the biggest banks were working hard to influence Lincoln and her Agriculture Committee colleagues to go lightly on derivatives. Prominent bankers from Goldman Sachs and Morgan Stanley, for example, personally lobbied the Agriculture Committee staff. Reporting this on April 14, *The Wall Street Journal* explained the banks' intense interest: Derivatives trading had earned about $20 billion in profit for the big five banks* in the previous year.

Lincoln, however, was feeling a pressure much greater than any New York bankers could apply: the pressure created by fear. She had a tough primary opponent in Arkansas, Bill Halter, the state's lieutenant governor, who was challenging her from the left. Halter had the support of national liberal groups including MoveOn.org, and of organized labor. Polls that spring showed him closing in on Lincoln, whom he was attacking for being too cozy with big business. Her record gave him plenty to work with. She had cast herself as a Bill Clinton moderate, and regularly infuriated liberals with her votes. Lincoln had opposed environmental bills and a public option for health care, and had supported Bush tax cuts for the well-to-do. Labor and several national liberal groups raised millions of dollars for Halter; he began to look like the favorite in the race. Lincoln spent the Easter recess

---

* Bank of America, Citigroup, Goldman Sachs, JPMorgan Chase, and Morgan Stanley.

in early April campaigning in Arkansas and knew she was in trouble. The last thing she needed was a public fight over derivatives with the Obama administration.

So she changed course. She abandoned the attempt to find a bipartisan position with Chambliss and instead embraced a radical new approach. It would have required all banks to spin off their derivatives trading operations completely. "The dark days of deals are over," Lincoln said in a melodramatic statement on April 14. "Financial institutions will have to decide if they want to be banks or if they want to engage in the risky financial trading that caused the collapse of firms" like AIG.

The Treasury disliked this new proposal, which the administration thought could create new risks to the financial system by forcing derivatives trading into unregulated new entities. Despite its apparent toughness, Treasury thought the new Lincoln proposal, written largely by Pat McCarty, had numerous flaws. But the news media and several liberal groups embraced it as "tougher" than Dodd's language, though it wasn't, and Lincoln clearly enjoyed her new status as outspoken critic of the big banks. She didn't want to change the proposal. Her primary was imminent—May 18.

This maneuvering was frustrating for Chon, who saw her careful work on policy being supplanted by politics. She understood why the Lincoln language was problematic, but was unable to do anything about it. The Agriculture Committee approved Lincoln's new proposal on April 21.

The next day, the Democratic Policy Committee held a meeting. This body provided a forum for Democratic senators to discuss politics and policy over lunch. Its meetings were private. Several senators questioned Lincoln about her proposal to force banks to give up their derivatives trading desks. Then Maria Cantwell of Washington, a former high-tech executive and a loner in the Senate not popular with her colleagues, startled the gathering by accusing the old boys who ran the Senate of disrespecting her friend Senator Lincoln by failing to recognize the serious contribution she had just made to derivatives regulation. Cantwell—who had made derivatives a personal interest, pressing for tougher regulation—complained that Geithner hadn't even met with Lincoln to discuss her new position before it was adopted by the Agriculture Committee. She warned that it would be a serious political mistake not to include Lincoln's new derivatives language as part of the Dodd bill about to go to the floor. Senators present thought Cantwell was taking a shot at Dodd, implying that he was guilty of sexism.

When Amy Friend heard about this, she was livid. The idea that Dodd, who had given her so much authority to write the regulatory reform legislation, somehow looked down on women was ridiculous.

Cantwell persisted. The next day she organized a letter to Harry Reid arguing that the Agriculture Committee's derivatives section should be the "foundation" of the final bill, which was meant to reflect the work of both Agriculture and Banking. Unless the provisions of Lincoln's bill were included, the letter warned ominously, "we would find it difficult to support comprehensive reform legislation." The letter was signed by six Democrats and, surprisingly, one Republican, Olympia Snowe of Maine. Dodd realized he had to take it seriously, because he would need every vote.

Meetings ensued between the Dodd and Lincoln staffs, Treasury and CFTC officials. The Dodd people were alarmed to learn that Lincoln wanted to substitute a new "Lincoln-Dodd bill" for Dodd's draft when the measure came to the floor, an obvious ploy to draw attention to herself. Dodd wanted to collaborate on the derivatives section, but no more. Michael Barr from Treasury had joined the conversations, which continued over a weekend. The goal was to add a new derivatives section to the bill that was an amalgam of the two committees' positions. The talks got off to a reasonable start but broke down on the second day. The Dodd people were upset, particularly with McCarty, for being combative and territorial. This was no way for fellow Democrats to behave, they thought.

Friend believed Lincoln's primary was the problem. The senator had publicly staked out a "tough" line and couldn't abandon it. Treasury and the Dodd team agreed to finesse the outstanding issues for the time being. "There was no agreement about how to proceed," Barr recalled. "We decided that trying to reach resolution at that moment would produce a worse outcome than letting it ride. We decided basically not to resolve the issues at that time." Instead, Lincoln's language—disliked by Treasury and by Dodd's team—was incorporated into the bill. Treasury and Dodd reassured each other that they would fix this later in the process.

One of the disputes in these discussions that alarmed Julie Chon was over jurisdiction, the issue that Frank had worked so hard to avoid in the House. The Senate Agriculture Committee staff took on the role of promoter of the CFTC, working relentlessly to increase its—and by extension, the Ag Committee's—importance by broadening its jurisdiction over regulation of financial products that traditionally fell under the SEC. Gary Gensler, a former Goldman Sachs banker who had hoped to be chairman of the SEC in the Obama administration, was offered the CFTC instead and took it. He worked with the Lincoln staff to try to enhance his agency's powers.

Chon understood the perverse political motivation for senators involved in this fight: An expanded jurisdiction over derivatives for the CFTC would likely produce more campaign contributions for Agriculture Committee members from the financial institutions dealing in derivatives.

At the end of the weekend negotiations, this issue was finessed by sticking to language on jurisdiction from the Obama administration's original draft bill, which was neutral on the question of SEC versus CFTC in regulating derivatives, giving both a shared role.

Pat McCarty was the principal figure in this drama, and he was defying one of the cardinal rules of the Senate: Always be open and honest in your dealings, with friend or foe. "The Senate is about trust and human relationships," in the words of Kara Stein, senior aide to Rhode Island's Jack Reed, the Senate's leading expert on derivatives and an active participant in this episode. Stein, a mild-mannered and likable lawyer, had written a bill for Reed creating a regulatory system for derivatives that he had introduced in 2009, before Dodd offered the first version of his reform bill. Reed's called for making the SEC the lead agency, at the expense of the CFTC. This made Stein and Reed the enemy for McCarty, and McCarty was the dominant figure on Lincoln's staff. At one point the Lincoln people told Chon to stop bringing Stein to meetings; they refused to deal with her. This shocked both Chon and Stein.

Two days after the final compromises had been reached, nearly all of them in Lincoln's favor, Chon and everyone else involved in the negotiations received an e-mail from the Agriculture Committee staff saying that the compromise version, now the official bill introduced for Senate consideration in a day or two, contained "a huge mistake . . . that must be fixed right away." She contacted Lincoln's staff director Holifield and asked for an explanation. It was the provisions on jurisdiction again. Holifield, she recalled, said it was "a purely technical matter." He said McCarty was drafting "a fix."

She, Friend, Silverman, and Jonathan Miller, handling the bill for

Dodd, were taken aback. "We can't pull the bill now. Why don't you offer up an amendment?" she said to Holifield. No, he said, "We can't risk it."

"Of course," Chon said, "Senator Dodd agreed, as he does often, to accommodate his colleagues." He told his staff to let Ag make its changes. "Then the next day, I woke up in the morning and the leadership office had already distributed the new, revised bill." McCarty and Holifield had failed to share their work with the Dodd team or Treasury, though the changes they had made were to Dodd's bill. After studying the new language, Chon concluded, "Not only did they not execute [the agreed-to] changes properly, they used the opportunity to make changes that were never discussed by the group, ever." One of their changes created a new loophole in the requirement for exchange trading of derivatives by changing the definition of a "swap execution facility"—an exchange for trading these instruments. It made the definition ambiguous, leaving room for legal disputes and uncertainty about who and what was covered.

"Our position was to include more descriptive, robust requirements [for exchange trading] and Ag wanted more nebulous requirements. I felt they were trying to dance with many different partners on K Street. They would tell certain people [lobbyists], you know, we agree with you, but they would tell people on the opposite side, we agree with you. So they would end up with a nebulous definition. This was one of those areas."

Several reporters seized on this change as a sign that the bill had been weakened at the last minute, and at least one news story said that Dodd was responsible. Then reporters began calling Chon to ask about the change. Several told her that Holifield had said the changes were made at her request. Then she saw e-mails from Ag staff that made the same statement. She was furious.

In all, the latest Ag draft made "about a dozen" significant changes. "They were serious," Chon said, "because, number one, they were a complete violation of what the entire group had agreed to coming out of those negotiations—a very disturbing outcome for a legislative process. And then number two, the substance. The changes involved either weakening the requirements or totally changing jurisdiction out of the hands of not only the SEC, but grabbing into other areas as well, such as the bank regulators, and moving bank-regulatory functions to the CFTC."

It was too late to change the draft again; it was never fixed, though it was improved later as we will see. The news media never caught on; only a few people realized what had happened, and none of them had an interest in making it known before the bill was acted on. Revealingly, no one in Washington read the bill carefully enough, or understood its terms well enough, to blow a whistle. The Obama administration and Dodd's team hoped to fix the text later in the legislative dance—on the floor of the Senate perhaps, or later in a conference committee that would have to resolve differences between House and Senate versions of the bill.

One element of Lincoln's bill did get public attention—her proposal to force banks to spin off their derivatives trading desks. The Federal Reserve and the FDIC publicly endorsed the view Treasury had expressed in the negotiations that this was a dangerous move that could leave derivatives trading in unregulated corners of the financial industry. Lincoln wasn't moved by these concerns.

So a seriously flawed bill would go to the floor of the Senate. Chon was heartsick. This had been "a truly horrible experience," she said. "It was not something I wanted to be part of."

Dodd had pacified Lincoln and her allies. The cost of doing so was higher than the public ever knew. But his overriding concern then was holding the sixty votes he would need for cloture—to cut off a Republican filibuster. What worried him most on the weekend of the final negotiations was Cantwell's Friday letter threatening to withhold support for the bill if Dodd failed to incorporate Lincoln's provisions. "I sat at this desk all day that Saturday," Dodd said later in a conversation in his Russell Building office, "finding all seven [senators who signed the letter], to make sure they would vote for cloture." While his staff negotiated, he made those phone calls and extracted the assurances he sought. All seven would stay in line. For this man of the Senate, eager to crown his career with one last big achievement, something he thought his country needed, getting those sixty votes for cloture was what mattered most.

CHAPTER TWENTY-ONE

The Senate Acts

As politics supplanted policy in the pecking order of senators' concerns over the previous three decades, the fate of controversial legislation became increasingly dependent on the political environment in which it was debated. Chris Dodd called it "the context." It can be difficult to define or explain, but talented practitioners can feel it. On the eve of floor debate on his bill, Dodd knew he had been blessed with a favorable context.

He benefited most from the lingering effects of the Great Crash, and the obvious public appetite for some form of retribution for those who caused it. Passage of health care reform, as we have seen, also heartened and emboldened Democrats supporting reform, and discouraged Republicans. The travails of Goldman Sachs, combined with its huge profits, put another arrow in Dodd's quiver. Opinion polls consistently showed public support for reforms.

Dodd worried that all these factors had emboldened his liberal Senate colleagues, some of whom, he feared, wanted to use Dodd's bill to score political points in an election year. Dodd wanted a bill, not a political argument.

As May began, the shrewdest participants in this legislative enterprise, both Republicans and Democrats, shared the view that the tides were running against the big banks and in favor of relatively tough reforms. Gregg, Corker, and Shelby all said publicly that they expected

Dodd's bill to pass. The smarter lobbyists working for the big banks began to poor-mouth their chances of "improving" the bill for their clients, to prepare them for an uncongenial outcome. For months they had calculated that Shelby would be able to moderate the bill as the price for reaching a bipartisan consensus with Dodd. Ed Yingling, president of the American Bankers Association, said in a March interview, "the longer this goes on, the stronger Shelby's hand is." By early May they realized this had been a miscalculation.

Nevertheless, Shelby was still engaged. He was negotiating with Dodd on the "too big to fail" provisions in the first two titles of the bill that described how regulators would put failing financial institutions out of business without bailing them out. Dodd had the impression that in the course of the many caucuses held in late April by Senate Republicans, Shelby had promised to produce a deal with Dodd on these provisions, even if the idea of a bipartisan bill had died. Apparently, Shelby wanted to demonstrate that he could still leave an imprint on the bill. The Dodd and Shelby staffs kept discussing this through the weekend of May 1–2. Debate was to begin on Tuesday the 4th, and Dodd wanted to have this deal in hand when it began. Staff was assigned to make the deal.

But Amy Friend and Ed Silverman were frustrated with Duhnke and Oesterle, who would never come to a final agreement. All through that weekend, Dodd worried. He believed this deal would be the key to getting his bill through the Senate. With it, he calculated, the Republicans would lose their only politically useful argument—that Dodd's bill would somehow permit more bailouts. Silverman, who loved his boss, called this ploy "a stroke of genius." Dodd admitted to Silverman and Friend that he was worried Shelby would figure out what he was doing before a deal was made, and back off.

No agreement had been reached when the Senate began its debate on the bill on Tuesday, May 4. Barbara Boxer of California offered the first amendment, written to provide a definitive answer to the accusation that the bill would allow for more bailouts. Boxer's amendment said, "All financial companies put into receivership . . . shall be liquidated. No taxpayer funds shall be used to prevent the liquidation of any financial company." But McConnell told Dodd and Reid that the Republicans would block a vote on this amendment until Dodd and Shelby made a deal on specific new provisions for winding down failing firms.

That day and into the night, Friend and several associates swapped ideas with Duhnke, Oesterle, and others from the Republican staff. Finally, Duhnke came to Friend and said, as she recalled it, "Look, we can negotiate this thing for another week. So we're going to give you a take-it-or-leave-it proposition."

Friend replied, she said later, " 'All right, but we may have questions about your take-it-or-leave-it proposition, are you guys going to be around?' He said, 'Yup we'll be around.' So when Duhnke delivered their offer we spent about half an hour reading it. Then we went to find them to ask them questions, and they were gone."

Friend was furious. The Republican offer was unacceptable. It was now after midnight. She was afraid to call Dodd to report this turn of events for fear that once she told him, he would never get back to sleep. "We were supposed to go to the floor the next day with this thing, and it was twelve steps back from where we were. It was abominable . . . unworkable . . . internally inconsistent." So she drove home.

Shortly after 2 a.m. her BlackBerry vibrated. It was Dodd e-mailing her. She recounted what happened next.

" 'Did you get anything?' he asked. And I said, Yes, do you want to talk? And he said, Yes. So this is about 2:15 in the morning. When we got on the phone I was trying to explain it to him. And I said, Now is the time to just get angry, we've just got to strengthen our resolve. I'm having a glass of wine, you should do the same thing and go to bed."

Then she sent an e-mail reporting the night's events to Silverman, who was at home in Alexandria, Virginia, kicking himself for leaving the office too early that night. Friend wrote, "I am PISSED! Have a nice night." Silverman thought this was the best line of the year.

The next morning, Dodd admitted that he hadn't gotten back to sleep. He looked awful, and he was anxious—the Dodd-Shelby amendment embodying their still elusive deal was supposed to be brought up for debate in a few hours. Impatient, he asked Silverman and Friend, "Can't we just agree to this [the take-it-or-leave-it proposal]?" Friend replied, "As your lawyer, my recommendation is no, because it is so fundamentally flawed." Dodd was worried about the politics; Friend's concern was the substance.

Shelby was also anxious. He called Dodd and said he wanted to come to his office. "What was interesting was, Shelby came with Oesterle, but without Duhnke," Friend recounted. Duhnke was Mr. No in her experience, so this was encouraging. "And they started to talk. And I just lit into Oesterle. I said this [take-it-or-leave-it proposal] makes no sense, this was like one step forward, twelve steps back—I was really on little sleep and very upset. And Dodd was looking at me, and Shelby was looking at me, and I just said this just doesn't make any sense.

"And both Dodd and Shelby said, Okay, well, work it out—can't you work it out? Shelby was saying, 'The two of you [Friend and Oesterle] need to stay together until it's worked out, we've got to get it done.' And my impression then was that Shelby had made promises to his caucus that we had a deal. And Dodd was also very anxious to have a deal. . . .

"So we did it. We ended up striking a deal. I came back here [to her office on the fifth floor of the Dirksen Building], met with Oesterle, there was a few of us here, and Andrew Olmem [a lawyer on the Republican staff] kept pushing back on what I said, and Oesterle said, 'Forget it, we'll do what you want,' he kept cutting back Olmem. So to me it was very clear that Shelby had said don't mess around, get this done. Within half an hour it was done. At no other time in all the discussions we had with them did I ever get that sense that Shelby had said, 'cut a deal' the way he did this time."

As this drama unfolded, Dodd took an unexpected phone call on his BlackBerry as he walked through the tunnel from the senators' parking garage to the Russell Building. "It was Harry Reid, Bob Menendez, Chuck Schumer, and Dick Durbin," Dodd recounted. These were four leaders of the Democratic caucus, all on the phone together. "They said we don't want you to make any deal with Shelby, forget about it." Dodd was taken aback, but unmoved. "I'm going to do this," he said, laughing a small, nervous laugh as he told this story of defying his leadership. "There were always those elements in the [Democratic] caucus who thought fighting would be better than getting a bill. I think that's what I was getting in that call, and I just was not going to accept it. It was out of the question. . . . It [the deal Friend had negotiated with Oesterle] was as good as I thought we could get, and it was taking the bailout issue off the table!"

This telephone call illuminated a cardinal weakness of the modern Congress, one aggravated by the demands of the twenty-four-hour news cycle for constant posturing on the big issue of the moment, and by the fact that most members both know and care more about politics than about substance. Dodd thought the senators on the phone were willing to jeopardize his bill to score political points. He was not.

The most significant substantive element of the Dodd-Shelby compromise eliminated the $50 billion fund—to be provided by big banks—that McConnell had wrongfully ridiculed a fortnight earlier in his floor attacks on the Dodd bill. Some Democratic senators, including the four who made that phone call to Dodd, had decided that the fund should be kept in the bill for political purposes. As Friend put it, "Democrats were saying, 'That's a great issue! We're going to say it's the big banks that are paying for any future bailouts.' " Dodd understood his colleagues' argument. He even thought that in an ideal world, the bill would contain the fund—compulsory contributions might persuade the big banks to behave more conservatively, one of his key goals for the bill. But once Shelby made an issue of the fund, Dodd concluded it wasn't worth fighting for.

"It was never about substance here," Dodd said. "It was about trying to kill us. I knew I had to get resolution of Title I and Title II [the sections covered by the compromise with Shelby] or the bill would die."

Dodd said "I knew," but of course he couldn't know for sure. On the other hand, and with good reason after thirty years of experience, he had confidence in his own tactical judgment. He wanted to take the bailout argument off the table.

So the compromise Friend and Oesterle produced eliminated the fund. Instead the money for the resolution of a failing institution would be borrowed initially from the Treasury, then repaid by selling whatever assets remained in the failed firm. If such sales did not produce enough to cover the costs, then big financial institutions would be assessed to make up the shortfall. The compromise also included new provisions making it harder for the Federal Reserve to provide emergency assistance to firms in trouble, and restricting the freedom to maneuver of the regulators charged with resolving a failing firm. The bill gave this power to the FDIC, which had extensive experience resolving banks that failed.

The compromise was quickly converted into legislative language and rushed to the Senate floor. But its arrival set off another unexpected drama that briefly alarmed Dodd and his staff. Someone at Americans for Financial Reform, the pro-reform group created by trade unions and consumer groups as a counterweight to the banks and their lobbyists, misread the amendment and fired off an e-mail to AFR's liberal allies in the Senate. The e-mail said the deal would exempt GE Capital, the financial arm of the General Electric Co., from any kind of systemic risk regulation, so was a bad idea.

This was a mistake. The amendment had nothing to do with GE Capital. "They just misread it," Friend said. But the e-mail "almost blew up on the floor," she added. She was on the floor at the time; key staff are permitted to join senators on that piece of exclusive real estate. A small section of chairs in the southeast corner of the hall is reserved for them. Friend saw half a dozen liberal senators "in the corner, near where the staff sits. They all had this e-mail in their hands. Somebody said, 'We can't vote for this, look at what this is going to do, this is going to get GE out from any kind of regulation.' " She realized this was a serious problem and reported it to Dodd, who in turn engaged Harry Reid. She and a colleague, Charles Yi, began explaining the situation to staff members of the alarmed liberals, and to the senators themselves.

Upset, Reid called Americans for Financial Reform to ask for its help to correct this mistake. An AFR staff member called Bernie Sanders of Vermont, the Independent who called himself a socialist but voted with the Democrats, who was one of the agitated liberals. The caller explained that the original e-mail was wrong, there was no problem with the amendment. Sanders passed the word to like-minded colleagues and the storm subsided.

But it had terrified Friend: "It was just so perilous—like you could feel emotions were so raw, and this had the ability to spark twelve people to vote against this for the wrong reason." Sending that e-mail "was just like lighting a match," Friend said. "You could see it spreading. So it was very helpful to be there and watch this and try to stop it."

As Ted Kennedy had written, "ninety-five percent of the nitty-gritty work" of the Senate was done by staff.

Friend was too discreet to make the obvious point: that a liberal interest group could write an e-mail that spooked perhaps a dozen members of the Senate, too many of whom seemed willing to accept its guidance without asking any questions. But this was the way the modern Senate often worked. Lobbyists could provide information that swayed the votes of senators who had neither the expertise nor the inclination to acquire it that would have enabled them to evaluate the information themselves. The best defense against this happening was the one that materialized that afternoon on the floor of the Senate—intervention by knowledgeable staff.

With this storm becalmed, the Senate could begin actual consideration of amendments to Dodd's bill. It was nine days since Reid first called the bill up—before the filibusters and cloture votes. The Boxer amendment, the first to be considered, passed 96–1. Next up was the Dodd-Shelby amendment, which was barely debated before Shelby and Dodd asked for the yeas and nays. It was approved 93–5. Just as Dodd had hoped, its success altered the atmosphere on the floor. McConnell, who had so harshly criticized Dodd's bill, was suddenly mollified. He said the amendment eliminated the bailout problem he had earlier perceived. It was "a good first step."

Dodd was exhilarated. Not only had he taken the Republicans' best talking point away from them, he had pacified them. They cooperated with his effort to "let the Senate act like the Senate," one of his favorite expressions, by considering a string of amendments under the "regular order." This meant no threats of filibusters, no demands for sixty votes to approve an amendment. Dodd was the floor manager for the bill, which made him, in effect, the majority leader for the duration of the debate. He agreed with McConnell to call up amendments in pairs, one from a Republican, one from a Democrat.

Dodd knew the drill; he had managed dozens of bills in his long career. He occupied the majority leader's desk in the front row, and hooked a microphone that resided on the edge of the desk into the breast pocket of his suit jacket. In the past, he had always had a Republican partner to comanage with him, but there was no Republican this time. Nor did any senior Democrat stick by his side throughout the proceedings. Of the twelve other Democrats on the Banking Committee, only the very junior Mark Warner of Virginia was a regular presence on the floor, chatting with Dodd and offering any help he could provide through much of the debate on amendments. Sitting beside Dodd in a chair next to the majority leader's desk was Friend or Silverman, his most important colleagues throughout this process.

The next day, May 6, Republicans called up an amendment to sharply limit the scope and alter the nature of the new consumer agency, making it part of the FDIC and focusing its attention on non-bank mortgage companies. It was easily defeated, 61–38. Two Republicans, Olympia Snowe of Maine and Charles Grassley of Iowa, joined all the Democrats in voting no. Later the same day, an amendment offered by two liberals, Sherrod Brown of Ohio and Ted Kaufman of Delaware, that would have forced the breakup of the biggest banks was also easily defeated, 61–33. This was the first sign that despite the anti-bank environment, the Senate was disinclined to approve fundamental changes in the banking industry. Like the House, the Senate preferred to try to improve the status quo, not toss it out.

There was also an ominous development on May 6 that Dodd noticed, but reporters generally ignored. Russ Feingold of Wisconsin, an ornery and independent-minded liberal, said in a speech on the floor that the Dodd bill had to be improved with the Brown-Kaufman amendment, the proposal to restore Glass-Steagall, and an amendment offered by Byron Dorgan of North Dakota to ban "naked" credit default swaps—exotic financial instruments that allowed investors to bet on the fate of bonds they did not actually own. Brown-Kaufman was defeated soon after Feingold spoke, and Dodd hoped and expected that the other two would also be beaten. Could the difficult Feingold become the only Democrat to vote against his bill? Dodd feared that he might.

The mood during these first days of voting on amendments was calm. Few senators came to the floor except when they had to vote. Dodd was able to move steadily through these and other less substantial amendments. Throughout, Dodd remained determined to be as magnanimous and accommodating to colleagues from both parties as he possibly could. Friend was struck by the way Republicans responded to him. "He's genuinely liked," she said of her boss. "Sitting there on the floor with him, Republicans would come up and say, 'I'm going to say nasty things [about the bill] but it has nothing to do with you.' "

And despite Harry Reid's announced eagerness for a quick conclusion to work on the bill, the Senate stuck to its usual relaxed schedule. It did not meet on Friday, May 7, and held no votes on Monday the 10th, so members could have their usual four-day weekend at home.

When business resumed on Tuesday the 11th, the subject that most animated the swarm of lobbyists "working the bill," to use their terminology, was the provision forcing banks to spin off their derivatives trading operations that Blanche Lincoln insisted be incorporated into Dodd's bill. This one was easy to explain: It would force banks to give up trading desks that made billions of dollars in profits—more than $20 billion in the previous year. The five big banks deployed more than 150 lobbyists to try to persuade senators and staff that this was a bad idea that would force derivatives trading overseas, or into unregulated corners of the American financial system. They had the support of Paul Volcker and Sheila Bair of the FDIC, who agreed that pushing derivatives desks out of the banks would make it harder to regulate them.

But as we have seen, this was not the banks' season. In March, when Dodd introduced his bill, the Securities Industry and Financial Markets Association (SIFMA), Wall Street's trade association in Washington, produced a list of about thirty items in the draft that it hoped to get changed. They won changes in just half a dozen, none very significant. And they got nowhere trying to undo the Lincoln provision.

This had nothing to do with the merits of their case. As their list of allies suggested, the banks had a strong argument on the merits. But for Dodd, Reid, and other Democrats, Blanche Lincoln's electoral fate was more important than any substantive argument. Her primary was imminent—just a week away—and no Democrat wanted to embarrass her before the voting began. Control of the Senate would be at stake in November, and it was widely assumed that the centrist Lincoln had a better chance of winning in conservative Arkansas in November than her liberal opponent. For Dodd the seven signers of Maria Cantwell's letter were more important than fixing the derivatives provisions at this stage of the process. Embarrassing Lincoln could put votes at risk; Dodd wasn't going there.

So the only chance the Senate got to modify the derivatives provisions came in a vote on an amendment offered by Chambliss of Georgia with support from Gregg and Corker. It would have substituted for Lincoln's provisions the much weaker language that Chambliss had offered in the Agriculture Committee, putting minimal new restrictions on derivatives trading. The Democrats easily defeated this Chambliss amendment on a party-line vote. No other attempt would be made to improve the flawed derivatives section of the bill.

Two other amendments backed by Republicans were approved on the 12th; both were also part of Dodd's tactical plan. One was offered by Kay Bailey Hutchison of Texas, whom Dodd hoped might be a secret supporter of his bill and who could conceivably be persuaded to vote for cloture, if not for final passage. (Once cloture was achieved, Dodd needed only fifty-one votes to pass the bill.) Her amendment, cosponsored by Amy Klobuchar of Minnesota, a Democrat, restored the role of the Federal Reserve as a regulator of small banks. Dodd's bill had taken the Fed out of regulating all but the biggest banks and bank holding companies, the last remnant of his earlier hope to consolidate bank regulation into a single new agency, long since abandoned. Now Dodd decided he had to accept the Hutchison-Klobuchar amendment as well. It passed 91–8.

The second amendment was offered by Olympia Snowe of Maine with Mary Landrieu, a moderate Democrat from Louisiana. It exempted all small businesses outside the financial sector from the regulations of the new Consumer Financial Protection Bureau. This was part of Dodd's months-long effort to cultivate Snowe; he wanted her to feel some ownership of the bill. After he embraced her proposal, it was approved by unanimous acclamation.

On the 13th, senators got a chance to whack the banks on another front altogether when Dick Durbin of Illinois, the Democrats' deputy leader, offered his "Interchange" amendment. This was an old crusade of Durbin's to reduce the fees merchants had to pay to card issuers every time a consumer used a debit card to make a purchase. For the banks this was a huge business; it brought them billions in revenue every year. These fees had nothing to do with the Great Crash, a fact opponents of the bill mentioned often. But the Senate had no rule requiring that an amendment to Dodd's bill be germane or relevant to the underlying bill, so Durbin could offer his plan now.

Retailers, from big ones such as Walmart and Target to the small businesses that had effective lobbyists in Washington, all agreed with Durbin that the "swipe fees," as they are called—typically about 2 percent of the price paid for a product or service by a debit card user—were too high. Merchants lobbied intently for his amendment, which authorized the Fed to limit the fees to levels "reasonable and proportional" to the cost of processing these charges.

The big banks, small community banks including Cam Fine's Independent Community Bankers of America, and credit unions fought Durbin fiercely. Many of them issued debit cards of their own. Just before his amendment came up for a vote, Durbin altered it to exempt the smaller banks with assets of less than $10 billion, but this did not end their opposition. Hometown bankers swarmed the Senate office buildings to press their case.

Despite their traditional influence, on this issue the community banks and credit unions were easily defeated, in part by the lobbying of small businesses that would benefit from Durbin's proposal. Every state had more small businessmen than small bankers. Durbin's amendment passed 64–33. Seventeen Republicans joined Durbin and forty-six other Democrats to pass the amendment. Bankers were stunned by this outcome.

On the same day, the Senate considered an amendment offered by Jeff Sessions of Alabama, ranking Republican on the Judiciary Committee, that would have replaced the new system for winding down failing financial firms that the Dodd-Shelby amendment had created with new provisions in the bankruptcy code, cutting out the role for the FDIC that Dodd-Shelby created. Under the Sessions provision, a giant financial firm would have to go through bankruptcy court, an idea Dodd and the Treasury Department considered cumbersome and, in a future crisis, much too risky. Dodd was flabbergasted when Shelby and Corker, who had both worked on the Dodd-Shelby amendment, supported the Sessions proposal. "To have Bob Corker and Richard Shelby, who were so involved in writing that part of the bill, vote for an amendment that basically stripped out all their work left me sort of dazed," Dodd said later. Both men chose to align themselves with their Republican colleagues, not with Dodd. Sessions's amendment was defeated on a party-line vote.

Both parties held caucus meetings on the 13th to discuss the debate on Dodd's bill. Many members had amendments they were eager to see considered on the floor—too many, Dodd felt. He pleaded with members to hold back. He already had sixty pending amendments, and scores more had been submitted. "We run the risk of losing this bill, that's the reality," Dodd said that morning on the floor. "This is not hyperbole."

Friend explained his concern: "People were constantly in his face, saying, I want my amendment, I want my amendment. I think what he was trying to say was, there are a hundred senators here and everybody has a great idea, but there's just so much this bill can take. He was very conscious of trying to maintain a balance. He couldn't get a bill through with just the Democrats. He told me when we . . . came out of committee that the bill was 'in equipoise.' I thought that was an excellent description. We had walked this line. On our Democratic side we had some of the most progressive members, and some of the most conservative members, and everybody found something in the bill that they were happy with. . . . It just was like this [she made a gesture of precarious balance with both hands]. He was very conscious of the fact that it can't go too far left or too far right. How do you keep all the Democrats and then pick up some Republicans?"

The 13th was a Thursday—the last day of the senatorial workweek. Reid was determined to hold a cloture vote to end debate the following week. So Dodd decided he had to keep dealing with the pending amendments that he and McConnell could agree on.

He called up an amendment from Al Franken, the new Democratic senator from Minnesota, to curtail the discretion of the ratings agencies that had given Triple As to the junklike mortgage-backed securities that played such a big role in the Great Crash. Next came an amendment sponsored jointly by Republican George LeMieux of Florida and Democrat Maria Cantwell of Washington state that eliminated from federal laws all references to the ratings given out by the agencies Franken sought to curtail. Both these passed easily, with bipartisan support.

The Senate worked into the evening. Attendance was sparse, but Dodd was able to dispose of one important matter with a voice vote on an amendment that few if any members beyond its sponsor fully understood. Dodd brought this one up at about 9 p.m. It had been offered by Susan Collins of Maine, the Republican to whom Dodd had paid the most attention for months. The provision had actually been written by Sheila Bair and her staff at the FDIC. Bair had friendly relations with Collins, a former bank regulator herself in Maine. Bair saw the amendment as a way to require big banks to hold as much capital, proportionally, as small banks, but its wording alarmed the banking community because it seemed to ban the use of "trust-preferred securities," a cousin of preferred stock, as part of a bank's "Tier One," or core, capital. It was an esoteric point but an important one to the big banks. Dodd himself hadn't mastered the issue, but he knew one thing: Collins wanted this amendment, and he wanted Collins's support for cloture next week. Collins's amendment was approved by voice vote with no significant debate.* The Senate adjourned for the weekend.

On Monday Reed filed a formal cloture petition, which requires the signatures of sixteen senators. "The end must come," Reid said. Under the rules, the motion could be voted on forty-eight hours later. The majority leader, with Dodd's encouragement, wanted to put an end to the consideration of amendments.

On Monday evening Dodd worked through several more insignificant ones, and one—proposed by Mark Udall of Colorado—that did a favor for consumers, guaranteeing them free access to their credit scores.

---

* This Collins amendment survived in the final version of Dodd-Frank, and caused problems for banks and regulators long after it was enacted because of its language.

When the Senate reconvened on Tuesday it looked as though a vote would be taken on one of the most substantive outstanding amendments, Merkley-Levin. This was the work of Jeff Merkley of Oregon, a freshman, and Carl Levin of Michigan. It was their attempt to incorporate the Volcker rule into the bill by prohibiting banks from using their own capital to make bets in the financial markets, either conservative stock investments or risky derivatives plays. It also banned banks from owning hedge funds or private equity funds.

The banks disliked this nearly as much as Lincoln's provisions on derivatives, because proprietary trading had become an important source of bank revenue, worth billions of dollars a year. So their lobbyists agitated against it during these days when the bill was on the Senate floor. But the proposal enjoyed bipartisan support. Shelby had told Merkley personally that if the amendment came up for a vote, he would support it.

Merkley-Levin had an interesting history. Jeff Merkley played the leading role. He grew up in a working-class neighborhood in Portland, the son of a lumber mill worker. He was the first member of his family to attend college—Stanford University, where he earned a BA. He acquired a master's degree in public policy from Princeton, traveled around Central America, won a fellowship to work in the office of the secretary of defense in Washington, then returned to Oregon. He ran the state branch of Habitat for Humanity for several years, a job that took him deep into housing issues. Then he ran a nonprofit agency that helped low-income Portland residents find affordable housing to buy or rent. In 1998, at the age of forty-two, he won a seat in the Oregon legislature. Just eight years later he was the speaker of the Oregon House, elected unanimously. In 2008, he challenged an incumbent Republican senator, Gordon Smith, and beat him by 3 percentage points.

Though no slouch at electoral politics, Merkley was more interested in policy, which set him apart from many of his new colleagues in Washington. He cared about poverty, housing, international relations. When Dodd heard him speak about housing issues at a caucus of Senate Democrats, he asked Merkley to join the Banking Committee. Merkley had already signed up for three other standing committees, but Harry Reid allowed him to break the usual rule and join a fourth.

Merkley had a wonkish streak and liked to read policy studies. Soon after he arrived in Washington at the end of 2008, he read a report on the causes of the financial crisis prepared by the Group of Thirty, an informal lobby of former central bankers and finance ministers that promoted its members' views on policy choices. One of its recommendations was to limit the activities of banks in the capital markets by restricting their proprietary trading. Merkley thought that made sense. The Group of Thirty was led by Paul Volcker, who was a principal author of the document that Merkley read and admired.

As his Banking Committee aide, Merkley hired a bright, energetic young graduate of Harvard College and Hastings Law School in San Francisco, Andrew Green. Merkley's interest in proprietary trading and Volcker's recommendation for new regulations led Green to Anthony Dowd, a West Point graduate and private equity trader who had gone to work, pro bono, as Volcker's aide to help with his duties as chairman of President Obama's Economic Recovery Advisory Board, a group of economists and business executives with no clear responsibility, but an opportunity at least to influence policy. Volcker hoped to influence the new administration's approach to regulatory reform.

Dowd and Green hit it off. Merkley and Green were the first people from the Senate to show serious interest in banning proprietary trading, Dowd said later. In the summer of 2009 Merkley pursued his interest in a ban with Dodd. Friend and her colleagues were writing the original Dodd discussion draft at the time, and included in it a provision calling for a study of the issue by the Government Accountability Office, the auditing arm of Congress.

After President Obama publicly embraced the Volcker rule—his term for the ban on proprietary trading—in January, Merkley thought the idea was ripening. In February he sent a "Dear Colleague" letter to every senator, soliciting cosponsors of an effort to block "taxpayer-backed gambling" by the big financial institutions that enjoyed the protection provided to banks by the FDIC and the Fed. Carl Levin of Michigan responded, saying he would like to join Merkley's effort; his aide Tyler Gellasch became Green's partner. Levin wanted to add a provision banning banks from betting against financial instruments they themselves created and sold—the sort of conflict he thought Goldman Sachs had engaged in and which he denounced in his subcommittee's hearings in April. Merkley agreed.

Merkley saw their amendment as "a modest form of Glass-Steagall," the Depression-era law that had separated commercial banking from all forms of investment banking, including proprietary trading. "We

decided this was really worth investing a lot of energy in." He personally lobbied eighty of his colleagues, and kept a chart that recorded
every senator's views on proprietary trading. Many admitted to him
that they didn't really understand the subject, he said later.

Volcker was happy to help find votes for the idea, though he cast
himself always as an educator, not a lobbyist. It was not a meaningful distinction; because of his stature in Congress (which matches
his physical stature—Volcker is six feet, seven inches tall), he was a
formidable lobbyist. His renown in Congress was remarkable. In the
spring of 2010 he was eighty-three years old, but looked much younger
in his custom-tailored suits and shirts. In his years as Fed chairman
(1979–87), Volcker made economic history by taming the worst inflation of modern times and putting the economy on course for a great
boom. Of the former chairmen of the Board of Governors of the Federal Reserve Board, only Alan Greenspan had built a reputation as
formidable as Volcker's, but Greenspan's standing had crashed along
with the financial markets in 2008–9. Volcker's was the sort of record
that intimidated congressmen and senators regardless of party, and the
banks knew it.

But they had one key ally: Mitch McConnell. The Republican
leader was determined to block Merkley-Levin. Discussing his ada-
mant opposition, Merkley recalled the visit McConnell and Senator
Cornyn had recently made to Wall Street, and surmised that opposing
the amendment was a way to curry favor with the bankers they hoped
would become major contributors to Republican Senate candidates.
Merkley said many of the Republican senators he approached "saw the
logic" of the amendment and were sympathetic, but were reluctant to
vote for it and undermine McConnell's efforts to cultivate Wall Street.
"They didn't want to be caught in the middle," as Merkley put it.

As the amendment attracted interest from other senators, Merkley and Levin, and their aides, Green and Gellasch, agreed to negotiate changes in it to win more votes. They also consulted often with
Dodd's staff and the Treasury, both now supporters of Merkley-Levin,
to keep everyone on the same page. The amendment's restrictions
on banks' activities got more flexible during these negotiations, but
Merkley and Levin decided that compromise was needed to win the
necessary votes. "We accommodated a range of Republican, Democratic, and industry concerns," Green said, without undermining the
important impact of the amendment. The banks were not happy with

the result, but were grateful for changes that would allow them to continue managing hedge funds and private equity funds for their clients when they could no longer run either with their own capital.

These negotiations took time—too much time as it turned out. "We probably spent too long negotiating," Green said. The polished version wasn't ready until the 17th, the day Reid filed the cloture petition that signaled the imminent end of the debate. There would be time, at best, to consider a few more amendments before the cloture vote, and Merkley-Levin was one of a number waiting in line. But McConnell would not agree to let it come to the floor on the 18th. When the Merkley and Levin camps realized what was happening, they decided to offer theirs as a "second degree amendment"—an amendment to another amendment—to every other popular proposal waiting in line. It was a clever trick that gave Merkley-Levin a better shot at getting a vote.

Negotiations about which amendments would get to the floor were conducted by four groups of staff: Reid's and McConnell's floor staff, who manage the flow of legislation for the two party leaders, the Shelby staff, and aides to Dodd. The two leaders' principal floor assistants, Lula Davis for Reid and David Schiappa for McConnell, had enormous influence on the workings of the Senate, yet no one outside the Senate even knew their names. McConnell and Reid disliked one another—an unusual situation in modern times, when Senate leaders have tended to get along reasonably well—but Davis and Schiappa made the trains run regardless, and were widely admired. Schiappa was also envied—by golfers in the Senate and on the staff. His handicap was five.

As time was running out, Friend recalled, "each side identified a bunch of amendments they wanted considered and then figured out how to pair them," one Democratic and one Republican.

The pending amendment that seemed to have the most support was one offered by Sam Brownback, a Kansas Republican, to exclude auto dealers from the purview of the new Consumer Bureau. This was the equivalent of the Campbell amendment the House had approved earlier. Auto dealers had appeared on Capitol Hill in droves during May to lobby for this exclusion, and a large number of senators were inclined to support them. But by offering their amendment as, in effect, part of Brownback's, Merkley and Levin put McConnell and his team in a box. They realized that Merkley-Levin enjoyed strong support—at least sixty votes, by Merkley's head count—and could pass. Brownback approached Levin and Merkley on the floor to ask them to detach their amendment from his; Merkley said he was willing provided McConnell would agree to votes on both separately. But McConnell had already told Brownback he would not allow a vote on Merkley-Levin.

As the debate drew to a close, Amy Friend had one last creative impulse—a gimmick that might solve the problems created by the section of Lincoln's derivatives provisions that would force the big banks to spin off their derivatives trading operations. Why not offer an amendment, she suggested to Dodd, that would leave that section in place, but empower the new council of regulators created by the bill to study the idea for two years, then decide if it should in fact be implemented? The council, chaired by Geithner, would probably kill the idea, the best outcome in Friend's opinion. She drafted the amendment. Dodd signed and submitted it just three minutes before the final deadline for amendments to his bill, at 11:57 a.m. on Tuesday the 18th.

But it was a little too clever. Lincoln, whose electoral fate was being decided that very day in the Arkansas Democratic primary, came out against the idea.* So did the big banks, who took the amendment's language literally, and foresaw two years of uncertainty about their derivatives business. They preferred to try to fix the derivatives provisions on the House-Senate conference committee that would have to follow Senate passage of a bill, and made that known through their lobbyists. So after a flurry of excitement, Dodd's amendment died before being considered. The flawed provisions on derivatives would remain in the bill.

Most of the 18th was wasted as the backstage negotiations over amendments continued. The classic Senate time killer, quorum calls, filled much of the day. The Constitution says a majority of members must be present to conduct business in the House or Senate, a rule mostly honored by ignoring it. In the Senate, fifty-one senators are rarely on the floor at the same time, but this only impedes the conduct of business if a member rises and suggests "the absence of a quorum." At that point the clerk must call the roll to establish how many mem-

---

* Lincoln came in first in the primary, but won fewer than 50 percent of the votes, so would face a runoff election in early June. Her colleagues would therefore have a continuing reason to try to protect her politically.

bers are present. When the majority leader or the floor manager of a pending bill is ready to resume business, he or she can ask the chair to suspend the quorum call. But another member can request its resumption at any time.

The scene on the floor is a reminder of how different the Senate is from the House. At one point on this afternoon Dodd wandered over to the Republican side for a back-slapping, laughing interlude with Gregg and Kit Bond of Missouri, another Republican. Then Dodd shared a joke and a laugh with John McCain. Such good-natured banter, often accompanied by slaps on the back, hugs, and arm massages, had survived in the era of partisan warfare, and Dodd loved it. He also knew how superficial such goodwill could be. The day ended without an agreement on substantive new amendments.

When the Senate convened on the 19th, Reid was ready for the cloture vote. He scheduled it for 2 p.m. "We have a few hours before cloture," he said. "I hope cloture will be invoked. If it isn't, we will continue working until we finish this legislation."

When he spoke Reid knew that Russ Feingold was probably going to vote against cloture, and he was worried about Cantwell too. But Brown of Massachusetts had told him directly that he would abandon his party and vote for cloture. Reid knew that the women from Maine, Snowe and Collins, were going to do the same. With their votes and those of all the Democrats besides Cantwell and Feingold, Reid would have the sixty he needed.

But he soon learned that Senator Arlen Specter, who had been a Democrat for just a year, was in his home state of Pennsylvania and would not get back in time to vote. Specter was in a foul mood; the day before he had lost a primary election, ending his Senate career.* That meant Reid needed Cantwell or Feingold to win the vote. By lunchtime he realized he couldn't count on either of them, so he postponed the vote and called an emergency caucus of Democrats instead.

It was a tense meeting. Reid began with praise for Dodd's handling of the bill, noting that he was managing it by himself. Reid said the Democratic Policy Committee had been working on the messaging—words to use to make the bill sound good at home. He

---

* Specter switched parties rather than face a popular conservative in a Republican primary. But Pennsylvania Democrats did not accept him as one of their own, and voted instead for his rival in the 2010 primary.

noted that the press had supported the bill throughout the debate. He reported that Specter would miss the vote, and that Collins and Snowe would vote for cloture. He apologized for the fact that not every Democratic amendment would get a vote—that was just impossible. But the real question was, What is better—this bill, or no bill? That was now the choice, Reid said. Then he invited Dodd to speak.

The next day's papers, Dodd predicted, could have one of two headlines: Democratic divisions block the bill, or Democrats prevail. He acknowledged the partisan warfare, noting that "this is the first time I've brought an important bill to the floor without a Republican partner." The last ten years in the Senate have been really difficult, Dodd said. But it would be "tragic" if we did nothing to help the people who have suffered so much because of the financial crisis.

Half a dozen others spoke up for the bill. Mark Warner of Virginia observed that it contained some important and tough provisions, allowing regulators to break up big firms or require them to maintain adequate capital to cope with a future crisis. Barbara Boxer of California urged her colleagues not to "snatch defeat from the jaws of victory." Members like herself who were running for reelection needed this bill to be passed—it was something for them to brag about.

The targets of all this rhetoric were Feingold and Cantwell, but they were not moved. Feingold wasn't even there. Dodd knew he was a lost cause after one brief conversation. Feingold was also running for reelection, and had decided that his image as an independent outsider in the Senate required him to oppose the bill unless it was much tougher. In a body of large egos, Feingold's was one of the biggest, and he put the image he cultivated ahead of any party concerns, or any substantive issue. "You can tell with some people whether it's worth it or not to have a second conversation" to try to get their vote, Dodd said later. "It just wasn't going to happen."

And Cantwell was just difficult. The Senate is a body of politicians—men and women with good people skills—but she was an outlier, prickly and stubborn. At this caucus she quoted a *New York Times* editorial of that morning that called her amendment a "must-pass" provision—evidence, the Banking Committee staff thought, that the *Times* did not understand the amendment or the derivatives market. The staff was also convinced that Cantwell herself did not understand the amendment, which was inspired by a controversial law professor named Michael Greenberger.

Cantwell did not say she would oppose cloture, but she did ask her colleagues how she could explain supporting the bill if it did not include Merkley-Levin, her amendment on derivatives, and the restoration of the Glass-Steagall Act, which was contained in another amendment that hadn't gotten a vote that she cosponsored with John McCain. As she left the caucus, however, she did announce that she would vote against cloture. She wanted the debate to continue with votes on her amendments.

Reporters in the hallway outside the Lyndon B. Johnson caucus room a few steps from the Senate floor could see in the faces of the Democrats leaving the meeting that it had not gone well. The tension was palpable. Reid decided to go ahead with the vote, knowing he might lose it.

As in the House, a roll call vote attracted more senators than almost any floor debate, because every member is trying to cultivate the image of a diligent senator, and casting recorded votes is one of the few ways to document one's diligence.

The crowds that gather for a vote on the House floor generally divide on partisan lines, but the Senate is different. Members congregate, joke, and laugh without much regard for party affiliation, more like members of the same club than partisan warriors. They gather in knots on the blue carpet decorated with red circles and white crosses, sometimes talking serious business, sometimes just fooling around. There is a physical division—Republicans sit on the north side of the hall, Democrats on the south. On both sides, senior-most members sit behind individual desks in the front rows, while the newest senators sit in back. The act of voting in the Senate has never been modernized; a clerk calls the roll, and members respond "Aye" or "No." But in modern times it has become fashionable not to actually respond to the roll call, but to wait until the clerk has read all one hundred names, then catch the clerk's eye to mouth "Aye" or "No," or just to flash a thumb up or down. With each registered vote, the clerk will intone, "Mr. Dodd votes Aye," or "Mr. Shelby votes No."

On this afternoon Cantwell sat at her desk in the back half of the Democratic section. There wasn't really steam coming out of her ears, but the expression on her face suggested that there should have been. Several members came up to try to persuade her to vote for cloture, but she wasn't budging. At one point she said to Reid, loudly enough to be heard in the Press Gallery twenty-five yards away, "Jesus Christ, Harry!" Feingold also refused to be persuaded.

As the votes were cast, reporters in the Press Gallery, located on the west side of the hall, above the dais where the presiding officer sat, began to realize that Reid could lose the vote. This hadn't been predicted—with at least two Republican supporters (Collins and Snowe) and fifty-nine Democrats, the majority leader was supposed to win. Specter's absence and Cantwell's stubbornness were both surprises. As the last votes were tallied on the preprinted sheets that reporters used to keep score—sheets listing every senator's name in alphabetical order, divided by party, the way the clerk called their names—it became clear that the fifty-ninth and sixtieth votes had eluded Reid.

The majority leader asked the chair to change his vote from "Aye" to "No." Under Senate rules, this would enable Reid to call up the cloture motion again when he thought he had the needed votes—a right reserved to members who voted no the first time it was considered.

After Cantwell and Feingold voted "No," so did Scott Brown of Massachusetts, who had changed his mind at the last minute. Reid was furious, as he made clear to reporters after the vote. "I know how to count votes," he said. "And I'm not going to be giving any names and verses, but a senator broke his word with me." For Reid this was a cardinal offense. Even in these difficult times dominated by partisan warfare, the orderly operation of the Senate depended on members keeping their word. The neophyte from Massachusetts, in his fourth month as a senator, had indeed told Reid he would be voting for cloture. But McConnell was pressing for maximum Republican opposition, and Brown blinked.

Reid had warned that if cloture failed, the Senate would resume work on the bill. Dodd returned to the work of considering amendments. Only a few had been approved by both parties for consideration. As a gesture to Cantwell, Dodd sought unanimous consent to bring up her amendment on derivatives, but Shelby quickly blocked it. One that was allowed to come up, sponsored by Snowe, required the new consumer bureau to consider the economic impact of its regulations on small businesses before issuing them. Consumer groups didn't like this, but Dodd had to have Snowe's support. It carried by a voice vote.

An amendment sponsored by Sheldon Whitehouse of Rhode Island also got to the floor. Its fate confirmed the inability of the liberals to win substantially tougher regulation that departed from past practice. Whitehouse wanted to allow the states to impose their own interest rate caps on credit card issuers, undoing the 1978 Supreme Court decision that created a single national market for credit cards and made double-digit interest rates on credit card debt routine. That was the same decision that made South Dakota a center of the credit card industry. The Whitehouse amendment was defeated 60–35.

The failed cloture vote embarrassed Reid because it was the sort of mishap his colleagues expected him to avoid. The majority leader never cast himself as an expert on policy, or as a national political leader. His job was to manage the Senate efficiently and effectively, to help his fellow Democrats in any way he was able to, and to count votes. This limited job description was an important reason why Reid remained the consensus choice of his colleagues as their majority leader. In a body of large egos—the Democratic caucus—his predilection for self-effacing management made him an easy choice. No one felt threatened or overshadowed by Reid.

He knew he had to do everything he could to get those sixty votes, by tomorrow if humanly possible. His first target was Brown, whose failure to keep his word had shocked Reid. Brown, obviously nervous about his role, said publicly he wanted to vote for a reform bill, but was worried about the impact of this one on Massachusetts financial firms.

Reid and Dodd decided they needed help from Brown's Massachusetts colleagues. They recruited Barney Frank and John Kerry, the senior senator from Massachusetts. On the evening of the 19th they tracked Frank down in the House gym, where he was working out. "Brown and Kerry and Reid are all over me!" Frank told Jeanne Roslanowick on the phone. He ran back to her office in his gym clothes, and the two went to work. Frank called all the principals; Roslanowick called Ed Silverman at the Senate Banking Committee.

Brown wanted some political protection in return for keeping his original promise to Reid. Frank was willing to provide it if he could. The upshot of all these conversations was a letter to be sent by Frank to Harry Reid and Chris Dodd in which Frank promised to look out for the interests of big Massachusetts financial firms in the conference committee that would go to work after the Senate acted.

Frank was not impressed with Brown's behavior under pressure, but he understood how dramatically his new colleague's status had been transformed by his recent move to Washington. In Massachusetts, Frank observed, Brown was "one of seven Republican [state] senators" in a body dominated by thirty-three Democrats, "so he had very little say in major policy matters." Now in Washington, quite suddenly, "he goes to being the decider. It's overwhelming for him." Frank told his staff Brown was behaving like "a high-schooler trying to pretend he was in college."

Dave Smith got the assignment to draft the letter, which he began at 6:30 the next morning. Smith's objective was to make no new, substantive commitments to placate Brown while creating the impression that the senator's concerns would be met. The resulting letter testified to Smith's skills as an obfuscator. In it Frank said, "I am confident that working together we can produce a final product that . . . does not inadvertently impair prudent practices that have built the vital financial sector so important to our state." It reviewed the contents of the House bill, emphasizing that it would do no harm to well-run institutions. It promised nothing concrete.

The letter was delivered on the morning of the 20th. Brown's office then raised a new concern, obviously prompted by lobbyists for banks, about the possible inclusion of a version of the Volcker rule. Brown asked Frank to provide assurances that when the conference committee met, he would reject a provision banning proprietary trading by banks. Frank was unwilling to do so. He actually favored such a provision. But he wanted to sound sympathetic to Brown. Smith drafted a second letter to be signed by Frank that included the assurance that his House bill would "not prohibit depository institutions or their parent holding companies" from helping their clients make trades or sponsor "limited" investment funds on their clients' behalf. Again the letter promised nothing specific, and only summarized the House bill. Roslanowick called it "whimsical." All the back-and-forth had been "hysterical," Roslanowick said that day—"just a zoo."

But for a nervous new boy, the letters were enough. Brown again promised to vote for cloture, insisting that this time he would not change his mind.

At 2:20 p.m. Dodd turned on his microphone, hooked it into the breast pocket of his suit jacket, and announced a vote to "reconsider" the previous day's vote that failed. The tense atmosphere of the previous day had evaporated. Dodd looked calm, even serene. So did Silverman and Friend, both with him on the floor. As the clerk called the roll, Arlen Specter, absent the day before, was on the floor accepting backslaps, hugs, and handshakes from commiserating colleagues expressing sympathy for his defeat in the Pennsylvania primary. Shelby sat at his desk playing with his large hands in a way that evoked an old-time preacher—rubbing them together, pushing one back at the wrist, then the other, rubbing them as if applying hand lotion. Warner, still trying to be helpful, kept an eye on the clerk's official tally sheet to make sure everyone was voting as expected. Cantwell and Feingold again voted no; Brown said "Aye," as did Collins, Snowe, and Specter. "On this vote," the presiding officer intoned when all senators had been heard from, "the ayes are sixty, the nays are forty." Cloture had been achieved. Reid pressed for a final vote on the bill that same night.

Which amendments might still get a vote remained unclear. Negotiations among staff continued through the late afternoon. For much of the time, quorum calls were the only activity on the floor. Then it became clear that McConnell would block a vote on Merkley-Levin. Its two authors came to the Senate Press Gallery at 7:15 p.m. to try to get reporters' attention for what was happening. By then they knew that McConnell had prevailed on Brownback to withdraw his popular amendment, rather than allow their second degree amendment to it—their legislative maneuver to get a vote on Merkley-Levin—to reach the floor.

"If you needed any additional evidence about the power of Wall Street [on] this body," Levin told the dozen or so reporters who gathered around to hear their remarks, "this is it." In fact, the power of Wall Street was working on just one man: Mitch McConnell. The "body" was ready to vote against the banks.

Shelby had one more speech to read. It was another nasty oration evidently written by staff and reminiscent of the eighteen-minute tirade of the previous November, though a third longer. He deplored "a fundamental failure of this body to do its own due diligence before we even attempt such a significant undertaking as we are about to tonight" by passing the bill. The speech criticized the committee for "outsourcing" the drafting of the bill to "the Fed, Treasury, O.C.C., S.E.C. and C.F.T.C.," all of which had indeed helped write language in the legislation. Shelby denounced Dodd's failure to address the problems of Fannie Mae and Freddie Mac, a new Republican rallying cry, though Shelby had implicitly accepted this omission throughout his long negotiations on the bill, never suggesting any provisions to cover those government-supported enterprises. The new consumer bureau, Shelby announced, would be "massive . . . populated by thousands of bureaucrats," a notion unsupported by anything in the bill.

Dodd had sat stoically through the original eighteen-minute tirade, but he decided he would not do that again. As Shelby began his denunciation of the work of his "good friend," Dodd and Amy Friend, who had been sitting beside him, stood up and walked off the Senate floor.

Corker also had one final speech to deliver. Completion of the bill would finally end what he had considered the finest moment in his four years as a senator.

"I think this bill had good things in it; there's no question. And I appreciate the thrust. . . . I think the process on the floor has been good. I do wish that we had spent more time developing a bipartisan template. I think there were plenty of missed opportunities there. I'm proud of the role I was able to play in this bill and feel like I've had some input in its shaping, but I really wish the policy was far different than it is."

Corker ended with a pipe dream: "It's my hope that in the next six months or so there will be a little different balance in this body where we take each other a little more seriously than we do now, and we actually end up with centrist policies that are middle-of-the-road policies." He was thinking about the next election in November, when he hoped more Republicans would be elected to the Senate. Corker saw that as improving the chances for "centrist" policies. He was oblivious to the meaning of the partisan warfare that raged all about him, warfare that made bipartisan centrism about as likely as snow on the Fourth of July.

At 7:50 p.m. Reid came to the floor to explain the final plan to complete action on the bill. He announced the terms of a "unanimous consent agreement" negotiated by his and McConnell's staffs. Such agreements grease the legislative process; without them the Senate would be mired in endless debate. Reid spelled out this agreement in the arcane language of the Senate, a strange means of communication that can only be appreciated by experiencing it:

> Mr. President, on behalf of the Republican leader, and I and the managers of the bill and a number of others who worked long and hard on this consent agreement, I now ask unanimous consent that all post-cloture [debate] time be yielded back; except for 5 minutes for the Republican leader or his designee to raise a budget point of order against the Dodd-Lincoln substitute amendment

No. 3739; Senator Dodd or his designee be recognized to waive the applicable point of order; that the Senate then vote on the motion to waive the budget point of order without further intervening action or debate; that if the waiver is successful, then all pending amendments be withdrawn; the substitute amendment, as amended, be agreed to; the bill, as amended, be read a third time; and the Banking Committee then be discharged of H.R. 4173, the House companion [that is, the bill the House passed in December]; that the Senate then proceed to its consideration; that the text of the Senate bill, as read a third time, be inserted in lieu thereof [in place of the House bill], the bill be advanced to a third reading and the Senate then proceed to vote on passage of the bill; that upon passage, the Senate insist on its amendments, request a conference with the House on the disagreeing votes of the two Houses; further, that on Monday, May 24, it be in order for Senator Brownback to be recognized for a period not to exceed 10 minutes, and Senator Dodd for the same period; prior to Senator Brownback offering a motion to instruct the conferees with respect to H.R. 4173 on the subject of auto dealers; that after the motion is made, the Senate then proceed to vote on the motion to instruct . . .

Yes, they really talk this way on the floor of the Senate. The "budget point of order" that Reid mentioned is the means of enforcement of the Congressional Budget Act of 1974, a law once seen as a way to impose fiscal discipline on Congress, now honored mostly in the breach. Under it a senator can raise a point of order to argue that a particular bill will spend more money than Congress has authorized for it, but even if that is true, the law can be "waived"—ignored—if sixty senators vote to waive it. That is what happened in this case.

Under Rule XIV, paragraph 2, of the standing rules of the U.S. Senate, a bill must be read three times before it is passed, twice when introduced and a third time before a final vote "by title only," meaning only the titles of sections of the bill. This rule too is honored in the breach; bills are never actually read in full. To have read this one—all 1,500 pages of it—would have taken days. But with unanimous consent this rule is easily finessed.

The reference to Brownback was Reid's concession to McConnell, and to the many members in both parties who wanted to give a break to auto dealers. The idea here was to allow a vote on "instructions to conferees" telling the senators who would serve on a conference committee to work out differences with the House bill to accept the House provision—the Campbell amendment—excluding auto dealers from the purview of the consumer bureau. Such instructions are not binding on the conferees, but this was a way to signal to the auto dealers that the Senate had heard them, and wanted to be responsive.

When Reid was finished, the Republicans made the anticipated budget point of order; Dodd moved that it be waived, and the Senate voted 60–39 to waive it. At 8:25 p.m., the final vote on the bill was the pending business. "I ask for the yeas and nays," said Dick Durbin of Illinois, the deputy majority leader.

"Is there a sufficient second?" asked Mark Udall of Colorado, the junior member then taking his turn presiding over the Senate. The Constitution itself (Article I, Section 5) stipulates that "the Yeas and Nays of the Members of either House on any question" shall be formally recorded "at the desire of one fifth of those present." In the Senate this has long been taken to mean one fifth of a quorum, or eleven senators in modern times, when a quorum has consisted of fifty-one senators. When Udall asked that question, well over a dozen senators raised their hands. "There appears to be a sufficient second," Udall said. "The clerk will call the roll."

Robert Byrd of West Virginia, ninety-two years old and in failing health (he would die a month later), was absent; so was Specter of Pennsylvania. Of the ninety-eight who voted, fifty-nine supported the bill, thirty-nine opposed it. Four Republicans joined the majority: Brown, Collins, Snowe, and Chuck Grassley of Iowa. Two Democrats, Cantwell and Feingold, voted no.

As the voting continued, members of both parties came up to Dodd to congratulate him. Lamar Alexander of Tennessee, a Republican, was particularly effusive. Some senators made a point of congratulating Friend and Silverman as well. But most members left the floor as soon as they voted, rushing to the airport in hopes of catching a late flight home. It was Thursday night, after all. The workweek should have ended hours earlier.

Dodd's wife and two young daughters were among the only spectators in the family gallery at the north end of the hall. As the final vote was tallied, Dodd waved to them, beaming, then pointed to the big clock at the back of the hall, as if to say, note this historic moment: 8:45 p.m.

on May 20, 2010. Dodd's sense of satisfaction fairly radiated from the floor of the Senate. He had done something tricky and complicated and important. The job wasn't finished yet—he and Frank would have to work out a common text that could pass both houses, and that would be tricky too. But for now he could just enjoy the moment.

Future historians who looked back at the month-long floor debate would be frustrated by the fact that it actually featured very little substantive debate. The Senate had just approved an enormous piece of legislation, one that would profoundly alter America's financial markets and disrupt traditional ways of making money on Wall Street. The bill created a new institution, the council of regulators, with vast powers to tell private firms how they could conduct their business. It created a new substitute for traditional bankruptcy to allow regulators to put failing firms out of business before they collapsed and contributed to a crisis. It created a powerful new consumer agency with its own source of funding that would be able to make bilking the public with bad financial products much more difficult. And it contained some bad mistakes, particularly Lincoln's ill-thought-through derivatives provisions, that Dodd decided had to be left in this version of the bill as a price of getting the bill approved.

If the Senate truly was "the world's greatest deliberative body," an oft-heard description that flattered the institution, it would have actually deliberated on these big changes, considered their impact and their necessity, and debated alternatives. But in this case, as we have seen, the deliberations were cut short. The Banking Committee was the natural venue for them, but it never held a substantive discussion of the bill's provisions. That was the price of Shelby's decision to offer no amendments in committee. On the floor the discussion was focused on the amendments that were allowed to come up. Only two of them addressed the biggest issues covered by the bill—the consumer bureau and the derivatives provisions—but they were partisan amendments whose only purpose was to eliminate the reforms Dodd's bill proposed. Neither got a serious debate, and both were disposed of on party-line votes after brief, perfunctory discussion.

Dodd managed to get his bill through the Senate by working assiduously to let Republicans participate, and by accepting many Republican suggestions—dozens of them appeared in the final bill. But in the end only those four Republicans broke from their caucus to support the legislation.

When the Senate adjourned that night, Dodd and Reid made their way to the Radio-TV Gallery. Every seat was taken. Staff crowded into the aisles on both sides of the relatively small room.

Reid began with the observation that "the details of Wall Street reform are complex—that's an understatement!" He himself never really understood them. But, he continued, their import was simple: "When this bill becomes law, the joy ride on Wall Street will come to an end." When he completed his remarks, Reid excused himself, asking Dodd to preside over the rest of this media event. Reid had hoped to be with supporters in Las Vegas on this Thursday night at a fundraiser with Vice President Biden. Instead he would join them by telephone. Reid faced a difficult reelection campaign, and like any modern senator, he knew he had to give priority to raising money to pay for it, even at this triumphant moment.

Dodd then thanked everyone who had helped him, naming "Amy Friend and Eddie Silverman" specifically. "I wanted to demonstrate that the Senate of the United States could still conduct our business much as the Founders intended," Dodd said. "We did that."

Reid's staff had invited Lincoln to speak too, hoping to give her some publicity. Her primary runoff election was scheduled for early June. "This is an historic reform," she declared, boasting that her derivatives provisions "will bring a six-hundred-trillion-dollar market out of the darkness."

Dick Durbin of Illinois also spoke. Durbin had an unusual hobby for a modern senator: He read books, especially on American history. He recalled Franklin Roosevelt's legislation to prevent a recurrence of the Great Depression, comparing this bill to those. And he perceived "a deciding moment in terms of the political parties in this country." It was remarkable, Durbin said, that just four Republicans would join this effort to reform the financial markets that had caused so much damage.

When the news conference broke up, Dodd passed the word among his aides that he wanted to take them all onto the Senate floor to thank them personally. About twenty men and women walked down the marble staircase from the gallery level to the floor. Dodd invited them all to sit down at the desks of senators. He told them how proud he was of the work they had done, and how grateful he was for it. This was a grand gesture by an old pro, and it made everyone in the group feel important. It also reflected the realities of the situation: Dodd understood that without the efforts of those people, he would have had no bill.

The Dodd gang then decided to adjourn to Johnny's Half Shell. Silverman recalled later that much was eaten and drunk, and "despite the fact that I was a poor staffer, I picked up the tab."

In the days that followed the Senate vote, different players announced differing explanations for what had happened. Barney Frank had a characteristic analysis: "Money is influential [in Congress], but votes will kick money's ass any time they come up against each other. In the Senate, once public opinion got engaged, it blew away the lobbyists, the money, campaign contributions. Public opinion drove that bill."

Administration officials happily took much of the credit for success in the Senate. Both *The Wall Street Journal* and *The Washington Post* published accounts of how the bill got through the Senate that were based in part on interviews with officials who put themselves in leading roles. Wrote the *Journal*: "In early May, Treasury officials created a war room at their headquarters next to the White House, where officials met at least three times a day to scour amendments, determine which ones would be targeted for attack and report back to Capitol Hill. Mr. Geithner made frequent trips to Congress to persuade individual senators." The *Post* story noted that "Democrats needed only to pick off a couple of Republicans whom Geithner and others had courted for months."

This self-congratulating infuriated Dodd, who understandably believed that it was his management of the process that produced success. He considered the administration's officials clumsy at politics, and often counterproductive. And he had received a complaint from Susan Collins of Maine about these newspaper stories that suggested the whole thing was a successful White House operation.

Collins symbolized Dodd's efforts to cultivate support for the bill wherever he could find it. He spent hours with her, and his staff spent more hours with hers. She had told Dodd how she wished she could have been his Republican partner on the bill. When she expressed dismay to Dodd about the administration's boasting, he tracked Geithner down on the other side of the world to vent. "I don't know what time it was for him in China," Dodd said just five days after the Senate passed his bill. "I was on the phone with Geithner for about an hour last night, just saying, Hey, if you do this one more time you're on your own. I worked my head off up here to try to get this right and you idiots down there . . ."

Dodd knew his job was not yet complete. He was likely to need Collins's vote again on one more cloture motion before a conference committee report could finally be enacted. Dodd's method was never to boast, but rather to work the human angle.

"I never took a political science course in my life," he said in that same conversation, "but it's just making the calls. My father once said, All politics is is good manners. That's all it is. Not just in terms of your relationships with your colleagues—it's also your relationship with your constituents, your staff. Do you pay attention to people? Do you listen? Do you pretend to listen? Being mindful of what are the factors that are going on in people's lives that have an influence on what their decision-making process is. That's what good manners are. It sounds kind of trite, but there's a lot of veracity in the notion that that's where this all is. So those calls, those times you spend with people, the socialization of the process has really had as much of an impact on how business is done here as anything else."

CHAPTER TWENTY-TWO

Conference Committee

Senate passage of Dodd's bill set up an event that had fallen out of fashion, like sideburns or bouffant hairdos—a "conference committee." Conferences were popular when legislating was still a creative process and compromise was not a dirty word. In those days, before the outbreak of partisan warfare, when the House and Senate passed similar but not identical bills on the same subject (the usual pattern), the leaders of both houses chose "conferees," members who had worked on the bill being "conferenced."

The conferees were generally the best-informed members of both houses on the subject at hand. The substance of the issues under consideration typically prevailed over partisan political considerations, though of course politics colored the conferees' views. Conferences were private; horse-trading and compromise were natural and normal. When the conferees reached agreement, they sent a new bill back to both houses for final approval.

It was an imperfect system. Rank-and-file members often felt powerless to influence conferences, which could be dominated by senior members and special interests. In a closed-door conference, conferees could abandon positions taken on the floors of both houses without being accountable for their actions.

The traditional conference reflected the decentralized powers of the Congress in the era of relaxed party discipline, which lasted into the 1980s. Party discipline then was difficult, usually impossible, to impose because the two parties had such diverse memberships. The Senate of the 1960s and 1970s included liberal, moderate, and conservative Republicans, and liberal, moderate, and conservative Democrats. Coalitions across party lines were the norm. Committee chairmen were the most powerful figures in both houses; the speaker and majority leader were only as influential as they were persuasive. Their direct power over individual members was limited.

The balance of power shifted profoundly in the House when Newt Gingrich became the speaker in 1995. Gingrich and his team put a premium on party discipline. They thought the Republicans could only preserve their new majority in the House if they stuck together on all big issues. His members, awed by the fact that Gingrich had led them to a huge victory that put them in charge of the House for the first time in four decades, deferred to him. Because Gingrich blew up the seniority system and chose committee chairmen himself, every chairman understood where his new power had come from.

Gingrich had no interest in supporting the traditional conference committee, not least because it gave a role to minority members—the hated Democrats whom he had demonized in order to win the Republican majority. He insisted that the Senate negotiate differences in legislation with him and his colleagues in the leadership. The minority party had no legal rights in the process; their only recourse was to vote against the final version of a bill, which they did again and again, with no practical consequence.

When Democrats regained control of the House after the 2006 elections, they took to heart lessons Gingrich had taught them. The new speaker, Nancy Pelosi, was less authoritarian, but she retained many of the powers Gingrich had claimed as speaker. Conference committees actually became rarer in the Democratic 110th Congress (2007–8) than they had been when the Republicans were in charge, in part because Republicans in the Senate sometimes tried to block the appointment of conferees by filibustering votes on them. Just 2 percent of the laws passed in that Congress were based on conference committee reports. The rest were worked out in private negotiations between the two houses and the passage back and forth of multiple versions of the same bill until there was one that both House and Senate would embrace. This back-and-forth was dubbed "ping-ponging" or "pinging." It became the most common way to resolve House-Senate differences.

The Senate was no more eager than the House to use conference committees in the years of partisan warfare. When Republicans controlled both houses, as they did most of the time from 1995 through 2006, the Senate was happy to use direct leadership negotiations instead of conferences.

For traditionalists, of whom there were fewer every year, the demise of conference committees was another sign of the collapse of "regular order," the traditional way of doing congressional business. Regular order meant an orderly consideration of issues, collaboration across party lines, and adherence to established procedures. Neither Frank nor Dodd could say they had followed regular order rigorously with regard to this legislation. In the House, Republicans wouldn't collaborate on anything; in the Senate they decided not to have a real markup of the bill, so passed up the opportunity to work over its provisions with care.

For many months, Frank's staff assumed that there would be no conference on financial regulatory reform. They had avoided one on the credit card legislation in 2009 by accepting the Senate's bill— a tougher version than the House had passed, to Frank's pleasant surprise. Dave Smith, the chief economist for the Financial Services Committee, said in April, when the House was waiting for the Senate to enact its version, "I don't want a conference." His rationale was revealing: "I don't want to leave big issues to a conference where people [members or special interests] have to get something [i.e., show off their accomplishment]. Items which are otherwise already settled in an agreeable way are on the table and available for horse-trading in a conference. There's another reason to be wary of a conference: They take time. We don't want time; time is our enemy now, it gives more opportunities for bad people to pick up the phone." He meant opportunities for special interests to intimidate members and get their way. Smith thought the only justification for holding a conference would be if "something on our no-go list comes out of the Senate"—a provision that Frank considered totally unacceptable, and couldn't vote for. Dodd and his staff began work on their bill also assuming that a full-blown conference was unlikely. Friend noted that there had been no conference on any bill she worked on since coming to the Banking Committee at the beginning of 2007.

But by March, even before the Senate Banking Committee reported out its bill without a proper markup, Frank had decided that he wanted a conference. He thought an open conference would strengthen his hand, especially if Dodd had to make a deal with Shelby on a bill that was weaker than the House version. "The public was on our side," Frank said. The more public the proceedings, he believed, the harder it would be to oppose the reforms that Wall Street still hoped to dilute.

On March 5, Frank put his intentions on the record in an interview with Maria Bartiromo, the CNBC anchorwoman. Characteristically using a wisecrack to support a serious point, Frank told her: "I'm going to suggest something very radical—that once the Senate has passed its bill, we have a House-Senate conference. We used to have those all the time. I would look forward to taking the House bill with other members of the House, Democratic and Republican, and senators, Democratic and Republican, and sitting in a public forum the way we used to do it, and go issue by issue that is different between us and have a big public debate." A few days later he suggested that the conference be broadcast live on C-SPAN. This would "pressure the Democrats to do the right things, and diminish Republicans' ardor" for opposing the bill.

Frank's conviction that public pressure would be his natural ally was strengthened after Congress gave final approval to Obama's health care reforms on March 21. With health care off the table, he thought, the news media would look for the next big conflict—financial regulatory reform. "Media attention helped revive an anti–Wall Street atmosphere," he said, and put a stiff political wind at their back.

By the time the Senate passed its bill, everyone involved had embraced Frank's idea—there would be a proper conference. This meant the Dodd and Frank staffs had work to do. So Jeanne Roslanowick, Dave Smith, and Michael Beresik from the House staff sat down with Dodd's key committee aides: Ed Silverman, Amy Friend, and Jonathan Miller. The two teams felt each other out, discussing how the conference might proceed. "We did the little dance you do," Roslanowick recalled. She and her House colleagues went into the meeting believing it was "the House's turn" to chair a banking conference, because the Senate chaired the last conference they could remember, from 2002. That would mean Frank would be the chairman, a role he coveted. Roslanowick acknowledged sheepishly a little later that they had been reminded of another, subsequent conference chaired by the House, but by then it was too late: The Senate staff, then Dodd himself, agreed that Frank could chair the conference. This and subsequent meetings of the two staffs were held on neutral territory—in the enormous cafeteria of the Capitol Visitor Center, a grand and extravagant underground facility built beneath the park on the east side of the Capitol.*

In return for accepting Frank as chairman, Dodd wanted the House to accept the Senate bill as the "base text" for the conference. "Our text was better," Dave Smith believed, but they agreed because of the big gorilla in the room—the fact that Dodd would need sixty votes to eventually enact a bill. The House staff realized he would need help to find those votes; using the Senate text was one way to help.

But the Senate text as passed wasn't entirely acceptable to either staff. Dodd's people wanted to add to it the hundred pages of small changes that they drew up as a manager's amendment but couldn't offer because Shelby's staff never agreed to let it be voted on. And there were important elements in the House bill that were not part of the Senate version. One was the title on mortgages and predatory lending, based on the separate housing bill the House originally passed in 2008, which imposed stiff new regulations on the mortgage brokers who had made such a big contribution to the Great Crash. It made illegal most of the unconventional practices that became commonplace during the housing bubble of the 2000s—the "no doc" (no documentation) loans, variable rate mortgages with ballooning interest rates, special rewards for mortgage brokers who sold the most expensive mortgages, and more. In ordinary times, this by itself would have been a major piece of legislation. Now it became just "T-14"—Title 14 of a huge piece of reform legislation.

The special provisions Frank added to the House bill to mollify the Congressional Black Caucus had no equivalent in the Senate version, and Frank insisted that they be included in the base text as well. This was a revealing fact of life in the modern Congress: The forty-two members of the Black Caucus in the House constituted an important bloc of votes, and Frank had made promises to them. The Senate included just one African American, the hapless Roland Burris of Illinois, who had been appointed to serve out the term of Barack Obama. Burris had no influence in the Senate.

The staffs had to spend long hours harmonizing minutiae in the

---

* The Visitor Center was a classic Washington boondoggle. Its original proposed cost was $71 million; its final real cost was $621 million. Work began in 2000, and the project was supposed to be completed four years later. It required eight years.

two huge bills—thousands of small details. When the base text was completed, the House Committee issued a press release enumerating some of the changes that had been made in House-passed provisions in this harmonization process. A typical example reported a change in the House position on the legal liabilities of mortgage originators: "Mortgage originators (i.e., individual mortgage brokers and loan officers) are subject to damages for violations of the compensation restrictions, duties of care and anti-steering provisions to no more than three times originator compensation." This was the gobbledygook of financial regulatory reform. Few members understood it and reporters generally ignored it, yet its impact on specific industries and institutions could be substantial.

The trade-offs that the staff negotiated without the participation of members of either body were ratified in one phone call between Dodd and Frank. As their aides acknowledged, neither man fully understood what they had agreed to, but both trusted their staffs to work it out properly.

Before the conference committee could begin work, it had to have members. Who would they be? Frank proposed to Pelosi a list of the eight Financial Services Committee Democrats. She accepted all eight, but said Frank needed more votes to protect his bill against any challenge from Republicans, or from the Democratic conferees she had to appoint from the other committees whose jurisdiction included some aspect of the bill. She decided to make it clear from the outset that those additional ten members could vote only on the issues that were in their committees' jurisdiction. "She had thought it through better than I had," Frank said. Republicans would get eleven members.

In the Senate, Harry Reid was not so careful or considerate. "Chris got an unpleasant surprise from Reid on conferees," as Frank put it. Reid named seven Democrats to the conference committee, four from the Banking Committee (responsible for thirteen titles in the fourteen-title bill, and half of the fourteenth as well), and three from Agriculture (responsible for just that other half of the derivatives title). McConnell would name five Republicans, so the party breakdown was seven to five. Reid allowed all seven Democrats to vote on all issues, meaning Dodd's control over the Senate conferees was minimal, at least on paper. If he lost one Democrat on any issue and the Republicans remained united, he would have a tie vote. Under the rules, no motion carries on a tie vote, so Dodd could too easily be hamstrung.

The fact that Reid made the Agriculture Committee Democrats "conferees on the whole bill . . . kind of spooked me," Dodd said later, though he absolved Reid of any hostile intentions. "He just wanted this thing over with." In fact, Dodd, the master cultivator of relationships, wasn't too worried.

"The good news was, I had Tom Harkin [of Iowa], with whom I have a good relationship, and I had Pat Leahy [of Vermont], whom I have a good relationship with. [Both were members of Agriculture, as well as chairmen of their own committees.] I talked to both Leahy and Harkin and they understood. They gave me a commitment that they wouldn't go south on me without having a serious conversation with me." In other words, characteristically, Dodd thought he could count on the loyalty of these old friends to maintain control of the Senate conferees. Leahy had been his colleague throughout the thirty years Dodd had served in the Senate; Harkin for twenty-five years.

Frank saw the conference chairmanship as the capstone of his career. He had decided that his next campaign for reelection, in 2010, would be his last. In the spring of 2010, Frank had shared this decision with close friends, but not with his staff, his colleagues, or his constituents. He understood that this bill would likely be his last hurrah, and he relished the opportunity to pull off something big and important.* He wanted to be a forceful, efficient chairman.

He set a rigorous schedule: seven meetings of the conference committee, the first on Thursday, June 10, the last two weeks later, on June 24. The staffs would spend many hours working on the necessary paperwork. Staff would also prepare scripts for every meeting, laying out the procedure for dealing with each section, giving Frank the words he would use to move from topic to topic. (He didn't always use the scripts.)

---

* After the Democrats got clobbered in the 2010 election and lost their House majority, Frank briefly changed his mind. Pelosi and other colleagues pressured him to stay on and help them regain a majority, and Frank announced his intention to run once more and serve until 2015. But he changed his mind again in November 2011, after the Massachusetts legislature radically altered his district and he realized he would have to win over tens of thousands of new voters whom he had never represented, and then, if he won, leave those voters high and dry after a single term. So he went back to his original plan and announced that he would not run again.

The conference was a Washington spectacle, and drew a crowd of reporters, lobbyists, and curious citizens to the first floor of the Rayburn House Office Building, where the Financial Services Committee's mammoth hearing room was located. The first four sessions would be held there, the next three in the Dirksen Senate Office Building, and a final one back at Rayburn. Cameramen and reporters took up positions in the hallway. The lobbyists were easy to identify in their bright silk neckties and expensive shirts, but there were no seats for them inside. They were shunted off to overflow rooms nearby, where the C-SPAN images were projected on large screens. Only three C-SPAN cameras were allowed inside the conference room. It was the first televised conference committee anyone could remember. The networks were free to use C-SPAN's pictures.

The hearing room—fifty-five feet wide and forty-six feet deep under a ceiling just shy of thirty feet high—had been reconfigured for the conference. The descending banks of black leather swivel chairs normally occupied by members were reserved for administration officials, staff, and reporters. The members sat at long tables set up in a rectangle in the area normally occupied by seats for the public and a table for witnesses. So the spectators looked down on the principals, as in a Roman amphitheater. Dodd and his Senate colleagues faced the audience. Frank's bald spot and unruly white hair was all that could be seen of him from the spectators' seats. Large television screens hung on the walls at each end of the room allowed everyone to see what C-SPAN viewers were seeing. The unusual arrangement contributed to a sense of excitement in the room; this was something new.

But the congressional knack for smothering excitement quickly came to the fore. Senator Dodd brought the first session to order, and announced that it would be devoted to "opening statements," the pompous and predictable pronouncements that members could not resist delivering, especially when television cameras were present. These comments never made the news shows or the newspapers, nor added anything of substance to the proceedings, yet they had become a permanent fixture of congressional hearings—evidence of the perpetual triumph of ego over substantive accomplishment.

Dodd nominated Frank to be chairman of the conference committee, which he accepted with a characteristic wisecrack: "I will put forward as a major qualification for this job my impatience, which I think will serve us all very well." His colleagues chuckled.

Dodd and Frank both emphasized that the conference would be

an "open" proceeding. "Nothing will be put into this final bill that is not advanced, openly debated, be subject to amendment by the conference process and then voted on," Frank said. He noted that the House-Senate conference was "a unique process," because America's was the only legislature in the world that has "genuine bilateralism" of two equal houses, with no legal mechanism to force them to agree. Achieving consensus "requires a degree of give and take and conciliation. I think we are all committed to making that work."

In his opening statement Shelby challenged Frank's description of openness. "I suspect there have been a number of private meetings where legislative language has been coordinated and drafted without any public access or Republican input," he said. Of course he was right. Frank's promise meant that debates and votes on proposed changes to the bill would be conducted in the open, but the hard work of hammering out compromises would, as always, be done by staff—Democratic staff—in meetings far from any television cameras. "It appears," Shelby said, "that the only facet of this conference that will be public is when the Republicans get our . . . chance to amend what has already been decided by our Democrat colleagues behind closed doors." Shelby expected to lose all of those votes.

Shelby accurately described a process dominated by the party that held large majorities of the seats in both houses. Shelby had missed his chance to seriously influence the bill in the Senate when he decided he could not take the political risk of compromising with Dodd or confronting the divisions among his Republican colleagues. Now his leverage had evaporated. The Democrats didn't need him.

Republicans, as always, were more disciplined than Democrats, and had worked out a party line for the conference, which was first displayed in their opening statements. One prominent Republican talking point was the failure of the bill to solve the problems of Fannie Mae and Freddie Mac, now federally owned institutions still hemorrhaging billions of dollars that Dodd, Frank, and the Obama administration acknowledged needed to be reformed. But because Fannie and Freddie were still centrally important to the national housing market and no one had a good idea for how to replace them, the Democrats said this was a matter to take up next year. As the conference continued, Republicans returned to "Fannie and Freddie" again and again. By the final sessions the reporters covering the meeting began to groan every time they heard another Republican invoke the F words.

Another Republican talking point, apparently irresistible even at this late stage, was "bailouts." Spencer Bachus, for example, decried "the bailout authority this legislation institutionalizes." The provisions of the Dodd-Shelby compromise in the Senate bill that were designed to finally bury that issue—and which Shelby and McConnell had both embraced—did not deter these references.

Bachus confessed to a committee aide that his remarks had been prepared for him by the Republican leadership. "I'm just reading the script handed down from above," the aide quoted Bachus as saying. Bachus remained an object of suspicion for the conservative leadership, and he kept trying to mollify them.

Perhaps the most striking comment made in an opening statement came from Tom Harkin, the liberal Democratic senator from Iowa: "I defy anyone here on this conference committee, I defy anyone on Wall Street or in New York, to show me one person, one trader, one whiz kid . . . who lost their home, their money and everything and were put out on the street because of what happened [in the Great Crash]. . . . [But] we can show you hundreds of thousands of Americans who lost their homes, lost their businesses, are out on the street because of what Wall Street did. It is up to us to make it right."

Harkin captured a reality that was rarely mentioned in this final stage of the legislative process. Something truly awful had happened in the previous two years, victimizing millions of Americans but very few of the perpetrators. Those victims rarely made more than a cameo appearance in the arcane debates over derivatives and the Volcker rule and the proper role of the Fed—the principal preoccupations of these senators and House members, all of whom had numerous constituents who had been battered by the Great Crash. Though the Great Crash created the context that made this legislation possible, few members tried to connect the tribulations of their constituents to the subject matter of their deliberations. This is a recurring problem for the modern Congress, whose machinations often seem remote from everyday American life.

Because the House and Senate bills had both been modeled on the Obama administration's proposals and turned out to be so similar, and because the Dodd and Frank staffs had now melded them into one, there was little room for drama in the conference committee's deliberations. Staff could resolve most of the outstanding issues. Frank began the conference with the least controversial topics and handled them expeditiously in the first four meetings.

The methodology was straightforward: Conferees from the House would put forward an "offer" to amend the bill to the conferees from the Senate, who would accept or reject it, or counter with a modification of their own. Or the Senate would initiate the process with its offer. Members could also offer their own amendments independently. Proceeding in this way the conferees agreed, for example, to make permanent an increase in the size of bank accounts insured by the FDIC to $250,000. Later House conferees "offered" to eliminate a provision in the Senate bill, sponsored by Jack Reed of Rhode Island, to require Senate confirmation of future appointees to the job of president of the Federal Reserve Bank of New York. The House position carried, and Reed's proposal died. On party-line votes, the conference rejected Republican amendments designed to weaken the Consumer Financial Protection Bureau.

These were nuts and bolts that provoked little controversy. The presence of C-SPAN's cameras seemed to improve the manners of the participants, though the partisan sniping periodically reappeared. At every session, while members sat still in their seats, staff bustled about behind them, carrying papers and negotiating language. Officials from the Obama administration were often in the room, obviously involved in the staff discussions. The tensest negotiations went on out of sight, usually in the offices of the negotiators—the staff.

The two most difficult topics were the subject of strained and complicated backstage negotiations: the Volcker rule and Blanche Lincoln's derivatives provisions.

The Senate had passed a version of the Volcker rule banning proprietary trading by banks—that is, forbidding banks from gambling with their own capital on investments in the financial markets. The House bill gave regulators the authority to ban such trading, but was vague about when the authority should be invoked. Frank said publicly he would accept a tough Volcker rule in the conference. Dodd wanted to strengthen this section with a version of the Merkley-Levin amendment that McConnell had blocked in the Senate.

But Dodd knew that the Republicans would insist again on a cloture vote to bring the final version of a bill to the floor of the Senate. To win that vote, Dodd assumed he would need the support of the same sixty senators who had supported cloture in May. That meant winning the vote of Scott Brown once again.

Brown saw the Volcker rule as a political opportunity. He had heard from Massachusetts financial institutions, particularly the State Street Bank and the Bank of America, which had a big presence in the state, that the Volcker rule could disrupt their businesses if it banned them from putting their own money into investment funds to support clients that ran them. The big banks wanted to loosen this rule, and Brown agreed to try to help them. He saw it as his job to help home-state institutions. And of course, bankers make good campaign contributors, and limits on a Volcker rule would be welcomed by banks far beyond the borders of Massachusetts. Dodd knew he had to listen to Brown.

Frank blamed the fact that Brown had to be satisfied on the stubborn refusal of Senator Russ Feingold of Wisconsin to agree to vote for cloture, on the grounds that the bill wasn't tough enough. This drove Frank to distraction. How could a liberal Democrat who claimed to favor stricter regulation of Wall Street exploit the Senate's most anachronistic rule, Rule XXII, allowing filibusters and requiring sixty votes to bring a controversial measure to a vote? Feingold's insistence on preserving his own political purity only had one substantive effect: It empowered every Republican senator who was willing to vote for cloture to make demands on Dodd and Frank that they could not afford to ignore.

Frank called Feingold to complain that by his actions he was encouraging Republican senators—specifically Brown, Susan Collins, and Olympia Snowe, the three who voted for cloture when the Senate passed its bill—to insist on changes that weakened the legislation. "And he [Feingold] said, 'Well, you know, I'm up for reelection, I can't be inconsistent,' " Frank later recounted. Frank argued with him: The bill was strong, he said, if not as strong as Feingold would have preferred, and Feingold's position would make it weaker. Frank sharpened these arguments in a personal letter, he recounted, but Feingold did not reply. He also refused to take a phone call from Paul Volcker, who wanted to try to persuade him to reconsider. "He's just been appalling in this," Frank said.

So Frank assigned Jim Segel, his political aide, to work with Brown's staff on possible deals. Segel had befriended Brown's legislative assistant, Nat Hoopes, whom he first contacted "in a collegial spirit" shortly after Brown's election in January. As the conference got under way, the backstage negotiations with Brown had become tense. Brown wanted the final bill to include a "de minimus"—minimal, or, by implication, insignificant—exception to the Volcker rule that would allow big banks to invest up to 5 percent of their capital in hedge funds, venture capital funds, or private equity funds as partners of the bank's clients. Volcker wanted to ban banks from investing their own capital in risky ventures of all kinds.

Volcker had become an important player in this drama. Mark Warner of Virginia called him "the 101st senator." Members of the House committee staff wryly referred to him as "God."

"He was out there when the mood shifted and people wanted to be tough," Frank explained. "He became the most visible expert with specific, tough ideas." More than visible, he became a kind of arbiter. If Volcker was for it, then Frank, Dodd, and nearly all the liberals who supported tougher regulation could be for it too. His opposition, on the other hand, would give the same members pause.

"Volcker is really an extraordinary man," Frank observed. "He has less pomposity and sense of self than anybody that important has a right to have. Of all of us Paul probably had the purest motives, in the sense that he could say, I'm going to do what I think is right for the public because what the hell else? I've got all the money, all the prestige I need, I'm eighty-three years old. And that radiated."

Volcker opposed the de minimus exception that Brown and the banks wanted. Five percent of the capital of the biggest banks was a huge loophole amounting to billions of dollars that they could invest in speculative funds. Volcker told a reporter he did not want the rule to "look like Swiss cheese."

Volcker and his assistant, Anthony Dowd, were not impressed by members of the House and Senate who took positions on issues they did not comprehend. "The percentage of congressmen and senators who really understand how a bank works, or even what a hedge fund is, is small," Dowd observed. He recalled one conference call with members in which some participants were misusing the term "proprietary trading." He asked how they were defining it, and got some gibberish about secret trading formulas that banks used in the market—in other words, they had no idea what they were talking about. Nevertheless, when he realized that some compromise might be required to get sixty votes, Volcker was willing to entertain negotiations, but not changes that would produce that Swiss cheese.

Segel, who had worked in the financial sector himself and sympathized with the concerns of State Street, the last significant public financial institution headquartered in Boston, recommended to Frank that he support the 5 percent exception to help a Massachusetts institution without jeopardizing the safety of the banking system. But

Frank was reluctant to take a position he knew would be criticized by liberals who favored a tough Volcker rule. This was characteristic; Frank preferred to be in liberals' good graces. Segel thought Frank was being stubborn.

Blanche Lincoln's provision on derivatives was still part of the Senate bill, and was still a problem for Dodd and the administration. Lincoln won her primary contest in Arkansas on June 8, a surprise to her Democratic colleagues, which, Dodd told reporters, strengthened her hand with fellow Democrats who wanted to help her win reelection. But Dodd also knew that the administration was pressuring her to compromise on the derivatives language that her man McCarty had written. Dodd wanted it changed also, but both he and Treasury wanted to change it without embarrassing Lincoln.

Both the Treasury and Dodd's staff were convinced that Lincoln did not fully understand the issue, but liked the politics of being seen as tough on the banks. For substance she seemed to rely entirely on McCarty, who was openly distrusted by Dodd's aides and the Treasury Department. But everyone involved understood they had to keep looking for a compromise.

The conference plodded on. "Financial Conference Not Exactly Must-See TV," said a headline in *Roll Call*, one of the three Capitol Hill dailies, on June 21; no one could disagree. The presence of C-SPAN's cameras only accentuated the fact that parliamentary committees operate in a world of their own, using an unfamiliar language and relying on bewildering rituals. This subject matter was devoid of entertainment value, and the leading actors were short on charisma. "We'd have to set ourselves on fire to have anyone pay attention to us," Frank quipped at one point.

The conference never made the front pages of the papers. The major networks' news shows almost never mentioned financial regulatory reform. Neither National Public Radio nor *The NewsHour* on PBS paid much attention to the debate. The bill was more important than most of the legislation that got more media attention, but it was also vastly more difficult to explain. The process lacked conflict, the lifeblood of modern political journalism, and the esoteric subject matter sailed over the heads of most editors.

On June 22, the conference moved to Room 106 in the Dirksen Senate Office Building. Dodd and Frank had agreed to share the job of hosting the conference, to emphasize the equality of the two houses. This is one of the ritualistic clichés of Congress, disbelieved by members of both houses, who like to think that their body is superior to "the other body," the euphemism each uses.

Dirksen 106 was an even larger room than the Financial Services Committee's chamber—eighty-one feet by fifty-one feet, under a twenty-one-foot ceiling. It is paneled in wood stained a medium brown, like maple, with large panels of green marble at regular intervals. The principally blue carpet has a complex pattern designed, like the carpet in hotel ballrooms, to disguise dirt. The room has giant windows on its east wall, but they are perpetually covered with thick blue curtains, so the outside world never makes an appearance inside. For the conference, long tables set end to end formed a big square to accommodate all forty-three conferees. As in the House, this space was taken from the area normally used for spectators. The big horseshoe-shaped dais used in formal hearings was, for this occasion, occupied by staff and administration officials. Reporters sat at tables on the periphery of the big room.

When Frank called the conference to order on Tuesday morning the 22nd, he warned members that "we have to finish by Thursday." Dodd warned that they might have to meet "late into the evening" to complete the job. The principal business that day was to work out the final version of the consumer protection agency. The House conferees accepted the Senate proposal to call it the Consumer Financial Protection Bureau and put it under the roof of the Federal Reserve Board, which would finance its activities—an approach Frank had ridiculed when he first heard about it, but had come to appreciate as a clever idea. The Senate provision gave the Fed no authority over the independent bureau. Its director, to be appointed by the president, would have total freedom of action, and more power than the heads of nearly all the other regulatory agencies, most of which were run by bipartisan boards.*

The auto dealers' formidable influence showed up on this day. Representative Luis Gutierrez of Illinois proposed reversing the decision the Financial Services Committee had made in 2009 when it excluded auto dealers from the purview of the consumer agency. But three of

---

* The Office of the Comptroller of the Currency, the principal bank regulator of all but the biggest banks (which the Fed supervises), is the only federal regulator with comparable powers.

his House Democratic colleagues voted against him, enough—with unanimous Republican opposition—to defeat the idea on the House side of the conference by eleven votes to ten. Then the Senate conferees defeated it too. The auto dealers had prevailed.

Periodically Frank adjourned the conference for twenty or thirty minutes, sometimes because of votes on the House or Senate floor, sometimes to give staff the opportunity to write new language or negotiate a compromise. When members came back into the room, they typically engaged in banter with one another, while staff could be seen in pairs and groups intently working on substance.

The gulf that separated these two subcultures was visible: When staff members circulated, they almost invariably carried stacks of paper. Members were generally empty-handed. Staff of course had the obligation to actually execute the agreements being reached, recording them in language that legislative counsel—the lawyers on the House and Senate staffs whose job was writing legislation—could convert into the proper legalese. Members, by contrast, had no specific obligations to produce any work product.

The next day the atmosphere was tense. Nothing had gone wrong, but a great deal still had to go right, especially the final deals on the Volcker rule and on derivatives. Lincoln was under intense, though publicly unseen, pressure. Some of it was coming from the House. A group of moderate House Democrats, members of the New Democrat Coalition and others from New York with ties to the financial industry, had come together in opposition to Lincoln's Section 716, and were demanding changes. They had broad support from many experts who weren't particularly sympathetic to the banks. Volcker and Sheila Bair of the FDIC had both publicly criticized the section as a bad idea. That morning, a worried Frank, by his account, "went to Steny [Hoyer, the House majority leader] and Nancy [Pelosi] and said, 'I'm telling you, this will bring the bill down.' " He asked for their help.

Hoyer quickly arranged a meeting with Lincoln, Collin Peterson, her counterpart as chairman of the House Agriculture Committee, Harry Reid, Pelosi, Dodd, and Frank. As usual, aides also attended. This group convened late that morning in Pelosi's large conference room in the Capitol, overlooking the Mall—the room where Paulson and Bernanke had terrified the leaders of Congress with their account of a crumbling global financial system on September 18, 2008.

The room was tense. Frank warned that "the whole bill can blow up over this, and I don't think that's in any of our interests." Sixty or more House Democrats could defect if Section 716 weren't changed, he said. Lincoln's first response was to cite the support she had from other senators, naming Byron Dorgan of North Dakota and Bernard Sanders of Vermont, two of the most liberal senators on financial issues. Frank responded sternly that a serious effort was required immediately to try to pacify the New Dems and New Yorkers, indicating that Lincoln should meet with them. "She said I'll listen," Frank recalled. "I said, I hope you'll listen." The meeting ended shortly after noon.

About six hours later, Neal Wolin, from the Treasury Department, traveled to Capitol Hill to meet with Robert Holifield, the young Arkansan Lincoln had named staff director of the Agriculture Committee, and Pat McCarty, the former CFTC and SEC official who had annoyed so many colleagues in the Senate, and administration officials too. Wolin wanted to pin down a compromise on Section 716.

Wolin was an effective lobbyist for the administration. A round-faced, jovial man with curly dark hair, his relaxed talent for dealing with people disguised an intensely competitive personality. He was one of the few Obama administration officials involved in financial regulatory reform who had actual experience working in the financial sector. He was smart and floridly profane. His colleagues loved him.

Wolin realized that Lincoln and Holifield had not mastered the derivatives issue, and had allowed McCarty to dominate discussion. More than once in their previous dealings on the legislation, Holifield had agreed to something Wolin recommended, but then called him back with suggestions for changing their agreement. Wolin thought this was McCarty's influence at work. Something similar had happened earlier in June, when Holifield came to Wolin's office for a serious talk, agreed to a compromise on Section 716, and seemed to commit himself when Wolin took him next door to meet Geithner, his boss. Then he called back with reservations. Now time was running out; Wolin needed to pin down a final agreement.

Wolin offered a proposal that would allow the banks to continue much of their traditional trading of derivatives. Trading of riskier derivatives would be "pushed out" of the banks into new subsidiaries of the bank holding companies that own the big banks. These would be separately capitalized so they couldn't pose a risk to the federally insured banks. He asked Holifield and McCarty to agree to this plan.

Wolin wasn't operating alone. The White House had gone to considerable lengths to intimidate Lincoln without appearing to do so. Geithner called her. Rahm Emanuel summoned McCarty and Holifield to the White House for a stern conversation. Obama himself invited Lincoln to the Oval Office to tell her how important a compromise was. They all told her they wanted to help her defend her seat in Arkansas in the general election, but she would have to compromise on Section 716.

When he arrived on Capitol Hill that evening, Wolin was surprised to find Gary Gensler, chairman of the Commodity Futures Trading Commission, in the meeting. Holifield previously worked for Gensler and was relying on him for help with the derivatives legislation. This concerned Wolin, who understood Gensler's ambition to make the CFTC more important, but he realized that in this meeting Gensler could not oppose the position of the administration that had appointed him. Emanuel had already let Gensler know that the White House expected him to line up with the administration's positions.

In the meeting Holifield was accommodating. McCarty continued to fault Wolin's proposal, and Wolin finally asked, Who is in charge here? He was trying to provoke Holifield, and it seemed to work. The staff director asserted his authority, and after a meeting lasting more than two hours, he shook hands with Wolin on the deal.

The next day, the New Yorkers and New Dems continued to agitate for a change in Section 716. At Hoyer's request, Wolin came up to his office at about 4 p.m. to explain the situation to a group of the New Democrats, including Melissa Bean of Illinois, and Gregory Meeks and Joseph Crowley of New York, all of whom wanted to be responsive to the big banks' concerns. Wolin agreed with them that Lincoln's provisions were bad policy, and his plan was intended to minimize the problems they created. But, he told them, he was stuck in a bad place. He said he was happy to consider alternatives, but "it's got to work with Blanche Lincoln or all of us are screwed." One of the New Dems, according to a participant, responded, "Then we'll be screwed!"

After that session a group of the House members marched over to Lincoln's Senate office and demanded to see her. She met with them and heard out their complaints. Again she sounded an accommodating note.

Various aides to the interested members tried to write a new version of Section 716 that would be broadly acceptable. Meanwhile Hoyer kept working on the New Dems, hoping to persuade them to live with the Wolin-Holifield compromise. "Somehow, Hoyer prevailed,"

Wolin said later. He was impressed with the majority leader's accomplishment. The New Democrats stopped threatening to vote against the bill. But at 9 p.m. on the 24th, there was still no agreement on specific legislative language.

While the maneuvering on Section 716 continued, a compromise on the Volcker rule began to take shape. On the morning of the 23rd in a conversation with Dodd, Scott Brown accepted his suggestion that the de minimus exception allow banks to invest up to 3 percent of their capital in investment funds, jointly with their clients. Brown and the banks he was fronting for had proposed 5 percent, which Volcker rejected as too high. Merkley and Levin reluctantly accepted 3 percent as well, though won a few small strengthening provisions in a final round of negotiating at the end of the afternoon.

The principals all wanted Volcker's blessing. The final conversations went on between Dave Smith of Frank's staff, Volcker's assistant Anthony Dowd, and Volcker himself. Smith called Volcker to report the 3 percent idea. Smith said this was the best they could get from Brown, and without Brown there would be no bill—and no Volcker rule. Volcker asked for a few minutes to think it over. Smith asked him to call back when he was ready to accept 3 percent. Volcker soon called again. "Okay," he said, Smith recounted, "but you're making me sick." Then, ten minutes, later, "Paul called back and said 'I'm feeling better, you can put me on with Chris [Dodd].' "

Smith was in Dirksen 106 when he got this call. He walked over to Dodd and handed him his cell phone. Dodd explained the agreement to Volcker, who blessed it. They had a deal.

Late in the afternoon Dodd formally introduced the new proposal. Displaying his characteristic instinct for diplomacy, Dodd referred to the new section 619 as "Merkley-Levin," and praised those two for changes that "improve [the original Senate bill] substantially. We think the overall effect of the amendment we are offering is to strengthen the limitations on proprietary trading," Dodd said, accurately. This was what Volcker had sought and the banks had fought against so fiercely, right up until this moment. But Volcker had prevailed.

A more mundane issue was how long this session would continue. Frank had wondered about going late into the night, adjourning, and reconvening on Friday or Monday to finish, but Dodd had insisted on staying in session until the job was done—all night if necessary. Frank was game. So the word was passed to members of the conference committee that they would remain in session until the bill was complete.

"Give them a break, and all of a sudden they'll be back and want to start all over again," Dodd remembered thinking when he recounted the story later. "Those are all 'feel' moments," he added, meaning moments when he acts on instinct. "It could be a disaster too, you've got to be careful. But I really felt at that juncture, we were that close, at this point—it was Thursday. The danger over a weekend—Jesus, it's always a nightmare. Press accounts, stories of people hardening up, going back, why don't you do more." He meant members would react to the press accounts of what they were doing, and perhaps to other pressures as well. Better not to give them that chance.

When Dodd was asked to expound on the notion of a "feel moment," he replied with a brief lecture on the lessons of his thirty years in the Senate.

"In politics it's like anything else. Why is a doctor better after fifteen years of doing surgery than in the first year? It's things you can't teach anybody. It's just the acquired skill of an institutional environment . . . a collegial environment where everyone's equal, everyone is strong-willed, most of them are fairly talented human beings, fairly bright and quick studies. You have to understand how it feels, what the rhythm of the institution is—when you fold, and hold, and all that stuff. . . . You can have natural abilities, which are important, but it's the acquired skills that have an awful lot to do with this."

Michael Barr, the young assistant secretary of the treasury, was in Dirksen 106 that night, remaining taut and alert when others yawned and faded. He agreed with Dodd: "People could sort of see, the conference is working, it's going to reach closure, there's going to be a final bill, we're all going to stay here together until it's done, this is the kind of direction that history is going in. It was just this feel in the room."

At about 10:30 Dodd formally introduced the Senate "offer" containing the new Volcker rule language. Jack Reed of Rhode Island explained it. The Senate conferees approved it by a voice vote and sent it to the House. Thanks to staff coordination, Frank and his colleagues knew what was coming, and quickly responded with technical changes that were soon approved.

There was a revealing moment at 11:45 when the House delivered these final changes to the Senate conferees. "I'm told by staff," Dodd said, "that the technical changes in Title 6 [home of the Volcker rule] we're okay with?" He made it a question to be sure, and spun his chair around as he said it in search of Amy Friend. She was sitting right behind him, and repeated in a low voice, "The technical changes we're okay with," nodding affirmatively. So the first of the most difficult issues was resolved.

At midnight, Frank called on Collin Peterson of Minnesota, chairman of the House Agriculture Committee, to introduce the "House offer" on derivatives, including a new version of Section 716. This was a well-rehearsed moment, the product of intense maneuvering and negotiating over the previous two days. That afternoon, Peterson and Michael Barr had gone outside for a cigarette and a final conversation on the plan. Peterson was a smoker; the youthful Barr was not, but "I smoked several cigarettes," he recalled later. Barr was the Obama administration's point man in the negotiations over new legislative language, and he was relieved that the substance of the Wolin-Holifield compromise was part of the new section that Peterson would be offering.

When called on by Frank, Peterson announced that "the administration and several senators" had worked out a compromise—an odd formulation for a House committee chairman about to present a House offer, but also a factual statement. He would now describe that compromise. The original Section 716 required banks to spin off all their derivatives trading activities, but the compromise allowed some to remain in the banks. He enumerated the list, showing that Lincoln had accepted significant changes. Banks would be allowed to trade derivatives based on traditional bank assets, including "interest rate swaps, foreign exchange, credit derivatives referencing investment-grade entities that are cleared, gold and silver." These constituted most of the business that banks cared about. Dealings in derivatives based on commodities, sources of energy, stocks and bonds, and some others—"generally the more risky" items, as Peterson put it—would have to be spun off to new affiliates capitalized separately from the banks. "The rest of Section 716 remains," he said, a diplomatic gesture to Lincoln, since "the rest" was less important than what had been changed.

The House conferees quickly approved the new proposal and sent it across the table to the Senate. Again because of prior collaboration between the staffs, Dodd had a prepared script to read accepting most of the changes in the derivatives title—"eighty-five of the House's 110 proposals we accept, after modifying fifteen; we respectfully reject twenty-five."

Judging by outward appearances, all was proceeding smoothly toward a final conclusion. But appearances were misleading. Moments before Peterson began to speak, Barr got a copy of the language in his proposal. Wolin was with him, and they hurriedly read through it, and realized that McCarty—who had drafted what was supposed to be the compromise Lincoln accepted—had once again changed what they thought had been an agreed compromise. They were livid, and hurriedly told Dodd, Frank, Jeanne Roslanowick, and Amy Friend that it would have to be changed again.

Senator Schumer of New York, until now a relatively passive member of the conference committee, was also agitated by the change, which he thought undid the assurances given that day to the New Yorkers who met with Lincoln. Schumer angrily told Friend (who had worked for him years earlier) that the provision would have to be changed again.

There were three major problems. As drafted by McCarty, the latest version would have banned the Federal Reserve from providing any "liquidity"—short-term cash assistance—to the central clearinghouses that, in the new derivatives market the bill created, would facilitate trades, collect and hold collateral, and provide other important services. In a future financial crisis, the Fed and the Treasury both believed, such assistance might be crucial to avoid catastrophe. Second, McCarty's draft—sloppy and full of errors, in Barr's and Wolin's opinions—would have made it extremely difficult for bank holding companies, the corporate structures that control most banks, to trade derivatives, even those that the compromise supposedly allowed banks to trade. This was the provision that upset Senator Schumer. Third, the new language would have made it impossible for Treasury to continue to provide capital support to Fannie Mae and Freddie Mac because they were both active participants in derivatives markets. This, Barr believed, would have "cratered the housing market" by undermining all confidence in Fannie and Freddie.

Barr found Holifield, who was one of the crowd in Dirksen 106, and told him the language had to be fixed. Holifield asked McCarty to join their discussion, and a heated argument ensued. Barr hurriedly edited the proposal, making cuts and writing out, by hand, new language to repair at least some of the damage. Dodd was ready to send the Senate's response to the Peterson offer from the House. "We had only minutes to fix it," Barr recalled. Barr saw numerous other errors in the draft but knew there wasn't time to try to clean them up. McCarty insisted there was "no way Lincoln would accept" Barr's changes, but Holifield contradicted him. She has already agreed, he said, and he accepted Barr's changes. Amy Friend saw to it that Barr's handwritten fixes were part of the Senate counteroffer that Dodd now introduced.

This was "the most complex title in the bill," Dodd said, reading from another prepared script. "This one is profoundly important—that we get it right." The revisions were sent back across the room to the House conferees, who approved them. Those watching on television—if anyone still was—and the people in the room saw no hint of the drama that had just played out backstage.

Shortly before 1 a.m., Dodd asked Blanche Lincoln to comment on the new proposal. This was, Barr thought, a kabuki dance—stylized ritual, carefully scripted. Lincoln thanked Dodd and "Chairman Franks," and declared victory. This latest version "retains the core of both bills," she said—meaning her original version and the House bill. All she'd ever wanted was to make sure that "banks should be banks," not engaging in risky activities. This version was a victory for "common sense." She insisted, inaccurately, that it retained "the 716," the section that had been significantly rewritten, but said the bill was much broader than that, and people should pay attention to its other provisions, which would bring the secretive derivatives market into the open for the first time.

No one in the room wanted to correct or contradict Lincoln. Dodd particularly wanted her to declare victory, and to feel victorious. Frank was pleased too. They both were relieved that a disaster had been averted.

Section 716 got most of the attention, but Lincoln's version of the bill contained other sections that provoked strong opposition in the tiny universe of experts who understood how the new derivatives market would operate. Two of those were Senator Jack Reed and his assistant, Kara Stein. They had been stewing for weeks about provisions in Lincoln's bill that vastly enhanced the jurisdiction of the

Commodity Futures Trading Commission—overseen by the Agriculture Committee—at the expense of the much bigger Securities and Exchange Commission, overseen by the Banking Committee.

The Lincoln proposal would have made the CFTC the regulator not only of its traditional commodities-based derivatives like the futures market in corn and wheat, but also interest rate swaps and foreign currency swaps that banks and manufacturers used to hedge their risks. If the CFTC became the primary regulator of all derivatives—essentially what the Agriculture Committee proposed—then firms like Goldman Sachs or Morgan Stanley would lavish their lobbying attention on that one, small agency—and on the members of Congress who oversaw it. This would be a boon for the campaign war chests of members of the House and Senate Agriculture committees. But in the opinion of many experts and Jack Reed too, it was a terrible idea.

Reed was an atypical senator. A small, compact man with a formidable intellect, he did mountains of homework. He mastered complicated issues. He had three degrees: a Bachelor of Science from West Point, a master's in public policy from the John F. Kennedy School at Harvard, and a Juris Doctor degree from Harvard Law. He served as a ranger and paratrooper in the Army, retiring with the rank of captain to go to law school. Colleagues in both parties held him in high regard.

Reed and Republican Judd Gregg of New Hampshire and their staffs took seriously their role as Dodd's "working group" on derivatives. They had spent long hours over several months working on a proposal that both men could jointly sponsor. The senators liked and respected each other, and so did their principal aides, Stein for Reed and Jenn Gallagher for Gregg.

Stein, a graduate of Yale College and Yale Law School who looked thirty but was in her mid-forties, called the relationship between her boss and Gregg "an example of the best kind of Senate collaboration." Her relations with Gallagher were excellent. "We had good intellectual discussions for months to try to get the right answers. We didn't agree always, but the disagreements were intellectual, without animus."

In the end the Reed-Gregg partnership failed to produce a joint proposal. Gregg backed away from their bill after the banking interests made clear their preference for the original deal between Lincoln and Saxby Chambliss, which was gentler on the banks. Gregg also disliked the turn that public opinion took that spring, the rising anti-bank sentiment, which he thought was "populist" and irresponsible. He said Obama had gone too far by embracing this populism, and making regulatory reform another partisan issue.

But Reed and Gregg remained on good terms. After working together for months, they shared common views on many aspects of the derivatives provisions. Specifically, they agreed on the need to preserve the SEC's role as a regulator of derivatives against the Agriculture Committee's efforts to minimize it in favor of the CFTC. As the conference entered its final stage, Reed recruited Gregg to try to help fix the jurisdictional problem they both perceived in Lincoln's bill. Reed and Kara Stein had been working for weeks on amendments that would give both agencies shared responsibility for derivatives markets. Gregg agreed to support them in conference, and to try to persuade Republican colleagues to join him.

At 1:15 a.m. on what had become Friday, June 25, Dodd blandly recognized Reed to offer the changes Stein had drafted to restore the SEC's role. Someone watching on C-SPAN who didn't know the history of tension between Lincoln's staff and the Banking Committee would not have realized that they were witnessing a showdown between the two committees and the agencies they oversaw.

In brief remarks, Reed said the amendments would "restore the balance" between the two agencies by providing for "joint rule-making" on derivatives trading. Lincoln hadn't known what was coming until Reed's amendments were distributed to the committee a few minutes earlier. After whispered consultations with staff, including McCarty, she spoke up in opposition to Reed's proposals. They were "redundant," she said; Reed was trying to "micromanage" the regulators, and it wasn't necessary.

Reed gently but firmly disagreed. Lincoln's description of her own provisions was wrong, he said. They would encourage "organizational imperialism" between the CFTC and SEC, and weaken oversight in the process.

Gregg spoke up in support of Reed. "It's really critical" to force both agencies to work together, he said.

Reed's amendments were to a Senate "offer" to the House, so initially only the Senate conferees would vote on them. Dodd called for a vote. Chambliss, the senior Republican on Agriculture, supported Lincoln against Reed. Every other Republican conferee—all members of Banking—voted "Aye."

Julie Chon, the Banking Committee aide who handled derivatives issues, remembered sitting between the Democratic and Republican staffs. "For the first time in all of reg reform I saw the Republican staff energized, united, and enthusiastic about something," Chon recalled. "When they saw how we were succeeding in fixing these jurisdictional problems, people on the Republican staff side started to chant: 'Banking! Banking! Banking!' "

Lincoln caught on: "Clearly the Banking Committee is using its numbers here and wants to overpower us on its jurisdiction. . . . I can count," she said. Eight of the conferees belonged to Banking; four to Agriculture. All Reed's amendments were approved.

Reed said later this important moment was a sign that the bill really did include some Republican ideas, and enjoyed some Republican support. "The irony here is, it was a bipartisan bill, it just didn't get a bipartisan vote" on final passage. This was an exaggeration, since the Republicans who supported him on these votes were not backing the entire bill, just this section on jurisdiction of the regulators. But the outcome did show that Dodd's bipartisan working groups made a difference—only the Gregg-Reed partnership made these changes possible.*

At 3:30 a.m., nothing was happening. Finally Frank explained: "In the interest of transparency I want to announce that the current delay is because they ran out of Xerox paper. . . . We're getting ready our response on Title 7, on derivatives. The paper is on the way." The room was hot and stuffy—air-conditioning in the Dirksen Building is operated by a timing system; it wasn't meant to work in the middle of the night.

Finally the House delivered its last counteroffer. Frank again made clear what was really happening: "Senator," he said to Dodd across the twenty feet that separated them, "I believe that if you have a counter-counteroffer, we can probably accept what you send us back." Again, the staff had smoothed the path in advance.

To which Dodd replied, "Where did Julie go?" He needed his derivatives expert. Chon quickly appeared at his side, holding a piece of paper with the last proposed changes to the provision. She explained its contents to Dodd, who explained it to the conference. After a perfunc-

---

* Gregg, one of the last Republican moderates from the North in the Senate, retired at the end of 2010. He was replaced by a more conservative Republican.

tory voice vote Frank accepted it on behalf of the House. At 4:15 a.m., Title 7 was complete. The conferees had approved a transformation of the gigantic derivatives market that would alter the face of American finance.

The end was now in sight. At 4:30 Dodd allowed himself a long yawn. Staff scrambled to produce the final paperwork. While they worked, Paul Kanjorski of Pennsylvania asked for the floor. At 5:07 he moved that the bill they were about to complete henceforth be known as "Dodd-Frank," in recognition of the two chairmen who had made possible this "extraordinary, historic event." Frank mumbled that it would be inappropriate for him to respond to such a motion, and handed the gavel to Kanjorski so he could briefly preside. Kanjorski called for a voice vote, and his motion carried. Not a "No" could be heard. Members stood and applauded the two chairmen. Even some Republicans joined the ovation; Spencer Bachus was one of them.

One sticky issue remained, the "pay for." This became an example of Congress at its most ridiculous.

Paying for the things it spends money on has not been a specialty of the United States Congress in the modern era, when the government's debt has soared. In 1978, in the earliest days of partisan warfare, the U.S. Treasury owed its creditors about $770 billion. At the end of 2010, federal debt totaled nearly $14 *trillion*. In the modern era, the government's debts grew more than eighteen-fold.

This happened despite the relative success of a serious effort to control spending and slow the growth of debt during the 1990s. This was the result of PAYGO legislation adopted in 1990, part of an ambitious deal between President George H. W. Bush and the Democratic Congress. The two parties agreed then on tax increases and spending cuts that began to curtail the enormous deficits incurred in the Reagan years. The deal included a tough "pay-as-you-go" rule that required Congress to "pay for" any new spending with tax increases or other spending cuts. Bill Clinton and Newt Gingrich renewed this commitment later in the decade in one of the last examples of meaningful bipartisan collaboration. As a result of its success, when President George W. Bush came to office in 2001 he inherited a budget surplus. For the first time in decades, the government was taking in more than it was spending.

The requirement that Congress "pay for" all spending with tax revenue or other spending cuts expired in 2002, and deficits ballooned again, aggravated by the big tax cuts Bush promoted. Republicans who controlled Congress drove up the debt with abandon. When Democrats regained control of the House in 2006, they instituted a new version of PAYGO—Speaker Pelosi's attempt to look fiscally responsible. But her version exempted large parts of the federal budget, so permitted huge increases in spending without new revenues or cuts. It did, however, apply to the financial regulatory reform bill.

The Congressional Budget Office, a nonpartisan agency created by Congress in 1974 to provide statistical research for the House and Senate on budget issues, issued an opinion that the bill being worked on by the conference committee would cost $20 billion to implement over the next ten years. This was a made-up number; it came from an estimate of how many financial firms might fail and be shut down over the next ten years. Real or phony, the CBO's number could not be evaded. The conference committee needed to find $20 billion to "pay for" the legislation.

Frank had a simple idea for a "pay for" that he thought suited the anti-bank mood of the moment, and was good politics too. He proposed a new "assessment" to be imposed on the biggest financial institutions—the largest banks, and hedge funds with assets greater than $10 billion—that would raise $19 billion over five years, to be held in a special fund. Dodd and the administration went along.

The idea of creating this fund provoked new Republican criticisms of potential "bailouts." But in the predawn hours of June 25, Mark Oesterle, Shelby's longtime senior expert and aide, came up with an idea to address that concern: Why not hold the money for a long period of time—say twenty-five years—and then use it to retire a sliver of the federal debt? Dodd loved this idea, and loved the fact that it came from the Republican staff. Oesterle and Charles Yi of Dodd's staff worked out the language, which Dodd asked Yi to explain to the committee. The CBO accepted the plan as an adequate "pay for," though in the real world the $19 billion raised from big financial institutions wouldn't pay for anything for twenty-five years, and then would become, in effect, a contribution to the Treasury.

Just before the final vote on this proposal, Senator Corker, with a grin, suggested that it be called "the Oesterle rule," but Shelby said, "I object," also grinning. At 5:25 a.m., Dodd called for the vote. The seven Democrats said "Aye." All five Republicans, including Corker, voted "No," on the grounds that the assessment was really just a tax on financial institutions.

Now all that remained was final votes on the completed conference committee bill. First the House conferees voted, one by one. The twenty Democrats said "Aye"; all eleven Republicans voted "No." Then the senators: seven Democrats "Aye," five Republicans "No." The newly renamed Dodd-Frank Act had passed on a party-line vote of the conferees.

"I thank my colleagues immensely," Dodd said, as the sound of applause filled the room.

At 5:39 a.m., nearly twenty hours after he had opened the "last day" of the conference, Frank spoke one last time: "With the votes of the House and the Senate conferees in favor of passage of the bill, I declare the bill passed and the conference committee is now adjourned."

No one in the room could remember such an important congressional event occurring at such a preposterous hour. But Dodd's instinct had proven correct. His insistence that the conference work through the night had produced the result he hoped for.

Despite the uncivilized hour, both Dodd and Frank lingered to celebrate, and to preen a little before the small band of reporters who had made it through the night. Dodd's first move was to hug Amy Friend and Kara Stein, and to plant a kiss on the cheek of Blanche Lincoln. Frank gathered up his scrunched-up copy of the previous day's *New York Times* while his partner, Jim Ready, snapped pictures of him.

When a dozen reporters had gathered around the two men, Dodd began by thanking, by name, Jeanne Roslanowick, Jim Segel, Dave Smith, then Ed Silverman and Amy Friend. "We don't pay enough attention and recognize the staffs who put in a tremendous effort," Dodd said. Predictably, no story written by the reporters present mentioned this tribute to the aides.

Then, despite the fact that he had been awake for about twenty-three hours, Dodd made a coherent little speech about the bill, citing its principal provisions and praising Frank for helping bring them to the threshold of final enactment. "No one will know until this is actually in place how it works," he admitted, and "it took a crisis to bring us to the point where we could actually get the job done. That's a terrible way to have to do this, but because we did have the crisis . . . we have done something that has been sorely needed for a long time."

Then Frank gave a short version of the speech he'd been making that spring. The bill contained tough provisions that "were considered unachievable" just a year or two earlier, he said, but something remarkable had happened that was "a tribute to the way American democracy can work. . . . With the passage of health care [in March] the American public began to focus on this, with the help of you in the media. And I don't think there's any question that made an enormous difference. This is a better bill than it would have been in significant ways because the American people focused on it. . . . We worry about big money—I worry about big money having an influence [on Congress], but it is reassuring that when public opinion gets engaged, it will win. We just need to make sure that we have more cases where that happens."

After answering a few questions from the exhausted press corps, the reporters fell silent. "Hey, Chris!" Frank said. "We've worn them out!"

"I never thought I'd see that," Dodd replied with a grin. And they went home to bed.

CHAPTER TWENTY-THREE

Endgame

The idea that the conference committee had completed its work with that vote at dawn on Friday only survived for a few hours— until Scott Brown's office issued a statement in the senator's name: "I was surprised and extremely disappointed to hear that $19 billion in new assessments and fees were added in the wee hours of the morning by the conference committee. . . . These provisions were not in the Senate version of the bill which I previously supported. My fear is that these costs would be passed onto consumers. . . . I've said repeatedly that I cannot support any bill that raises taxes."

Brown was obviously enjoying his moment of leverage. Opposing the proposed bank fee gave him another opportunity to ingratiate himself with the Massachusetts banks, and banks everywhere. After establishing that Brown would not vote for cloture without a change in the "pay for" provision, Dodd knew he had to come up with another idea, and quickly. And Frank would have to reconvene the conference committee.

But that wasn't so easy. The Senate parliamentarian informed Dodd that under Senate rules, once a conference committee had approved its report and its members had signed the document, the rules precluded reopening the conference. Dodd couldn't believe it. "What rule am I breaking?" he remembered asking the parliamentarian, Alan Frumin. Frumin said reopening a conference would look "unsavory." He cited a precedent that involved a senator who had added an earmark in pencil to an appropriations bill after the conference committee had acted. It provided for a new Interstate exit ramp in his state. That led to an ethics rule that such changes were inadmissible. Friend argued that this was an entirely different situation. She and Dodd persuaded Frumin that they had to hold another session of the conference committee.

Dodd admitted later that he hadn't paid enough attention to the "pay for" problem, but the Treasury team did. With help from his administration colleagues, Michael Barr had several suggestions for how to find the $19 billion the Congressional Budget Office was demanding. The ideas were sophisticated gimmicks designed to satisfy the quirky demands of the CBO, not really to pay the costs of the bill, which in fact were unknowable. Dodd's and Frank's staff members embraced two of Barr's suggestions.

The first was to end the TARP program immediately. Under the original TARP legislation, Congress authorized expenditures of $700 billion to prop up banks, auto companies, and other institutions reeling from the Great Crash, but only $475 billion had actually been spent. That meant there was budget authority to spend another $225 billion under TARP. But if the program were ended at once that authority would disappear. CBO calculated that this would save $11 billion over ten years, which it estimated was the amount that the government would lose if it made another $225 billion in TARP loans. CBO reckoned that about 5 percent of all TARP loans would never be repaid. Five percent of $225 billion was just over $11 billion. All this in spite of the fact that the money might never have been loaned, and if it was, might have been repaid. That was the first gimmick.

The second was to increase the size of the Federal Deposit Insurance Corporation's insurance fund, which it draws on to pay the costs of winding down banks that fail and making good on the insurance extended to depositors in those banks. A new assessment of banks would bring in nearly $6 billion. Only big banks, those with assets of more than $10 billion, would be assessed; small banks would contribute nothing, another reflection of their political influence. CBO agreed that this money, to be collected by the FDIC and never used to reduce government spending, could nevertheless be "scored" as a savings to "offset" costs of implementing the Dodd-Frank bill.

The CBO, Frank acknowledged during discussion of this idea, "is a wondrous institution."

Republican senators on the conference committee expressed outrage when these gimmicks were proposed. Angriest of all was Judd Gregg, a former chairman of the Senate Budget Committee and an expert on spending issues. "This is a fraud on the American taxpayer," he said, because this "pay for" would not, in fact, pay any of the costs of implementing Dodd-Frank. He was right about that.

But similar frauds had been perpetrated again and again, by both Republicans and Democrats. The Republicans howling now had been authors of spending bills and tax cuts earlier in the 2000s that had added trillions to the national debt. Gregg himself had admitted as much. Republican complaints on this occasion had no resonance. A cynical public had long since stopped listening to the partisan exchanges about spending and taxes, one of the longest running shows in Washington.

Frank said he was sorry to lose the bank and hedge fund assessment, which he liked better than these new ideas. But "to get enough votes to pass this bill, we have to do this. And it is a very important bill. . . . [So] I am prepared to make some compromises." There, in a nutshell, was Barney Frank's philosophy of legislation.

At the end of the discussion, the conferees voted on the revised conference report. The outcome was the same as it had been early Friday morning: all Democratic conferees in favor, all Republicans opposed.

Dodd made sure in advance that Brown and the women from Maine would approve this "pay for." Dodd conducted "shuttle diplomacy" with all three Republicans, visiting each in his or her office, following up with phone calls and staff visits. During his visit to Collins she told him how much she admired the process he was conducting. With those three, Dodd thought he had sixty votes for cloture.

He almost had sixty-one, but a day earlier, Robert Byrd of West Virginia, a member of Congress since 1953, had died in a suburban Virginia hospital at the age of ninety-two. He had been a reliable Democratic vote for cloture, provided his wheelchair could bring him to the floor in time to vote. He was likely to have a Democratic successor because the appointment would be made by West Virginia's Democratic governor, but installing the new senator would take a fortnight at least. Byrd's death meant that Dodd could not meet the July 4 deadline he and Frank had publicly announced for final approval of the bill. Memorials for Byrd would fill the last two days of June, then Congress would take its July 4 recess, putting off a Senate vote until the middle of July. But the House, as always the more efficient chamber, would consider the conference report on June 30, the very next day.

As in December, the House debate on the rule and the debate on final passage were indistinguishable. On the Democratic side the rhetoric was straightforward and unexciting. The majority wanted to praise its accomplishment and get to the finish line.

Republicans once again came armed with talking points, the product of the GOP's messaging operation. They were designed to score political points, and often had little or no connection to what was actually in the bill under consideration. For example, the most popular was to refer to the bill as "a job killer," the theme House Republicans had adopted for 2010. They argued that President Obama and his Democratic supporters in the House were passing complicated legislation but ignoring what the people really wanted: jobs.

"This is a job killer, pure and simple," said Jeb Hensarling of Texas. He said it four times. Most Republicans who spoke used some version of the phrase. The argument was never spelled out; new regulations would inevitably cause firms to hire fewer people, but no one explained precisely how.

Just as popular was the accusation that the bill would perpetuate "bailouts," the accusation that would not die. The bill actually precluded bailouts of the kind that had angered the public in 2008 (when the Republican administration provided them), but for this debate the House Republicans subtly redefined the term. Spencer Bachus, the ranking Republican on the Financial Services Committee, offered this redefinition in his remarks: "This bill will institutionalize AIG-type bailouts of creditors and counter-parties," he said. It was a formulation that experts could understand, one obviously intended to invoke the memory of the huge bailout of the least popular beneficiary of Hank Paulson's and Ben Bernanke's largesse, AIG.

But Bachus was not saying that Dodd-Frank would allow the government to bail out a firm like AIG in a future crisis—the bill actually made that impossible. Instead he was referring to the fact that under Dodd-Frank, regulators could, in a future crisis, dissolve a failing firm that threatened the stability of the financial system in a way that could entail paying off its "creditors and counter-parties." The law made this possible so that regulators could limit the destabilizing impact of a firm's collapse. Creditors were institutions and individuals that had lent the failing firm money. Counter parties were those who had ongoing deals with the failing firm that the firm could no longer honor. In an emergency, Dodd-Frank would allow the FDIC, the agency that would resolve a failing firm, to borrow money from the Treasury for such payments, to try to avoid a wider meltdown.

But as Frank pointed out when he replied to Bachus, Dodd-Frank would only allow this kind of help for a firm when it was on its way to dissolution, after its stockholders had lost the full value of their investment, and the board of directors and management had been fired. "This is not AIG," Frank said. The powers in the bill could not be used "to keep an institution going" the way AIG had been kept alive, but only to kill it off. And if the FDIC had to use cash to resolve a failing firm, it would initially be borrowed from the Treasury; the bill stipulated that large financial firms would be assessed for every dollar used.

Another popular Republican talking point was the failure of Dodd-Frank to deal with Fannie Mae and Freddie Mac. Roy Blunt of Missouri, a member of the Republican leadership, used this one: "The root cause of the problem we have in the economy today was caused by these entities," Blunt asserted, a proposition no serious economist would endorse. "They are not addressed" by Dodd-Frank, he continued, proof of the bill's inadequacy.

Judy Biggert of Illinois, once a relative moderate who had been pushed out of her job as ranking member of one of the subcommittees of Financial Services by the conservatives, declared that Dodd-Frank "increased taxes on community banks, manufacturers, small businesses, consumers, and American families." The bill, of course, contained no new taxes.

So the House debate ended much as it had begun eighteen months earlier, with members of the two parties talking past each other, often dealing with different versions of reality. Once again, many of the most significant provisions of the bill were ignored or skimmed over in favor of rhetorical flourishes designed for political benefit.

In a few minutes, the House would enact an enormous piece of legislation that would fundamentally alter what had become the single most important industry in the United States, changing the rules of the great financial game that had been in place for years or even decades. Most Americans had no idea what was happening, or what it meant, either to the titans of Wall Street or to themselves. This was how the system worked. Even the men and women in this old hall, the House of Representatives of the United States, who would now vote on the bill had, with a few exceptions, only a vague sense of what the new law would mean.

No matter. It was nearly 7 p.m. "The question is on the conference report," the acting speaker intoned. First a voice vote: "The ayes appear to have it," the acting speaker announced.

"Mr. Speaker," said Frank, the floor manager of the bill, "I demand the yeas and nays"—a roll call vote. Members materialized on the floor like ants drawn to spilled marmalade. They trooped to the electronic voting devices to insert their plastic members' cards. The results were projected onto the wall above the speaker's rostrum. As each member's vote was registered, it was recorded for all to see. When everyone had voted, the acting speaker reported: "On this vote there were 237 yeas and 192 nays. The conference committee report is agreed to."

Three Republicans voted for the bill: Michael Castle of Delaware, a moderate former governor who was running for the Senate and would be defeated in the Republican primary by a Tea Party activist ten weeks later; Joseph Cao of Louisiana, an accidental congressman from New Orleans who won his seat by running against a convicted felon, and would lose it overwhelmingly in November; and Walter Jones, a populist maverick from North Carolina who thought Wall Street deserved tougher regulation. This was three more Republican votes than Frank's bill had received in the House six months earlier when it passed 223–202.

Nine Democrats, mostly liberals, who voted against Frank's bill in December switched to "Aye" this time. Five Democrats who didn't vote in December also voted "Aye" on final passage. Three Democrats who voted "Aye" in December voted "No" in June.

"I am very happy," Frank said the next day. "The vote yesterday was very good for us. The votes on the left came back. . . . The bill came out better than I thought it would. I won all the important things that I needed. It is by far the most dramatic increase in consumer and investor protection in American history."

On the day the House was completing its final action, Chris Dodd was nervous. He would have to wait two long weeks before the Senate could take up the bill—more than enough time for something else to go wrong. Scott Brown's demand that had forced him to reopen the conference shook Dodd's confidence. Where would the next pothole appear? He decided to go to the floor of the Senate to make a speech.

Kirstin Brost, his press aide and sometime speechwriter, had drafted remarks for him to read, but Dodd didn't need a text. He knew what he wanted to say. First he reviewed the human toll of the Great Crash, mentioning the trillions in savings wiped out, the retirement funds lost, the eight and a half million jobs that had disappeared.

"Seven million of our fellow citizens have had their homes fall into foreclosure," Dodd said. "Imagine coming home one night and facing your family and telling them that the house you have lived in—where you have played, you have eaten, you have dreamt, you have laughed, you have cried, you have done all of the things that building enshrines in the American family—is no longer yours . . . despite all of your efforts. For seven million of our fellow citizens that night has happened."

This bill couldn't undo the damage done, but it could help insure that the next economic crisis—"and we will have another economic crisis"—would not "metastasize" the way the last one did, Dodd said. "If we can control it, identify it early enough, begin to address the problems that it poses, then we might avoid the kind of catastrophic effect" we had this time—"the most significant in almost 100 years."

The bill wasn't perfect—"I am not overly enthusiastic about every provision," he said. But that was inevitable. Congress consists of 535 people, the affected businesses were big and important, the administration and the regulators also had interests of their own. "It is difficult to try to fashion a piece of legislation that accommodates the various interests and allows us to move forward. But that is what we have tried to do," Dodd said.

He described his emphasis on bipartisan participation, beginning with his invitation to Shelby to come to the first White House meeting in early 2009. "This has been a truly inclusive, collective effort." The conference with the House was unique, "the only time I have ever seen a conference conducted with the public viewing every single second of it" on television. "I do not know what else I could have done to make this more inclusive," Dodd said. "I urge you, I plead with you to give us the vote on this bill," he concluded. The process he followed, "by which everyone gets a chance to participate, ought to be the model of how the Senate conducts its business. I hope my colleagues will not underestimate the value and importance of that approach we have taken with this bill."

This was "right from the heart," as Amy Friend put it later. "The process was so important to him. He wanted this to be part of his legacy. . . . You could hear his concern that somehow he could lose all of this"—lose the cloture vote in two weeks' time, and lose the bill.

Dodd's anxieties proved unwarranted. By the time the Senate finally took up the conference committee report on July 15, Brown, Collins, and Snowe had all announced publicly that they would vote to end debate and bring up the bill for final passage. All Democrats but Feingold would do the same. As the Senate convened that morning, Dodd and Harry Reid looked relieved and relaxed. Under the rules, the Republicans were entitled to demand thirty hours of debate after a cloture vote and before final passage, but Reid had outmaneuvered them by timing the cloture vote for a Thursday. If they wanted the full thirty hours, they would lose the weekend. So they settled for two and a half hours. Dodd and his staff were hoping for a quick and easy final day.

First there would be one more staff-written Shelby speech attacking the bill and, implicitly, Dodd and his staff. Dodd-Frank was a partisan bill, Shelby said, blaming that on "decisions made by the Obama administration," a formulation calculated to wound Dodd. Shelby again assailed Dodd for failing to hold hearings to explore the causes of the Great Crash, again regretting the failure to match the Pecora Commission of the early 1930s. In his speech at Oxford University in the fall of 2009, Shelby spoke confidently about how the system needed to be reformed, as though he had no doubt about what had gone wrong to cause the crash, but in this speech, as in the eighteen-minute diatribe of the previous November, he chose to play dumb, as though what had caused the disaster was a mystery.

Shelby accused Dodd of acting deviously and in bad faith: "The majority knows that this bill is a job killer and will saddle Americans with billions of dollars in hidden taxes and fees," he said, an assertion with no established basis in fact. "It became apparent early on to me that the administration and the Democratic majority were not interested in regulatory reform. All they were trying to do is exploit the crisis in order to expand government further and reward special interests. The Dodd-Frank bill will not enhance systemic stability. It will not prevent future bailouts of politically favored institutions and groups by the government." Shelby read this partisan boilerplate without blushing.

This time Dodd would not bite his tongue. "I feel as if I am listening to the first [Shelby] speech back in November," he said—the eighteen-minute diatribe—"and wonder if we have been in the same chamber and same city over the last several years." The Banking Committee held eighty hearings over the previous two years, "with countless efforts to reach out and bring in people," Dodd said. Half the amendments to the bill approved on the Senate floor came from Republicans. Shelby's Republicans "never offered" a substitute bill. And "we didn't need a Pecora Commission to find out what was going wrong. We had mortgages being sold in this country to people who couldn't afford them, marketing them in a way that guaranteed failure, securitizing them so [their creators] could be paid and then skipping town in a sense. I didn't need to have hours of hearings to find out what was the cause of it."

Dodd did not mention a fact that he had thought about more than once during his frustrating dealings with Shelby over the previous eighteen months: that during 2003–7, when Shelby was the chairman of the Banking Committee and the housing bubble grew to the point of bursting, Shelby held no hearings on the subjects of housing, "no-doc" home mortgages, Fannie and Freddie, the risks being taken by banks or anything else that either helped foresee or helped mitigate the impact of the Great Crash. "I must say I'm rather stunned, I've never seen a line written about" Shelby's do-little tenure as chairman, Dodd said later. But bringing it up himself was not his style. "My job as chairman is to produce a good product. The role is to govern. Why create barriers to that conclusion?" Personal criticism never helps.

When Shelby and Dodd exchanged these words on the floor, they were the only senators present. Friend and Ed Silverman sat with Dodd. The empty chamber revealed the total absence of tension or excitement; the outcome of the final vote was not in doubt. A few more speeches followed, including a recitation of the Republican talking points from McConnell. Then at 11 a.m. it was time for the vote on cloture. The script held: There were sixty votes in favor of ending debate and proceeding to the final vote. Brown, Collins, and Snowe joined all the Democrats. Grassley, the sometimes ornery Iowa Republican who voted for cloture when the bill came up for a Senate vote in May, lost his appetite for disloyalty, and voted "No."

The 150 minutes left for debate were filled with perfunctory comments on both sides. At one point Barney Frank appeared on the Senate floor, an unusual visit by a member of the other body, but he left before the final roll call, which produced the same result: sixty votes in favor, thirty-nine opposed. Byrd's successor still hadn't been sworn in, so the Senate was one member short. When the presiding officer announced the vote, Dodd grinned at his wife and daughters in the gallery, kissed Amy Friend and shook Ed Silverman's hand. It was a calmer, quieter scene than the congratulatory scrum that had followed passage of the Senate bill in May.

Only the ritual meeting with reporters in the Radio-TV Gallery remained. This too was more restrained than in May. Reid and Dodd were the only senators present. Reid was deeply engaged in a close reelection campaign, so his congratulatory remarks emphasized how good this legislation would be for Nevada. Reid heaped praise on Dodd, who reciprocated in kind—the usual senatorial malarkey.

The last act occurred six days later downtown, in the auditorium of the Ronald Reagan Building at 13th and Pennsylvania Avenue, two long blocks from the Treasury. Scores of people from Capitol Hill and the executive branch agencies who had worked on the bill filled the hall. President Obama and Vice President Biden arrived at 11:30 to warm cheers, and Obama read a speech from two TelePrompTers on either side of the podium.

From the beginning, the complexities of the legislation had frustrated its authors' efforts to summarize it cogently in a way that nonexpert citizens could understand and find appealing. That problem stymied Obama's speechwriters on this occasion. They wrote a workmanlike speech with little emotional content about an ambitious piece of legislation that constituted an unusually significant accomplishment, but it didn't sound so important in Obama's remarks. When the speechwriter looked for a way to relate the bill to everyday life, he used an example not from Dodd-Frank, but from the credit card bill passed in 2009 that made it harder for card issuers to jack up the interest rate on existing customers. A different president who wanted to put himself squarely on the side of the little people who suffered most from the Great Crash and against the financial interests that caused the disaster could have used this occasion to deliver an emotional oration, but not

Obama. He spoke about an end to "taxpayer bailouts," and also praised the financial sector for the important role it plays in American life. Characteristically, he struck a note of evenhanded moderation.

Obama took credit for the substance of the bill. "Even before the crisis hit, I went to Wall Street and I called for common-sense reforms to protect consumers and our economy as a whole," he said, recalling his speech as a candidate for president at Cooper Union in New York in March 2008. "And soon after taking office, I proposed a set of reforms to empower consumers and investors, to bring the shadowy deals that caused this crisis into the light of day, and to put a stop to taxpayer bailouts once and for all. Today, thanks to a lot of people in this room, those reforms will become the law of the land."

Those "thanks" took the edge off Obama's claim that the reforms in the bill were his idea. And Obama elaborated on the thanks. "For the last year, Chairmen Barney Frank and Chris Dodd have worked day and night—" At that the big room erupted in cheers and applause, even a few whistles. Frank grinned like a little boy who had just found a five-dollar bill on the sidewalk; Dodd beamed too. They and a dozen of their colleagues stood on the stage a few steps from Obama and everyone applauded and reached out to touch them. They reached out to each other. After a prolonged interruption, Obama returned to his text: "Barney and Chris have worked day and night to bring about this reform. And I am profoundly grateful to them." The staff who worked for and loved both men especially appreciated those words.

When his speech was finished, Obama sat down at a table to sign the bill. He used eleven pens to write out the eleven letters that spell Barack Obama, so there would be souvenirs aplenty—another Washington ritual. With his signature the United States code had grown by another two thousand pages. The world had changed. The Great Crash and its consequences, the awe and fear that Hank Paulson and Ben Bernanke so effectively conjured in Nancy Pelosi's conference room just twenty-two months earlier, had been channeled into a consequential, even historic act of Congress.

CHAPTER TWENTY-FOUR

Still Broken

It would be heartening in these cynical times to seize on the enact-ment of Dodd-Frank as evidence that even in an era of partisan strife and congressional dysfunction, the House and Senate are not really broken. After all, Congress did enact the most significant changes in the rules governing America's banks and financial markets in eighty years. Isn't that grounds for hope?

Hope perhaps, but not optimism. The story of Dodd-Frank does demonstrate that Congress still *can* work and it shows how, but only in extreme circumstances—so extreme that they are unlikely to recur for a long time. This bill could be enacted because disparate stars in the political firmament had aligned in precisely the right arrangement—a perfect constellation. This coincidence of historical and political cir-cumstances might never have happened, and might not happen again for years. The fact that they all came together this once did not repair our Congress, whose many shortcomings appeared again and again during this story.

The historical context made Dodd-Frank possible. In 2008 and 2009 the country suffered a catastrophe, in part because of Congress's own negligence—its eager complicity over nearly three decades in the systematic deregulation of the American financial system. In the 1980s, 1990s, and 2000s, deregulation became the consensus position in Washington. Republicans and most Democrats supported legisla-tive and policy changes that undid many of the regulatory restrictions enacted in the 1930s as part of the New Deal. Banks and large financial institutions won victory after victory in Congress. Finance became an ever larger sector of the American economy, and the biggest source of corporate profits.

After the crash of 2008 this history didn't look so good. Almost no one in Congress denied that something had to be done to improve regulation of financial markets. Even the staunchly pro-market, anti-regulation conservatives who dominated the Republican minority on the House Financial Services Committee offered their own proposal for regulatory reforms. Senator Shelby was blunt about the need for more regulation. "We were blinded basically by the fact that there was inadequate regulation, if any regulation," he said in a conversation in May 2009, "especially of new [financial] products, and I think a lot of that brought us to where we are today." In his Oxford Union speech in November 2009, Shelby called for "new rules . . . and clear procedures for resolving failure [*sic*] of large financial firms"—financial regulatory reform.

Dodd and Frank, both liberals who believed that strong rules, effectively enforced, would mean stronger, more stable markets, jumped at the chance to legislate changes, and from the beginning, history seemed to be on their side. Just as the Great Depression made possible Franklin Roosevelt's presidency and the New Deal, Dodd and Frank hoped the Great Crash of 2008 would make effective new regulations possible. President Obama did too.

It was the failures of President Herbert Hoover and the Republican Congresses of those years that produced big Democratic majorities in the election of 1932. The failures of George W. Bush and the three Republican Congresses that served from 2001 to 2007 similarly enabled Democrats to win what became decisive majorities in the House and Senate after 2008. This was another circumstance that made regulatory reform possible.

It also helped that the substance of possible reforms was visible long before the legislative process began. As we have seen, Obama had publicly supported changes in the rules that were also endorsed by Republicans, most prominently Paulson and his Treasury staff. They were reforms based on a consensus among many professionals and academics who followed the issues of financial regulation. That consensus did not cover every detail, but it narrowed the targets for reform to nearly all the subjects that the final bill ultimately covered. The existence of a bipartisan, expert consensus made it easier for three

Republican senators ultimately to support the bill. Legislation whose provisions enjoyed the support of Hank Paulson, prominent Republican and former head of Goldman Sachs, wasn't easily dismissed as a radical, left-wing idea.

The fact that Dodd and Frank held the key chairmanships that made them responsible for the regulatory reform effort was another fortuitous coincidence. Both men demonstrated the skills of resourceful and effective leaders in a Congress where true leadership is rare. Frank's standing with his colleagues, his success mimicking the techniques of Lyndon Johnson to win the loyalty of the Democratic members of his committee, and his ability to master the arcane subject matter of regulatory reform made possible his success. "I am amazed at how well Frank knows these subjects," said Rodgin Cohen, the leading banking lawyer in New York, who had extensive dealings with all the players. Frank's capacious intellect enabled him to lead the conference committee through the final stages of the legislative process without a serious slipup. His stamina helped too. Democratic members of the House committee, every one loyal to the chairman, said repeatedly that Frank was the only member who could have pulled off what he accomplished.

Dodd's personal attributes were even more important. He was not as brilliant as Frank, but he was bright enough to handle the subjects of regulatory reform, and his gifts as a politician were formidable. He was one of the Senate's most popular members, and he knew it. But from the beginning Dodd took nothing for granted. He put in exhausting hours cultivating colleagues, and never complained that he had wasted time. He disagreed that it had been of no help to spend countless days and nights in conversation with Shelby (and Mrs. Shelby too), because even after the failure of their efforts to write a bipartisan bill, Shelby was willing to agree on the Dodd-Shelby compromise on how to put a failing financial firm out of business. Dodd considered that deal a key to his ultimate success on the Senate floor. "The role is to govern," Dodd explained—not to score points or win arguments, but to do the serious work of managing a complicated country.

Dodd obviously believed that cultivation of colleagues was his principal job. He did it patiently, and brilliantly. His method involved more than good manners; he looked for ways to accommodate the substantive concerns of his colleagues, especially Republicans, so the final bill contained many provisions inspired by Shelby, Corker, Collins, and Snowe. In this regard the Senate differed fundamentally from the House. Frank never worried about pleasing Republicans, and the Republicans' contributions to the House bill were insignificant.

Dodd fought not just for financial regulatory reform, but for a vision of how the United States Senate ought to do business. His discipline was remarkable. He never lost his temper with a colleague or an aide. He never lost his confidence that the method by which he got a bill through the Senate was as important as the substance of the bill. His approach was utterly old-fashioned, and at odds with the bellicose culture of the permanent campaign that had come to typify the Senate in his last term of office.

The fact that it was his last term was important. Without his decision to abandon his reelection campaign, pushing a strong bill through the Senate probably would have been impossible. "If I'd been a candidate it would have been very hard to pass this bill," Dodd said after Obama had signed it. Had Dodd remained in the race, he knew he would have been a target of a vigorous Republican effort to defeat him, because—as his poll numbers confirmed—he was vulnerable. The 2010 elections, like every congressional election since 1994, would be a contest for all the marbles—control of the House and Senate. In such an environment, when every seat might be decisive, Mitch McConnell would have spared no effort to deny Dodd a big victory on regulatory reform that might have improved his chances of reelection. Once Dodd had dropped out of the race, he was a much less interesting target for Republicans.

One way to think about the importance of Dodd and Frank is to imagine that neither was on the scene. That would have made Paul Kanjorski of Pennsylvania the senior Democrat and likely chairman of House Financial Services, and Tim Johnson of South Dakota the chairman of Senate Banking. Kanjorski, erratic and self-absorbed, enjoyed little respect in the House, and Johnson, who was still recovering from a stroke-like medical event that impaired his ability to speak, was best known as a friend of the big banks that had set up their credit card operations in his state. Neither had the personal standing, political skills, or intellectual capacity to lead such a complicated legislative effort.*

"Chris Dodd might have been the only person who could have car-

---

* Because Senate Democrats continue to respect seniority when selecting chairmen of committees, Johnson became chairman of the Banking Committee in January 2011 after Dodd's retirement.

ried this off at this time, in this Senate," observed Jack Reed, Dodd's admiring colleague. Why? "One, his rapport and relationship with everyone. Two, his sense of timing, legislatively, built up over thirty years—when to [say], Okay, let's take some more time, let's listen to what you have to say, but also, We've got to move. We've got to do it, today's the day to do it. Very, very sophisticated. And also, he put his whole being into this. You know, he wasn't preoccupied with a campaign because he had stepped out of it. This is what he wanted to do, and get it done right. I think with anyone else on that committee [in charge], it would not have come out as well, or at all."

Most members of Congress leave office without ever having put their personal imprint on a significant piece of legislation. For the modern senator or House member, success in elections usually has nothing to do with legislative accomplishments. The political consultants who shape campaigns for Congress shy away from substantive debate about legislative issues, instead looking for emotional slogans that can move voters. Very few members or challengers overrule the strategies of their political consultants. Legislating is no longer the principal preoccupation of our legislators—politics is. Most commonly, it is politics by sound bite.

But not for Dodd and Frank, who were willing to try to lead their colleagues to difficult decisions about complicated issues. In the 1960s and 1970s members with strong policy interests regularly made such efforts, but in the era of partisan warfare, substantive leadership in Congress has become as rare as bipartisan harmony. Its decline has come with the ascendancy of politics over policy that has transformed the House and Senate over the last generation.

Dodd and Frank shared the policy leadership role with the talented group from the Obama administration that worked on regulatory reform. Over the course of the last three decades leadership on policy has usually come from the administration "downtown," and that was true in this case. We have seen the Obama administration's handiwork at every stage. Geithner, Wolin, and Barr at Treasury and Diana Farrell in the White House were especially important players. They set the framework for reform in their June 2009 white paper, then provided the first drafts of legislation, and many subsequent drafts as well. Although Congress altered many of their original proposals and rejected several during the legislative process, the final bill covered all the major topics in their drafts. After Dodd-Frank was signed into law, Treasury put out a three-page press release asserting that the bill "achieves the core goals laid out by the Obama Administration last June," enumerating them in detail. It is a persuasive document.

Not that the relationships were always easy. Barr, a brilliant but sometimes abrasive law professor turned government official, regularly annoyed both members and staff. "Barr is a smart man with no political judgment," Frank observed in December 2009, just after the House passed its version of the bill. But Barr learned over time, and could acknowledge his own shortcomings. "This job gives one ample opportunity to learn humility over and over and over again," he said after the bill had been finally passed. By the end, as we saw, Barr the nonsmoker was smoking cigarettes and schmoozing with Collin Peterson, chairman of the House Agriculture Committee, on the long, last day of the conference, just like an old-fashioned politician.

Wolin was a more natural pol, and on several occasions his intervention was crucial. He pacified Melissa Bean of Illinois in the House debate on preemption, when she could have caused Frank great misery and Frank needed Wolin's help to make peace.* He helped pacify the New Democrats and New Yorkers who threatened to revolt in the last days of the conference over provisions in Blanche Lincoln's derivatives provisions. And he pacified Lincoln herself, a tricky job that Dodd was happy to leave to Wolin.

President Obama was a player too. From his first meeting in the White House on February 25, 2009, with Dodd, Shelby, Frank, and Bachus, Obama made the cause of regulatory reform his own, and made it a priority for his administration.

The president's avid support was most helpful in the House. Some members of the big Democratic majority were ambivalent about their new president, but most accepted his agenda and his leadership. In the Senate, Obama's backing made Dodd's effort to find Republican collaborators more difficult. McConnell, as we have seen, thought that his first job was to frustrate Obama, to insure that his presidency failed, so he would not be reelected.

Dodd had to give up on finding a Republican partner, which ironically resulted in a tougher bill, because what Dodd called "a sixty-vote

---

* Bean's relatively meaningless provision that she negotiated with Wolin was included in the House bill, but dropped in the final version. She never raised her voice to complain.

bill" could be closer to his and the administration's desires than a bipartisan version based on compromises that might have attracted seventy-five or eighty votes. After Obama surprised everyone in Washington by winning the fight for health care reform, his stature among Democrats in Congress rose, and the confidence of Republicans sank. The health care victory created momentum behind regulatory reform.

Ultimately, Dodd and Frank could not have pushed their bill over the finish line without the Obama administration's help. And calling the bill Dodd-Frank could not change the reality that the Obama administration had written or helped to write most of it.

If Obama administration officials were important, the staffs that worked for Dodd, Frank, and other members of their committees were absolutely critical to the success of the legislation. The biggest contributors were Jeanne Roslanowick, staff director of the House Financial Services Committee, and Amy Friend, counsel to Senate Banking. After Dodd and Frank, these two played the largest individual roles in the legislative process. They were more important than any other members of either committee because they were in a better position than any member to influence their bosses and the bills they were trying to enact. Friend and Roslanowick—personal friends for many years—provided walking, talking proof of the dirty little secret that Ted Kennedy revealed in his memoir—the overwhelming amount of legislative work done by staff.

On the final day of debate in the House on the conference committee report, Frank submitted for publication in the *Congressional Record* a list of the Democratic staff who had worked on the bill. It included forty-four employees of House Financial Services, and thirty-two from Senate Banking. Secretaries and junior clerks were on the list, but also the several dozen professionals who did the substantive and political work that made Dodd-Frank happen.

These people, many with years of experience and extensive academic and professional credentials, spent thousands of hours on the peculiar forms of labor that create an act of Congress. Drafting the bill in the proper format, identifying the existing laws that had to be modified by the new one, making sure paragraph 14 of the third section of Title VII (an invented, hypothetical example) did not contradict paragraph 4 of the preamble to Title V—this sort of task ate up the working hours of staff members for a year and a half. Weekend and late-night work was routine. Frank liked to say that "the taxpayer got a real bargain" from the staff who were willing to work so long and so hard for relatively modest financial rewards. Friend's salary in 2010 was $169,349.16; Roslanowick's was $172,500. Members of Congress earned $174,000 in 2010.

Much of the work the staff did never made it into the final product, of course. An amendment that was rejected took just as much effort as one that was adopted. Much of the work that did end up in the bill came not from employees of the House and Senate, but from scores of officials at the Treasury, White House, Federal Reserve, Securities and Exchange Commission, Commodity Futures Trading Commission, Office of the Comptroller of the Currency, and the Federal Deposit Insurance Corporation, all recruited at different times to help out with the drafting. Some of the amendments offered by members were drafted by lobbyists and their lawyers, or interest groups. The lawyers on the staffs of the House and Senate offices of legislative counsel acted like editors, making sure the final versions of the bill's provisions were properly worded to fulfill the formal goal of the nonpartisan office of "leg counsel," as it is known on the Hill: "the achievement of a clear, faithful, and coherent expression of legislative policies."

In Friend's words, "It takes a village, both inside and outside Congress, to draft the thousands of details" in a bill of this importance. Not one of the villagers was a member of the House or Senate, however. A few members, especially Dodd and Frank, made the policy decisions that the drafters would memorialize, but neither they nor any other members—save perhaps those who previously worked as congressional aides*—knew how to actually write a bill.

Public opinion was another of the stars that aligned to make the success of regulatory reform possible, but not in the most obvious way. There was no groundswell of public support for a new systemic risk regulator, or for a new way to put failing financial firms out of business, or for the regulation of derivatives, a "product" very few citizens understood. The most obviously popular piece of reform legislation in the 111th Congress was the credit card bill that made it harder for card issuers to jack up their interest rates arbitrarily, but it was enacted before work on broader regulatory reform began. A new consumer protection agency enjoyed broad public support, according to opinion

---

* There were seventy-five former aides serving in the House in 2010.

polls, and it was the aspect of reform that supporters most often discussed in public.

But opinion was important in a subtler way. Poll after poll showed that Americans wanted to hold Wall Street to account for the Great Crash. A typical example was a Bloomberg News poll in the spring of 2010, which found that 56 percent of Americans agreed that "individuals in Wall Street banks whose actions helped cause the financial crisis should be punished by the federal government by limiting their compensation or banning them from working in the industry." This was a much harsher remedy than Congress ever considered. Voters were angry at Wall Street and at the recipients of government bailouts, and any competent politician knew it.

That hostility was the basis of Frank Luntz's memorandum to Republican lawmakers suggesting the words they should use to oppose regulatory reform, words like "big bank bailout bill." But Luntz's verbal gymnastics could not alter the underlying reality: The public favored tougher regulation. A *Washington Post*–ABC News poll in April 2010 found, for example, that two-thirds of the public supported "stricter federal regulations on the way banks and other financial institutions conduct their business." Some Republicans acknowledged as much, and more knew it was true. Bob Corker, the Tennessee Republican, for example, consistently took the position that a strong, comprehensive reform bill would be good both for the country and for his party. "It's good for Republicans to be for good financial reform," Corker said in January 2010.

In the end, McConnell had to accept the political reality: Opposing reform was not a winning issue for Republicans. He dropped his attempt to filibuster consideration of Dodd's bill in June 2010 because he knew that several of his Republican colleagues would not defy public opinion to support him. Throughout the eighteen months that regulatory reform was before Congress, its supporters knew that the public mood put the wind at their backs. So did the opponents.

Another less obvious factor that helped the reform effort was the inability of "industry"—the euphemism used on Capitol Hill to describe the big banks and financial institutions—to work its usual magic on Congress. For the previous three decades, Wall Street and the bankers usually got what they wanted on Capitol Hill. The crash changed that. Edward Yingling, the president of the American Bankers Association and the bankers' principal lobbyist in Washington, developed a spiel that he repeated at bankers' meetings all over the country in 2009 and 2010. He told them, "We had four strikes against us at the beginning of 2009," and enumerated: "First, the worst recession since the Great Depression, and one centered on the financial sector." Second, the TARP bailouts for the banks, "just a disaster" for banks and bankers, because they were stigmatized as undeserving recipients of taxpayers' money. Third, "an unfriendly Congress." And fourth, "a president who was a former community organizer"—in other words, not a natural friend of the banks. When he gave these talks to bankers, Yingling was trying to prepare them for the fact that the regulatory reform process was unlikely to end well for them.

The big banks and Wall Street institutions never gave up trying to shape the bill to serve their interests, but they had little success. "The big banks got nothing," Frank said with evident satisfaction.

They did a better job spending money on lobbying than they did on influencing the final version of Dodd-Frank. Financial firms including banks and credit unions, securities dealers, private equity funds, and finance and credit companies acknowledged spending nearly half a billion dollars on lobbying the 111th Congress, according to the statistics of the Center for Responsive Politics in Washington. This sounds like a lot of money, and it did represent a substantial contribution to the economy of metropolitan Washington, but for the companies in this sector, which earn billions and billions, it was a pittance. Goldman Sachs alone made more than $21 billion in profits in 2009–10.

Because—and only because—all of these components and circumstances coincided in 2010, something unusual happened: Congress passed quite a good bill that will have sweeping consequences. It will significantly change American financial markets, and—if it isn't repealed or radically rewritten—has a reasonable chance of making them safer and more stable. Dodd-Frank should induce more prudent behavior on Wall Street.

Predicting the consequences of new legislation is a risky enterprise, in part because many of the most important decisions about how the bill will be implemented lie with the regulatory agencies that must turn Dodd-Frank's mandates into practical requirements, and then must enforce them. Congress does not try to specify the details of how a new law should be implemented, leaving that job to those agencies. The rule-writing process is cumbersome, partly because it allows interested parties to lobby the agency writing the rules. In this case the big banks and many others lobbied intensely. More than two years after Dodd-Frank was enacted, the Federal Reserve, SEC, CFTC, Treasury, and others were still finalizing the regulations.

The final rules the regulators establish will be controversial; some may be challenged in court. Some will have unintended consequences—they are inevitable. And when they are agreed to, enforcement isn't automatic—regulators must be vigilant to be effective. They weren't vigilant for years leading up to the Great Crash.

But Dodd-Frank will certainly change the world. Bank profits will suffer, especially because of changes in the derivatives market, which in its unregulated state was a source of rich profits that will now be substantially slimmer. Big banks will have to hold more capital, which will also hurt their earnings, because they can't loan out the money they have set aside as capital reserves. The next Lehman Brothers, if there is one, should not collapse in an unplanned bankruptcy and cause turmoil across the world. The Consumer Financial Protection Bureau has begun to issue new rules intended to protect the public.

The way this story unfolded did not follow a civics book model of how Congress should work. Instead the plot line reflected the realities of the modern Congress.

The first of those is decidedly un-modern: Congress is a reactive institution, and always has been. This was what the founders wanted: a legislative branch that would proceed with caution, part of a system of checks and balances that discourages rash action and the exercise of arbitrary power. The founders got their wish; the country got a government that can be frustratingly slow to confront problems before they become crises.

A reality in the modern era has been the ascendancy of the executive branch at the expense of Congress. Presidents since Theodore Roosevelt and Woodrow Wilson have undermined the founders' intention that the presidency described in Article II of the Constitution be subordinate to the Congress described in Article I. Presidents propose, and Congresses dispose—that is now the standard operating procedure, as it was in this instance.

Dodd and Frank, both fiercely proud of their institutions, were determined to influence the legislation, and they did. But their institutional pride and loyalty, typical of their generation of senators and

House members, is much less common now, and they have both retired from Congress. In the era of partisan warfare, loyalty to party is usually stronger than loyalty to the institutions of Congress. Dodd's concerns for preserving an old-fashioned way of doing bipartisan business in the Senate, an expression of his institutional loyalty, seemed antiquated in the Senate led by Harry Reid and Mitch McConnell, two partisan warriors.

Dodd and Frank both cared about governing, and about policy, neither a typical concern in Congress now. One of the most revealing episodes in this story was the urgent phone call Dodd received from Reid, his deputy Dick Durbin of Illinois, New York's Chuck Schumer, and Robert Menendez of New Jersey—most of the Democratic leadership of the Senate, all on the phone at the same time—in May, when Dodd was trying to find a compromise with Shelby on the "too big to fail" section of the bill. They told Dodd not to make any deals with Shelby. But Dodd considered that deal crucial to his chances of getting the bill enacted. The senators who called him weren't as worried about the fate of the bill—they wanted to score political points. Dodd, exploiting his own stature and seniority, ignored them.

Only the big Democratic majorities in both houses (which disappeared in the elections of 2010) allowed Dodd and Frank to legislate such broad reforms. They prevailed against the culture of the modern Congress, which undermines collaboration across party lines and minimizes the chances of commonsense, good-government solutions. House Republicans, as we have seen, had no interest in collaboration. A few Republican senators did, especially Bob Corker of Tennessee, but he did not have the standing in his own caucus to bring along allies, or to defy McConnell and Shelby.

Olympia Snowe of Maine, one of the last Republican moderates and one of the three Republicans to vote for the bill in the Senate, announced her retirement eighteen months after Dodd-Frank was enacted. In interviews she complained that the "sensible center" had disappeared from the Senate, along with bipartisan collaboration. "Congress is becoming more like a parliamentary system," she wrote in an article for *The Washington Post* explaining her decision, "where everyone simply votes with their party and those in charge employ every possible tactic to block the other side."

Snowe was describing the triumph of politics over policy. This is the distinguishing characteristic of the modern Congress, and its impact is profound. It affects every member, because the permanent campaign requires nearly every one of them to devote a day or two of every week to fundraising, a dreary and demeaning task. It surely affects the decisions of serious citizens about whether or not to run for Congress in the first place.

In a conversation on this subject, Dodd observed that the country still produced serious people who cared about policy issues, "but the problem is, they just don't gravitate to politics. That's the unfortunate part." If you mention the idea of running for Congress to many such people, Dodd said, "they look at you like you absolutely lost your mind." Who is eager for a job that requires asking strangers for money? And requires service in a "democratic" institution that doesn't operate on the basis of majority rule? Some good people still decide to run for the House or Senate, but many of the most serious—like Dodd and Snowe—go in the other direction.

So Congress is dominated by people with political skills but limited expertise. Of the 535 members of House and Senate, those who have a sophisticated understanding of the financial markets and their regulation could probably fit on the twenty-five-man roster of a Major League Baseball team. Members' ignorance empowers lobbyists and staff. In this case it empowered Dodd and Frank, who both enjoyed deference from most of their Democratic colleagues on their committees who were happy to leave the details to them.

The people members like to call their bosses—the voters—are also ignorant about complicated policy issues such as financial regulatory reform. Americans are an apolitical people. Many—recent polls suggest it is a majority—are reflexively hostile to politicians and government, and disinclined to make the investment of time and energy necessary to become informed voters. If they could come back to visit us today, the founders might find this aspect of American life the most disappointing. They were optimistic men of the Enlightenment who thought their fellow citizens would jump at the chance to participate in the affairs of the new republic they were creating. Instead we have a country where thousands of school districts have stopped teaching civics altogether, a minority of citizens understands how their government works, and a large fraction of the population never bothers to vote.

Congress is more representative today than it was in the early years of the republic, when suffrage was restricted to white men who owned property. But now it is representative in every sense of the word. It represents ignorance and emotion as well as nobler qualities of the electorate. We don't get a House and Senate that are better than we are.

Numerous features of congressional life discourage bipartisan collaboration and reinforce the partisan warfare. Members rarely have opportunities to socialize together, and rarely make friends across the partisan divide. They don't reside in the Washington area, but scurry home to their states and districts as often as possible, usually every weekend. And their weekends typically begin on Thursday and end on Tuesday. Trips overseas by congressional delegations historically provided opportunities to make friends from the other party, but those trips, often criticized in the news media, have become rarer and rarer.

The principal deterrent to bipartisan collaboration has been the ascendance of partisan warfare. Partisan warriors, often beginning with the party leaders in both houses, actively discourage efforts to build bridges. Ray LaHood, a moderate Republican from Illinois who served in the House from 1995 to 2009, then became President Obama's secretary of transportation, tells the story of how he and Rahm Emanuel, then a Democratic congressman from Chicago, organized dinners during 2008 for seven or eight House members of each party as a way for them to get to know one another. When the Republican leadership got wind of these affairs, they "castigated" LaHood, as he put it. "Leaders in my party called me up and said, Were you crazy? One time I had a Republican colleague come up to me on the floor and say, 'What are you doing having dinner with the devil?' "

LaHood did not identify the colleague who considered Democrats the devil, but it could have been one of many. Republicans like LaHood—moderates who believe in effective government and are eager for bipartisan cooperation—are all but extinct in the House, and rare in the Senate. The Grand Old Party—a nickname for the Republicans born in the 1870s, when it was still the party of Lincoln, and still young—is not what it used to be even in the 1980s when Ronald Reagan was president. The GOP has moved further and further to the right, and by 2012 was dominated by an anti-government faction preoccupied with preserving low tax rates, minimizing the role of the federal government, and waging political war against the Democrats.

These new Republicans believe in enforcing ideological discipline. As a result of concerted efforts by conservative groups and the fervid Republican "base" voters, now predominantly evangelical Christians, the moderates who provided Republican leaders for decades have been marginalized or drummed out of the party. Political scientists who study polarization in Congress have found that, judged by the votes they cast, Republican members have become steadily more conservative over the last generation, and have moved to the right more quickly than Democrats have moved to the left.

Congressional Democrats are also more ideologically consistent than at any time since World War II. They are mostly liberals who defend the policies and programs of Democratic presidents since Franklin Roosevelt, and promote government as a defender of the weak and provider of opportunity. Democratic members of the House and Senate are appalled by the anti-government faction of the Republicans, and rarely try to engage its members. The most conservative Republicans are appalled right back. The breakdown of comity and repeated failures to find bipartisan solutions to the biggest problems, including financial regulatory reform, reflect this polarization. Increasingly, Republicans and Democrats just disagree, fundamentally, about nearly everything.

When they express their disagreements the way political parties do in the parliaments of Europe—with virtually unanimous votes for or against proposals advanced by the government of the day, or in this country by the president's administration—then the system envisioned by the founders cannot work. The founders rejected a parliamentary system, and chose instead a Congress of two different bodies and an independent president. They assumed that this Congress would work the way their Constitutional Convention worked—by negotiation and compromise involving all factions. If negotiation and compromise are ruled out, as they so often are in Washington today, and if one party is not in control of the government the way the Democrats were in 2009–10, then dysfunction and stalemate are inevitable.

A final curiosity about Dodd-Frank: This big, substantial, and consequential new law never really penetrated the public consciousness. As we've seen, it wasn't even well understood by most of the members of the House and Senate who voted for or against it. All of its complex provisions were never carefully dissected in House or Senate hearings, or by the popular news media.

"Dodd-Frank" was quickly reduced to the status of political symbol. Every Republican presidential candidate in 2012 came out against the new law, though none spelled out his or her objections in any detail, or said what, if anything, should take its place. President Obama boasted that the bill was tough on Wall Street and would help prevent another financial crisis; it became part of his campaign for "fairness."

And the bill itself remained an enigma. More than two years after the law was enacted, few citizens understood, for example, that the new Financial Stability Oversight Council, chaired by the secretary of the treasury and consisting of the heads of eight regulatory agencies and one public member, was given unprecedented powers to instruct regulators to limit specific risky behaviors by financial firms—in other words, to order them not to engage in practices deemed too perilous. The council can even order the FDIC to close down a financial firm if it decides, by a two-thirds vote that includes the treasury secretary's, that the firm's risky behavior endangers the stability of the financial system. Someday the use of this extraordinary power could have enormous consequences, but it never got much attention in the legislative process that produced Dodd-Frank.

One reason for this lack of public understanding is that Congress has awful public relations. Members rarely connect with voters on complex, substantive issues. Even talented members like Dodd and Frank slip into a Capitol Hill argot when they are talking to constituents about legislation, no doubt baffling their voters. Congress operates behind a sort of curtain in a world of its own, a world of mumbo jumbo: subcommittee and committee hearings, markups, Rules Committee rules, motions to recommit, amendments in the first and second degree, cloture votes, and all the rest. The mumbo jumbo describes the legislative process as members of the House and Senate have shaped it over the years. It can be learned, but not without study and effort. Very few citizens outside the Congress master this Byzantine world. As a result, there is only a tiny attentive audience for what goes on in Congress—perhaps ten or fifteen thousand professors, journalists, lobbyists, government officials, and lawyers, in a country of more than 300 million.

The members of that tiny informed audience, like members of the House and Senate, tend to accept the mumbo jumbo as just the nature of the beast—standard operating obfuscations. So the House and Senate go on doing business in ways that citizens might disapprove of strongly, if they really understood what was happening. Would the public support the Senate's Rule XXII that permits nearly unlimited filibusters, thus assuring that the majority does not rule in the United States Senate? Would the voters endorse the stern party discipline that has prevailed in the House for nearly two decades, making bipartisan collaboration so rare? These are important matters; changing them could transform Congress and make it less dysfunctional. But members are almost never asked to explain their positions on "process" issues like these. They just play the old games behind the curtain. They know that almost no one is paying close attention.

But even without studying it carefully, the country has made up its mind about Congress: Americans think their House and Senate are dreadful. According to repeated Gallup polls, fewer than 50 percent of the country has approved of the way Congress does its business since a brief burst of patriotic enthusiasm after 9/11. In recent years Congress's numbers have descended precipitously, down to 10 percent approval in early 2012. Gallup had never recorded a lower number.

The gridlock in the 112th Congress (2010–12) brought the number so low, but approval of Congress never rose above 25 percent after 2010 began. The country was still reeling from the Great Crash, the public mood was sour, and Congress was an easy target. Years of negative stories about congressional corruption, lobbying, earmarks, and sleazy campaign contributions had taken a toll. So had Congress's many substantive failures, beginning with its habit of spending more money than it was willing to raise from taxes, year after year.

So Dodd-Frank was an anomaly—an accomplishment produced by a catastrophe, and by the fear engendered by that catastrophe. There will be other catastrophes in the future, and they may again push this clumsiest, least efficient of American institutions into action. But our Congress is still broken.

Acknowledgments

A book like this one can be written only if the people who know what happened are willing to talk about it. Thanks to Chris Dodd and Barney Frank, I had the best possible sources for this story, so my acknowledgments begin with them.

Both met with me repeatedly in 2009 and 2010 to talk about what was happening with the legislation that became the Dodd-Frank Act. I recorded our interviews, then transcribed them; I preserved more than 110,000 words of Dodd and Frank, enough to fill a book almost as big as this one. Frank also took the time to dictate notes over two months in 2009 and shared them with me. Many of the most revealing anecdotes in this book come from those interviews and notes.

Dodd and Frank also told their staffs that they could talk freely with me. This allowed me to avoid one of the implicit rules of modern Congress: that staff must disappear from public view. All attention from the news media, especially, must go to their bosses, the members of the House and Senate—this is fundamental. When you read or hear news stories about acts of Congress in the future, notice how often you are given the name of a staff member other than a designated spokesperson. This will be easy, because you will rarely get a name. Staff are invaluable sources for reporters on Capitol Hill, but they invariably speak anonymously, "off the record," and usually give their bosses all the credit for ideas, deals, even words that the staff actually produces.

I hope that in this book you get a fuller picture of the critical role that staff play. Thanks to the dozens of staff members who spoke to me, I certainly did. Amy Friend, Jeanne Roslanowick, Ed Silverman, and Dave Smith were invaluable; each answered hundreds of questions. Michael Beresik, Julie Chon, Andrew Miller, Jonathan Miller,

Jim Segel, Kara Stein, Lawranne Stewart, Charles Yi—these and many others in the House and Senate helped me understand the legislative process and their role in it. I am extremely grateful to every staff person on Capitol Hill who helped me.

Members also gave me a lot of their time, often in repeated interviews or over meals, and provided a rich education. I particularly thank Senators Richard Shelby, Bob Corker, Judd Gregg, Jack Reed, and Mark Warner; and Congressmen Spencer Bachus, Ed Perlmutter, Jim Himes, Bill Foster, and Jeb Hensarling, who each gave me multiple interviews. Representative Jim Cooper of Tennessee, whom I have known since he was an undergraduate at the University of North Carolina in the 1970s, shared much wisdom. Over the two years I worked on this book, I spoke to several dozen other members as well.

From the executive branch, Michael Barr and Neal Wolin of Treasury and Diana Farrell of the White House staff were especially helpful. Gary Gensler of the Commodity Futures Trading Commission gave me a long and useful interview.

I would like to acknowledge several participants in the story who provided significant help: Rodgin Cohen, Camden Fine, Travis Plunkett, Paul Volcker, Elizabeth Warren, Edward Yingling, and Mark Zandi. Douglas Elliott, a retired investment banker now at the Brookings Institution, was a guide and teacher. A number of banking lobbyists also helped, but asked that their names not be mentioned. Donald A. Ritchie, the official Senate historian, filled many gaps in my knowledge.

As it has for nearly half a century, *The Washington Post* gave me invaluable assistance. No one has had a better employer. Don Graham, the proprietor, Katharine Weymouth, the publisher, Marcus Brauchli, executive editor, and many colleagues have given me support and encouragement. When the words "from *The Washington Post*" appear after your name, your calls get answered, your requests for interviews are nearly always granted. Brady Dennis, the talented young reporter who covered the evolution of Dodd-Frank for the *Post*, was a generous colleague and a good sounding board; special thanks to him. Alice Crites, an extraordinary researcher and sleuth, helped me with this project, as she has with so many over the years.

The Woodrow Wilson International Center for Scholars in Washington gave me a comfortable perch for a year that allowed me to complete my interviews and begin writing this book. Retired congressman Lee Hamilton was the center's president when I arrived, and he became a helpful source. He organized a bipartisan lunch of ten other former members of the House and Senate to discuss how Congress has changed in the modern era, a memorable event. Michael Van Dusen, the Wilson Center's chief operating officer, was generous with his time and with good advice. The Wilson Center, now run by former congresswoman Jane Harman, is an island of intellectual rigor in a town where that is too rare.

I also want to thank Kathryn Dunn Tenpas, a professor and director of the University of Pennsylvania's Washington Semester Program. She introduced me to four of her best students who did research projects for me: Alex Bolton, Clare Foran, David Gurian-Peck, and Justin Rand. The work of these four saved me many hours, and enriched this book. Working with them was an invigorating experience.

Amanda Urban, my loyal literary agent, was skeptical about this project when I first proposed it, but she believes in supporting her writers, and she has certainly supported me. This is my third book with Jonathan Segal of Knopf, one of the smartest, most thorough editors in New York, who pushes me when I need pushing, and wields his pencil—yes, he still uses a pencil—with uncommon skill. His assistant Joey McGarvey gave me some extraordinary help way beyond her normal duties, and I thank her for that. The entire Knopf team consists of all-stars; I am proud to benefit from their talents.

Four friends read the manuscript and made good suggestions for how to improve it: my best friend for half a century, Thomas Powers; Jonathan Davidson, now chief of staff to Senator Michael Bennet of Colorado; Steve Weisman, a former *New York Times* reporter who is a fellow at the Peterson Institute for International Economics; and Len Downie, my colleague and pal at the *Post* since we were summer interns together in 1964.

Hannah Jopling, to whom this book is dedicated, is one of nature's wonders. A creative anthropologist, she is also one tough critic. She made this a better book, just as she has improved every aspect of my life for nearly five decades. Our daughters, Emily Thelin and Charlotte Kaiser, and their splendid husbands, Josh Thelin and Nick Peterson, and my miraculous grandson, Linus Hazard Peterson, provide my emotional armor. They are the greatest.

All of the mistakes are mine.

Notes

CHAPTER ONE *"I Could Hear Everyone Gulp"*
I interviewed Hank Paulson, Chris Dodd, Barney Frank, Spencer Bachus, Steny Hoyer, Richard Shelby, David Smith, and four staff members who attended the September 18 meeting and shared their notes with me but asked not to be identified. Bachus also gave me the notes he made on the meeting. Dodd shared a manuscript that he and a colleague wrote describing the meeting.

5   *"There was an almost surreal quality"*: Hank Paulson, *On the Brink* (New York: Business Plus, 2010), 240.

5   *"I'll call him and set up"*: Steny Hoyer interview with the author.

6   *"Madame Speaker"*: Nancy Pelosi on *60 Minutes*, September 29, 2008.

6   *"We need legislation"*: Paulson, *On the Brink*, 255.

6   *"He hadn't called us!"*: Hoyer interview with the author.

8   *"They'll kill me up there"*: David Wessel, *In Fed We Trust* (New York: Crown Business, 2009), 203.

8   *"This is only going to work"*: Andrew Ross Sorkin, *Too Big to Fail* (New York: Viking, 2009), 442.

9   *"If we don't act"*: Wessel, *In Fed We Trust*, 204.

9   *"It is a matter of days"*: Paulson, *On the Brink*, 259.

9   *"Our tools are not sufficient"*: Wessel, *In Fed We Trust*, 204.

9   *"This is a save-your-country moment"*: Spencer Bachus notes from the meeting.

9   *If the expected actions:* Ibid.

9   *"I kind of scared them"*: Wessel, *In Fed We Trust*, 204.

9   *"I've never seen"*: Notes of a participant, confidential source.

9   *Congress, Paulson said:* Notes of a participant, confidential source.

9   *"an eerie, jaw-dropping silence"*: Chris Dodd unpublished account of the meeting.

10   *"a salutary effect"*: Notes of a participant, confidential source.

10   *"big enough to make a difference"*: Bachus notes.

10   *"Chris, they should have"*: Chris Dodd unpublished account and interview with the author.

11   *"If you put in"*: Bachus notes.

11   *"Heaven help us all"*: Notes of a participant, confidential source.

11   *"the meeting was starting"*: Notes of a participant, confidential source.

11   *"If you want something"*: Bachus notes.

11   *"If you think"*: Ibid.

11   *"It takes me two weeks"*: Notes of a participant, confidential source.

11   *"If what is at stake"*: Notes of a participant, confidential source.

11   *"We have to have"*: Notes of a participant, confidential source.

11   *"If we don't help homeowners"*: Bachus notes.

12 *"This is a national crisis"*: Ibid.
14 *"We're told not to worry"*: "Area's Lawmakers Evenly Split on Bailout Plan," *Los Angeles Daily News*, Sept. 30, 2008.
15 *"Undermining the basic principles"*: Tom Price press release, September 29, 2008.
15 *"I've been talking"*: Paulson, *On the Brink*, 287.
15 *"The specter had been raised"*: Liaquat Ahamed, "Did Lehman's Fall Matter?," *Newsweek* online, May 18, 2009.

CHAPTER TWO   *The Man Who Wasn't Gray*
I interviewed Barney Frank, Lee Hamilton, and Jim Segel. *Barney Frank* by Stuart E. Weisberg, published in 2009 by the University of Massachusetts Press, was very helpful.
19 *"Long before peace marchers"*: Weisberg, *Barney Frank*, 51.
20 *"My short attention span"*: Ibid., 117.
20 *"Even as a freshman"*: Jim Segel interview with author.
20 *"He was depressed"*: Ibid.
21 *"I was worried"*: Ibid., 193.
21 *"Part of our job"*: Quoted in Weisberg, *Barney Frank*, 193.
21 *"I'm not sure his staff"*: Segel interview with the author.
22 *"Anyone who tells you"*: Quoted by Jeffrey Toobin in *The New Yorker*, January 12, 2009.
22 *"People busted their ass"*: Weisberg, *Barney Frank*, 223–24.

CHAPTER THREE   *What Is to Be Done?*
I interviewed Barney Frank, Jeanne Roslanowick, and David Smith.
28 *"Ninety-five percent"*: Edward M. Kennedy, *True Compass* (New York: Twelve, 2009), 486.
29 *"I can remember"*: Jeanne Roslanowick interview with the author.
29 *nearly four hundred defeated or retired members:* Figures compiled by the watchdog group LegiStorm and available at http://www.legistorm.com/pro/revolving _door.html.
29 *"an extraordinary combination"*: Barney Frank interview with the author.
29 *"To write good laws"*: Roslanowick interview with the author.
30 *"I needed someone"*: Frank interview with the author.
30 *"Forgetting that these"*: David Smith interview with the author.
36 *"I'm going to start"*: Barney Frank dictation for the author.
37 *"the president did gently but clearly"*: Ibid.
37 *"If there is this view"*: Ibid.

CHAPTER FOUR   *An Orgy of Outrage*
I interviewed Barney Frank, Paul Kanjorski, Ed Perlmutter, Spencer Bachus, Jeb Hensarling, Dave Smith, and Jeanne Roslanowick.
39 *$182.3 billion:* GAO report at http://www.scribd.com/doc/20015353/GAO -Report-Status-of-Government-Assistance-Provided-to-AIG.
40 *"would be disastrous"*: Wessel, *In Fed We Trust*, 195.
42 *expressing "outrage"*: Paul Kanjorski press release.
43 *"You better take good care"*: Barney Frank interview with the author.
44 *"totally surprised me"*: Barney Frank dictation for the author.
45 *$2.7 trillion:* "Downgrades and Downfall," *Washington Post*, December 31, 2008.

46 *This was the first time:* "Rage at AIG Swells as Bonuses Go Out," *Washington Post*, March 17, 2009.

46 *"death threats and angry letters":* Ibid.

47 *"There's a tidal wave":* The transcript of this hearing can be found at http:// democrats.financialservices.house.gov/hearings111.shtml. A tape of the hearing is at http//financialserv.edgeboss.net/wmedia/financialserv/hearing031809 .wvx.

51 *"politicians are motivated":* R. Kent Weaver, "The Politics of Blame Avoidance," *Journal of Public Policy*, Vol. 6, No. 4 (October–December 1986), 371–98.

52 *"serious reservations about":* Frank dictation for the author, April 19, 2009.

52 *Geithner and Bernanke gave testimony:* The transcript of the hearing can be found at http://democrats.financialservices.house.gov/media/file/hearings/ 111/111-20.pdf.

CHAPTER FIVE   *A Politician for Life*

I interviewed Chris Dodd, Barney Frank, Ed Silverman, Douglas Bennet, and Morgan McGinley.

60 *"There was nobody to talk to":* "Dodd's Other Campaign: Restoring Dad's Reputation," *New York Times*, September 24, 2007.

61 *"Having not always lived up":* "Political Debt and a Son's Enduring Loyalty," *New York Times*, March 9, 1989.

61 *"Lest there be":* "Dodd Announces Candidacy," *The Day*, May 18, 1974.

65 *in polls, Dodd was never favored: Washington Post*–ABC News polls available at http://www.washingtonpost.com/wp-srv/politics/polls/postpoll_121107.html.

66 *Dodd's Banking Committee:* "Dodd on Trail, Committee on Hold," *Washington Post*, November 7, 2007.

66 *Frank was frustrated:* Barney Frank interview with the author.

66 *"Things were turning sour":* "For Harried Chris Dodd, It Was Iowa Where Things Started Unraveling," *Hartford Courant*, January 7, 2010.

CHAPTER SIX   *Back in the Game*

I interviewed Chris Dodd, Amy Friend, Edward Yingling, Barney Frank, Richard Shelby, Annette Shelby, William Duhnke, Mark Oesterle, Mike House, and Carter Eskew.

67 *several dozen reporters:* "Senate Time Tolls Against Candidates," *Washington Post*, January 24, 2008.

68 *"It was the Kennedy magic":* Amy Friend interviews with the author.

71 *"I had not known":* Paulson, *On the Brink*, 11.

73 *seven of them came to dinner:* Tim Johnson, Evan Bayh, Mark Warner, Jack Reed, Charles Schumer, Jon Tester, and Robert Menendez.

75 *"The basis of this bill":* Chris Dodd interview with the author.

75 *"I remember thinking":* Friend interview with the author.

76 *"something better":* Edward Yingling interview with the author.

76 *"had no substantive thing":* Barney Frank dictation for the author.

77 *"failed us":* Richard Shelby interview with the author.

77 *"He's from across the tracks":* Mike House interview with the author.

77 *"I liked his energy level":* Annette Shelby interview with the author.

79 *"We had footage":* Carter Eskew interview with the author.

81 *"Whoever thought this place":* Chris Dodd interview with MSNBC, Sep-

tember 13, 2010, transcript at http://www.msnbc.com/id/39085380/ns/politics
-the_exit_interviews/.

82 *"This is going to be difficult"*: "Narrow Vote Hurts Card Reform Bill," *American Banker*, April 1, 2009.

CHAPTER SEVEN *"Downtown" Takes the Lead*

I interviewed Michael Barr, Diana Farrell, Neal Wolin, Jeanne Roslanowick, David Smith, Amy Friend, Ed Silverman, Barney Frank, and Chris Dodd.

84 *"This is a bill"*: Diana Farrell interview with the author.

85 *"intense, blank-sheet-of-paper sessions"*: Ibid.

86 *"modernizing the system"*: Ibid.

86 *"there was simply no room"*: Michael Barr interview with the author.

86 *"They are farther along"*: Jeanne Roslanowick interview with the author.

87 *"Rahm and I have a very good relationship"*: Barney Frank interview with the author.

89 *In the two years leading up to the elections of 2008:* The numbers come from the Center for Responsive Politics' opensecrets.org website. They include donations from political action committees (PACs) sponsored by companies and industry groups, and from individuals identifiable as working for firms in the two sectors. The financial sector includes finance, insurance, and real estate.

89 *"It is theoretically possible"*: Frank interview with the author.

90 *"A New Foundation"*: Text of the white paper can be found at http://www.treasury.gov/initiatives/Documents/FinalReport_web.pdf.

91 *"Historic Overhaul of Finance Rules"*: *Wall Street Journal*, June 18, 2009.

94 *"I look forward"*: Obama's speech can be found at http://www.whitehouse.gov/the-press-office/remarks-president-regulatory-reform.

CHAPTER EIGHT *A Rich Variety of Humanity*

I interviewed Barney Frank and Jeanne Roslanowick. Frank also dictated notes that he shared with me, as noted below.

96 *"It's the old version"*: Barney Frank interviews with the author.

98 *"So I called her"*: Ibid.

98 *"a silly idea"*: Jeanne Roslanowick interview with the author.

99 *"The single biggest thing"*: Barney Frank dictation for the author, April 19, 2009.

106 *"Let me just ask you"*: From the transcript of the hearing.

CHAPTER NINE *Politics First*

I interviewed Barney Frank, Elizabeth Warren, Travis Plunkett, Michael Barr, Neal Wolin, Jeanne Roslanowick, and David Smith. Frank also dictated notes that he shared with me, as noted below.

108 *"For example"*: Barney Frank dictation for the author.

108 *"these financial people"*: Barney Frank interview with the author.

110 *"As a result"*: "In Crisis, Banks Dig In for Fight Against Rules," *New York Times*, May 31, 2009.

113 *"They pay more in interest"*: Elizabeth Warren interview with the author.

113 *"They all told me"*: Ibid.

114 *"financial product safety commission"*: *Democracy*, No. 5, Summer 2007, available at http://www.democracyjournal.org/5/6528.php.

114 *he knew Warren personally:* Michael Barr interview with the author.

114 *consumer protection should be:* Neal Wolin interview with the author.

115 *"The extent to which"*: Frank dictation for the author, February 28, 2009.

115 *"It was only"*: Warren interview with the author.

116 *"If what they were feeling"*: Jeanne Roslanowick interview with the author.

117 *"Kanjorski and I"*: Frank interview with the author.

CHAPTER TEN *An Impotent Minority*
I interviewed Spencer Bachus, Bob Corker, and two confidential sources on the staff.

120 *He agreed that:* Spencer Bachus interview with the author.

122 *"They've done that all over"*: Ibid.

122 *At one point:* Ibid.; Bob Corker interview with the author.

123 *"Then we'll blow this thing up"*: Confidential source on Financial Services staff.

CHAPTER ELEVEN *Peddling Influence*
I interviewed Camden Fine, Edward Yingling, Barney Frank, Chris Dodd, and four banking lobbyists who asked to remain unidentified.

128 *more than $40 million:* Center for Responsive Politics, http://www.opensecrets .org

128 *Political action committees and individuals:* Ibid. Data can be found at http://www .opensecrets.org/industries/totals.php?cycle=2012&ind=F.

128 *a total of $62.9 million:* Based on Center for Responsive Politics statistics. Original press release can be found at http://www.campaignmoney.org/press room/2009/07/08/analysis-house-financial-services-committee-received-62–9 -million-in-campaign-contributions-from-financial-.

129 *financial sector donations of $1,041,298:* Center for Responsive Politics calculation at http://www.opensecrets.org/industries/summary.php?ind=F&cycle=2008 &recipdetail=S&memY.

129 *Dodd received $6,081,836:* http://www.opensecrets.org/industries/summary.php ?ind=F&cycle=2008&recipdetail=S&mem=Y.

130 *"does affect legislation"*: Quoted in Brooks Jackson, *Honest Graft: Big Money and the American Political Process* (New York: Alfred A. Knopf, 1988).

130 *more than $3.1 million:* http://www.opensecrets.org/lobby/lobby_topcontribs .php?cycle=2010&type=L.

133 *"a new and powerful agency"*: Obama's speech of June 17 can be found at http://www.whitehouse.gov/the_press_office/Remarks-of-the-President -on-Regulatory-Reform.

134 *$5 million hardly compared:* More detailed figures from the Center for Responsive Politics are available at http://www.opensecrets.org/lobby/list_indus.php.

135 *"When the CFPA proposal"*: Edward Yingling interview with the author.

137 *"We'll have this debate"*: Barney Frank interview with the author.

137 *From the outset:* Yingling interview with the author.

141 *in a letter written*: Barney Frank provided a copy of Fine's letter.

CHAPTER TWELVE *"We've Got an Opportunity Here"*
I interviewed Chris Dodd, Barney Frank, and Ed Silverman.

142 *"The members don't want"*: Barney Frank interview with the author.

143 *still in serious political trouble*: Quinnipiac University polls of Connecticut voters can be found at http://www.quinnipiac.edu/institutes-centers/polling-institute/ connecticut.

144 *The first, in* Portfolio *magazine:* *Portfolio* magazine went out of business. Its article was reported in *The Wall Street Journal*, "Dodd Tied to Countrywide Loans," June 13, 2008.

144 *published a column:* Kevin Rennie, "Dodd's 'Cottage': A Cozy Purchase," *Hartford Courant*, February 22, 2009.

144 *a subsequent* Courant *news story:* "A Few Real Estate Deals Among Friends," *Hartford Courant*, March 15, 2009.

148 *"First of all the subject matter":* Chris Dodd interview with the author.

148 *When Dodd asked Shelby directly:* Ed Silverman interview with the author.

CHAPTER THIRTEEN   *In the Legislative Weeds*

I interviewed Barney Frank, Andrew Miller, and Jeanne Roslanowick.

150 *"They're busy":* Barney Frank interview with the author.

150 *"The substance has problems":* Jeanne Roslanowick interview with the author.

151 *"The administration badly over-drafted":* Frank interview with the author.

152 *more than 2,700 individual lobbyists:* More detailed figures from the Center for Responsive Politics are available at http://www.opensecrets.org/lobby/list_indus.php.

153 *"Floyd Stoner could take me out":* Roslanowick interview with the author.

156 *"coherent and comprehensive information":* Jeanne Roslanowick memo to the author.

158 *"You have to put everything":* Andrew Miller interview with the author.

CHAPTER FOURTEEN   *Making Sausage*

I interviewed Camden Fine, Barney Frank, Jeanne Roslanowick, Jim Segel, and Elizabeth Warren.

160 *"I got a call":* Camden Fine interview with the author. He also provided his e-mail to the board.

165 *"You play to the anger":* Jeanne Roslanowick interview with the author.

165 *"Barney went through it":* Ibid.

166 *"how it really works":* Elizabeth Warren interview with the author.

166 *"If you're a Democrat":* Barney Frank interview with the author.

168 *"This is only a markup":* Jim Segel interview with the author.

170 *"In some cases":* Frank interview with the author.

170 *"This notion":* Ibid.

172 *on this occasion:* A webcast of this markup session can be found at http://financialserv.edgeboss.net/wmedia/financialserv/markup101409.wvx.

177 *When asked about this:* "Campbell's Car Dealer Exemption Chastised," *Orange County Register*, October 23, 2009.

178 *"I knew I couldn't win":* Frank interview with the author.

181 *"public and private companies":* "Black Caucus Seeks to Ease Radio's Woes," *New York Times*, December 3, 2009.

184 *she raised a third of her campaign cash:* Center for Responsive Politics statistics, available at http://www.opensecrets.org/politicians/industries.php?cycle=2010&cid=N00024875&type=I&newmem=N.

CHAPTER FIFTEEN   *Looking for a Path*

I interviewed Amy Friend, Andrew Miller, Ed Silverman, and Richard Shelby.

189 *"When you put something":* Amy Friend interview with the author.

191 *"I can't imagine":* Ed Silverman interview with the author.

192 *"was appalled":* Andrew Miller interview with the author.

193 *"The staff produced":* Silverman interview with the author.

197 *"I believed that the American people":* The full text of Shelby's speech is at http://shelby.senate.gov/public/index.cfm/newsreleases?ID=0da0c344–802a-23ad-4f44-c4821774fb52.

CHAPTER SIXTEEN   *The House Acts*

Quotations from floor debates and speeches are available in the Congressional Record, which can be accessed at http://www.gpo.gov/fdsys/browse/collection .action?collectionCode=CREC.

207   *leaked word of it:* "House Republicans Huddle with Lobbyists to Kill Financial Reform Bill," *Roll Call* website: http://www.rollcall.com/news/-41311–1.html.

223   *"to have a record vote":* Quoted in "The Motion to Recommit in the House: The Creation, Evisceration, and Restoration of a Minority Right," a 2003 paper by Donald R. Wolfensberger of the Woodrow Wilson Center for Scholars, available at https://www.msu.edu/~rohde/Wolfensberger.pdf?q=recommit.

CHAPTER SEVENTEEN   *Searching for Consensus*

I interviewed Mike House, Richard Shelby, and Ed Silverman.

228   *"We're meeting":* Richard Shelby interview with the author.

229   *"He'll drive":* Mike House interview with the author.

233   *$13.2 million:* Center for Responsive Politics statistics for 2009. Numbers can be found at http://www.opensecrets.org/pfds/averages.php.

237   *"Perception is reality":* Quoted by Nicholas Lemann, "The Word Lab: The Mad Science Behind What the Candidates Say," *The New Yorker,* October 16–23, 2000.

239   *"It looked like":* Ed Silverman interview with the author.

CHAPTER EIGHTEEN   *More Tactical Maneuvers*

I interviewed Bob Corker, Jonathan Davidson, Chris Dodd, Barney Frank, Amy Friend, Tom Griscom, Tom Ingram, Ed Silverman, Nathan Steinwald, and Mark Warner.

242   *"A great opportunity":* Bob Corker interviews with the author.

244   *"There were a lot":* Tom Ingram interview with the author.

244   *wrote a column:* Tom Griscom, "Primer on Dissecting the Senate," *Chattanooga Times Free Press,* Nov. 12, 2006.

244   *An independent poll:* Mason-Dixon poll cited in ibid.

245   *"tenacious, persistent, questioning":* Ingram interview with the author.

247   *But turning the quest over:* Chris Dodd and Mark Warner interviews with the author.

247   *The two men and their aides:* Dodd and Corker interviews with the author.

248   *From their first meeting:* Amy Friend interview with the author.

249   *The Democratic staff:* Jonathan Davidson, Nathan Steinwald, Amy Friend, and Ed Silverman interviews with the author.

255   *"I never expected it":* Corker interview with the author.

264   *"put the wind":* Barney Frank interview with the author.

264   *"They've got to give me":* Silverman interview with the author.

265   *"a one hundred percent chance":* "Reg Reform Gets a Shot in the Arm from Health Care," *American Banker,* March 25, 2010.

CHAPTER NINETEEN   *On the Senate Floor at Last*

Quotations from floor debates and speeches are available in the Congressional Record, which can be accessed at http://www.gpo.gov/fdsys/browse/collection.action? collectionCode=CREC.

267   *nearly 60 percent:* Center for Responsive Politics statistics are available at http:// www.opensecrets.org/news/2010/08/financial-industry-related-politica.html.

267   *a Fox Business News reporter:* Charlie Gasparino.

267   *"About 25 Wall Street executives"*: Gasparino's account is at http://www.foxbusiness
      .com/markets/2010/04/12/street-execs-pols-earful-financial-reform/.
268   *more than $150,000:* Numbers from Federal Election Commission findings.
271   *"Republican leaders"*: "GOP Fights to Unify Opposition to Bill," *Wall Street
      Journal*, April 15, 2010.
271   *"perpetuate bailouts"*: "Bair Says Reform Bill Will Make Bailouts 'Impossible,' "
      American Banker, April 15, 2010.
273   *"that represents the best negotiating position"*: "GOP Fights to Unify Opposition to
      Bill," *Wall Street Journal*.
273   *"The single most important thing"*: "Top GOP Priority—Make Obama a
      One-Term President," *National Journal*, October 2, 2010.
273   *"We worked very hard"*: Quoted by Joshua Green, "Strict Obstructionist," *Atlan-
      tic Monthly*, January–February 2011.
274   *Susan Collins of Maine:* "GOP Fights to Unify Opposition to Bill," *Wall Street
      Journal*.
276   *"We've seen misleading arguments"*: "Obama Makes a Strong Case for Financial
      Reform," *Washington Post*, April 23, 2010.
277   *One quoted Shelby: Congress Daily*, April 15, 2010.
277   *"We're getting closer"*: "Senators Close to a Deal on Financial Regulation Bill,"
      Washington Post, April 22, 2010.
278   *This was possible because:* Sarah A. Binder and Steven S. Smith, *Politics or Prin-
      ciple? Filibustering in the United States Senate* (Washington, D.C.: Brookings
      Institution Press, 1997).
280   *"all the trappings"*: "Goldman Sachs Hearing: Senators Seek, Fail to Get an
      Apology," *Wall Street Journal*, April 28, 2010.
282   *"suggested that they saw"*: "Republicans Allow Debate on Financial Overhaul,"
      New York Times, April 29, 2010.

CHAPTER TWENTY   *Staff Warfare*

I interviewed Michael Barr, Julie Chon, Amy Friend, Kara Stein, and Neal Wolin.
289   *"refused to be buffaloed"*: Michael Lewis in an interview with the Motley Fool,
      available at http://www.fool.com/investing/general/2008/12/01/michael-lewis
      -on-the-hedge-fund-manager-who-saw-it.aspx.
292   *"we couldn't support it"*: Michael Barr interview with the author.
292   *Reporting this on April 14:* "Banks Fight to Block Rules," *Wall Street Journal*,
      April 14, 2010.
293   *"The dark days of deals"*: "Obama Calls Together Congressional Leaders in Push
      for New Financial Regulation," *Washington Post*, April 15, 2010.
293   *The next day:* "How 'Hard to Fathom' Derivatives Rule Emerged in U.S. Sen-
      ate," *Bloomberg News*, May 7, 2010.
294   *six Democrats and, surprisingly, one Republican:* The signers besides Olympia
      Snowe and Maria Cantwell were Sherrod Brown of Ohio, Tom Harkin of Iowa,
      Bill Nelson of Florida, Byron Dorgan of North Dakota, and Dianne Feinstein
      of California.
294   *"There was no agreement"*: Barr interview with the author.
295   *"The Senate is about trust"*: Kara Stein interview with the author.

CHAPTER TWENTY-ONE   *The Senate Acts*

I interviewed Chris Dodd, Anthony Dowd, Amy Friend, Andrew Green, Ed Silverman, and Edward Yingling. Quotations from floor debates and speeches are available

in the Congressional Record, which can be accessed at http://www.gpo.gov/fdsys/browse/collection.action?collectionCode=CREC.

299 *"the longer this goes on"*: Edward Yingling interview with the author.

299 *"a stroke of genius"*: Ed Silverman interview with the author.

300 *"Can't we just agree"*: Amy Friend interview with the author.

302 *"It was never about substance"*: Chris Dodd interview with the author.

305 *In March:* "Banks Lobby to Rid Finance Bill of Ban on Trading in Derivatives," *New York Times*, March 10, 2010.

311 *Merkley and Green were the first people:* Anthony Dowd interview with the author.

315 *When the Senate convened:* Account based on Amy Friend's contemporaneous notes on the meeting, which she attended.

CHAPTER TWENTY-TWO   *Conference Committee*

I interviewed Michael Barr, Julie Chon, Chris Dodd, Anthony Dowd, Barney Frank, Jack Reed, David Smith, and Neal Wolin.

336 *His colleagues chuckled:* All the public sessions of the conference committee are preserved on C-SPAN's website and can be easily watched or sampled. The first day's session can be found at http://www.c-spanvideo.org/program/293998–1. There are links from this page to all the other sessions.

340 *"And he said"*: Barney Frank interview with the author.

341 *"The percentage of Congressmen"*: Anthony Dowd interview with the author.

344 *"went to Steny"*: Frank interview with the author.

346 *"it's got to work"*: Neal Wolin interview with the author.

347 *"Okay," he said:* David Smith interview with the author.

348 *"People could sort of see"*: Michael Barr interview with the author.

354 *"for the first time"*: Julie Chon interview with the author.

354 *"The irony here"*: Jack Reed interview with the author.

CHAPTER TWENTY-THREE   *Endgame*

I interviewed Chris Dodd, Barney Frank, Amy Friend, and Jeanne Roslanowick. Quotations from floor debates and speeches are available in the Congressional Record, which can be accessed at http://www.gpo.gov/fdsys/browse/collection.action?collectionCode=CREC.

359 *"I was surprised"*: Scott Brown press release available at http://www.scottbrown.senate.gov/public/index.cfm/2010/6/statement-of-u-s-senator-scott-brown-on-financial-reform-conference.

361 *Gregg himself had admitted as much:* In an interview for a 2009 *Frontline* documentary on PBS; transcript can be found at http://www.pbs.org/wgbh/pages/frontline/tentrillion/etc/script.html.

361 *Dodd thought he had sixty votes:* Chris Dodd interview with the author.

366 *"right from the heart"*: Amy Friend interview with the author.

367 *"I must say"*: Dodd interview with the author.

CHAPTER TWENTY-FOUR   *Still Broken*

I interviewed Michael Barr, Rodgin Cohen, Bob Corker, and Ray LaHood.

372 *"I am amazed"*: Rodgin Cohen interview with the author.

375 *"This job gives one"*: Michael Barr interview with the author.

377 *"the achievement of"*: Mission statement of the House office is available at http://opencrs.com/document/RS20735/.

378 *A typical example:* This and many other polls on attitudes toward Wall Street and reform can be found at http://www.pollingreport.com/business.htm.

378 *"It's good for Republicans":* Bob Corker interview with the author.

379 *nearly half a billion dollars:* The center's numbers are available at http://www.opensecrets.org/lobby/index.php.

381 *"Congress is becoming":* Article is at http://www.washingtonpost.com/opinions/olympia-snowe-why-im-leaving-the-senate/2012/03/01/gIQApGYZIR_story.html.

383 *"castigated":* Ray LaHood interview with the author.

384 *Political scientists who study:* The leading academics studying this phenomenon are Nolan McCarty of Princeton, Keith T. Poole of the University of Georgia, and Howard Rosenthal of New York University. Their work can be found on their blog, www.voteview.com/blog/.

386 *Gallup had never recorded:* The Gallup Poll numbers can be found at http://www.gallup.com/poll/1600/congress-public.aspx#gdcontent.

Index

Illustration Credits

Page 1: Official White House photograph by Pete Souza (top left); David Brody, Bloomberg via Getty Images (center right); Harry Gural (bottom right).

Page 2: United States Senate Committee on Banking, Housing, and Urban Affairs (top right); Harry Gural (center left); Office of U.S. Senator Mark R. Warner (bottom right).

Page 3: Melina Mara, *The Washington Post* (top left); United States House of Representatives Committee on Financial Services (center right); Bill O'Leary, *The Washington Post* (bottom left).

Page 4: Amy Friend (top left); Amy Friend (center left); Harry Gural (bottom right).

Page 5: French Ministry of Foreign Affairs (top left); Tom Williams, Roll Call/Getty Images (center right); Kendall Whitehouse (bottom left).

Page 6: American Bankers Association (top left); Preston Mack (center right); Stephen Crowley/*The New York Times* (bottom).

Page 7: Harry Gural (top right); Charles Dharapak, Associated Press (center right); Office of U.S. Representative Spencer Bachus (bottom).

Page 8: Jim Ready (top); Official White House photograph by Lawrence Jackson (bottom).